ALSO BY ED WALTON

This Date in Boston Red Sox History
Red Sox Triumphs and Tragedies

The Rookies

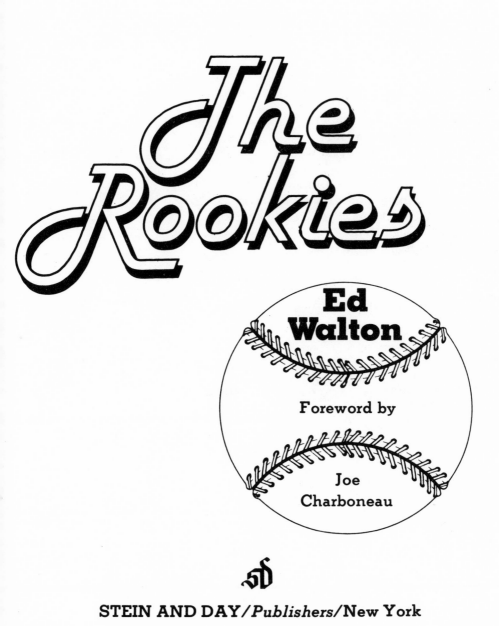

Ed Walton

Foreword by

Joe Charboneau

STEIN AND DAY/*Publishers*/New York

First published in 1982
Copyright © 1982 by Ed Walton
All rights reserved
Designed by Louis A. Ditizio
Printed in the United States of America
STEIN AND DAY/*Publishers*
Scarborough House
Briarcliff Manor, N.Y. 10510

Library of Congress Cataloging in Publication Data

Walton, Edward H., 1931-
    The rookies.

    1. Baseball players — United States.   2. Baseball
clubs — United States — History.   I. Title.
GV865.A1W323   796.357′092′2 [B] 80-5892
ISBN 0-8128-2778-3   AACR2

For my Mom and Dad
who saw me through my rookie years

"A player shall be considered a rookie unless, during a previous season or seasons, he has (a) exceeded 130 at bats or 50 innings pitched in the major leagues; or (b) accumulated more than 45 days on the active roster of a major league club or clubs during the period of the 25 player limit (excluding time in military service)."

—1980 Major League Rule

CONTENTS

Illustrations between pages 156 and 157

ACKNOWLEDGMENTS

No book of this magnitude could be put together by one person without the help, cooperation, and encouragement of others. The hours spent in research became staggering at times and the keys to completion were provided by many. A special tip of the old baseball cap must go to them.

My good friend Tim Samway of Hampton Falls, New Hampshire, helped hatch the rookie idea; and it was he who rode herd on me until its completion, continually advising, verifying, and checking what was being done. So enthused was he over the various rookies that he placed a radio-telephone call from the wilds of Alaska to find out the baseball news. His support meant a lot when things were dragging, and is sincerely appreciated.

Fred Ehrhardt of the Varsity Sports store in Fairfield, Connecticut, provided the back room and coffee for many discussions on rookies put forth by the gang of baseball buffs who gather there.

Bill Gavin of South Weymouth, Massachusetts, provided a list of memory-jogging names. I suspect he enlisted his sister Eleanor to help him with the pages of names he researched for me and with his checking of the manuscript.

That stickler for detail, Frank Williams of Bridgeport, Connecticut, verified every fact as many times as it took to set me straight.

Anne Lukachik had to figure out my writing and put it in typed form while correcting the world's worst spelling; Art Ballant, my editor at Stein and Day, advised and counselled; and Rich Marazzi provided a few rookie tales from his expertise on the '50s. Smokey Joe Wood, former Boston Red Sox and Cleveland Indian discoursed on those rookie camps of long ago, with an occasional comment from his son Bob.

ix

My thanks go also to the following: Boston Red Sox rookie pitcher Steve Crawford, who kept me informed of his thoughts as he moved from double A ball to the majors, and to his Bristol manager Tony Torchia, for his insights; Boston Red Sox rookies Ed Jurak, Mike Smithson, John Tudor, Joel Finch and wife Karen, Win Remmerswaal, Jerry King, Brian Denman, Jim "Willie" Wilson, and Otis Foster for their thoughts about life in the minors and majors; Pawtucket Red Sox owner Ben Mondor and minor league pitching coach Lee Stange, scorers and P.A. announcers Bill George, Bob Kirschner, and George Geer, and Cincinnati Red farmhand Mickey Duval; and certain Seattle Mariner farmhands. And to Joe Charboneau, American League Rookie of the Year, for his Foreword.

These Public Relations departments require special mention: Boston Red Sox, New York Mets, Detroit Tigers, Kansas City Royals, Cincinnati Reds, Minnesota Twins, Houston Astros, Montreal Expos, Los Angeles Dodgers, California Angels, Toronto Blue Jays, San Francisco Giants, San Diego Padres, Philadelphia Phillies, and the Chicago White Sox, with a special tip of the cap to Mary Jane Ryan of the Red Sox, Stu Smith of the Giants, and Tim Hamilton of the Mets. The teams listed also supplied some of the fine photographs in this work.

And last, but not least, to my family, who had to bear with me through late hours and periods of no communication throughout the project, but who continually understood my devotion to baseball.

To all a special thanks. Your help and friendship mean a lot to me.

Ed Walton
Fairfield, Connecticut
December 1980

FOREWORD

I knew that it wasn't going to be easy. The major leagues are hard for any rookie, even if you hit .350 like I did for two straight minor league seasons.

In the minors I didn't have to worry about slumps or pressure. If I didn't hit for a while, I knew that I would stay in the lineup until I came out of my slump. But with the Indians, I felt that I had to produce every day or someone was going to jump in and take my job. A few hitless days would have me thinking about being farmed out to Tacoma. When you are a rookie, you feel that you have to produce every time you play.

The Rookies is an excellent account of what it is like to break into the majors. So much of what I have experienced is contained in these pages.

No matter how good you are or what you did in the minors, you will always be a rookie in your first year, and this book makes that point very well. There is always a line between the rookies and the rest of the team. It is as though the other players are waiting for you to prove yourself, to stand the test.

They say that you never really feel secure in this game, and that is especially true in your rookie year. You look around and see so much talent on your team and the other clubs. It can overwhelm you and shatter your confidence if you let it.

For these reasons, I am glad that my rookie year is over with. Don't misunderstand, I had a great time in 1980. But the second time around has to be easier. I have faced almost all of the American League pitchers. I have played in every stadium and been to every city. The feeling of awe is gone.

But most importantly, I now know that I can play in the majors. Before, I only thought so. When you are in the minors, you dream and talk about playing in the Big Show. All the players sit around and talk about what they will do in the majors if only they get the chance. But you can't be sure if you will cut it until you make it through your rookie year.

My rookie season is now history and I feel that I did well for the Cleveland Indians. I hit .289 with 23 homers and 87 RBIs, but I felt I could have done a lot better. Winning the Rookie of the Year Award was really a great thrill.

The Rookies captures the excitement of being a rookie, and I am sure that you will find reading it an interesting and rewarding experience.

—Joe Charboneau

Introduction

The annual midwinter trek to Florida and Arizona is not entirely made up of tourists seeking a moment in the sun and escape from the February snows of the North. There is a smaller migration each year of fuzzy-faced young men carrying baseball bats, gloves, spikes, and battered suitcases, driven along by the common desire to win wealth and fame in the major leagues.

Each year brings a new crop to the training camps. Today they are all under contract, but not so many years ago they would arrive with little more than a hope and a prayer, only to tramp from one big-league camp to another begging for a chance to show their "stuff." All had the common characteristics of determination and a will to learn, and asked only a chance. Some luckily stayed. For others it was the all too familiar telegram home: "Send money, they started to throw curves today, be home soon." It is said that rookies progress from prospect, to suspect, to reject. We have all read the advance notices with such observations as: "Young Billy Slider is the fastest pitcher since Bob Feller"; or "Thurman Jones fields his position with the grace of Marty Marion"; or "With his pair of hands Tom Fielder may be our best second baseman since Bobby Doerr." Long forgotten are these comparisons when Slider, Jones, and Fielder wind up in the Cotton States League. Oh, how our hopes soared when the sportswriters led us on with those glowing headlines! They always return the following spring to rave again about a new collection of rookies. It's all part of the game. The first youngster who puts a strike past Joe DiMaggio shows promise, draws sighs from his manager, and gets bold headlines in the papers.

It isn't only the sportswriters. How many managers have hung the "can't miss" tag on the rookie when it turns out that by late April the youngster "isn't missed"? Leo Durocher once described a rookie's curve as "breaks like a ball falling off a pool table" and the pool hall was probably where the kid wound up. Astute baseball men have been known to sing praises, such as "That guy hit .352 on the coast and will burn up the League," only to have him hit almost a hundred points less when he gets his chance. It's not always that way. Once in a while a Pete Reiser or a Mickey Mantle comes along, but very seldom. There are many, many more who turn into busts than into stars.

Reiser was the sensation of the Brooklyn Dodger camp of 1941. Many insist there never was a rookie with more promise. "Pistol Pete" took the nation— Dodger fans or not—by storm. The first eleven times he batted in the spring games he got a hit. It appeared that there was no way to get him out. Everybody raved about him. He tore through the National League that season, winning the batting championship, becoming the youngest (age 22) player to do so. Poor Pete developed the unlikely habit of trying to run through outfield fences and never really matched that rookie season, but what fun it was while it lasted. And then there was Mantle. He stepped onto the New York Yankee training camp diamond at Phoenix, Arizona, and in no time had been turned into a national hero, who it was figured would make people forget all the heroes of the past. Surely, he would beat a path directly to the shrine at Cooperstown—but that is getting ahead of our story.

Good for ticket sales at the old home ball yard: Is that why we hear all this springtime ballyhoo? Get the phenoms away from the cash customers so they really can't be seen until the image is created, of course. Stimulate early spring enthusiasm among the paying fans. Owners see this and realize it takes the fans a while to whip up interest. A little TV, some radio, but mostly press notices all add up at the turnstiles. Sure, it is a golden opportunity for the youngsters. What does the publicity do to the young athletes? Some can handle it. Some are of a temperament that succumbs to publicity and as a result never reach their potential, although it seems more likely that they would have flopped anyway.

When the St. Louis Cardinals' Branch Rickey, often called the father of baseball's "farm system," embarked on establishing his vast network of minor league clubs, his methods were new to baseball and different from today's techniques. His method was to scout the city playgrounds and the cow pasture lots of the countryside and sign the youngster who demonstrated any flash of talent and send him out, sometimes burying him deep, into the vast Cardinal system, which numbered better than 50 clubs and nearly 800 players. And, oh, how these young men with dreams eagerly signed on! It was rumored some played for as little as sixty dollars per month. Over the years, Rickey's system paid handsome dividends as a seemingly endless flow of talent reached the Cardinals (Hafey, the Deans, Mize, Slaughter, Moore, Marion, the Coopers, Musial, etc., etc., etc.). Many developed at very little cost. Rickey kept talent available at all times, and when he felt he could keep them down no longer would sell or trade them off for substantial sums to other teams.

Why a book on rookies? Because here we have the typical American story—the young man fighting his way, against the establishment, to the top. Some are successful, some are not; but their story is one the American baseball public can relate to. Who among us at one time or another has not had that "rookie feeling"? A new school, the first day on the job, a recruit entering the service—all experiences we can relate to. The odds seemed so great. So it is with the rookies: Only a handful make it; but for those the drum beats loudly.

Years ago, *The Saturday Evening Post* had a cover by Norman Rockwell that portrayed the typical wide-eyed, freckle-faced rookie on his initial appearance in the Boston Red Sox clubhouse at Sarasota, Florida. There he was, a farm boy with his cardboard suitcase, mail order suit, bat and glove. He was becoming part of his dream. Maybe the rookie never really was like that; certainly he no longer resembles the Rockwell version. Today he may show up with his agent, outwardly sure of himself and saying that no one awes him. Don't believe it! Inside, he is tied in knots, his heart is pounding, and he doubts if he is good enough. Outside he appears different, but his first day in spring training is perfectly preserved in his mind. No matter how long he stays in baseball the memory of that first major league camp stays with him forever.

Who were these boys of spring and where did their journey lead? Let's take a look and recall what they did and what was said about them.

A Look
at Some
Rookies Past

While we will actually start our journey in 1942, no book on rookies would be complete without touching briefly on some of the lore of the past, the stories and traditions which surround the youngsters of the earlier years.

The rookie of the early 1900s found himself an outcast at the spring camp. The vets, fearful of losing their jobs, made life as unbearable as possible for the newcomers. Helpful they were not. Throwing up roadblocks in the paths of the rookies was common. The rookie played second fiddle in the field or on the mound and had to fight his way to get a chance at batting practice. How many found their gloves cut to pieces, shoes nailed to the floor, uniforms torn, bats sawed in half? How many were sent on wild-goose chases to find the keys to the batter's box, or employed by the groundskeeper to help him put out the foul lines? Forced into isolation at the hotel and feeling the veteran players' wrath on the field, each rookie had a tough row to hoe. Many became discouraged and went home; others would not give in and prevailed.

The early training camps had a few bats, some scuffed baseballs, and some meager other equipment, nothing like what one would expect in today's complexes. No pitching machines, fancy batting cages or trainers' rooms. At the first spring camps the players would arrive around 10 A.M. and work out until about 12:30 P.M. Everyone would take a turn at bat, except the pitchers. Each man would hit in turn four or five times, getting about 15 hits. The pitchers would soon be worn out and batting practice would be over. A few warm-up exercises and an infield practice would be held while the out-fielders shagged flies. This lasted about 15 minutes and it was called a day. After about 30 days of this routine, spring training would end.

While most of the camps had only one daily workout in those days, there

3

was the exceptional manager who would have two workouts, usually a morning session and an afternoon session. Managers had no coaches and had little time to spend on the personal instruction of any player. The rookie either had it or he didn't have it; he made the team or he didn't make it. He was on his own. A smart one watched the established player, and when he saw the veteran doing something more effectively than himself, he would imitate in an effort to improve. Today, of course, all this is changed. Coaches and special instructors abound at the camps. Each player is studied carefully, and routines are worked out whereby he is, hopefully, converted into a genuine major leaguer.

Now that we have the setting and a feeling for how these camps operated, let's take a look at some of the things that happened to the rookies who were there. The trading of ballplayers has created some very strange and curious deals. Players have been traded for all types of things, from racehorses to sacks of oysters. It was once reported that San Francisco bought a first baseman by the name of Jack Fenton for a box of prunes. The payoff on all screwy diamond deals may have come when the Red Sox left a young rookie outfielder at Little Rock in 1908 as payment for the rent they owed on their spring training site. There was the stipulation that if he developed, Boston would have first crack at him. The rookie came on fast that season and batted .350 and was being eyed by several major league clubs. Little Rock owner Mickey Finn, true to his gentleman's agreement with Boston, gave them first chance at this fleet-footed fly chaser. The Sox bought back the phenom for five hundred dollars. His name—Tris Speaker, now a Hall of Famer and one of the game's all-time greats.

The old St. Louis Browns pulled the same trick when they left infielder Buzzy Wares behind in Montgomery, Alabama, as payment for the spring use of the ball park there. My, how times have changed!

Trading in today's game has become quite sophisticated, but it wasn't always that way. Consider that one of the greatest left-hand pitchers of all time was once, as a rookie, traded for a wooden fence. When Lefty Grove was pitching with the Martinsburg, West Virginia, team it seems that their ball park was badly in need of a wooden fence. When Jack Dunn of the Baltimore Orioles approached the Martinsburg club owner about the purchase of Grove, the price was set as the price of a new wooden fence for the ball field.

One of the earliest rookie stories concerns a young lad sent for a tryout with the Cleveland club in 1883. Not impressed by what he saw, the Cleveland manager sent this youngster, Hugh Daily, to the mound, ordering him to toss batting practice. The batters swung at the lad's offerings and missed, batter after batter. The manager, now interested, told his batters to bear down against the rookie. No use, most of them just whiffed the air as Daily threw strike after strike. Daily had played some ball previously with Buffalo, but this show so impressed the Cleveland manager that he signed him onto the club for the season. Daily went on to star with a 23-19 record and remained in the big time for five more years. He tossed a no-hitter against Philadelphia, and once struck out 19 batters in a game. It has been said that he pitched in various minor leagues until he was 50, but what was remarkable about Hugh Daily was that his pitching arm was his only arm. A boyhood accident had caused him to lose his left arm.

Then there was the rookie who complained to his manager that he was going home because when he threw his very best fastball the veterans on the club were spitting tobacco juice on it as it went by the plate. I wonder how the catcher felt? Or how about the Cincinnati rookie, when asked by Manager Birdie Tebbetts what position he played, replied, "Infield." "What position?" asked Birdie. "Stooped over," the rookie replied. And there was the rookie who argued with Branch Rickey over his new contract. Rickey made an offer and the youngster countered with another. Thus it went for an hour or so. Finally Rickey said, "Your trouble, son, is that you can't hit a happy medium." To which the rookie replied, "What do you mean, I can hit everything they throw."

Then there was Blondy Ryan, who had appeared in a few games with the 1930 Chicago Cubs before he surfaced again with the 1933 New York Giants. The rookie left the Giants because of a contract dispute early in the season. When the Giants became involved in a hot pennant race, causing Ryan to reconsider, he sent a wire to Manager Bill Terry: "We can't lose, I'm on my way." He did arrive and helped the Giants win the flag, lasted four more years in the big time, but never appeared as a regular again.

Rookies come in all sizes and shapes and are usually thought of as youngsters. Consider two rookie pitchers who appeared with the 1937 Boston Bees. Lou Fette was 30 years old and won 20 games. He was joined by 34-year-old Jim Turner who also won 20 games. Their combined efforts could only raise the Bees one spot in the standings, from sixth in '36 to fifth in '37. Despite this fact, I suppose you could say the Bees came up with a couple of honeys. Fette lasted four more years in the majors, managing only 21 more wins, leaving the majors with 41 wins and 40 losses. "Milkman" Jim Turner spent eight more seasons in the majors with a moderately better record, having won a total of 69 games and dropping 60 before passing from the major league scene. Interestingly, four other rookie pitchers named Turner have appeared in the big leagues over the years, and none lasted more than one season, and between them won only one game. A year later, in 1938, a rookie appeared in the Boston American League camp and found himself being farmed out to Minneapolis. But as a parting blast at the Red Sox veteran outfielders, Ben Chapman, Doc Cramer, and Joe Vosmik, he vowed he'd be back and make more money than all three put together, and he did. That was the temperamental rookie, Ted Williams. In a game against the St. Louis Cardinals one day, a Pittsburgh Pirate rookie missed several steal signals. Called into Manager Fred Haney's office after the game, he was asked if he knew the signals. He replied that he did. "When you were given the steal sign three times, why didn't you run?" Haney asked. "I thought you were trying to confuse the Cardinals," came the serious reply.

Long forgotten is the originator of an old baseball story that has been told about so many rookie pitchers. The bases were loaded, none out. The catcher went through the list of pitches not once, but twice, each time only to be shaken off by the pitcher. Finally, the catcher walked to the mound explaining to the rookie that he had gone through every pitch in the book and had been shaken off. "What do you want to throw?" he inquired. "Frankly, nothing," the rookie replied. "I want to hold on to the ball for a while because the way they are hitting me, they are going to knock me and the ball right out of the park no matter what I throw."

In 1924 a rookie joined the Braves in Boston just before they headed for a series in New York. Knowing little about big city customs, the rookie was assigned to the sixteenth floor upon arrival at the New York hotel. Entering the elevator with his roommate, Casey Stengel, he noticed Casey slip the elevator operator a dime upon arrival on their floor. Assuming it was the custom, the rookie followed Stengel's example. Some time later, Brave manager Dave Bancroft encountered the rookie at the fourteenth floor exit, all tuckered out and breathless. "What's the matter, you look all in?" asked Bancroft. "Mr. Bancroft, I ain't got much money with me and can't afford to pay a dime everytime I ride the elevator," the rookie replied. "Who told you that you have to pay a dime?" inquired Bancroft. "Casey Stengel did." With a slight smile on his face Bancroft said, "Never mind paying any more, the club has a charge account here, and we will take care of your fare."

The old catcher Joe Sugden once told about the rookie pitcher who had a repertoire of so many pitches, he couldn't figure how he would ever give all the signs. "Hold on kid," he said. "I wear a glove on one hand and have only five fingers on the other." "So what," the kid replied. "Take off your shoes and start using your toes."

Then there was the rookie pitcher who was having all sorts of control problems. When his manager inquired as to why, he learned that the rookie's nervousness caused his hand to sweat so that he was having trouble gripping the ball. So like all good managers, he hauled out a resin bag for the youngster's use. The control problem continued, much to the manager's dismay. "Didn't that resin bag help?" he asked the rookie. "I don't know," came the reply. "I couldn't get the darn bag open."

Tales abound about Joe Jackson, but once in his rookie season while playing an exhibition game in a bush league park, he complained about the broken glass bottles in the outfield and how they were cutting the covers of the baseballs. Jackson was playing in his stocking feet at the time. Joe also had the strange habit of ordering what his teammates did in restaurants. It is believed he couldn't read the menus and this was his way out.

Then there was the rookie who finally got his chance to pitch and was shelled, earning a ticket back to the minors. Before leaving he asked his manager for a recommendation. "Sure," the manager said and wrote, "To Whom It May Concern, this rookie pitcher pitched one game for me, and I am satisfied."

While scouting young Moe Berg for the Brooklyn Dodgers in 1924, Mike Gonzalez sent off a wire which has often been repeated in baseball lore, "Good field, no hit."

George Whiteman was a fancy-fielding outfielder who played professional baseball from 1905 to 1929 playing well over 3000 minor league games, but only 85 in the majors. He played three games for the 1907 Red Sox and eleven for the 1913 Yankees, so he was really a rookie when he appeared for the 1918 wartime Red Sox. Appearing in 71 games, he was nothing spectacular during the regular season. The Red Sox that year won the American League championship and met the Chicago Cubs in the World Series. Winning the series four games to two, the Sox hero was Whiteman, whose five hits were made at opportune times and his great catches in the field were game-savers. An unsung rookie turned hero. One of the most famous rookies of all times was the Chicago Cubs' Lou Novikoff. One night he made a great steal of third base, the only problem was that the bases were loaded at the time. When asked why he had done such a foolish thing, the "Mad Russian" explained, "I couldn't resist, I had such a great jump on the pitcher."

One day Red Sox rookie pitcher Red Ruffing brought a sandwich with him to the bullpen. Before he could finish it, he was called upon to relieve against the Yankees. "Who do they have coming up?" he asked. "Ruth, Gehrig, and Meusel." He laid down the sandwich and implored his bullpen mates not to touch it as he said he would be right back.

There was the rookie pitcher, who in all innocence replied to a question by his first big league manager. "How did you go down in the minors?" "By bus most of the time."

Lefty Gomez said that he was so skinny when he first joined the Yankees they had to give him a single-digit number, as he wasn't wide enough to carry two digits on his back.

In 1929 the New York Yankees brought up a youngster named Sam Byrd, a fine fielder and a hard hitter. For six years he remained with the Yanks in a role which never seemed to change—a late inning replacement for Babe Ruth. When the Babe left the Yankees, Byrd was no longer needed and was sent off to Cincinnati. Sam never really made it in the Ohio city either. Then one day he decided to forego baseball and turn to a career in golf and became one of the great golfers of the early forties—a rookie who might have starred on many teams, but had to play a secondary role until he switched sports.

Speaking of Babe Ruth, he was like most rookies of his time when he joined the Boston Red Sox, except he could hit the ball harder than most and eat more than many. Some of the veteran Red Sox decided to teach the brash young rookie how to act and hazed him continually, until in fury the Babe challenged the whole team to a fight. This lessened the abuse somewhat, although his being farmed out to Providence just five weeks after his arrival probably had the greater effect.

Back around the end of World War I, two rookies appeared at the Boston Red Sox tryout camp. One from Kansas City was a happy-go-lucky player, always in the middle of things, joking and laughing his way through the tryouts, keeping everyone else laughing with his jokes. The other was a very serious young college boy who had starred at Holy Cross. The college boy worked hard, but somehow things weren't breaking right for him and he felt he was a failure. The Kansas City rookie would console him saying, "We can't all be big leaguers." Finally the youngster from Holy Cross decided it was best he give up baseball. He thought, one more chance, I'll give it my all tomorrow. But things didn't get any better, and he retired to the bench discouraged. As he sat there he watched the kid from Kansas City and noticed how clumsy he really was. The veteran players were saying that the kid from K.C. would make the majors. Well, this just burned up our college boy, who made up his mind if the K.C. joker was a big leaguer, he certainly could be also. Well neither made the Red Sox, but our college boy finally made it with the Pittsburgh Pirates, where he played for 17 years with a lifetime batting average of .320 for those years. In 1948 Harold "Pie" Traynor made it into baseball's Hall of Fame. In the long run the kid from Kansas City dropped out of baseball, never making it to the majors to fulfill the prediction of the Red Sox veterans. He did however continue his comedian role and became a star in his own right. You will remember the name Joe E. Brown.

Major league club owners are often painted as heartless, cold individuals who care little for the players they employ. Not always so. Consider Connie Mack, owner-manager of the old Philadelphia Athletics. In 1914 a wild kid came to the Athletics named Sam "Red" Crane. He played only two games for Connie that season, but returned again during the next two seasons, although he only managed to appear in ten games. The young infielder drifted to Washington and then into the National League with Cincinnati and Brooklyn. Then one night tragedy struck. In an insane fit of jealousy, Sam murdered his ex-girlfriend and her escort. Off to prison Sam went for a long time, quickly forgotten by the baseball world, all that is, except his first major league manager, Connie Mack. For years it was Mack who went to visit Crane, wrote to him and campaigned for another chance for his former rookie. Finally, Mack's efforts were successful; Crane was released from prison, and it was Connie who gave him a job and a helping hand to make good.

Lady Luck often smiles on rookies with a break here and a break there. One such rookie was shortstop Charlie Hollocher of the 1918 Chicago Cubs. In a bind for a shortstop, manager Fred Mitchell checked the minor league records and came up with Hollocher's name—an obscure ball player in the Pacific Coast League. For a small sum Charlie was purchased and brought to Chicago. Lady luck had smiled on the rookie and the Cubs. Hollocher hit and fielded brilliantly and inspired the Cubs to the National League championship. For seven years this unknown rookie played shortstop for the Cubs, but suddenly the young man decided that playing ball was ruining his health. Despite the doctor's okay, Charlie disappeared from the major league scene refusing to ever return. Lady luck had smiled on Charlie Hollocher for the last time. Sixteen years after his last major league game, he was found shot to death on a St. Louis street in August, 1940.

Have you ever heard about Norfolk's famous rookie visitor of 1900? The New York Giants purchased this rookie pitcher from the Norfolk club, but without a tryout he was sent back to Norfolk. Soon he was drafted by the Cincinnati Reds. Never given a chance with the Reds, he found himself involved in a trade that sent him back to the Giants. So here he was, in one season he went from Norfolk to New York, New York to Norfolk, Norfolk to Cincinnati, Cincinnati to New York. Upset at this point, he asked the Giant manager, Buck Ewing, for a final chance and convinced him to the point where he was retained by the Giants. It was one of the best moves the Giants ever made, as this rookie won 373 games over the next 17 years for them. He was Hall of Famer Christy Mathewson.

Parents often worry about their sons as they march off to the baseball wars. When Smokey Joe Wood, the famous Boston Red Sox pitcher and Cleveland Indian outfielder, was to report to the Hutchinson, Kansas, club as a 17-year-old, his dad went along with him to make sure the environment was proper. There was another lad of 17 in the late '30s who signed on as a Giant farmhand and was assigned to a club in Louisiana. Later, this same boy signed a Boston Red Sox contract and was assigned to the Albany, New York, club. This started me wondering what had happened in Louisiana. Since the boy was from the East, I figured perhaps he had become homesick. "No way," he replied when asked. "My dad didn't feel that was the proper environment for a 17-year-old, and he came down there and hauled me home."

While rookies usually signed on with a particular team because of the money offered, Hall of Fame outfielder Harry Hooper, a college graduate with an engineering degree, signed with the Sacramento club of the California State League because they promised to get him a surveying job.

While a college education led to Hooper's baseball career, baseball led to catcher Chief Meyers' college career. While playing in a baseball tournament in Albuquerque, Meyers met Ralph Glaze, who later pitched (1906–08) for the Boston Red Sox. Glaze, who had attended Dartmouth College, told Meyers of a fund set up at Dartmouth to provide education to American Indians. Meyers applied and was accepted. While he didn't finish college, he did attend for a year before the call of the diamond got the better of him. Meyers caught nine years in the big time, mainly for the New York Giants of John McGraw.

Most rookies dream of hitting a homer in the big leagues. In 1929 the Detroit Tigers had a rookie infielder named Frank Sigafoos who had had "a cup of coffee" with the A's in 1926. The dream came true for Frank, but as the ball sailed into the stands and he started his trot around the base paths, he was called back by the umpire. Seems a balk had been called on the pitcher—no home run. Given a second chance—you guessed it—he struck out. Oh, yes, he never hit a home run again during his major league career.

Just a little sidelight here, but did you ever wonder who started the idea of spring training, the place where most of our rookies are first showcased? It was Cap Anson of the Chicago White Stockings, a great baseball innovator who in 1886 summoned his ballplayers to Hot Springs, Arkansas.

The Cincinnati Reds once gave a chance to a big husky pitcher who showed some fine promise. Suddenly he left camp, and the Reds could not convince him to come back. He had found a new sport he liked better. Probably the next time he was seen in a big league dugout was with Jimmy Collins of the Boston Pilgrims at the old Huntington Avenue Grounds in Boston, where he was a regular visitor as the former heavyweight boxing champion, John L. Sullivan. Boston seemed to attract heavyweights as fans, as some 50 years later Rocky Marciano would often attend their games.

Lou Gehrig was so shy as a rookie at his first New York Yankee camp in

New Orleans that when he ran out of money he took a job in a local drugstore, rather than ask for an advance on his pay.

A young left-handed pitcher turned up at a Detroit Tiger camp and showed a fine screwball pitch. A well-meaning Tiger coach and several veterans advised him to give up the pitch before he hurt his arm. They told him he would never make the majors with it. After these trials in 1926 and 1927, he was released outright to Beaumont of the Texas League, but in 1928 he appeared at a New York Giant camp and remained with the New Yorkers for 16 years, becoming a famous pitcher and Hall of Fame member. Carl Hubbell's best pitch all those years was his screwball.

In 1926 a 17-year-old rookie walked into New York manager John McGraw's office, referred by a friend of McGraw's. "What do you play kid?" inquired McGraw. "I'm a catcher," said the kid trying to appear adult. The next day McGraw was impressed by the 17-year-old's batting. "Ever play outfield?" McGraw asked. "Yes sir," said the unassuming youngster. "When I was a kid." This was a young Mel Ott considering himself an adult.

When Hall of Famer Honus Wagner reported to his first Pittsburgh Pirate spring training camp, he was also considered somewhat shy. These were the tough days for rookies, who had to battle for what they wanted with the hostile veterans. The regulars gave nothing to Wagner. He couldn't even get a chance in the batting cage. One day the Pirate owner visited the camp and wanted to know why Wagner was not hitting. Honus explained how his teammates wouldn't let him. The owner said, "Make them let you." So up strolled Wagner, bat in hand. One of the Pirate vets said to him in no uncertain terms to "beat it." "Who do you think you are?" Our shy rookie replied, "I think I am the next batter, and either I hit or I bat your head in. Which do you choose?" He had no further trouble.

While it was generally accepted in the early days of baseball that the old established players would not help the rookie, there were, from time to time, exceptions. I believe there may have been more exceptions than is thought today. Like many yarns, they grow with time; sometimes the exceptions become the rules as years go by. Certainly veterans didn't want to lost their jobs, but on the other hand they also wanted to keep or make their team a winner. For instance, Tris Speaker credited veteran Red Soxer Cy Young with spending hours in hitting fly balls to him to perfect his outfield skills. An old gentleman who once had a tryout with the Detroit Tigers told me that Ty Cobb was tough on rookies until he could evaluate them, and if he determined they had some promise, he would slyly offer them advice, sometimes by example, but always trying to maintain his image of toughness.

Perhaps there was a heart beneath that image after all. Rookie pitcher Rube Foster enjoyed little pitching success with the Boston Red Sox until veteran pitcher Smokey Joe Wood took him aside and showed him how he threw the fastball. Foster did a turnaround and became a successful pitcher for several years after accepting Wood's hints. This was not always the case, but it did happen in many instances.

Of course, there are tales of rookies turning the tables on the veteran. One often told story is the one of what young Earl Whitehill did to Babe Ruth when the Detroiter faced the New York Yankees for the first time. Whitehill got two quick strikes on the Babe when he left the mound and walked in toward the plate for a conference with Johnny Bassler, his catcher. Talking just loud enough so the Babe could hear, Whitehill said to Bassler, "Don't forget to let me know when Babe Ruth comes to bat." "Okay," said Bassler. This infuriated the Babe, and while he was complaining about the fresh rookie, Whitehill slipped strike three past him.

Some rookies have a mind of their own. Johnny Broaca had a fine record at Yale University. Then one day Yale had an exhibition game against a semi-pro team in which Yale coach Joe Wood planned to pitch Broaca. Johnny said he would not waste his time pitching against semi-pros, and when Wood insisted, Broaca walked off the field and the team. Because of his fine record at Yale, the New York Yankees signed him, but their manager, Joe McCarthy, farmed him out to the Newark Bears for seasoning. "No way," said Johnny while threatening to quit baseball. McCarthy wasted no time in recalling him, and Broaca won him 12 games—one year out of Yale.

Rookies often wind up short careers in strange ways. Consider Joe Borden, who in 1875 won several sensational games for Philadelphia, including what has gone down in baseball history as the first no-hitter. Boston lured Borden away after that great rookie year and dreamed of him as winning game after game for them. Perhaps he was the first victim of "the sophomore jinx," because he could not win consistently in Boston and wound up his second season as the groundskeeper in Boston's ball park.

In most seasons only a few rookies make it successfully into the big leagues. But as incredible as it may sound, consider all of these great players were rookies in 1925 (several had been up for a cup of coffee before, but all made it to stay in '25): slugger Jimmie Foxx, catcher Mickey Cockrane, second baseman Charlie Gehringer, pitchers Fred Fitzsimmons, Red Ruffing, and Lefty Grove, outfielder Chick Hafey, and first baseman Lou Gehrig. All except Fitzsimmons are members of Baseball's Hall of Fame. Fitzsimmon's record wasn't bad at all—19 years, 217 wins against 146 losses, and better than 3200 innings pitched. Quite a vintage year, that of 1925!

In 1915, a young rookie pitcher off the campus of the University of Michigan arrived at the St. Louis Browns' camp. Now in that year the big pitcher in the American League was Walter Johnson of the Washington Senators. The St. Louis rookie beat Johnson 1 to 0 in their first encounter. To prove that this was no fluke, he again defeated Johnson in a great pitching duel, 2 to 1. An amazing start for a rookie. He won only four games that year because his manager made him give up pitching and switch to first base, where he became one of the greatest of all time—Hall of Famer George Sisler.

The results of the first season spent in the major leagues are not always an indication of what the future may hold, considering what some Hall of Famers did. Ty Cobb batted a .240. Eddie Collins did not perform well at second base and hit only .235. Tris Speaker hit only .150 on his first try and .224 on his second tour, while the great Rogers Hornsby batted .246.

Former Los Angeles Dodger manager Walter Alston had a very short rookie career. It lasted one game as a late-inning replacement for first baseman John Mize when both were with the St. Louis Cardinals. He made an error in the field and struck out in his only time at bat. Perhaps the rookie with the most appropriate name was pitcher Martin Walker. In his only big league game, he gave up two hits and walked three. That was with the 1928 Philadelphia Phillies. Consider these debuts: Doc Hamann with the 1922 Cleveland Indians, one game, six batters, three hits, and three walks; or Hareson Horsey, who worked four innings with the 1912 Cincinnati Reds and gave up fourteen hits; or Arliss Taylor of the 1921 Philadelphia A's. He allowed seven hits in two innings, but of all things, he struck out Joe Sewell who was among the all-time toughest batters to strike out.

Some rookies had successful debuts and some not so successful ones. Walter Johnson lost 3 to 2 to the Detroit Tigers, while the day before, as was customary, he had pitched batting practice for both clubs. Addie Joss hurled a one-hitter for Cleveland in defeating St. Louis 2 to 0. Ty Cobb doubled in his first at-bat in 1905 off New York pitching great Jack Chesbro. Leon Ames, New York Giant pitcher, pitched a five inning no-hitter against the St. Louis Cardinals. Casey Stengel, playing for Brooklyn, had four straight hits, stole two bases, and walked once. In 1902 the Philadelphia A's Danny Murphy had six hits, including a grand-slam home run. Brooklyn's Van Lingle Mungo pitched a 2-to-0 shut out, struck out twelve, allowed three hits, and knocked in both of the Dodger runs.

In 1890 Cy Young three-hit Chicago as Cleveland won 8 to 1. Chicago White Sox infielder Sam "The Dixie Thrush" Strang collected seven hits in a doubleheader. Yankee pitcher Russ Van Atta not only shut out the Washington Senators 16 to 0, but went 4 for 4 at the bat. Dizzy Dean three-hit

Pittsburgh and allowed only one unearned run in a 3-to-1 victory. First baseman Fred Luderus of the Philadelphia Phillies had a home run, a double, and two singles in four at-bats. Boston Red Sox rookie pitcher Buck O'Brien got off on the right foot in 1911, blanking the Philadelphia A's 2 to 0. He kept it going by besting the Cleveland club 3 to 0, and ran his shutout innings pitched to 20 before allowing a run. This was a record that stood until 1945, when another Red Sox rookie, Dave Ferriss, came along to toss 22 scoreless frames. When Hall of Fame catcher Roger Bresnahan made his major league debut, it was as a pitcher, and he defeated Washington 3 to 0. The Dodgers' Jack Dalton had five straight hits in his first game in the big show. All of his hits came off the Giants' pitching great, Christy Mathewson. Cecil Travis of Washington also went 5 for 5 in his first game.

The Pirates' Larry French had his first pitch in the majors hit for a home run, and though in the second inning, his first pitch was also hit for a homer, he still won the game over the Giants 3 to 2. Who can ever forget that Cleveland Indian pitching great, Bob Feller, who struck out 15 St. Louis Browns in his first game? Rapid Robert was only 18 at the time. In 1905 Irv Young, a rookie left-handed pitcher, joined the Boston Braves (Red Stockings then) and must have wondered if he would get paid overtime. In his first game he shut out the St. Louis club 2 to 0, then defeated Pittsburgh 4 to 2 in ten innings, and then he had to go 15 innings to defeat the Chicago Cubs 3 to 1. He was a 20-game winner that year, but dropped 21 games.

When pitching great Carl Hubbell pitched his first game in the big time, he lasted only until the second inning when the Pittsburgh Pirates drove him from the mound with five runs. That was in July 1928. Revenge came the following season, when on May 8 at New York's Polo Grounds King Carl no-hit the Corsairs, 11 to 0. Ernie Shore, the big right-handed pitcher who was a star for the Boston Red Sox from 1914–17, got his big league start for John McGraw's National League Giants in 1912. It was the only game he pitched in the National League, which was understandable because in the one inning he worked, the ninth, the Boston Braves knocked out eight hits and scored ten runs against him. He had a 19-run lead when he entered the contest; the New Yorkers held on to win 21 to 12.

Shore wasn't the only rookie pitcher to get off to a shaky start. The Giants' Rube Marquard was racked up by the Cincinnati Reds for six hits and five runs in four innings during a 7-to-1 New York loss. The great Christy Mathewson, who won none and lost three in his first season, gave up a single, hit a batter, and allowed two runs in a relief role in his debut. Outfielder and evangelist Billy Sunday whiffed four straight times in his first game. Or how about Brooklyn's Nap Rucker, who in 1907 was beaten by Boston in his first start, 3 to 2. He distinguished himself by making two wild pitches, two wild throws on fielding plays, and stood on the mound holding the ball while Boston's second sacker Claude Ritchey stole home with the winning run. Billy Herman, long time Chicago Cub infielder, while batting was hit on the head by his own foul ball and knocked unconscious in his second time at bat in the big leagues. One W. J. Duggleby became the first rookie to hit a home run in his first at-bat. That was way back on April 21, 1898, for George Stallings' Philadelphia club. Outfielder Johnny Bates of Boston did it on April 12, 1906, to be the first National Leaguer to accomplish it since 1900. The first American Leaguer to do it was Cleveland's Earl Averill on April 16, 1929. Boston ball clubs proved to be the downfall of two Hall of Famers in their major league debuts. After walking four batters in the fourth inning against the Red Sox, Lefty Grove of Philadelphia headed for an early shower. And while the Phillies' Grover Cleveland Alexander won 28 games in his first season, the Boston Braves handed him a 5-to-4 loss in his first game. Cuban catcher Mike Gonzales watched the Giants steal four bases off him in his only game for the 1912 Boston Braves. Prince Hal Schumacher's first game for the New York Giants lasted one and one third innings, as he gave up seven runs on seven hits and a walk. The Chicago Cubs could only manage one run off relief pitcher Lefty Roy Boggs of the Boston Braves on September 17, 1928. Boggs didn't give up a hit that day, yet he hit three, made two wild pitches, and walked a batter. Bob Ewing of the 1902 Cincinnati Reds didn't fair much better against Chicago when he walked ten Cubs, seven of them in the fifth inning.

Now before we move on to the more modern-day rookies, we must tell the most incredible rookie story of all time, that of Charlie Faust. There have been many versions of the Faust story, and while I have heard a number of them, there certainly is an underlying thread of a story running through each one. As time goes on and the story is retold, I guess it changes, as in the old game we played as kids in which you would whisper a short story into the ear of the next player, he to the next, and so on until after a number of players the resulting story would be repeated and all would laugh at the new version of the original. At any rate, there is no question that there really was a player (well, I guess that too is questionable, as we shall see) named Charles Victor Faust, sometimes referred to as Charles "Victory" Faust.

Charlie was a 30-year-old rookie with John McGraw's New York Giants during the 1911 season. Ballplayers for years have been known as a superstitious bunch, and Charlie's career was an outgrowth of this fact more than anything else. It certainly wasn't his playing ability. He was an unconsciously funny character, but took himself most seriously. Charlie was a tall, lanky fellow who first appeared out of the grandstand one day while the Giants were visiting in one of the circuit's Western cities. Picture this individual walking out of the stands, a tall, lanky guy dressed in a suit and wearing a black derby on his head, asking to see Mr. McGraw. Introducing himself to McGraw, he related a story of how he had visited a fortune teller who had told him that if he would join and pitch for the Giants they would win the pennant. McGraw, being one of those superstitious people, was interested in Faust's story and invited him to remove his hat and coat and show his pitching abilities. So here was Charlie whirling his arms in all directions, leg poised high in the air, tossing pitch after pitch to McGraw. No matter what pitch McGraw would call for, the ball came in the same way, straight, no speed at all. McGraw finally threw away his glove and caught the young man from Kansas bare-handed. It wasn't long, of course, before McGraw realized he had a real character in his midst. Inquiring of Faust as to his batting prowess, he learned that Charlie considered himself pretty good.

Word was passed among the Giant players to humor McGraw's new find. So here he was, in his best suit, at bat. The pitch was lobbed in, and Faust hit a slow roller to short. But the forewarned Giants let him beat out the hit, deliberately chasing Charlie around the bases, letting him slide into each base all the way to home. Great enjoyment was had by all as the Sunday suit took a beating at each base. That evening when the Giants boarded their train en route to their next playing date, there was Charlie Faust. McGraw informed his squad that he was taking Charlie along to help them win the pennant. Every day from then on, Faust was in uniform warming up, certain he was going to be called upon to pitch and save the day for the Giants. When the Giants would fall behind, down to the bullpen would go Charlie to warm up but never to pitch. Now it seemed more often than not the Giants would rally once Charlie began throwing. Their good luck charm seemed to work. A superstition, sure, but unexplainable as it was, when Faust started throwing the Giants started hitting. Finally, late in the season, Faust was put into a couple of games long after the Giants had won the pennant. In all seriousness, Faust was sure of his ability, never realizing that the opponents were aware of the situation. Their wild and furious swings were, he felt, certainly a tribute to the speed of his fastball and the break of his curve. Appearing in two games, he completed two innings and recorded two strikeouts. Many of the accounts of Faust's career say that he did get into a game as a batter, repeating the base-sliding show that he had put on for McGraw during his tryout. I can find no record of his appearance at bat, so I must discount these reports. I do remember hearing once that his appearance at the plate occurred after three were out and the other team stayed around while Charlie performed his base-running prowess. The Giants went on to meet the Philadelphia Athletics in the World Series, losing four games to two with Faust seriously claiming that had he been used they would have won. When the 1912 spring training season rolled around, there was Faust ready to go. Again, game after game, there he was warming up, spinning his own particular brand of magic. Another pennant for the Giants in 1912, another loss in the World Series, this time to the Boston Red Sox, and again Charlie was bemoaning the fact that had he pitched, surely they would have won.

1913 arrived, and as sure as could be, there was the old vet Charlie Faust, now a great drawing card with the fans. Not even a theatrical contract for a Broadway appearance could keep him away from his beloved Giants. Again, McGraw kept stalling him from game to game. Finally, after the Giants had won the 1913 pennant, McGraw tired of his good luck charm and released him. In quest of a job, Faust went on to visit other big league training camps the next season. There were no takers. Finally his money ran out, and he had to return to the Midwestern farm from which he had come. Surely as he left the big leagues he was convinced of two things—that he really never was given a chance, and that he was truly a great pitcher by virtue of his two hitless innings.

Maybe our story should end here, but it has a postscript. After three straight pennants, the Giants, without Charlie Faust, slipped to second place in 1914, finishing ten-and-one-half games behind the "Miracle Boston Braves." Two years later, on June 18, 1915, Charlie Faust died. I only hope it wasn't from a broken heart, for surely Charlie Faust was an unusual rookie, one worth remembering in any book on baseball.

1942:
A Bumper
Crop

To the surprise of many, the Brooklyn Dodgers (now in Los Angeles) were the pride and joy of the nation in 1941. Just the mention of Brooklyn or their superb outfielder Fred "Dixie" Walker would bring down the house on any radio show, or for that matter, at any place where a group might gather. Oh, how Dodger fans suffered during the World Series when their catcher, Mickey Owen, let a Hugh Casey spitball get past him on a third-strike call. This miscue allowed the Yankees' Tommy Henrich to move safely to first base and ignite the New Yorkers to still another world championship under that old master Joe McCarthy. Joe DiMaggio, Bill Dickey, King Kong Keller, Red Ruffing, all names to signal fear in the hearts of their opponents—kings of the American League and baseball were these New York Yankees.

War clouds were well over the horizon during 1941, but only a small trickle of players were wearing the uniforms of Uncle Sam. This was soon to change. Brooklyn's bubble was soon to burst, as an up-and-coming St. Louis Cardinal team was being put together out in the Mound City. The Cardinals would reign for three years, until wartime priorities would put an end to what appeared to be a dynasty in the making. The Yankees continued to march along stubbornly, failing to give in to the holes in their ranks being made by Uncle Sam.

What a wonderful array of rookies appeared at the 1942 training camps, and what talent still lay in the lower minors, most of it not to appear until victory had been achieved on the war front. Who were the drums beating for during the 1941–42 winter? Let's take a look back at that long-ago spring and its cast of characters.

In a wartime season, rookie stars were apt to change scenes suddenly.

19

When the 1941 season ended, the major leagues were looking forward to a rich harvest from the farms. Two shortstops were supposedly the cream of the crop. Claude Corbitt was on his way from Montreal to Brooklyn to make Pee Wee Reese hustle to hold the job he had recently taken from Leo Durocher. John Pesky had arrived in Boston to relegate Red Sox manager Joe Cronin to a utility role. Uncle Sam beckoned and these two outstanding prospects were the object of his call. Corbitt never arrived in Brooklyn until 1945, and then for only two games before moving on to Cincinnati where he never filled more than a utility role. Pesky had a fine rookie season in '42 when he banged out 205 hits while batting .331. John, of course, returned from service to help the Bosox to the 1946 pennant and played for ten more years in the American League. Still active as a coach, Pesky has also served Boston as a manager, and has had a term in the broadcasting booth.

Entering the 1942 season, the Boston Red Sox had another prospect by the name of Lancelot Yank Terry. He was better known as Yank Terry, a name—some speculated—Boston owner Tom Yawkey would have changed from this constant reminder of his New York nemesis, the Yankees. Terry was bound to Boston from the Pacific Coast League. It was felt that the aces coming from the Coast League were often overrated, as the Sox had learned a year earlier when one Oscar Judd, a highly touted left-hander and a big winner, wound up on option in Louisville. Judd did return to win eight games for Boston in '42. However, Terry led the West Coast circuit in wins (26) and ERA (2.31), walked only 74 and whiffed 172. The big right-hander was 29-years-old, a far cry from the age of today's average rookie, but not at all unusual for the days when players put in a longer apprenticeship down on the farm. Until he reeled off the 26-8 record in 1941, his high-water mark for his previous eight campaigns had been 16 victories. Remember, the Coast League played a long 178-game schedule. Yank had a brief stint with the 1940 Red Sox and did win one game in four appearances. Among his qualifications for the majors was an odd sense of humor. Possessor of a fine set of upper dentures, when the going got tough he would remove these and proceed to make faces at the opposing batters—a sight which not only gave the batter a laugh, but also caused much distraction. This oral strategy, eagerly anticipated at Fenway Park, did not seem to work, as in four seasons (1942–45) with the Red Sox, Yank managed only 19 wins while dropping 28 before departing the major league scene.

Down at the Polo Grounds in New York, the Giants and new manager Mel Ott were eagerly awaiting the arrival of a slick-fielding second baseman from Atlanta named Connie Ryan. Ott felt he would need a fielder of Ryan's ability to replace the departed Burgess Whitehead, who had failed badly in

1941 and had been sent packing, and to make up for the lack of range of first baseman John Mize, recently obtained from St. Louis. Ryan had been the main reason that the Crackers had reached the playoffs with Nashville, the ultimate winner. Giant shortstop Billy Jurges needed a keystone partner with Ryan's ability as much as Mize needed a fielder on his right. With veteran Billy Werber at third base, the Giants rightfully felt their infield problems were over. It didn't work out that way. Ryan appeared in 11 games, hit .185, and wound up in Jersey City, while another rookie, Mickey Witek, took over the second base chores. In April of 1943, Ryan was joined by catcher Hugh Poland on a train ride to Braves Field in Boston, with catcher Ernie Lombardi heading to Gotham. Perhaps the Giants made a mistake, as Ryan remained in the majors for 11 more seasons to star with the Braves, Reds, Phillies, and White Sox.

Ryan wasn't the only minor leaguer awaited at the Polo Grounds. A four-letter man from the University of West Virginia, Herbert "Babe" Barna was on his way from Minneapolis where he had hit .336 with 24 home runs and 22 doubles. Barna had had a cup of coffee with the Phillies in '37 and '38 and with the Giants in '41, and the big heavy hitter, it was felt, would fit in well with the "new" Giants. He did team up with Ott and fellow rookie Willard Marshall in the outfield for '42, but in '43 he was sent over to the American League Red Sox where he ended his major league stay after 30 games. Babe made a hit on his first trip to the plate as a Giant. It landed in the right field seats at the Polo Grounds—his biggest claim to fame. A 21-year-old lefty pitcher who had made four appearances with the '41 Giants was also returning for '42 after being hotly pursued by the rival American League Senators, Red Sox, and Yankees. Dave Koslo joined fellow left-handers Carl Hubbell, Cliff Milton, and Tom Sunkel to give the Giants an awesome array of portsiders. Described as cold, practical, unemotional, and humble, this brilliant prospect won three and dropped six before Uncle Sam called. He returned in 1946 to star for years for Horace Stoneham's nine, but little remembered today was his arrival in '42.

In Detroit they were talking about the son of former major league catcher Howard Wakefield. The son, an outstanding hitter, who had signed for a reported $52,000 bonus, had batted seven times for the Tigers in '41, although he spent most of the summer with Winston-Salem of the Piedmont League. Detroit owner, auto body tycoon Walter Briggs, had engaged with the Cleveland Indians in a bidding war for this young man as each time he took batting practice, fellow players would gasp at his power. Dick Wakefield spent '42 with Beaumont of the Texas League, but oh how they raved about the second coming of Ty Cobb, Hank Greenberg, and Charlie Gehringer all rolled into one. He returned to the majors in '43 to stay for eight years, but never really approached his advanced billing.

In Chicago, the White Sox were touting a six-foot-three, 200-pound Polish southpaw named Stan Goletz. Somewhat of a rarity, he not only had won 15 games at Oklahoma City, but had also batted .300. Called up to Chicago in September of '41, he had made his major league debut not as a pitcher at all, but as a pinch hitter, a trick he did five times, getting three hits. Not only did "Stosh" become A-1 in the hearts of the White Sox faithful, but in the eyes of his draft board as well. He never appeared in another game at Comiskey Park. Imagine what might have been had this good-natured rookie been permitted a chance to take the mound in the Windy City. One of many players to come down the major league trail in the tradition of Babe Ruth, those who can hit and pitch, Stanley lacked running speed, which seemed to insure a mound career, but fate dictated otherwise.

The talent-rich New York Yankees were high on three outstanding pitching prospects. One was Hank Borowy, the nation's most sought after collegian, whose blazing fastball was chalking up no-hitters and shutouts while he pitched for Fordham. Hank reported to the Yankee camp with an 18-10 record at Newark. Coming along with him from the Bears was Johnny Lindell with an outstanding 23-4 record after an 18-7 record in Kansas City. Rated better than both of these by scouts was another right-hander, Mel Queen, who was 14-5 at Binghamton. All three faced the formidable task of cracking a staff already heavy with the likes of Ernie Bonham, Spud Chandler, Atley Donald, Lefty Gomez, Johnny Murphy, Red Ruffing, and Marius Russo. There were three other rookies of whom much was expected, Rugger Ardizoia, Al Gettel, and Milo Candini. Borowy turned out to be the best of the group, winning 15 and losing 4. Strangely, after successful '43 and '44 campaigns in New York, winning 14 and 17 respectively, he reeled off 10 wins in 1945 before he was suddenly traded to the National League Cubs. There he added 11 more wins to total 21 for the year and led the Chicago nine to the National League championship. Lindell won two games and lost one before he was switched to the outfield where he performed until 1950. The Yankees then sent him to the National League where he summered for several more years. Queen won one game and returned in '44, but never gained the success predicted for him. Despite a career which sent him to Pittsburgh and lasted until 1952, he showed only 27 victories against 40 losses. Of the other three, Ardizoia returned in 1947 to make ten appearances with no record. Gettel returned in '45 with fair success. Candini popped up in 1943 with the Washington Senators.

The Chicago Cubs were presenting a different story in one Louis Alexander Novikoff, better known as the "Mad Russian." Lou had appeared in 62 games for the '41 Little Bears after five highly successful minor league seasons. 1942 turned out to be his best season in the "bigs," as he appeared in 128 games batting .300. One of the all-time great minor league players, he averaged .337 for his minor career, but never really made it in the majors. It seems he went fishing too often, mostly for curve balls, few of which landed anywhere but in the catcher's mitt.

Depending upon your definition of a rookie, the man most touted for the 1942 season was a tall slender southpaw pitcher for the St. Louis Cardinals named Howard Pollet. Yes, those of you who remember 1942 will recall another Cardinal rookie pitcher turned outfielder who over the long run turned out to be a Hall of Famer, Stan Musial. It was not Musial but Pollet who was drawing the notices in early '42. "The best pitcher to come along since Bob Feller," they said. Joining the Cards on August 15, 1941, he had a 20-3 record at Houston, with 151 strikeouts and an ERA of 1.16, a new league record supplanting the 1931 record set by Whitlow Wyatt (1.53). Appearing in nine games for the '41 Redbirds, he was 5-2, and in '42 he was 7-5. While he did help the Cards to the pennant, he was not the living legend he was expected to be. In fairness to Howie, he did stay in the majors for 14 seasons and won 131 games, among which were a 21-win season and 20-win season. Now, the less heralded Musial was a sore-armed class C league pitcher who was converted to an outfielder. He played 12 games for the '41 edition of the Cardinals. Boasting some long-ball power, there were reports that he might turn out to be the surprise of the year or that he might very well lead Rochester or Houston to minor league championships. Surprise it was. Who would expect that he could break into the outfield of Enos Slaughter (.311), Terry Moore (.294), and Johnny Hopp (.303)? As mentioned earlier, the Cardinals had sent their '41 first baseman, John Mize, to New York opening up that position on their club. Enter John Hopp at first base and young Mr. Musial into left field where he hit .315 with ten home runs, both second to Slaughter's team-leading .318 and 13 round trippers. Thanks in a big part to "Stan The Man," the Cardinals won the National League crown. He remained in the Cardinal dugout for 22 seasons and four World Series, entered the Baseball Hall of Fame in 1969, and is regarded as an all-time baseball great, something that was not predicted in the winter of 1941–42. It should not pass without noting that the Cardinals were into one of the great periods in their history, winning three pennants from '42 to '44, and again in '46. They might have also won in '45 if it were not for the war (Musial, among others, was in the service). Many consider the '42-'43 Cardinals among the all-time great teams in baseball history.

These then were the heralded ones, the supposed cream of the crop, the sure bets who got the bulk of the ink. As our chapter title suggests, it was a "bumper crop." There were others less ballyhooed, who though appearing to have promise, were not considered blue-chippers. What a mistake! Consider the other boys of the summer of '42 and draw your own conclusion.

Waiting in the wings of the minor leagues were such as the Cardinals' pitchers Johnny Beazley (21 wins for the '42 Cardinals), Harry "The Cat" Brecheen, Murray Dickson, Red Munger, and first baseman Ray Sanders. The other St. Louis entry, the Browns, had a power-hitting shortstop in Vern Stephens and a curve-balling pitcher, Clarence "Hooks" Iott. Also coming to the Browns was a big former railroad worker who had put in a hitch with the CCC before turning his attention to baseball. Frank Biscan had won 20 games with Lima, Ohio, in 1940. With the '42 Browns he won none and lost one and closed out his stay in the majors in 1948 after another trial in '46, with a 7-9 record. Chuck Stevens was another rookie the Brownies had a look at in 1941, but in 1942 he could not move the vet George McQuinn off first base and was returned to the Toledo Mud Hens where he enjoyed little success. Uncle Sam stepped in, and off he went until 1946, when he did return to hold down the first base job, replacing McQuinn who had been traded to Philadelphia after the 1945 campaign. Speaking of St. Louis, there was another rookie of note in the Cardinal camp, a local St. Louis native who, of all things, was a former table tennis champion. He had gained the title of the best second baseman in the Pacific Coast League. Buddy Blattner played only 19 games with the Redbirds, but after the war returned to play with the New York Giants.

The Giants had several highly regarded rookies, but two of them, both catchers, were a strange pair. They were not only cousins, but one was named after a former Giant great. Bill Clemensen and his cousin Larry Doyle Smith never made it to the Polo Grounds. Smith, the son of Doc Smith (a pre-war catcher) was the more highly regarded of the two. Off the campus of North Carolina State, he appeared to be the Giants third-string catcher behind Harry Danning and Rae Blaemire. Giant farm director Bill Terry was singing praises for reliever Hugh East, who once fanned seven of nine men to face him in a minor league game. East appeared in four games for the '42 Giants, 13 the following season, and left the bigs with a 2-and-6 record. Terry was also boosting a couple of potential Jewish stars from his Jersey City farm. He hoped that 14-game winner Hank Feldman would form an all Jewish battery with Danning, while Sid Gordon would patrol the outfield. Feldman made it and played until 1946, posting a 35-35 record. Gordon played six games in '42, stuck in '43, went into the service, returned in '46, and starred for the Giants, Braves, and Pirates for 11 more seasons. Right-hander Rube Fischer, who had a look-see in '41 and won one game, was back in '42, but summered in Jersey City, returned for the war years to win 15 more games, but was tagged with 34 losses during that period.

The Giants' arch-rivals, the Brooklyn Dodgers, had a large group of prospects for the '42 season, none of whom had much major league success. Dodger fans will remember: Les Burge, who was going to make us forget Dolph Camilli; catcher Cliff Dapper, who was heralded for his handling of pitchers but had a tendency to drop too many baseballs; slugger Jack Graham (son of the old Braves catcher Peaches Graham), who had led Montreal into the Little World Series; or pitchers Bob Chipman, a native of Brooklyn who did survive 12 National League summers; Ed Head, who pitched through the wartime seasons and was coming off 18 wins at Montreal; Chet Kehn, who was Larry MacPhail's answer to the Cardinals' Pollet and appeared in three major league games with no won-lost record; and Emile Lochbaum, a Louisiana State University graduate known as "Sweets" because of his fondness for candy, a big winner in Atlanta who never made it and returned to New Orleans where he taught math and coached high school football. Then there was pitcher Jack Kraus, also known for his hitting, a lefty, who had won 18 at Durham and later popped up with the '43 Phillies. Outfielder Tom Tatum was not expected to unseat Pete Reiser in centerfield, but this right-handed power hitter, who once hit Atlanta pitching for three home runs in one day, was expected to receive outfield consideration. He didn't make it until '47 when he was traded to Cincinnati where he played 69 games.

The Chicago Cubs were singing praises for some rookies you may remember. Certainly anyone from Puerto Rico will remember pitcher Hi Bithorn because one of the best baseball fields in the Puerto Rican League is Hi Bithorn Stadium. It is located in Santurce, and is named for this big right-handed pitcher who was 9 and 14 for the '42 Cubs and enjoyed moderate big league success during four seasons. A couple of other players from south of the border were vying for jobs in Wrigley Field during 1942. Jesse Flores, a native Mexican, had been a two-year mainstay for the Cubs' Los Angeles Angels farm club. Known as a strikeout pitcher, Jesse once put together 18 consecutive scoreless innings in the Pacific Coast League. He appeared in four games for the Cubs, but boasted a 14-5 record at L.A. and wound up with the Philadelphia A's in '43 where he starred during the war years. The other Latin trying to make the Cubs was a 25-year-old Cuban catcher, Chico Hernandez. He is an interesting story. Until the present regime of Fidel Castro came along, Cuba was shipping some pretty fair ballplayers into this country. Castro, himself a ballplayer, put an end to this. There is, however, a parallel in the Hernandez story. Chico was in his freshman year at the University of Havana in 1936 when Colonel Fulgencia Batista overthrew the Gomez government. Batista, with his sugar strikers and well-armed soldiers, marched into Havana in December of that year, and the first order of business was to close the university. He had no use for any student strikers. Fleeing the country, Chico came to the U.S., thus starting a baseball career born of a revolution. He played with moderate success for the '42 and '43 Cubs. Among the bumper crop of the Cubs was Cy Block, a Brooklyn boy out of New York University who had led the Sally League in batting and RBIs. He managed only 17 games in three years in Chicago. Joining Block in the battle against Cub third baseman Stan Hack was Glen "Rip" Russell, back from winning the Texas League MVP for a second chance. He made it, but seldom appeared at third. Another in the Cub camp was one Wellington "Wimpy" Quinn, named after the comic-strip character, Popeye's sidekick. Cut from the Babe Ruth mold, Wimpy performed at first base, in the outfield, and pitched. He had made three appearances with the '41 Cubs, and that ended his career. Perhaps the best of the Cub hopefuls was outfielder Harry "Peanuts" Lowery, who split the '42 season between Chicago and then minor league cities Milwaukee and L.A. He finally stuck in the Windy City and became a genuine star. Signed by the old minor league star Jigger Statz, Lowery was a little man, 5'8½", 170 pounds, but carried a big bat for 13 National League seasons. The remaining Chicago prospects were pitchers: Glenn Gardner, who made it in 1945 with the Cardinals; a local Chicago boy, Emil Kush, who got into one game, went to Milwaukee, the service, and returned in 1946 for five more seasons; and Russ Meers who had a similar story. Then there was left-hander Johnny Schmitz, a young man from the woods of Wisconsin who had won two games for the '41 edition of the Cubs. He was up to stay for 12 more years and to become one of the better pitchers in the big time. He had the distinction of pitching just one pitch to one batter and getting his first win in his first big league try. Relieving in the top of the ninth against Brooklyn, with the Dodgers ahead 4 to 2 and one out, Brooklyn batter Cookie Lavagetto (the same who ruined Bill Bevens' World Series no-hitter) grounded the first pitch to short for a double play. The Cubs staged a three-run rally in their half of the inning to give them and "Bear Tracks" Schmitz the win.

The Pittsburgh Pirates were boasting two rookies, both of whom had had a cup of coffee in '41, pitcher Bill Brandt and outfielder Culley Rickard. Both later played briefly in Forbes Field. The other Pennsylvania entry in the National League, the Philadelphia Phillies, had a native Pennsylvanian named Ron Northey. He was a former high school star who had left Duke University after his freshman year to play in the Eastern League at Williamsport where he led the league in RBIs. This long-ball-hitting outfielder made the jump to Philadelphia and stayed in the majors for 12 seasons.

The New York Yankees had a young catcher, Ken "Ziggy" Sears, son of the umpire, but he couldn't budge Bill Dickey or Buddy Rosar out of the catching job. Detroit had outfielder Bob Patrick tabbed as a future star. Nine games in two years was their reward. The Tigers also had outfielder-infielder Don Ross, who had had previous tries with Detroit and the Dodgers. He made it and stayed around for five more years. Also on the Detroit roster was infielder Billy Hitchcock, a product of the Yankee farm system. Big, strong, with good range and a fine bat, Billy remained and played with several teams until 1953. The White Sox listed Harrisburg first baseman Harvey Johnson and shortstop Leo Wells. Of the two, only Wells stuck around as a part-timer, and then only for two seasons. The Cincinnati Reds listed their prime prospect as pitcher Jim Prendergast, a much-traveled minor leaguer. Jim didn't make it until 1948, and then with the Boston Braves where he was 1-1. The Boston Braves had the highly regarded shortstop Nanny Fernandez, billed as a better shortstop then Eddie Miller. The slugger also was supposedly a better hitter than the Red Sox' Ted Williams. His rifle arm, great hands and range did win him the third base job with Sebi Sisti. The other Boston entry, the Red Sox, listed first baseman Paul Campbell, catcher Bill Conroy, and infielder Eddie Pellagrini. The first two were replacing aging vets, while the latter replaced shortstop John Pesky who was headed to the service.

The aged sage of Shibe Park and the Philadelphia Athletics, Connie Mack, had four fine rookies, all of whom made it. In addition to right-handed pitcher Fred Caliguiri, there was right-handed pitcher Russ Christopher, of whom little was predicted, though he would last in the majors for seven years. Another righty with good speed and a good curve was Dick Fowler. He stayed for 10 years, and on September 9, 1945, no-hit the St. Louis Browns. Then there was a chunky little outfielder who had had two previous short trials and hailed from Czechoslovakia, Elmer Valo. He roamed big league ball parks for 20 years, most of which were spent with Connie in Philadelphia. Elmer was one of those unusual players who batted left-handed and threw right-handed. He was a favorite with fans everywhere for his great catches, most often made while smashing into outfield walls, thus earning himself the name Elmer "Valiant" Valo.

Perhaps more than those of any other team, the best groups of rookies coming up in 1942 were those of the Cleveland Indians and the Washington

Nats (also known as the Senators). Any serious baseball fan will recognize the youngsters in these two groups and remember their accomplishments. Consider what Cleveland offered—catchers Otto Denning and Jim Hegan, first baseman Les Fleming, outfielders Otis Hockett and Hank Edwards, and pitchers Steve Gromek and Red Embree. All stayed around the major league scene for a number of years. How many teams can boast of such a class of rookies all arriving in the same season? Denning, Fleming, and Hockett all stepped right into starting roles. The Nats also boasted a quality group: pitchers Early Wynn and Roger Wolff; the two Cuban outfielders Roberto Ortiz and Bobby Estalella (who had put in parts of five previous seasons); and infielders Stan Galle, Charlie Letchas, Bob Repass and Hillis Layne. Not quite as high quality a group as the Cleveland gang, they were nevertheless a group not to be overlooked. Of course, the cream of this Washington crop was Early Wynn, who pitched for 23 years in the majors with Washington and Cleveland, reaching the charmed circle of those pitchers who won 300 games. Early retired in 1963. Signed as a 16-year-old while he was in school at Panama City, Florida, he entered the Hall of Fame in 1971 and is one of a select few who have played in three different decades.

There they are, the bumper crop of 1942. It will take quite a year to come close to the quality they represented. Surely the war had its effect on them, but still they represented the last of the prewar harvest from the farms. Before we leave 1942, it should be mentioned that in the lower minors there were others already making their presence felt, who were waiting for their day in the sun, delayed by the war. We will get to them later, but you will surely recall some of the names: Frank Shea and Charlie Wensloff at K.C.; Joe Wood, Jr. and Lou Lucier at Louisville; Eric Tipton and Billy Johnson at Newark; Heinz Becker at Milwaukee; Lou Klein, Ted Wilks and Preacher Roe at Columbus; Frank Biscan and Fred Sanford at Toledo; Wes Westrum at Minneapolis; Dick Culler at St. Paul; Larry Jansen and Ferris Fain at San Francisco; Blix Donnelly at Sacramento; Willard Marshall at Atlanta. And so many other familiar names: Joe Hatten, Joffre Cross, Austin Knickerbocker, Jim Russell, Howard Moss, Earl Harrist, Tom De La Cruz, Ralph Hodgin, Walt Dubiel, Ed McGah, Ralph Kiner, Gene Woodling, Hank Wyse and Ellis Kinder, to name a few.

1943-45:
The War
Years

The effects of the Unites States' entry into World War II in late 1941 made their presence felt on the world of baseball in 1942, but it was not until 1943 that the face of the game really changed. By the time the spring training camps opened in 1943, more than 25 percent of the entire playing personnel had left the major league scene to enter the various branches of the armed forces. Some had reached the front-line fighting; others were contributing to the war effort in other ways. It was only natural that many of the players could be found in the military's vital physical training program. A look at the rosters of the teams on our military bases showed many of the top players from both the majors and the minors. Of course, many of the young players who would have been the top rookies of the 1943 to 1945 period were among this group. The parade of players who entered the service in 1942 was only the beginning, the end was not in sight, but baseball would continue as long as nine men could be put onto the field.

The reports from the minor league scene were even more devastating as to the immediate future. Entire new looks prevailed, as more than two thousand young players traded their flannels for the khaki of the military. With this large number of players marching off to war, there was a wholesale abandonment or suspension of franchises along the minor league front. Add to this the travel restrictions imposed by the government and you can see why many minor league team owners found it difficult to operate their clubs. The minor leagues folded at an alarming rate. From some 31 leagues in operation in 1942, only 10 operated in 1943 and 1944. As the GIs began to return from the war in 1945, the number of leagues in operation grew to 12. This reduction of the minors, of course, meant that there were fewer rookies of quality arriving on the major league scene.

29

Baseball moved on through these years without fear and asking no favors. Imagine the problems that would face any other sport or business suffering the same percentage of losses among its top performers or reserve forces. Surely any of the others would have had to close up shop entirely. Actually, the 1943 season began with some players of decent quality still performing on the diamonds. As the season progressed, more and more of these players began to disappear. The major league clubs were forced, for the first time, to train in the North and forego their annual trek to their spring playgrounds in the South. That the game was able to continue at all during the war years was due to the ardent fan in the White House. Franklin D. Roosevelt took time out from his duties as commander in chief to write what has become known as his "Green Light" letter of January 15, 1942, to then baseball commissioner Judge Kenesaw M. Landis. In this letter the president expressed his belief that baseball should continue as an important morale booster during the crisis. While Roosevelt did not advocate the deferment of baseball players (baseball did not ask for it either), he felt the game could continue with the use of older players. This was exactly the course that baseball followed. Onto the scene came many aging rookies, reactivated retired veterans, and those players who for one reason or another were deferred from military service. While it certainly seemed that the draft boards were practically camping in the baseball locker rooms, baseball forged on. As it had done during World War I, baseball survived and exerted its influences upon the country.

One of the most effective morale-building posters during the war pictured a young soldier who was declaring, "I'm fighting for my right to boo the Dodgers." He was talking about his inalienable right to freedom of speech, expressed by the fans' heckling of that lovable baseball team from Brooklyn, which had long been famed for its slaphappy fans. "The Brooklyn Symphoney," "Moider the ump," and "Kill the bum" were the fans' trademarks. On the war fronts, baseball scores continued to be the most popular news items among the troops. The nation's sports pages were full of pictures of battle-weary soldiers and sailors huddled around a radio in some far away place listening to World Series games. At the major league ball fields at home, foul balls no longer became the prized souvenir of those who retrieved them, but were faithfully returned to the usher, who would place them in a conveniently placed receptacle, later to be shipped off to our boys in service. GIs were admitted to ball games free of charge, and baseball survived.

Landis summed up the game's position when he said, "We do not want baseball in America exempt from the liabilities of common life in America. We want the same rules applied and enforced on us as on everyone else. This is baseball's position, and I take full responsibility for it. I don't want any man in the stands to think that any man on the field is exempt from any law or rule or statute. About the question of whether baseball is going to die or is going to live, I've formed the habit of living." In Washington, Elmer Davis, director of the Office of War Information, stressed his opinion, "If there is no baseball, my customers—those million and a half soldiers in foreign lands—are going to put up a hell of a squawk. We will see baseball, and if it isn't as good as it used to be, it will still be good enough to do." Servicemen wrote home from overseas telling of their interest, and even men who at home would ordinarily not read about baseball in the daily newspapers were avidly following the game. Their interest did not end here, as witnessed by the quantities of uniforms, gloves, shoes, balls, bats, and equipment provided by the baseball fund for their use.

Baseball scores as usual may have been an important factor in maintaining the morale of the servicemen listening to the radio everywhere from Guadalcanal to the Rhine, but putting together and holding together a club in wartime was no cinch. Good teams are the result of carefully training men to play as a unit. Take away the key players and anticipate that more will leave and the result could easily become chaos. Fortunately, the men running the clubs did not let this happen. Many baseball historians tend to characterize wartime baseball as made up of rejects, fading veterans, patched-up ball clubs, and error-making youngsters. To some extent this was true, but on the other hand there were many greats whose careers were not interrupted by the service. I do not believe that the game was as as diluted during the war as is generally believed. I think this is an important fact to remember when we discuss the men who appeared as rookies during this era of baseball, and I propose that the brand of baseball played in 1943, '44, and '45 may not have been as bad as some people have claimed. Certainly it was not as top-notch as it was in the years following the war, but then again, in today's world of expansion baseball, it is entirely possible that some of those performing in the major leagues would have had their problems holding down a regular position during the era under discussion. Before we get to the rookies of the war era, I feel we should examine the competition these players faced. How else can we put them into perspective?

As surely as the St. Louis Cardinals dominated the National League scene from 1926 to 1934, they rebounded to build a dynasty during the 1942 to 1946 period. During the war, they captured the National League flags in '43 and '44 to complete three successive pennants. Gone were "Ol' Diz" and his brother Daffy Dean, and "Wild Horse of the Osage"—Pepper Martin. Gone too were Jim Bottomley, Ducky Medwick, and Rip Collins. They were replaced by the likes of young Stan Musial, the Cooper brothers, Harry Brecheen, Marty Marion, Howie Pollet, and company. Consider that this new group of Redbirds won 106 games in 1942, and 105 in both 1943 and 1944, all years in which they won the National League crown. In 1945 they dropped back to second place, but still managed to win 95 games. In any era this was an outstanding record. These were good Cardinal teams. The 1945 team had lost several stars to Uncle Sam, including Stan Musial, Walker Cooper, and George Munger, while Mort Cooper had been traded to the Boston Braves. With them the Cardinals may have made up the three game margin of the Chicago Cub victory in the pennant race. With the return of the servicemen, the Cards made it four pennants in five years by winning in 1946.

The 1945 championship Cubs had some quality players who would have made a good showing in any era. They continued as regulars after the war, as the National League clubs returned to prewar strength; Phil Cavarretta, Stan Hack, Bill Nicholson, Andy Pafko, Peanuts Lowery, Claude Passeau, Hank Wyse, and Hank Borowy to name a few.

Consider also some of the other players in the National League during these years: Eddie Miller and Bucky Walters at Cincinnati; Bill Herman, Arky Vaughn, Eddie Stanky, Whitlow Wyatt, and Kirby Higbe at Brooklyn; Preacher Roe, Bob Elliott, Rip Sewell, and Al Lopez at Pittsburgh; Buddy Kerr, Mel Ott, Ernie Lombardi, and Bill Voiselle at New York; Tommy Holmes, Eddie Joost, Phil Masi, and Al Javery at Boston; Pinky May, Ron Northey, and Ken Raffensberger at Philadelphia. The weakness of these wartime clubs was on the bench. It was here that the aging vets resided side by side with untried rookies. This is pretty much true today, as expansion has weakened the second line of attack.

In the American League we had three different champions during this era: The New York Yankees in '43, the St. Louis Browns in '44, and the Detroit Tigers in '45. Despite losing many of its '41 and '42 championship players to the service, the Yankees repeated as the junior loop champs, mainly on the arms of pitchers Spud Chandler, Tiny Bonham, and Charlie Wensloff. The St. Louis Browns won their only American League pennant in 1944 and followed it up by scaring the feathers off their National League counterparts in the World Series. This was a unique series when you remember that it was the last where all the games were played in the same ball park, and the last between two teams from the same city—unless you want to consider Brooklyn and New York as the same city. Unless the New York Mets and Yankees or the Chicago Cubs and White Sox can, in some future year, manage to do it, it may be the last time a city series will ever happen. It seems certain that the

'44 season will be the last in which the competing clubs share the same stadium.

For some reason, the Browns of 1944 have been put down over the years and made a symbol of ineptitude. In actuality, they were not the poor team they have been made out to be. There was a time when the Browns were not the doormat of the American League, but were a respected contender for the flag. They boasted such ballplayers as Bobby Wallace, George Sisler, Ken Williams, Jimmy Austin, George Stone, and Urban Shocker. They experienced a steady decline in the late '30s, but under the capable field-leadership of manager Luke Sewell and front office guidance of Bill DeWitt, they regained respect in 1944. They were a good team made up of a collection of well-recruited players. They proved they belonged, when after losing an early season lead, they met and defeated the Yankees in the final four games of the season. It was one of the finest clutch performances in major league history, a fact often overlooked today. They had a good-fielding, strong-hitting first baseman in George McQuinn, who performed well both before and after the war. Their second baseman was Don Gutteridge, another player who was capable of performing in any era. At shortstop was the hard-hitting Vern Stephens, who led the league in RBIs three times and played for 15 years (1942–1955) before hanging up his spikes. He was hardly what has been characterized as a wartime ballplayer. At third base was Mark Christman who put in nine years in the American League, two before and four after the war. Among the outfielders were Al Zarilla, a .299 hitter in '44 who proved his worth after the war by hitting .329 in 1948, and .325 in 1950 and stayed around the big league scene for ten years. Outfielder Mike Kreevich, the only Brown to hit over 300 in '44, had hit even higher three times in the more competitive pre-war period. The pitching staff included such established major leaguers as Jack Kramer, Nelson Potter, Bob Muncreef, Denny Galehouse, and Sig Jakucki. In the World Series that year, they averaged seven strikeouts per game. Sure, there were some journeymen ballplayers on the club who, if it were not for the war, might have been in the minor leagues and their lack of bench strength hurt the Browns, but basically, like their National League counterparts, the Cardinals, they were a good ball team.

The 1945 American League champions were the Detroit Tigers, who won the flag by a game-and-one-half margin over the Washington Senators, mainly due to the return from the service of slugging outfielder Hank Greenberg. Their roster included a number of proven major leaguers also: first baseman Rudy York, second baseman Eddie Mayo, outfielders Roy Cullenbine, Doc Cramer, and Jimmy Outlaw, catchers Bob Swift and Paul Richards, and pitchers Prince Hal Newhouser, Dizzy Trout, Al Benton, and

Stubby Overmire. While they, like all wartime clubs, had little depth, they did boast a fairly good first string.

Now that we have set the background for the war years, who were the rookies who were trying to make these clubs? Remember in these years that the clubs were training in the North, with most of the early workouts taking place inside various college field houses. They were not necessarily private affairs, as on one occasion in 1943 better than 2500 fans showed up to watch the Boston Red Sox work out at Tufts College in Medford, Massachusetts. Perhaps the prize rookie of 1943 was George "Snuffy" Stirnweiss, a shortstop-second baseman for the New York Yankees. Stirnweiss, a former University of North Carolina football hero, was a fleet-footed, sure-fielding lad up from the Newark farm club. Stirnweiss threw a scare into Yankee general manager Ed Barrow and field manager Joe McCarthy when he was called for an induction physical in late March of '43. Recently married and long suffering from ulcers, he was rejected from the service. He hit .319 in 1944, dropped to .309 in 1945, but led the league in hitting with the lowest average ever, until Boston's Carl Yastrzemski hit a league-leading .301 in 1968. Six years after his last game, Snuffy tragically met his death as a railroad train he was on plunged off a bridge into Newark Bay in New Jersey.

Detroit had the slugging Dick Wakefield back after a fine year at Beaumont in the Texas League where he hit .345. He made the Tiger club in '43 and led the league in at-bats, hits (200), and doubles (38) while hitting .316. He entered the service after 78 games of the 1944 season, returned in 1946 and stayed around for six more seasons. The former University of Michigan student never really lived up to his advanced notices. Wakefield, with a reported $52,000 bonus in his pocket, was an immediate success and hero in Detroit. In his first season, he won the annual All-Star Game after American League manager Joe McCarthy named him to his squad. Wakefield had been in the league only three months. Baseball reports began to compare Wakefield with Boston's great slugger Ted Williams, and Dick set his sights on out-hitting the Red Sox blaster. When the two met during the 1945 offseason, it was reported that Wakefield wagered a chunk of his 1946 salary that he would out-hit Williams, a fact which sent Baseball Commissioner A. B. Chandler hurrying off to the Red Sox' camp at Sarasota, Florida, to start an investigation. It ended when he became convinced the two sluggers were just employing a figure of speech common among baseball players who loved to merely make fictitious big bets. Nevertheless, it was an item of some speculation during the early days of 1946.

The New York Yankees were unveiling a rookie battery in 1943. A big left-hander came up from their Newark farm club named Tommy Byrne.

Tommy stayed around the American League for 13 years, winning more often than he lost. It was often believed that part of his success was a result of his wildness, which certainly kept the batters on their toes. He led the league three years in a row (1949-1951) in walks, and overall he walked 1037 while striking out 766. On the receiving end, the Bronx Bombers had rookies Ken "Ziggy" Sears from Kansas City and Aaron Robinson from Newark. Sears made it for 60 games, while Robbie appeared only once. Robinson returned in '45 for eight more American League seasons, while Sears surfaced in St. Louis for seven Brownie games in 1946.

There were other American League rookies of note in 1943. Tom McBride, who in seven minor seasons never batted below .300, was vying for a Red Sox outfield position. He made it and stayed for six American League campaigns. His greatest claim to fame is a trivia expert's delight, being the first and last batter in the 1946 World Series. Another Red Sox hopeful was Johnny Lazor, also an outfielder, who played for four years in Fenway Park, leading the American League with a .310 average in 1945, but failing by five at-bats to qualify for the batting championship.

Out in Chicago, there was talk of a young outfielder named Thurman Tucker who had a look-see of seven games in 1942. No one really expected he would stay, but he fooled them all and closed out a pretty fair career eight years later with Cleveland. Out at the Wigwam on the shores of Lake Erie, there were two rookie pitchers of whom little was expected. There was a former teammate of Manager Lou Boudreau's at Illinois, a brilliant young rookie who was 15-8 at Indianapolis, Ray Poat. There was also a young pitcher, a real Indian, who had appeared in two games in '42. He made the team in 1943, winning 11 and losing 12. In 1947 he was traded to New York, where he hurled two no-hitters and led the Yankees to a number of championships. He was Allie Reynolds, the "Superchief." The Yankees, in addition to the aforementioned Stirnweiss, introduced another Newark Bear, Billy "Bull" Johnson, at third base along with his Bear teammate Bud Metheny in the outfield. In Philadelphia, Connie Mack introduced a big right-handed pitcher named Don Black and talked about people named Tal Abernathy, Fred Caligiuri, Sammy Lowry, Jimmy Pofahl, Irv Hall, Jim Tyack, and Felix Mackiewicz, several of whom briefly appeared in American League box scores, but none of whom were candidates for the Hall of Fame. The St. Louis Browns, as hard hit as all teams by service call-ups, were presenting as rookies a number of former major league veterans a la Paul Dean, Archie McKain, and Woody Rich, along with a cast of returning players from '42. There was also a long-time minor leaguer with the imposing name of Welty Seinsoth, who had won 24 games in 50 appearances with

New Orleans. He was as impressive as Connie Mack's collection of rookies. It is a rare occasion when a major league batter hits for the cycle, but that is just what rookie outfielder Leon Culberson of the Boston Red Sox did in early July 1943. There were other rookies on the rosters of the American League clubs who die-hard baseball fans recall—not all made it in '43. Remember Herb Bremer, Vince Castino, Guy Curtright, Russ Derry, Ford Garrison, Anton Karl, Roy Partee, Vic Wertz, and Joe Wood, Jr?

The senior circuit also was presenting an array of newcomers in 1943, some of whom turned out to be blue-chippers. The depths to which wartime teams were reaching was illustrated by the plight of the Brooklyn Dodgers, who were holding their spring training sessions at Bear Mountain, New York. There was the strange tale of a 17-year-old busboy at the Bear Mountain Inn who was given a chance at pro baseball. Carl Kerkam was an employee of the inn when he caught the eye of Brooklyn manager Leo Durocher, who issued him a uniform and gave him a workout at first base. Dodger veterans Augie Galan and Billy Herman took the lad under their wing and coached him with hopes that he might make the Dodger farm club at Montreal. I wish I could say the youngster arrived at Ebbets Field to win a few games for the Dodgers, but he never did, and I am not certain what his fate was. This just serves to show what major league teams were up against. They left no stone—or in this case tray—unturned in seeking talent to stock their rosters.

The teams weren't the only ones seeking people for tryouts. The fans were also aware of the shortage and were known to take things into their own hands. The Dodgers were also the subject of one such attempt by a fan, in this case an 11-year-old boy from Pittsburgh. It seems young Richard Miller decided upon a baseball career and left his hometown to seek a major league contract instead of wasting his time on the sandlots at home. After watching a Pirate-Cardinal twin bill at Forbes Field, and without telling anyone, he headed for Detroit with $50 in his pocket. Arriving in the Motor City, he found that the Tigers were not playing. Unable to find Manager Steve O'Neill, he decided to try the Brooklyn Dodgers. He purchased a railroad ticket for New York and during a two-hour wait for the train purchased himself a bat, several baseballs, and—wishing to be well prepared—a first baseman's mitt (a Dolph Camilli model), a catcher's mit (Bill Dickey), and two fielders' gloves (Joe DiMaggio and Charlie Keller). Dragging his equipment behind him, he crawled into his upper berth and headed for New York. His downfall came at breakfast the next morning when he befriended a gentleman in the dining car of the train and told him of how he was headed for the Dodgers. Trudging up the exit ramp at Grand Central Station in New

York, he saw his breakfast partner speaking with a couple of New York's finest. Richard assured the police that Brooklyn manager Durocher would not mind seeing him. The railroad police beat Leo to the would-be rookie, and soon arrangements were being made to option Richard back to the Smokey City sandlots.

Branch Rickey had moved into the Dodger front office as successor to Lieutenant Colonel Larry MacPhail, but the only rookie of promise he could come up with was a Puerto Rican infielder, Luis Olmo. Olmo made the club and batted a .303 in 57 games and due to a shortage of outfielders, he performed there instead of the infield. Traded to the Braves in 1950, he left the big league scene in 1951.

Only six players who started the 1943 season with the Philadelphia Phillies were with the club when the season ended. Among them was a big left-handed rookie pitcher who they had picked up in a prearranged trade with the New York Yankees. Al Gerheauser had won 14 games for the Yank farm club at Newark. He became the workhorse of the Phillies' staff, winning 10 while losing 19. The New York Giants were trying out a number of rookie pitchers in '43, some of whom had been tested before. Remember Rube Fischer, Hugh East, Bobby Coombs, Ken Trinkle, Bill Sayles, and the two most successful, Bill Voiselle and Sal Maglie? Maglie was not aboard until 1945 and then only briefly, but he did stick in 1950 and remained on the big league scene for 10 years. Catcher Hugh Poland was the rookie catcher the Giants were hoping would handle this farm crop. Their hopes were not realized. A pretty good outfielder who arrived on a full-time basis at the Polo Grounds in '43 was Sid Gordon, who spent 11 more seasons in the National League.

The Pittsburgh Pirates were less fortunate than any other club in replacements for their players who were off to the wars. Outfielder Jim Russell made it, and they were counting heavily on two young pitchers, Wallace Herbert, who didn't, and one Xavier Rescigno who personifies our wartime rookies. He played during the '43, '44, and '45 seasons in Forbes Field, winning 18 and losing 22. In 1938, one Woodrow Wilson Williams had appeared in 20 games for Brooklyn, but in '43 Woody popped up in Cincinnati, where he spent most of the season on the bench. However, when he finally got into action, he tied a mark that had only been reached by seven National League batters in the senior loop's history. He whacked out 10 consecutive hits. The Boston Braves presented Chuck Workman and Butch Nieman as two-thirds of their outfield in '43. In Chicago, the Cubs were singing the praises of Robert McCall, a strong-armed fastballer who they snatched from Brooklyn's farm system and who was rated as the outstanding minor league prospect. His major league debut was postponed until 1948. They also had in tow a young infielder who had won the American Associations's MVP named Eddie Stanky. He made the club and toured around the National League with four other clubs for the next 10 years. The St. Louis Cardinals, the National League champions, hit it big with rookies. Buster Adams, an infielder, made it, but was traded off to the Phillies. Infielder Lou Klein captured the second base job, and pitchers Harry Brecheen and George Munger joined the pitching staff.

As the 1944 season dawned on the major leagues, it appeared that it might take some small miracle to find enough quality players to get things underway. The major leagues annually conduct a draft meeting in which the cream of the minors are taken for the major league rosters. This year a one-man "draft" meeting was being held by Uncle Sam. Far more than 250 major league performers had gone to war, with more waiting on a day-to-day basis to be drafted. Perhaps the St. Louis Cardinal boss Sam Breadon summed it up best when he said, "We don't know where we stand for 1944." Nevertheless, as related earlier in this chapter, the seasons got underway, and while the top clubs had fairly decent first lines, it was a lack of bench strength which was evident on all clubs. Despite Breadon's reservations, his Cardinals prevailed in the World Series over their American League counterparts, the St. Louis Browns. While most of the teams presented a new look in personnel, the Philadelphia National League club, long known as the Phillies, also presented something new in names. They were to be known as the Blue Jays, a name which shortly became a wartime casualty.

The Washington Senators got things rolling at the baseball winter meetings when they sent the veteran outfielder "Indian" Bob Johnson to the Boston Red Sox "to make room for the youngsters." To this day, who the youngsters were that Senator owner Clark Griffith was talking about remains a mystery. The Washington outfield in 1944 consisted of veterans Jake Powell, Stan Spence, and George Case. This was not a bad outfield and could well have performed in other than the war years, but in '44 they couldn't prevent Washington's collapse from second place in '43 to dead last. While Griff was making way for youngsters, the Cincinnati Reds were giving a really young man a chance. A 15-year-old Joe Nuxhall started the season pitching for his high school. A few weeks later, he was signed by the Reds and became the youngest player ever to play in the major leagues at 15 years, 10 months, and 11 days old. He appeared in one game (June 10, 1944) and pitched two-thirds of an inning in relief. He didn't win or lose the contest, but gave up two hits and walked five before manager Bill McKechnie approached the mound and took the youngster off the hook. Nuxhall left with a 67.50 earned run average, but returned to the big leagues in 1952 where he remained for 15 years, winning 135 games against 117 losses.

The New York Giants were trying a different approach to obtain ballplayers by giving tryouts to Latin American players. Manager Mel Ott was giving spring tryouts to third baseman Hap Reyes, catchers Andy Pasquale and Andy Fleitas, all from Havana, Cuba, and Andy Alemendro, a shortstop from Puerto Rico. Ott's experiment didn't work. Reyes played for a while but the only Latin to stick was the Cuban coach Dolf Luque. As opening day arrived, the National League was hoping for help from the following rookies: second baseman Emil Verban at St. Louis; third baseman Buck "Leaky" Fausett and pitcher Tommy de la Cruz at Cincinnati; pitchers Elwin "Preacher" Roe and Cookie Cuccurullo at Pittsburgh; and infielders George Hausmann and Hugh Luby in New York. The American League was touting fewer rookies, but the Chicago White Sox had pitcher Ed Lopat, and the Philadelphia Athletics had five rookies, one of whom became an American League standout at third base for 14 more years—George Kell. The others were the long forgotten Bill Burgo, Lew Flick, Ed Busch, and Elwood Wheaton. Not highly rated (although perhaps he should have been) was a 6'11" rookie named Ralph Stewart, who was at the Detroit Tiger camp in Evansville Indiana, perhaps the tallest rookie to ever appear on the major league spring training scene. In his second year with the Tigers that spring was Frank "Stubby" Overmire, another pitcher, who stood only 5'7" tall. Imagine him standing next to Stewart! Overmire stayed in the majors for 10 years. Stewart never made it.

When the dust settled on the '44 season, the best of the National League rookies turned out to be the following freshmen: Bill Voiselle, a big righthanded pitcher for the New York Giants, who almost reversed the record he compiled at Jersey City in '43. He was 10-21 with the Little Giants but was 21-16 at the Polo Grounds. In addition to wearing number 96 on his back, which was the name of his hometown, he also led the league in innings pitched, starts, and strikeouts. The St. Louis Cardinals were boasting about two fine rookies—pitcher Ted Wilks and outfielder Augie Bergamo. Wilks had starred at Columbus in '43 and became a star in St. Louis with a fine 17-4 record in '44. The experts were calling him the most effective twirler in the senior circuit, as his winning percentage of .810 led the league, and he finished 16 of his 21 starts. He also established a record for freshmen hurlers in the National League by winning 11 straight games. He stayed around nine more seasons in the big time. Bergamo came up from Columbus with a reputation as a power hitter. He filled a utility role with the Cards, but might have been a regular with any other team. Joining outfielder Bergamo was second baseman Emil Verban, who won the regular job when Lou Klein entered the Coast Guard. Augie stayed only two years, Emil until 1950. The Philadelphia Phillies had a hard worker in right-handed pitcher Charley Schanz, who won 13 games while dropping 16 with the eighth-place club. This bespectacled hurler wound up his career in 1950 with the Boston Red Sox. The Chicago Cubs were heralding several rookies. Catcher Billy Holm saw little action because of weak hitting. Don Johnson hit and fielded well at second base. Andy Pafko, who had been "all everything" in batting in the Pacific Coast League in '43, established himself in the Cub outfield, and despite some injuries and illness, hit .267 in 128 games. Pafko remained in the National League 17 years.

Over in the American League, the aforementioned Philadelphia third sacker George Kell lived up to his advanced billing. In June, when the A's first baseman Dick Siebert was injured, Connie Mack obtained Bill McGhee from Little Rock, and Bill sparked the Macks for weeks and wound up batting .289. Interestingly, McGhee at first refused to report when purchased from the minors, claiming he wasn't good enough, but he was persuaded to give it a whirl anyway. Perhaps Bill knew what he was talking about, as '45 turned out to be his last season. The Yankees kept starting a lad named Joe Page, but the youngster had trouble completing games. In 16 starts he was relieved 12 times. Someone must have seen the light, as it was decided that perhaps Joe could finish up what someone else started. So the next season they let him pitch only in the late innings, and it worked. Joe became the best reliever in the American League for a number of seasons. When Yank catcher Rollie Hemsley was called into the Navy in August, the New Yorkers called upon Mike Garbark, who came through with some timely hitting. Mike, the brother of the A's catcher Bob, lasted only as long as the war. The Detroit Tigers called upon a semi-pro pitcher named Chuck Hostetler, who arrived to play the outfield and to hit so well that he led the league for half the season and single-handedly picked up the slumping Bengals. He only lasted one more season. Pitcher Rufus Gentry also enjoyed his only good major league season for Detroit in '44. There were several others in the American League who were wartime players but enjoyed good freshman seasons: Myron Hayworth, with a modest batting mark, at St. Louis; Walter "Monk" Dubiel, at New York, who pitched 19 complete games with a 13-13 slate; Clem Hausmann, a slim right-hander, who was both a reliever and starter at Boston. The Red Sox also summoned two pitchers from the Pacific Coast League. Clem Dreisewerd, a southpaw twirler, was the top flinger at Sacramento when called. He had a slick curve and a fair slider to go with his ten years of pro pitching. He beat the Yankees twice, but lost four other games.

Then there was Rex Cecil, a big right-hander who cost Tom Yawkey a few bucks to obtain him from San Diego when Tex Hughson was called into service. With a record of 19-11 on the coast, he was much sought after. He arrived at Fenway Park in the midst of a doubleheader with St. Louis, was called upon to pitch four innings, and won his first game. He won only five more games while losing ten in the majors. Ed Klieman at Cleveland and Joe Berry at Philadelphia did acceptable relief work. Infielder Grey Clarke filled a utility role with Chicago, but was shaky on defense, and Al Powell did the job defensively, but didn't hit for Washington. Earlier we spoke of Chicago's Ed Lopat. The pitcher had spent seven years in the minors and did stellar work for a weak White Sox nine, but gave no indication of becoming the fine pitcher he was to become for 11 more years.

Perhaps one of the strangest seasons major league baseball has experienced was that of 1945. It not only saw the war turn the corner, but also baseball. The season started at a low ebb, but perked up before it concluded as the vets began to return from the service. Despite what has been written, the 1945 league champions, the Detroit Tigers and the Chicago Cubs, had some pretty fair players in their lineups. Detroit, in fact, was led to the championship by Hank Greenberg, who had returned from service. Joining him were the likes of second baseman Ed Borom, and pitchers Tommy Bridges, Walt Wilson, Les Mueller, and Al Benton. The World Series of that season produced one notable quote. A sportswriter when asked who he thought would win the series replied, "I don't think either of them can win." As the season ended, plans were being announced by big league clubs to resume spring training sites in '46 under Florida's sun. Stadiums were being renovated, installation plans for lights were being announced, and daily newspapers were carrying accounts of players being discharged from service and of rostered players being released to make room for the returnees. The Social Security offices must have been working overtime. Plans were being made for resumption of the wartime-plagued minor leagues; the Pacific Coast League was even announcing plans to seek major league rating. It began to look like baseball as usual. The farsighted could see expansion coming upon the baseball scene, even though the traditionalists would have no part of it. Consider what happened in Baltimore as a sign of things to come. Then a minor league city, their old ball park had burned down in 1944, forcing the International League club to move into the gigantic Municipal Stadium. War workers pushed Baltimore's population to record highs, and they flocked to the ball park in record numbers. One game drew more than 50,000 and that was done without the benefit of hard liquor or beer, which was not allowed on the premises. As war industries grew, population rocketed in the cities of Texas, and that area also became a possible expansion region. Air travel was envisioned as allowing expansion to the West Coast, as it was calculated that the time to cross the continent would be no longer than the train ride from Boston to Washington. Racetracks began to compete with baseball, forcing baseball to, believe it or not, reluctantly turn to night games. Professional football was slowly growing, but pro baseball was not well organized for the growth which lay ahead, a strange circumstance considering the threats to its very existence. So here we were in 1945 sitting around speculating on the chances of survival. Luckily there were a few baseball men who foresaw what was coming, and though it took a while to change, we can look back today and see what happened. But what about the rookies of that last wartime season?

The rookie class of 1945 came in all sizes and shapes and with all types of ability. This was evidenced by several incidents involving umpires. When veteran umpire Bill McGowan called out a batter on strikes, the lad turned on the umpire claiming he couldn't call him out on "that." The surprised McGowan looked down at the batter, as only he could, and said, "No? Well, buddy, you read tomorrow's newspapers, and you'll find out I can." Another veteran umpire, George Magerkurth, was having a bad day under a boiling hot sun in Cincinnati with a bunch of complaining ballplayers when a spectator in a nearby box joined in the fun. By now George had had enough, and he approached the fan in the field box, reached over and gave him a punch, followed quickly by an apology. That's the way it was in '45.

The Washington Senators finished second in the American League race, due primarily to four knuckleballers—Mickey Haefner, Roger Wolff, Dutch Leonard, and John Niggeling—who were winning 60 of their 87 victories. But their mound staff also had a prize rookie in a little (5'7", 153 lbs.) right-hander named Marino Pieretti. He was a regular starter from opening day on and was occasionally called upon for relief work besides. Appearing in 44 games, he had a 14-13 record and performed for six more American League seasons. The champion Tigers also had a little (5'8", 180 lbs.) rookie at third base in Bob Maier. He came up to the majors with a "should stick and click" label from Buffalo where he was very highly rated. After his initial season's work at the hot corner, it appeared he would stay around for a while. He hit .263 and fielded acceptably. Sadly, it was his only season in the big time, as the Tigers traded for the Philadelphia Athletics' rookie sensation of '43, George Kell, to play third for them.

The Chicago White Sox had a rookie infielder who was rated as a poor fielder and a weak hitter, but he proved everyone wrong by putting in 12 years in the big league with a .262 lifetime average. His name was Cass Michaels. They also had a couple of pitchers of note, Earl Caldwell and Frank Papish. Cleveland was hoping to get help from rookies with such names as Blas Monaco, Henry Ruszkowski, Ed Wheeler, Bill Bonness, Joe Desiderato, and a pitcher with the appropriate name of George Hooks (although it's not certain if his name was appropriate for what he threw or for what was used to pull him out of a game). None of these left any mark at all on the big league scene. It is doubtful that even the die-hard Cleveland fan will remember any of this group. The New York Yankees listed among their hopefuls one Joe Buzas, a shortstop who appeared in 30 games. While Joe never became a Hall of Fame candidate, he did, in later years, become an owner of several minor league clubs and a top minor league official. His daughter has also been listed as president of the Bristol Red Sox of the Eastern League. In addition, the Yankees resorted to pitching Paul Schreiber, a long-time batting-practice pitcher who 21 years earlier had a big league tryout. Philadelphia's Connie Mack had one rookie pitcher of some promise in Luther Knerr, a big Pennsylvanian who was listed as a starter but was relegated to a relief role. He once confided to the author that, while he would have relished a starting role, he was happy just to be in the major leagues. He realized that as baseball moved out of the war era, the role to be played by the relief pitcher would increase in importance, which it did.

The American League presented several other rookies of some note. The St. Louis Browns had Pete Gray, a one-armed outfielder up from Memphis. He had been the Southern Association's most valuable player, despite his physical handicap. He hit .333 and had a fielding average of .983 for the Chicks. A master at drag-bunting and a speed demon on the bases, he stole 68 bases at Memphis. Opponents learned early not to take chances with his throwing arm. He had cost the Brownies $20,000. Having lost his right arm in a childhood accident, he appeared in 77 games for the '45 St. Louis nine. In one doubleheader he had five singles. His first major league extra base hit was a triple. He was a remarkable player considering he had to both catch and throw with his left hand. He would make a catch with his glove touching only the ends of his fingers, then roll the ball across his chest as he shoved his glove under the stub of his right arm. Bringing his arm back, he rolled the ball into his hand to make the throw. He could return the ball to the infield almost as quickly as any outfielder. His batting average for the only major league season he had was a .218. He returned to the minors and played there until 1949. His manager at the time in St. Louis, Luke Sewell, was quoted as saying, "Gray knew he was being exploited, but no matter, you have to admire his courage." The Washington Senators were giving a tryout to a rookie first baseman named Bert Shepard, who was playing with a wooden leg. He had lost his right leg when his P-38 fighter plane was shot down over France early in the war. He was still a hospital patient at the time of his tryout and claimed he could run 100 yards in 14 seconds despite his handicap.

The rookie of the year in 1945, and one of the best ever, was a young man who had been discharged from the Army Air Force and was pitching for the Boston Red Sox—Dave "Boo" Ferriss. Before Dave burst onto the scene, another event occurred at the Fenway Park home of the Bosox that bears mentioning. On April 16 of 1945, something new was written into Boston baseball history when the Red Sox gave workouts to three young black ball-players. You will remember them even though they didn't make the Red Sox, which has to rate as one of the great mistakes in the history of that team. They were former University of California, Los Angeles, football and baseball star Jackie Robinson, the 1944 Negro-American League batting champion Sam Jethroe, and the star second baseman of the Philadelphia Stars of the Negro National League, Marvin Williams.

Back to Ferriss, the right-handed pitcher became the toast of the baseball world. His repertoire included a fine fastball, a baffling curve, and a great change of pace to go along with excellent control. In five weeks he had four wins in as many starts. He had pitched three shutouts and established a new American League record by hurling 22-1/3 scoreless innings to better the old mark of 19-2/3 innings set by another Red Sox pitcher, Thomas "Bucky" O'Brien, way back in 1911. The 23-year-old, 6'2", 200-pound freshman, who won 20 and lost 8 and batted .417 for the Randolph Field Ramblers in 1944, was hitting major league pitching at a .667 mark at the time. Dave went on to win 21 games against 10 losses, despite a loss of effectiveness suffered late in the season because of a serious sinus infection. Proving that he was no flash in the pan, he won 25 games in '46 to lead the Red Sox to the pennant, staying around Fenway Park as a player until 1950 and later returning for several years to coach other Red Sox rookies. So popular was he with the Beantown crowd that 28,000 of them turned out on a late-season Sunday to present their rookie ace with a new auto. Remember, new cars were not that easy to come by in 1945. As happens to so many who are tendered a day of honor, Dave lost the game, which was shortened to five innings because of a Boston Sunday law at the time regarding the hour after which an inning could not be started.

Ferriss, an ambidextrous thrower, relied upon his right arm to win the first eight games he pitched. He had a second eight-game winning streak, defeated each team in the league the first time he met them, and pitched five shutouts, four of them coming in his first six games. A few baseball experts felt the left-handed-hitting rookie was good enough to pitch left-handed and remain in the big leagues. A fine athlete, "Boo" was also a great passer and punter for his high school football team and held several Mississippi basketball scoring records. A fine fielder, he lost his first game on a rainy Sunday afternoon in Yankee Stadium when he slipped on the wet grass fielding a batted ball. Dave remained in the majors until a sore arm ended his career.

The National League could present nothing to match the American League heroics of Ferriss or Gray. The Pittsburgh Pirates had a small young outfielder named Al Gionfriddo who had been discharged from the service because of a physical disability. He was a first-year standout as a fielder, while batting .284. Gionfriddo played for the Pirates again in '46 and for one game in 1947 before being traded to the Brooklyn Dodgers. There he gained everlasting baseball fame for his great World Series catch of a Joe DiMaggio fly ball in Yankee Stadium. This catch was actually his swan song in the majors as he never appeared again after his World Series heroics. The Pirates also were praising another rookie in 1945, catcher Bill Salkeld. Bill appeared to take a liking to major league pitching, hitting .311, just 71 points better than his '44 average at San Diego. He took over as the Bucs' first-string catcher after toiling for eleven years in the minors. This should serve as an example for today's minor leaguers who often become discouraged if they haven't made the majors in four or five seasons. A blue ribbon receiver, Salkeld played two more summers in Pirate land before he went off to Boston for two campaigns, helping the Braves to a pennant in '48. One more game in 1950 with the Chicago White Sox ended his major league tour. Speaking of the Boston Braves, they had a fine performance from an outfielder who had two very short earlier tryouts with the Cardinals and the Dodgers. Carden Gillenwater was speedy, had a strong throwing arm and a potentially powerful bat. In that long-ago season, he was one of the majors' best fly catchers. What was baffling the major bigwigs was why he hadn't been a regular long before, as since the 1941 season he had a top-notch rating.

The Brooklyn Dodgers were singing a happy song about rookie hurler Cyril Buker who had a fine 11-3 record with St. Paul. When the young candidate left his teaching job in Wisconsin, Uncle Sam reclassified him 1A in the draft. The Dodgers were also hoping that rookie catcher Stan Andrews, up from Montreal, would be capable of ousting vets Mickey Owen, Clyde Sukeforth, or Ray Hayworth. He did not. The Flatbushers also had a rookie pitcher named Tom Seats who had appeared in a few games in 1940 for Detroit. He was their chief southpaw hurling hope, but first he had to see his way clear to move away from the shipyard job that he had held for several years. Working days at the yard, he had been pitching for the San Francisco Seals evenings, weekends, and on special occasions. On this schedule he won 25 games while losing 13, just about the best in the Pacific Coast League. Seats saw his way clear to leave his shipbuilding duties and won 10 while dropping 7 for the Brooks, but it marked his final season in the majors. Tops of all the promising Dodgers was Big Ed Stevens, who was brought up from Montreal midway through the season. Showing some power, he had 14 doubles, three triples, and four home runs while hitting .274 and fielding very well.

The Philadelphia Phillies, a wartime club hit harder by losses than most clubs, was perhaps typical of what the average fan considers the wartime teams to be like. The Phillies, or Blue Jays of that era, were made up of aging veterans, cast-offs, and untried rookies. They presented the likes of Jimmie Foxx, Anton Karl, Oscar Judd, Rene Monteagudo, Glenn Gardner, Jim Wasdell, Vance Dinges, Vince DiMaggio, Jake Powell, Gus Mancuso, Charlie Schanz, and Coaker Triplett. In 1945 they also had a couple of brothers as their keystone combination—Garvin and Granville Hamner. However, one Elisha "Bitsy" Mott appeared to play three of the four infield positions (he didn't play at first base). A fiery competitor with good speed, he won the shortstop job over the other two spots. He appeared to have a long career ahead of him, but his future started and ended in '45, his only big league season. The St. Louis Cardinals were finishing second in 1945, the only year in the five year span (1942–46) that they didn't cop the flag.

This fact did not deter them from coming up with a couple of good rookies, which seemed to be an annual event for them. Who will ever forget Red Schoendienst, who had gone to the Card tryout camp on a lark and became a great Redbird second baseman, playing in 19 big league seasons and later becoming a successful manager after his playing career had ended. He had suffered a splinter in the eye doing war plant work between seasons, which made him 4F in '45. The popular redhead played better than 2,200 major league games and had a lifetime batting averge of .289. He was perhaps best known for his defensive prowess. Want a surprise? How many remember that in his initial season he was primarily an outfielder? He was an infielder by choice, a shortstop, but he had the impossible task of moving the regular Card shortstop, Marty Marion, out of a job, so he wound up in left field despite an ailing arm. In '46 he moved to second base where he completed his career, 18 years and several clubs later. Also pretty much forgotten today is the fact that he led the National League in stolen bases in '45 with 26 thefts. The second Cardinal rookie to make it big was pitcher Ken

Burkhart who won 18 and lost 8. It took the war to get him out of the Cardinal farm system and to toss four shutouts among his victories. Of the 12 complete games he pitched, he won all of them. Two other rookies of some promise in Cardinal camp at Cairo, Illinois, were infielder Glenn Crawford and pitcher Henry Koch. The New York Giants had a large crop of rookies, the majority of which never made it. Does anyone remember any of them? Dale Mathewson, Bill Emmerich, Francis Rosso, Loren Bain, Ray Harrell, Mel Heiman, John Toncoff, Bob Barthelson, or Charlie Mead?

There was an interesting incident at St. Louis during a Browns-White Sox game that involved both vets and rookies. Known at the time as "The battle of the dugout," the incident or brawl—take your choice—occurred in mid June. The players on the two clubs had been "jockeying" and razzing each other during the game, a result of hard feelings engendered earlier in the season. The melee started during a White Sox rally in the eighth inning when Sox rookie and batting-practice pitcher Karl Scheel got on Brownie pitcher George Caster as he was being removed from the mound by St. Louis manager Luke Sewell. Caster took the baseball and threw it into the Chicago dugout. This caused Sox manager Jimmy Dykes to come out of the dugout, followed by his players, to protest to umpire-in-chief Art Passarella. At this point the Brownie players came out of their dugout causing the White Sox to retreat. The crowd then began to pour onto the field from the stands causing the umpires and police to act quickly to restore order before any serious damage was done. The Browns had now invaded the Chicago dugout in pursuit of ex-marine Scheel, who was then pummelled, requiring first aid. Order was restored, and Scheel had a police escort from the field. The Sox won the game 4 to 1 behind Eddie Lopat. Sewell, Caster, infielder Ellis Clary, and pitcher Sigmund Jakucki wound up being fined by American League president Will Harridge. Interestingly, the Browns' only run scored as a result of an extra base hit by the one-armed rookie Pete Gray, his first ever in Sportsman Park. Gray later scored when Vern Stephens brought him home with a double. So it went during the final wartime season—1945.

By 1950, only 30 of the 559 players on the major league rosters of 1945 remained active in the majors. That meant that 529 players had dropped out of the picture in the brief space of five years. The prominent rookie, Pete Gray, was released to the minors. The World Series winners, Detroit, had dropped all their heroes except Hal Newouser, Art Houtteman, Dizzy Trout, and Bob Swift. Their Series opponents, the Chicago Cubs, had only three players left, Bob Chipman, Phil Cavarretta, and Andy Pafko. In the American League, Boston and St. Louis had complete turnovers. Among the other clubs' players left were: Chicago—Floyd Baker and Cass Michaels; Cleveland —Lou Boudreau and Steve Gromek; New York—Joe Page, John Lindell, and George Stirnweiss; Philadelphia—Carl Scheib; and Washington—Dick Welteroth. Over in the National League, besides the already mentioned Cubs, the following players remained: Boston—Tommy Holmes; Brooklyn —Tommy Brown and Ralph Branca; Cincinnati—Howard Fox and Herman Wehmeier; New York—Andy Hansen; Philadelphia—Andy Seminick and Granny Hamner; St. Louis—Harry Brecheen, Max Lanier, Ted Wilks, Del Rice, Marty Marion, and Red Schoendienst; and Pittsburgh had none. The war years were in the record books, and a new era was about to begin for baseball.

1946: G.I. Joe Comes Marching Home

Back came the GIs, laying down their tools of war and marching to the strains of "Take Me Out to the Ball Game." A new era was about to dawn on the baseball world. The return of the prewar days, which fans everywhere were eagerly awaiting, would actually never occur, and, along with war years, were now relegated to history. Although few realized it, a great turning point in the baseball history was about to occur as the 1946 spring training camps opened. The careful observer of the baseball scene would detect changes which were now rapidly taking place.

Consider that new minor leagues were being hastily formed, not always because local conditions demanded or warranted it, but because the manpower in the majors, being increased by returning GIs, had to be shuffled downward. The major league clubs seemed not to want to part with their wartime players, lest one would develop true major league skills overnight. This movement signaled the start of the greatest era in the history of minor league baseball, with more leagues and more active players than had ever been seen. Virtually all of these new clubs had major league affiliation, as the day of the independent owner was about finished. Players were distributed with strings attached to the clubs at the top.

Fat wartime paychecks had allowed the major league clubs to wallow in increased gate receipts after mid-1945. This delightful predicament made the big league owners sit back and dream of what a baseball public, hungry for the return of their prewar heroes, would do for their postwar coffers. Few were spending any of this windfall money. Uncle Sam took a dim view of this and hit some club owners hard with an excess profits tax. More attention might have been paid to stadium improvements or player purchases. Many big league owners, instead of spending their excess profits, were on the telephone calling up wealthy friends along the minor league trail, convincing them to invest in a local club. Pacific Coast League owners were offering to match big league salaries in efforts to get top-notch players. The owners seemed to ignore the slow readjustment to peacetime production along with the influx of returning GIs into the job market, which cut into the funds available to the fans. The regular full-pay envelope might not always be available. Labor-management problems would eventually eat into the savings of the baseball public, a money shortage which would be felt at the turnstiles of the baseball world. The cost to maintain the farm clubs, from which our rookies would come, was actually hanging in the balance. Baseball seemed to be little aware of this as they prepared for 1946.

Owners with any foresight realized that former players returning from the service would only provide temporary relief and that more advanced thinking would be needed to insure good baseball. Scholastic coaches were up in arms over major league raids on their players. Arguing that education was being interrupted and youthful values being distorted, they were after assurances from Commissioner Happy Chandler that certain rule changes would be put into effect for the protection of their players. Chandler, in his first meeting with the major league owners, asked them to abolish the practice of signing high school players to contracts.

Another problem facing the owners was the demise, to some extent, of college baseball, now being overshadowed by interest and participation in football. Spring football and earlier scheduling of fall games was detracting from college baseball. This trend, while continuing until today, has been slowed by a new emphasis certain schools have put on their baseball teams. There was a time when a surprising number of major leaguers came off college campuses, and of late there has been talk of the majors again depending upon the lads from this source. One must wonder if today's talked-of trend isn't an effort on the part of the majors to cut down on expenses. What about those boys who have no desire or aptitude for college? An interesting debate. Perhaps the answer may hold the key to the future of the minor leagues and to where the rookies of the future will get their training. This is a subject too complex to get into in a book of this nature, but one to ponder. Whatever the outcome, its roots may well have started in 1946.

Certain farsighted owners were of the opinion, and rightly so, that baseball had better realize that it had two products to sell—the game itself, and those who actually ran the game. Their suggestions included motion pictures, advertising in every. town no matter how remote, speakers' bureaus, and instructors at baseball schools. These concerns would extend to schools and colleges, recreation centers, even to the sandlots, with these goals all being coordinated under the commissioner's office by men trained in such matters. The fact that such a plan might offer employment opportunities to players when their playing days were over and might induce youngsters to consider baseball as a profession was part of the plan. Like so many other well-intentioned plans, it was put on a shelf to gather dust along with the proposed Department of Promotion, Henry Ford's willingness to finance sandlot teams, and the American Legion's plan to expand its development work. The two major leagues, to some extent duplicating their efforts, did launch into token promotional programs, but it would seem they perhaps were afraid of losing their separate identities. As 1946 arrived, there were plans for the commissioner to tackle the promotional plans, but certainly not on the scale some of the owners had originally suggested. I wonder if they envisioned today's vast TV coverage and what might be possible with it. Perhaps increased night games were envisioned as a means of survival, but they were hardly the answer.

Other changes faced the owners as the war ended. There was the story of a game played in the Pacific War theatre in which a big, fireballing sailor was pitching a game against an all-star club. By the seventh inning he had struck out 13, when suddenly he was facing Joe DiMaggio with two outs and the bases loaded. The big fellow proceeded to whiff Joe on three pitches and immediately became the most talked about player in the service. Unknown to the fans back home, he would be in the minors in '46 blazing his fastball as he had earlier in the Pacific. Oh yes, he was a Negro.

A large step for the majors, which would forever change the talent pool, and was steadfastly resisted by the owners for years, occurred on October 23, 1945. Branch Rickey announced that the Brooklyn Dodgers had signed, to play for their Montreal (International League) farm club, the contracts of two blacks—Jackie Robinson, a shortstop from the Kansas City Monarchs, and Johnny Wright, a pitcher from the Newark Eagles. Robinson is a story in himself as we shall see later on. Wright soon disappeared. Certainly Rickey's shrewd handling of the black situation was saving organized baseball from the damage it was sure to suffer without such moves.

Rickey was further suggesting greater numbers of farm clubs, reportedly between 26 and 30 per team, to insure proper player development. This large number of clubs appeared to be too expensive an undertaking for most teams, as despite local ownership, the teams would have to be staffed by the big league clubs. Big league affiliation had to be purchased with big league capital, and the days of the independent team, as we have stated before, would soon become a rarity.

Over the years, major league baseball had been plagued by futile attempts to start a players' union. The history of labor relations in baseball and the controversial reserve clause is a whole story in itself, much too lengthy to delve into here. A good account is *The Imperfect Diamond*, written in 1980 by Lee Lowenfish and Tony Lupien. With the expanded minor leagues, these old problems were again raising their heads. Players' fears of being buried in the bushes was only one area to be addressed. Certainly the players would be looking for bigger paychecks and more individual rights. The whole baseball picture was ripe for the proper organizer to step in. Standardized pay, insurance, continued salary in the case of the injured, better equipment, meal and transportation allowances, laundry, transportation, etc., etc., would become the issues. The racial discrimination problem was yet another factor with which baseball had to contend.

While at the time it might not have been considered any more than sour grapes, an event took place on the baseball scene which would eventually lead to the players' organization of today. It would seem that the owners underestimated the seriousness of the action invoked by a 28-year-old ballplayer after his discharge fron the Navy. The aforementioned Tony Lupien, a first baseman with the Philadelphia Phillies, was initiating the first test case concerning a veteran's rights to his former job. Sold by Philadelphia to Hollywood of the Pacific Coast League, Lupien felt he was entitled to a year's employment with the Phillies (with whom he had played before entering the service) under the provisions of the veterans' rights act. The point of this is that the ramifications are still being felt by baseball today. This is mentioned here only to give the reader an idea of the problems baseball was facing in the first postwar season. Before we look at the rookies of the year, one other problem facing the majors should be mentioned. It was a short-lived problem, but was considered quite serious at the time. South of the border, down in Mexico, a couple of wealthy brothers named Pasquel had begun luring major leaguers to their Mexican League with offers of *mucho dinero*. Most prominent among the jumpers: the Giants' Danny Gardella and Sal Maglie; Max Lanier, Lou Klein, and Fred Martin of the Cardinals; Mickey Owen of Brooklyn; and Vern Stephens of the St. Louis Browns. Offers were made to such major league stars as Stan Musial, Ted Williams, and Pete Reiser, but they resisted and stayed in the U.S. The Mexican League soon collapsed, and some of the jumpers had nothing more than empty pocketbooks and five-year suspensions to show for their efforts.

In the National League, the St. Louis Cardinals were continuing their dominance by capturing their fourth title in five seasons, even though it took a playoff with the pesky Brooklyn Dodgers to do it. The '45 champion Chicago Cubs dropped back to third place.

In the American League the expected pennant race between the '45 champion Detroit Tigers and the New York Yankees never developed, as they finished second and third respectively behind the talent-laden Boston Red Sox who breezed to an easy pennant. It was quite a season for the pitchers in the junior circuit, as Hal Newhouser and Bob Feller each won 26 games, while the rookie sensation of 1945, Boston's Dave Ferriss, was posting 25 victories. Ferriss's teammate Tex Hughson had 20 wins, while New York's Spud Chandler equaled that number. The Redbirds from St. Looie took the World Series from the Red Sox in seven games.

As was expected, many of the would-be rookie heroes were forced to spend their season summering in the minors, as the returning vets captured most of the available spots on the rosters, which were loaded with a wealth of overwhelming talent. Spring training moved back to Southern areas to sort out this talent.

The Nationals seemed to have the better of the rookie crop. They came up with two players who had similar last names, one in Cincinnati, Grady Hatton, and one in Brooklyn named Joe Hatten. The Reds' talent hunters saw Grady hit a neat .500 in the 1944 National Semipro tourney and signed the young third baseman. He entered the majors without any minor league background. He hit .271 and led the Redlegs in RBIs with 69, not bad considering that a severe knee injury kept him out of action during the final month of the season. Hatton signed with the Reds even though the Red Sox, Cubs, Yankees, and Dodgers had been after him. Grady spent 12 years in the big time with the Reds, Red Sox, both Chicago clubs, the Cards, and Baltimore. Joe Hatten, Brooklyn's lefty pitcher, did have minor league experience, and while Leo Durocher's men had trouble scoring runs for him, he turned in 14 victories, twirled 222 innings with 13 complete games. He lost 11. He made it into two World Series and lasted seven years, winding up his career with the Cubs. Joining Hatten on the Dodger staff was Hank Behrman, who chipped in 11 wins, but lasted only three more seasons. A two-game trial in 1942 preceded another Reds' rookie pitcher, Ewell Blackwell, who despite the weak hitting of the Reds, made the All-Star team and led all National League pitchers in shutouts with six. Known as "The Whip," Blackie stayed around the big league scene for ten seasons, posting 22 wins in 1947 (9-13 in '46). This sidearmer was well respected by the hitters of his day. The Chicago Cubs had a first sacker who had finished out the 1941 season at Wrigley Field, and who in '46 moved the veteran Phil Cavaretta into right field. This was Eddie Waitkus perhaps better remembered as a member of the Philadelphia "Whiz Kids," and as being shot during the 1949 season by a distraught fan. The Cubs also had a good hit, no field outfielder in Marv Rickert. A couple of sluggers dominated the rookie honors for Pennsylvania's entries. At Pittsburgh, an outfielder named Ralph Kiner seemed likely to be the standout freshman of the year until he suddenly stopped hitting home runs in midseason. He had 16 at the halfway point, but then went homerless for almost six weeks. He wound up leading the league with 23, one more than New York's John Mize. The homerless streak was a rare occurrence, as Kiner, currently a New York Mets announcer, went on slugging for eight more National League seasons and one American League campaign. He was elected into baseball's Hall of Fame in 1975. Del Ennis came directly from the Navy to the Philadelphia Phillies' outfield and demonstrated a strong batting eye (.313), speed, and throwing accuracy. Del had 14 big league seasons before hanging up his glove. A native of Philadelphia, it was said he only cost the price of a streetcar token for the Phillies to sign. The Cardinals were blessed with Dick Sisler, the son of Hall of Famer George Sisler. He played in the majors for eight years, appeared in two World Series, and was manager of the Reds in 1964 and 1965. Brooklyn also had as a rookie, Carl Furillo, a hard-hitting outfielder, who went on to a distinguished major league career. Others of note in the National League before the season started: Cliff Dapper (a catcher), John Corriden, Jr., the Canadian, J. P. Roy, and John Douglas at Brooklyn; Mike Budnick, a pitcher with the Giants known for his temper problems; and Bobby Adams, Clay Lambert, Jesus Ramos, Jack Warren, and Clyde Vollmer at Cincinnati. Bill Rigney made it as an infielder with the New York Giants, who were also taking a look at Jaime Almendro (known as Poochie), Charlie Fox, and Bob Joyce (PCL-MVP 31 wins, 35 complete games). The Cubs were testing John Ostrowski, Russ Meers, and Charlie Adams. The Pirates had a crop with such forgettable names as Edson Bahr, Fred Clemence, Ben Guintini, Clark Henry and John Mayhew (Eastern League batting champ). The Phillies had people named Don Grate (who never was), Ed Murphy (once hit three successive homers with Portsmouth, Ohio), John O'Neill, Charlie Ripple (averaged 18 strikeouts a game in high school), and a rookie who scouted himself, Ed Walczak. The Boston Braves had high hopes for Thaddeus Cieslak, Al Treichel (6©5″ pitcher who had been with seven other clubs, including the Browns and White Sox), Jim Wallace, and Stan Wentzel (said to resemble Wally Berger). The talent-rich Cardinals also had Otis Davis, Jack McLain, Fred Martin (31-year-old), Conklyn Meriwether, and Joe Garagiola, now a popular broadcaster with NBC-TV. The American League was stocked with more veteran players, and while they had hopes for a number of youngsters, only several stood out in the crowd. Tops among the newcomers was Detroit's Walter "Hoot" Evers, a much-publicized outfielder. He started the year by breaking an ankle and a thumb in spring training which sidelined him for weeks. He did a great job when he finally made the lineup until he collided with second baseman Eddie Mayo. For his efforts, he picked up a broken jaw and a broken wrist. Returning in the final weeks of the season, he showed the skill and power that branded him for stardom. A four-sport athlete at the University of Illinois, the Pirates, Cubs, and both St. Louis clubs were after him until Detroit's Wish Egan relieved owner Walter Briggs of some of his cash to bring Evers into the fold. "Hoot" played 14 years in the American League, most of which was with Detroit, but he also performed briefly in Boston, Baltimore, and Cleveland and spent part of a season with the National League New York Giants.

The St. Louis Browns presented Chuck Stevens, a fine-fielding first baseman who had his troubles at the plate. The Washington Senators were looking for big things from Gil Coan. The young outfielder turned up at spring training wearing a pair of spikes that did not fit. The resulting blisters just about finished his rookie year, as he appeared in only 59 games, a true case of getting off on the wrong foot, or in this case, feet. The Chicago White Sox were giving a third try to the immortal Murrell "Jake" Jones. It wasn't any more successful than the season-and-one-half he spent with a different pair of Sox—those of the Red variety in Boston. In fairness, Jake suffered a broken arm almost as soon as the season started. The American League rookies seemed to be under the injury hex in 1946. Strange as it may seem, except for Evers, the top four clubs in the American League operated almost entirely with players of previous major league experience. The regular catching job at Cleveland was won by rookie Jim Hegan, as he ousted veteran Frankie Hayes. The Chicago White Sox boasted of a right-handed pitcher named Ralph Hamner, who later moved across Chicago to the Cubs for three years. The St. Louis Browns had a reserve third baseman named Bob Dillinger, a talented player who had started his career at second base. The bespectacled Dillinger developed into a pretty fair third sacker over the next five seasons. The Browns also took a preseason look at George Washington Bradley, an outfielder with ten years of minor league experience.

Bradley had the distinction on successive nights during his minor league career of fanning five straight times and coming back the next night to get five straight hits. The Boston Red Sox went to camp expecting big things from four returning GIs with Ernie Andres perhaps the most heralded of all the American League rookies in '46. Ernie attended Indiana, where he was a good baseball player and a regular on the Hoosiers' basketball five. Coming off two great seasons of service ball, Sox manager Joe Cronin was sure he would have Bostonians soon forgetting the departed regular third sacker Jim Tabor. Andres opened the season at third and departed 15 games later with an .098 batting average, wondering if perhaps he shouldn't have stuck to basketball. Al Flair had appeared in eight games at first base for the 1941 Bosox and after a long service career was back to battle Rudy York for the job, a battle the ex-GI lost. The third rookie was catcher Ed McGah, good defensively but not offensively. He played in only 24 games over a two year period. The fourth newcomer to Fenway Park was a native son, a shortstop named Eddie Pelagrini, who is still a popular figure in Boston coaching a local college nine. He had the unlikely task of moving Johnny Pesky out of the shortstop position, something he could not do. His advanced notices said he hit the long ball, which he did, as he became one of those rare rookies to hit a home run in his first big league at-bat. Eddie spent two seasons in a utility role in the Hub and split six other campaigns in the majors with four other clubs.

Meanwhile down in Philadelphia, Connie Mack was praising five of his farmhands. George Armstrong, a catcher the Brooklyn Dodgers had let get away, appeared behind the plate only four times for Connie. Lew Carpenter, a right-handed pitcher from Georgia Tech who was 22-2 as a minor leaguer at Atlanta in 1945, never threw a game in an A's uniform (he did appear in four games with Washington in '43). Gene Handley, brother of Pittsburgh's Lee, did fill an infield utility role for two seasons for the Mackmen. In contrast to today's rookies, Gene had played for Sacramento for five seasons before he got a try with the A's. Another Pacific Coast League prospect out of Portland was left-handed pitcher Wandel Mosser, but he didn't work out for Connie either. Catcher James Calvin Pruett, billed as the second coming of Mickey Cochrane, after nine games in the '44 and '45 campaigns never played in Shibe Park again. He had cost Connie Mack five farmhands to obtain.

Jimmy Dykes, the White Sox manager, picked up an infielder who had bounced around the minors since 1934 and once had a look-see with Pittsburgh and the St. Louis Cardinals. But that was all Charlie Biggs would get in the Windy City. Chet Hajduk, a bang-up first baseman and a native of Chicago, had played one game for his hometown White Sox in 1941 and that was the extent of his career, as he couldn't budge the veteran Hal Trosky in 1946. Cut loose by the Yankees, Gene Nance was rated a classy third baseman by the Pale Hose and perhaps they knew what class minor league ball they wanted him in because that is where he wound up.

On the lake front in Cleveland they were touting a native son, a fireballing pitcher who would make the baseball world forget Lefty Grove, but as it turns out he is the forgotten one today. Remember Bill Bonness? Cleveland, however, did have a couple of great rookies in addition to the aforementioned Hegan. They were much less ballyhooed, but turned out to be top-notch major leaguers, and they got their start with the '46 club. Catcher Sherman Lollar spent 18 years in the American League after being the International League MVP in 1945 at Baltimore, where he hit .367, had 34 homers among 169 hits for 302 total bases. He cost Cleveland $10,000, but was well worth the price. Pitcher Bob Lemon, elected to the Hall of Fame in 1976, was only fooling around with pitching in 1946. He had been a utility infielder and outfielder and rated only fair up until then. During the '46 campaign he appeared more often on the mound, and while it was little realized at the time, he was taking his first step toward the shrine at Cooperstown. There was more pitching interest in young Ralph McCabe, who had hurled a minor league no-hitter while a member of the Indian farm club at Wilkes-Barre. McCabe pitched four innings of one game for which he was tagged with the loss before departing forever from the Cleveland scene.

The New York Yankees were sending out press notices on two pitchers and two utility men. Tony Sobol and Dave Douglas were the guys who were to provide the backup for the better known first-string Yanks. Neither made much of an impression and are long forgotten today. The two hurlers, Frank Hiller, out of Lafayette College in Easton, Pennsylvania, and strikeout wizard Karl Drews enjoyed some success in the Big Apple, but both moved on to play a number of years with other clubs. Detroit had a tall right-hander by the name of Lou Kretlow, who was supposed to be the leading prospect to come out of the service ranks. He had more success with the Enid (Okla) army team than with the Tigers. He did last for ten seasons and played with four other clubs, posting a 27-47 mark over that period. Catcher Milt Welch continued the slump that began with Buffalo in '45 and never played with the Tigers at all in 1946. He had appeared in one game in '45. The Washington Senators had one of the finest defensive outfielders in the minors in slim Earl Wooten to go along with Gil Coan, but '46 was not Earl's year to stay in the Capital City.

So there they are, the problems, innovations, the rookies, and the clouds on the horizon that appeared in the first peacetime season since 1941. The GI Joes of the world of baseball had come marching home, and the national pastime was about to enter a period in its history that would prove to be one of the most interesting it ever had. Things were changing rapidly, growth abounded. The relative calm which had once prevailed in the baseball world would be gone forever. 1946 set the stage for the years ahead. Great rookies were just down the road, and they would bring with them great changes, new ideas, new records, but perhaps of even greater importance, new excitement to the grand old game as we shall shortly see. Baseball would never be the same again.

1947-49: A Man Named Robinson

Many exciting things were happening in baseball during the three years that wound up the turbulent decade of the Forties. Entering the ten-year span, America had enjoyed baseball pretty much as it had been for the previous thirty-nine seasons. As we have seen, World War II brought drastic, but necessary changes to baseball. It was nothing compared to the changes and new faces the 1947-49 period would bring.

Baseball on the minor league level grew like wildfire, surpassing the boom it had enjoyed in the post-depression era. The number of minor leagues reached all-highs, and cities who had not dared to dream of having their own team in organized baseball suddenly found themselves represented on the baseball map. Many of the returning GIs found summer homes in the baseball world, some to become the rookies of the late '40s, others waiting in the wings to make their debuts in the early years of the new decade of the '50s.

Although it was little realized in 1947, the two teams that emerged in league championships would dominate the baseball scene for the better part of the years ahead. They were the Brooklyn Dodgers in the National League and the New York Yankees in the American League.

In the spring of 1947, many questions confronted baseball fans. Would the Red Sox repeat? Could the Dodgers overhaul the St. Louis Cardinals? What rookies would break the monopoly held by the returning veterans of 1946? Could the great rookie home run hitter of 1946, Ralph Kiner, make a run at Babe Ruth's home run record?

Oh, what a season it was! Attendance records fell in eight of the sixteen major league cities (Boston, Brooklyn, New York, Pittsburgh and St. Louis in the National League, and Boston, Cleveland and Philadelphia in the

American League). It should be pointed out that every other team did not draw continuous record crowds either, as the St. Louis Browns drew a crowd of only 315 one afternoon in the final week of the season. While the teams under the big top were drawing just short of 20 million paid customers, 52 minor leagues were drawing more than 40 million fans to watch the better than 8,000 players they employed.

After losing the 1946 National League pennant to the St. Louis Cardinals in that league's first play-off necessitated by a tie, the Dodgers captured the National League flag in '47. The Cardinals not only failed to retain their championship, but in November, their long-time owner sold his beloved Redbirds, along with their nationwide farm system. In the American League, the New York Yankees ran away with the pennant, easily outdistancing the second place Detroit Tigers with the '46 winners, the Boston Red Sox, dropping back to third. As was the story with the Cardinals, the Yankees lost Larry McPhail, their temperamental and controversial president, general manager, and one-third owner, when he bowed out among tears after the World Series.

The 1947 World Series will always be remembered for two outstanding moments in World Series history. The highlight of the classic, and one of the great World Series moments, occurred in the fourth game, played at Brooklyn's Ebbets Field. The Yankees had a 2-to-1 lead entering the last of the ninth inning with their pitcher Floyd Bevens pitching his way to a rather shaky no-hitter. No one had ever pitched a World Series no-hitter, and now Mr. Bevens was standing on the brink of baseball immortality. He got the first batter of the ninth to fly out to Joe DiMaggio. The Dodgers' Carl Furillo then drew Bevens' ninth walk of the game. Jorgenson fouled out to Yank first sacker George McQuinn. Two gone now. Al Gionfriddo was sent in to run for Furillo. Pete Reiser was sent up to bat for Dodger pitcher Hugh Casey and received an intentional walk, a strange move by Yankee manager Bucky Harris, putting the winning run on base. It was even more unusual when you consider that Reiser was nursing an injured ankle which slowed his running considerably. The Bums countered by sending Eddie Miksis in to run for "Pistol Pete." Two on and two out, one out to go for Bevens' victory. Dodger second baseman and leadoff man Eddie Stanky was scheduled to be the next batter, but the veteran "Cookie" Lavagetto was sent up to pinch-hit for him. A good clutch hitter, "Cookie" promptly lined a double off the right-field wall, ending the game and the no-hitter all in one stroke of the bat. Strangely, Lavagetto had a chance again the following day in another 2-to-1 ninth-inning situation. The author, in attendance at the game, remembers well how wild old Ebbets Field went when the previous day's hero strode to the plate. The result was, of course, different as the Yankees' Frank Shea sent him back to the bench, a strikeout victim. It was as if the world had ended for the Brooklyn faithful.

The second historic event occurred during the sixth game when Dodger leftfielder Al Gionfriddo went deep to the bullpen wall in Yankee Stadium to make a spectacular catch of Joe DiMaggio's bid for a three-run homer. The catch gave the Dodgers a victory and forced the series into a seventh game. The Yankees won the seventh game, but ironically for the three heroes, Bevens, Lavagetto, and Gionfriddo, it was the end of their major league careers. None of the three appeared again in a major league game.

In that 1947 World Series, the Dodgers presented a rookie first baseman who would later be named rookie of the year. Jackie Robinson batted a .259 in the World Series, hardly record-breaking news. But Jackie did set a record of sorts, as he became the first black player to appear in a World Series. Not only that, he became the first known black to appear in the majors. There have been rumors that other light-skinned blacks may have been in the majors in earlier years, never letting on as to their race. To date there has been no proof of this. It was in late 1945, as previously related, that Branch Rickey had signed Robinson and John Wright, both blacks, to Montreal contracts. From the beginning, it was obvious that Rickey had tagged Robinson to be the first Negro to come into the majors. Despite what the baseball world thought, it needed players of Robinson's caliber. Rickey knew well that to break the color line he needed a player who possessed the qualities Jackie had—not only the playing ability of this former college football hero, but the intelligence and courage to face the tough road ahead. Robinson fit the bill to a tee. With strict racial laws still in effect in the South, Robinson found he often could not live, eat, or in some cases even play with his teammates. He was subject to racial taunts, attempted spikings, beanballs, and resentment from teammates, Northern and Southern alike. While some Dodgers asked to be traded rather than play alongside Robinson, others like shortstop Pee Wee Reese and second baseman Eddie Stanky, supported their new rookie teammate, possibly realizing what he would mean to Brooklyn. Rickey warned Robinson that to fight back would only hurt the act he was attempting. More important than Robinson or any single individual was Rickey's battle cry. Rickey passed up signing another black because he heard that the American League Cleveland Indians were interested in him. This was Larry Doby, who did appear in 29 games for the Indians in 1947, becoming the second black to appear in the majors and the first in the junior circuit. But it was Robinson who broke in first, Doby not winning a regular job in the Indian outfield until 1948. As we are aware now, all teams finally followed Rickey's example.

But consider that it was not until 1955 that Elston Howard became the first black to wear Yankee pinstripes, and the Boston Red Sox, who had a shot at Robinson, would not have a black until 1959, 12 years later, when Pumpsie Green appeared for Tom Yawkey's millionaires.

Robinson hit, fielded, and ran the bases with a daring that Brooklyn had not seen for years. As his teammates saw that he could put cash in their pockets, Jackie won their acceptance. A key situation arose on the Dodgers' first 1947 visit to St. Louis. Rumors were flying that the Cardinals would not take the field if Jackie played. To his everlasting credit, National League president Ford Frick stepped in threatening to suspend all the players who took such a position "even if it wrecks the National League for five years." The rookie Robinson appeared in 151 Dodger games, batting .297 and sparking his team to the championship, while outhitting and outrunning all other rookies. As time passed, Jackie was accepted and played ten seasons in the big leagues at a variety of positions, but primarily at second base. The ramifications of his making it to the top were tremendous, when we look back on them today. He opened the door for black players to play in the major leagues, a fact that would forever affect the major league brand of baseball for the better. Opening this door spelled the demise of the great Negro teams and their leagues, which had for years been a tradition in certain cities. What he did for the Negro and civil rights movements in this country may never be calculated. Just think about it for a moment. He easily is the most important rookie to appear on the major league scene and the most important included in this book. His efforts changed so many things forever.

Robinson, the former UCLA football hero and future baseball Hall of Famer, was not the only rookie of the 1947 season, however. New York's other National League team, the Giants, were singing the praises of a rookie who had all the qualifications to be a throwback to the zany days of early baseball. Perhaps not as well known and certainly not as well remembered as Charlie Faust of John McGraw's Giants, Clint Hartung arrived with abilities that led some to predict the second coming of Babe Ruth. Hailing from Hondo, Texas, Clint gained the nickname "Hondo Hurricane," perhaps the only thing that comes to mind when his name is mentioned today. A pitcher-outfielder, he joined other Giant rookies, infielder Jack "Lucky" Lohrke and Larry "Swede" Jensen, a 30-game winner for the San Francisco Seals. Giant manager Mel Ott was hoping for better things from this trio than from the hot-shot PCL hurler Bob Joyce, whom he had touted a year earlier. Joyce wound up summering in Minneapolis. When the Hondo Hurricane reported to the Giant camp in Phoenix, he had been described as an "an entire ball club in himself." The young zephyr was 23-years-old, stood

6'5" and weighed in at 215 pounds—a good natured, modest, big-eared guy direct from the ranch. Advanced billing said he could hit and pitch with the best. Signed by the Minneapolis Millers right out of high school, the all-state pitcher-first baseman was dispatched quickly to the class C Eau Claire club of the Northern League, where he proceeded to hit .358 while posting a 3-1 record on the mound. A call from Uncle Sam ended his minor league career, and Clint wound up playing for an Army Air Force team, winning 23 games while impressing some former big leaguers, including the St. Louis Cardinal Enos Slaughter. Transferred to Hawaii, his pitching improved while he was hitting tape-measure home runs. Word filtered back to the Polo Grounds and the Giants bought him sight unseen from the Millers. Expected at the 1946 spring camp, Hartung decided to remain in the service playing for Hickam Field, where he batted .567 while posting a 25-0 record as a pitcher. When he finally reached the Giant camp and homered in his first game, the Giants were already making reservations for him at Cooperstown. Manager Ott, liking what he saw, started him in right field on opening day. After several weeks of muffed flies and bobbled ground balls, Ott decided to try him on the mound, where by the season's end, Hartung had posted a 9-7 record. Hartung's problem was that he had only one pitch, a fastball. When Leo Durocher replaced Ott as the Giant skipper, he alternated Hartung between the outfield and the mound. Clint stayed around the major league scene until 1952 and showed a 29-29 record as a pitcher and a .238 lifetime batting average with 14 home runs, not quite up to Babe Ruth's standards. Gaining baseball immortality as a rookie, he also became the answer to baseball's most famous trivia question, "Who was on base when Bobby Thomson hit his famous 1951 home run to win the pennant for the Giants?" Whitey Lockman had doubled sending teammate Don Mueller to third, but when he was forced to slide, Mueller came up with a broken ankle. Who went in to run for him? You guessed it, the Hondo Hurricane, Clint Hartung.

As for the other two Giant rookies, Larry Jansen won himself 21 games while losing 5, giving him the National's best won-lost percentage. What made his freshman record outstanding was that he didn't start a game until May 10, due to a fractured cheekbone. Jansen pitched for nine years in the majors, recording a 23-win season in 1951. Infielder Lohrke stayed around for seven seasons, mainly in utility roles. His career was probably more distinguished by his nickname than by his feats on the field. Why "Lucky"? When he was in the minors, he missed a team bus one day and the vehicle later became involved in a crash. In the service, he was bumped from an airplane that met a similar fate. Strange, but true.

The third New York team had key plans for their golden boy from

Newark, Bobby Brown, whom they had signed for a $25,000 bonus. Brown, who is now a successful doctor, made the club, but was overshadowed by a couple of other newcomers. One, an outfielder who wound up a catcher, did a swell job for the Bronx Bombers, batting .280 with 15 doubles, 3 triples, 11 homers, and 54 RBIs in 83 games—Lawrence "Yogi" Berra was his name. Out with injuries on several occasions, but still able to lead the Yankee pitching staff with a 14-5 record, was rookie hurler Frank Shea. A cocky right-hander named Don Johnson, a 20-year-old, had a red-hot spring, and a great future was predicted. It turned out to be a 27-38 record in seven years with a number of teams.

Lest they not be forgotten, the Brooklyn Dodgers were hoping pitcher Paul Minner and outfielder Marvin Rackley would join Robinson, but it was one John "Spider" Jorgenson who did, capturing the third base spot.

The Boston Red Sox were looking to improve their American League champions by bringing up a young outfielder who was a former New York University baseball and basketball hero, Sam Mele. Mele had been the MVP in the Eastern League as a first-year outfielder for Scranton. Manager Cronin was hoping Mele would replace the aging Wally Moses in right field. Mele did, with some dependable socking (no pun intended), as he hit at a .302 clip and went on to spend a number of successful years in the league. He returned after his playing days were over to lead the Minnesota Twins into the 1966 World Series, but lost a seven-game series to the Los Angeles Dodgers. Mele now works for the Red Sox as a scout and minor league batting coach. Mele's teammate at Scranton was Tommy Fine, a switch-hitting right-handed pitcher who won one while losing three for the Red Sox in 1947. Speed, competitive fire, and a .389 batting average for the Atlanta Crackers earned future American League batting champion Billy Goodman a 12-game stay with the Red Sox. Pitcher Mel Parnell also joined the Red Sox and went on for 10 years to become their all-time lefty winner with 123 victories.

Cleveland expected big things from Eddie Robinson (it must have been a grand year for people named Robinson). Not exactly a rookie, Eddie had made the '46 Tribe when a bad knee sent him back to Baltimore, then of the International League, where he became the loop's MVP. A long-ball hitter, he was expected to join the Texas League's '46 batting champ, Dale Mitchell, with the Tribe. Mitchell was a success, leading all American League rookies and the Indians with .316 BA. Robinson never lived up to his National League namesake, but did make the club.

The St. Louis Browns were unveiling some hot prospects. Remember outfielder Paul Lehner, who despite the bad habit of going AWOL turned out to be a good find for the Brownies. His teammates at Toledo were catcher

Les Moss and a long forgotten first baseman named Jerry Witte. They all made the club. Dave Philley, after two short trials, was expected to nail down a Chicago White Sox outfield post. He did and spent a total of 18 years in the majors. In the City of Brotherly Love, Connie Mack had a couple of good ones in first baseman Ferris Fain and pitcher Bill McCahan, who put himself in the Hall of Fame by throwing a no-hitter against Washington on September 3.

In the National League, the Giants also had Bobby Thomson, previously mentioned, who proved to be a fine outfielder and a power hitter. "The Flying Scot" stayed around for 15 years with several clubs. The Philadelphia Phillies recalled Ralph LaPointe from Baltimore in late August, and he plugged the hole at shortstop and showed power at the plate, but after the season was traded to the Cardinals. The St. Louis Cardinals were predicting that Vernal "Nippy" Jones would solve their infield problems. The Cincinnati Redlegs were so sure of Pacific Coast League product Eddie Erautt that they shelled out $25,000 in cold cash for the 20-game winner with the sizzling fastball. Only 22-years-old, he had led the PCL with 234 strikeouts and also led in shutouts. Six years in the National League produced 15 wins, 23 losses, and no shutouts. Former Cleveland Rebels' basketball star Frankie Baumholtz also found a home with the Reds. Spring trials won a position for a highly recommended power-hitting first baseman for the Boston Braves, the bespectacled Earl Torgeson, and just about eliminated recruit Tom Neill with the same club. Neill, the Southern Association batting champion at .374 with the Birmingham Barons, was tabbed the real comer of the two. His major league career lasted 20 games over two seasons, while Earl stayed around for 15 years and two World Series.

In addition to Mele, NYU alumni who came into their own were Eddie Yost, "the walking man" of the Washington Senators, who at present is a Boston Red Sox coach, and a pretty fair pitcher who had had several trials over in Brooklyn, but in '47 won 21 games for the Dodgers, Ralph Branca. His path would cross that of Bobby Thomson in a few years in that famous season-ending game. So despite the number of returning GIs, who swelled the ranks of the rookies of 1946, it appeared the 1947 crop was better in quality as well as quantity. With Robinson, Berra, and Thomson, the New York teams appeared to have the best of it.

The 1948 season has to be remembered for the first American League playoff and for the prospect of the first all-Boston World Series. Led by their playing manager, shortstop Lou Boudreau, the Cleveland Indians defeated Joe McCarthy's Boston Red Sox in the first American League playoff to gain the World Series spot against the Boston Braves, who had won their first

National League crown since 1914. The win also ended any possibility of an all-Boston World Series. With the Braves and Indians meeting in the fall classic, you had the first series played in ball parks referred to as teepees.

Baseball people are pretty much in agreement that the 1975 season and the World Series of that fall did as much to revive interest in baseball as any season in recent history. It is also generally accepted that 1948 was the closest previous season to '75 to bring baseball into national prominence. Record-breaking attendance throughout the majors and the minors was perhaps the best sign that the product was healthy. Boudreau took care of the Boston Red Sox fantasy, despite the players who moved regularly from the St. Louis Browns to Fenway Park—Vern Stephens, Ellis Kinder, Jack Kramer and Billy Hitchcock. Commissioner Happy Chandler was freeing 10 Detroit Tiger farmhands on the grounds that they had been covered up by the Tigers. Actually, of the 10, Bill Serena may have been the best, as he surfaced with the Chicago Cubs in 1949 and played six seasons for the Little Bears. Another pitcher, Paul Hinrichs, got a reported $40,000 to sign on with the New York Yankee farm club at Kansas City. Paul never made it to Yankee Stadium, but wound up with the Red Sox for four games in 1951.

On August 16, 1948, the baseball world and the nation mourned the death of the game's most famous player, Babe Ruth. It was Boudreau, however, who was capturing the fancy of the nation's baseball fans by leading his Cleveland Indians to the American League crown. He had a season as remarkable as many of the Babe's. He became the last player-manager to win a world championship, the last shortstop to hit over .350 (.355), he led his league in fielding at shortstop for the ninth consecutive year, and as previously mentioned, he single-handedly led the charge against the Red Sox in the playoff. Strangely, the two shortstops in that playoff, Boudreau and Boston's Vern Stephens, almost didn't make it. The Browns had dealt Stephens to Boston before Lou's boss, Bill Veeck, could complete negotiations for a trade which would have sent Boudreau to St. Louis and Vern to Cleveland. I wonder what effect that deal, had it been completed, would have had on baseball? For one thing, the first American League playoff might not have occurred, Cleveland's fine rookie left-hander Gene Bearden might never have been heard from, and Boston's Denny Galehouse might never have been cast in the goat's role as the surprise starter and loser in that historic playoff.

Major league teams were paying out record amounts of money for young amateur players in 1948. These youngsters were to become known as "bonus babies." The Boston Braves and the Detroit Tigers went the highest in the bidding for these untried players. It was reported that the Braves shelled out $75,000 for an 18-year-old Rochester, New York, pitcher named Johnny

Antonelli, and the Tigers handed $75,000 plus two automobiles to a Besse-
mer, Alabama, catcher, Frank House. Both, of course, proved their worth in
the big time. The Philadelphia Phillies were handing Hugh Radcliffe, a
Georgia pitching phenom, and outfielder Stan Hollmig, of Texas A&M,
$40,000 and $25,000 respectively. Another youngster under contract to the
Phillies was posting a 9-and-1 record at Wilmington when a July call came
for him to report to Shibe Park, where he posted a 7-9 record. Remember
Robin Roberts? He stayed around for 18 years, won 286 games, and entered
baseball's Hall of Fame in 1976. The Boston Red Sox picked up a bonus baby
named Frank Quinn from Yale University for an estimated $50,000. What
they didn't know was that Quinn had arm problems. He arrived at Fenway
Park amid a storm of publicity in 1949, and during that season and the 1950
season appeared in nine games, neither winning nor losing a game. In
Philadelphia, the Phillies rose out of the National League cellar, finishing
ahead of both the Chicago Cubs and the Cincinnati Reds, and were laying
the foundations for their Whiz Kids, who we will meet later on. The miracle
of miracles was happening to the Phillies' American League counterpart, the
A's, as they reached fourth place, their highest finish since the days of Foxx,
Grove, and company.

In July of 1948, the Brooklyn Dodgers and the New York Giants, bitter
rivals, made one of the most startling switches in all baseball history. The
Dodger manager, Leo Durocher, switched over to the hated Giants, as the
New Yorkers "promoted" their club's all-time hero, the mild-mannered Mel
Ott, to a front office job. This prompted Leo to make his all-time famous
quote, "Nice guys finish last." Giant fans became outraged to think that the
man they had hated for so long would take over their team, while back in
Brooklyn, Dodger loyalists were somewhat confused to say the least.

The freshmen aces of 1948 in the American League were plentiful again.
The Boston Red Sox, in an effort to bolster their '47 team that had sagged
behind the record of their '46 champions, sent a brilliant rookie second
baseman, Al Kozar, to Washington along with veteran Leon Culberson in
exchange for the hard-hitting Stan Spence. Kozar won the regular keystone
sack assignment and fielded brilliantly while batting .250. It was all downhill from then on, and two seasons later he was gone forever. The Senators
also had the less-heralded Gil Coan back for a third chance. He had flopped
in '46 and '47, but redeemed himself with a hot season at Chattanooga,
hitting .340.

The champion Cleveland Indians had two interesting rookies on their
mound corps. One was a 42-year-old rookie, no stranger to baseball enthusi-
asts, the ageless, dark-skinned Satchel Paige. He was brought up and his skill

and poise helped the Indians to their pennant. Used as a relief hurler, he was 6 and 1. There are enough stories to fill several volumes alone about Paige, whom Dizzy Dean, Cardinal hero of the '30s, once called the greatest pitcher alive. In 1953 at age 47, Paige appeared in 47 games for the St. Louis Browns. Twelve years later, he made an appearance for Kansas City, tossing three innings of one-hit ball, "just to keep the juices flowing," as he would say. The other Indian was a national hero in October and their biggest surprise, Gene Bearden. Hero of the playoff, along with Boudreau, and star of the World Series, Henry Eugene Bearden won 20 while losing 7. As it turned out, this was Gene's only season in the spotlight, as he could never reach the heights he attained in '48 during six more seasons. However, it was Bearden who kept the Tribe in the thick of things in '48 by capturing seven of his first ten games. Obtained from the New York Yankees' Oakland farm club, where he had been 16-7, Gene teamed up with Bob Lemon to keep the Indians in the race when their ace Bob Feller faltered in the early going. Bearden had been badly wounded during the war and had spent a long time overcoming the crushed knee and fractured skull that he had suffered in action in the Pacific. To catch Bearden, the Indians found a rookie catcher, Joe Tipton. Cleveland also had a hard-hitting outfielder in Allie Clark, who followed Bearden to Cleveland from the Yankees. Clark had hit .373 in 24 games for the Yanks at the tail end of the '47 pennant race after his recall from Newark. He came in a trade for pitcher Red Embree.

Bearden wasn't the only war hero rookie of 1948. Connie Mack came up with one of the real finds for the year in Lou Brissie, a big southpaw hurler. Brissie won the hearts of baseball fans everywhere by his courageous triumph over a severe leg injury suffered in the Italian campaign. Brissie's left leg was all but torn away by shell fragments; only his great determination to play baseball again saved him from losing the leg. With the help of a heavy protective leg brace, Lou returned to the mound to win 23 while losing only five in the Sally League before arriving in Philadelphia. He won 14 while losing 10, leading Mack's pitchers in strikeouts with 127. In '49, he was 16 and 11, but it was downhill after that. He did put in seven big league seasons before hanging up his glove.

The Detroit Tigers came up with first baseman George Vico and a youthful Art Houtteman, who was one of the finest pitching prospects in the American League and a sure bet to take a regular turn on the mound in the Motor City and better his seven wins of '47. He fell to 2 and 16, but copped 15 victories in '49 and 19 in '50. Vico only remained two seasons in Detroit, but was sensational in his first year.

Dick Kokos, after only two seasons in the minors, was brought up by the

St. Louis Browns in mid '48. In the 71 games he played, he showed one of the finest throwing arms among the league's outfielders while he batted .300. A mid-season addition to the Browns was first baseman Hank Arft, who hit a triple and a home run in his first game, an American League record. Pitcher Ned Garver posted a 7-11 record for the Browns in the first of his 14 seasons in the American League. In 1951 he won 20 games for the last place Brownies.

In Boston, Billy Goodman came into his own as a utility infielder and the Concord, North Carolina, native showed signs that he could swing the bat by hitting at a .310 clip, a forerunner of his league-leading .354 in 1950.

The National League rookie crop was capturing the rookie of the year voters, and selectors were having trouble choosing between Boston's Alvin Dark and Philadelphia's Richie Ashburn. The Phillies were hard at work building a fine team in Clearwater, Florida, willing to spend as much as any club for new talent. The oufield appeared to be set when Harry "The Hat" Walker fouled a ball off his toe that put him on the shelf. Manager Ben Chapman, in need of another outfielder to fill in for his batting champion Walker, was sent a young kid named Ashburn. The blond-haired youth proceeded to win Ben several exhibition games with his bat and running abilities. Taking the lad North with the club proved to be one of Chapman's best moves, as Richie became a real gem in the Phillie outfield for years. The best base thief in over 40 years, he had Phillie fans thinking of the Cardinal's Pepper Martin with head-first slides, and they were thrilled with the way he covered center field. Batting in the leadoff spot, his speed was used to win many a game. Suppose Walker hadn't been injured? Ashburn might have spent one more season in the minors, but sooner or later his talent would have won out.

The Braves meanwhile found the answer to their shortstop problems when former LSU football star Alvin Dark was moved up from their Milwaukee farm club to replace Dick Culler and help lead the Bostonians to the pennant. Teamed up with second baseman Eddie Stanky, they formed an excellent double-play combination. With Earl Torgeson at first base and Bob Elliott at third, the Braves presented a very fine infield. Spurning pro football, Dark chose a baseball career which lasted 14 years as a player and 13 more as a manager in both leagues. He covered a good deal of territory in the field and batted a fine .322 to Ashburn's .333. Ashburn did lead the league in stolen bases with 32 and teamed up with Del Ennis and another rookie, Johnny Blatnik, in the Phillie outfield. Equally as impressive for the Phils was a young pitcher that Phillie ivory hunters had found in '47 on their back steps in Egypt, Pennsylvania. Signed right out of high school for a considerable amount, the youngster looked like no bargain at the start of the season.

He was as wild as any green rookie could be. Experience was all Curt Simmons needed, and this strong left-handed 18-year old pitcher came into his own in 1948. With improved control, he became the Phillies' number two hurler behind the old Washington Senator veteran, Dutch Leonard. Simmons played in the majors for 20 years with a year (1951) out for a stint in the service of Uncle Sam.

There were others in the senior circuit whose talents gained luster in the light of big-time competition. The Cincinnati Reds had a shortstop with excellent range in Virgil Stallcup, who had Red fans forgetting Eddie Miller, their former star. The Reds, in searching for a hard-hitting outfielder, brought back Hank Sauer, who had a brief trial in 1947 before he was returned to Syracuse where he hit 50 home runs and won the International League's MVP Award. Hank led all the major league home run hitters early in the year, with 22 of his season total of 35 hit by the end of June. Even Babe Ruth was wondering how many homers that Sauer might crank out, "What's this guy trying to do—beat my mark of 60?" Ruth exclaimed. The Reds also came up with a hometown product in pitcher Herman Wehmeier.

The New York Giants' outfield was graced with a fleet-footed, sharp-hitting youngster, who a year earlier had been heralded as a great rookie prospect, until he fractured his left leg during a spring training game at Sheffield, Alabama. Carroll "Whitey" Lockman appeared in the '47 lineup only as a pinch hitter during the final week of the campaign. Quite recovered from his injury, he came back strong in '48, blasting a career-high 18 home runs while batting at a .286 clip. He lasted in the big time for 15 seasons and returned later for three seasons at the helm of the Chicago Cubs. The Giants' eager search for a winning pitcher seemed to end when they uncovered Sheldon "Available" Jones who had turned in a decent year with Jersey City. The nickname "Available" had been acquired early in his career; when pitching in Texas, he would eagerly announce that he was "available" whenever any assistance was required on the mound. He once appeared in 19 consecutive games while in the minors. Giant manager Mel Ott found plenty of use for him as Jones posted a 16-8 mark.

While the Philadelphia Phillies were enamored with rookies Ashburn and Simmons, another young pitcher was making only a so-so 7-9 start with them. As it turned out, young Robin Roberts became one of the prizes of all time, although you might have had trouble convincing anyone of that in 1948. The careful observer would have seen the good curve ball and a humming fastball to go along with excellent control, everything to make him a star of the future. Two hundred and eighty-six victories, and six consecutive 20-win seasons with a high of 28 in 1952 led this all-time great into the Baseball Hall of Fame in 1976. Another Phillie find was Ralph Caballero, up from Utica. He took over the third base chores immediately and effectively. Not an outstanding hitter, he was a superb defense man.

The Pittsburgh Pirates came up with a pretty fair battery. Eddie Fitzgerald was the top backstop of the minors in 1947, batting .363 for Sacramento in 144 games. He continued to star for the Pirates, taking on their first-string receiving duties, showing a faultless defense and hitting a very respectable .267. Eddie spent 12 summers in the majors pretty equally divided between Pittsburgh and Washington. The other half of the rookie battery was Bob Chesnes, a right-hander who did much to make the Bucs the National League's miracle club of '48. Used both as a starter and relief specialist, he finished the season as the Corsair's top hurler (14-6).

In Chicago, strange things were happening for Charlie Grimm's last-place Cubs. In '47 the Cubs' third baseman was Peanuts Lowery, who actually gained greater fame as an outfielder. In '48 Grimm moved Lowery into left field and took his '47 center fielder, Andy Pafko, and stationed him at third base. This gave rookie Hal Jeffcoat, a Nashville graduate, a chance as the Bruin center fielder. Hal made plenty of mistakes in the early season and didn't impress anyone at bat in the beginning. Before the season ended, he found himself and became one of the best players on the Cub roster, hitting .279 and demonstrating speed not only in the outer garden but on the base paths as well. All this with a fine throwing arm made him a real find.

It would seem more than ever in 1948, that baseball was a young man's game. The veterans were fading, and the kids were laying the groundwork for the future. A baseball expert once said that out of every 100 minor leaguers, one rookie ought to be able to make it. A 100-to-1 shot is a pretty small target at which to take aim. Big league clubs were spending money on young players at a record pace in hopes of beating these odds. By today's standards, the amounts they were shelling out might not seem great, but in 1948 they were considered extravagant. The careful observer would note that major league pitching was far inferior to what it had ever been before, and top-grade pitchers were even more scarce than during the war years. So the clubs were battling each other with their bankrolls for untested high school chuckers. This was soon to change. The big collection of '48 rookies soon bloomed into bright futures. The emphasis was on youth.

The New York Yankees of 1949 were perhaps the major surprise of the decade of the '40s. They were somewhat of a failure in 1948 and were expected to again finish no higher than third in 1949. However, they overcame injuries and terrific opposition, especially from the late-season drive of the Boston Red Sox. The Sox took them to the final series and final game of the season, before the Bronx Bombers won out and moved on to the world championship over the Brooklyn Dodger, four games to one.

Actually, neither of the pennant races were decided until the final day of the season. The Yankees found themselves one game behind the Red Sox going into a final two-game series with the Sox at Yankee Stadium. The New Yorkers prevailed 5 to 4 in the first game to tie for the league lead, and then copped the flag with a 5-to-3 triumph on the last day. The Dodgers, with a one-game lead on the final day of the season, were forced into extra innings by the Philadelphia Phillies, but won 9 to 7 in ten innings, preventing a tie with the second-place St. Louis Cardinals. Strange as it may seem, both league champions wound up with identical 97-57 records. The World Series of 1949 was the first in which lights were used, a forerunner of things to come. With darkness setting in at the final game, on October 9 at Ebbets Field as the Yankees came to bat in the ninth inning, Baseball Commissioner Happy Chandler requested the lights be turned on.

For the world champion Yankees, it was the beginning of an incredible string of 14 American League pennants over the next 16 years. The first ten of these would be won under their new manager, Casey Stengel. No newcomer to the baseball wars, Stengel was replacing Bucky Harris at the New York helm, after years of managing National League teams where he did little but gain a reputation as a clown, and a character who could talk a language all his own. His postgame sessions often left sportwriters and newscasters walking away wondering exactly what the "Ole Professor" had been telling them. Perhaps more than anything, it was these verbal barrages, known as "Stengelese," which gained Casey his reputation. Maybe so, but he must have suddenly turned ingenious because 1949 marked the first of his record five straight world championships (1949-1953).

The Brooklyn Dodger ball club of 1949 now had the nucleus of the team that was to dominate the National League scene for the first half of the next decade. Loaded with right-handed hitting power to take advantage of the relatively short left-field wall at Ebbets Field, the Dodgers had seen rookies Gil Hodges, a hard-hitting first baseman, and Roy Campanella, a fine offensive and defensive catcher, come into their own in 1948. Hodges played 18 big league seasons and was a successful manager before his sudden death in 1972. Campanella had been behind the plate for ten years when an offseason auto accident in 1957 left him paralyzed, suddenly ending his brilliant career which led to the Hall of Fame in 1969. These two were blended with veterans Billy Cox at third base, Pee Wee Reese at shortstop, and our 1947 rookie Jackie Robinson at second base to form the fine infield combination that would make them the premier National League team for years to come. 1949 also saw Robinson named the loop's most valuable player, as he led the league in batting with .342 average and was its leading base stealer. In professional baseball for only four years, Robinson remained one of only five National League blacks. All were on New York teams— Robinson, Campanella, and Don Newcombe at Brooklyn, and infielder Hank Thompson and outfielder Monte Irvin with the arch-rival New York Giants. Irvin appeared in 36 games in 1949. Thompson had arrived in 1947, playing 27 games with the American League's St. Louis Browns, but did not come into his own until he appeared at the Polo Grounds in 1949. For some reason, it is Cleveland's Larry Doby who is best remembered as the American League's first black, but actually Thompson appeared during the same season though returning to the Negro National League for the 1948 season. In 1949 he joined the Jersey City Little Giants, where a good start earned him a promotion to Leo Durocher's Giants. In 1949, the American League had only two blacks, both with Bill Veeck's Cleveland Indians, Doby and Satchel Paige. Only three major league clubs out of the 16 had seen what the future could bring from this great pool of untapped talent.

Getting back to the Dodgers, their outfield consisted of two members who would be around for a few years to come. Duke Snider, who had been up briefly in 1947, came to stay in 1948, and really blossomed in '49, and Carl Furillo, who had arrived in '46 upon his return from service. They were teamed up with a journeyman outfielder, Gene Hermanski. Snider may well have been the backbone of these great Dodger teams, later immortalized in Roger Kahn's classic, *The Boys of Summer.* He was pretty much a complete ballplayer; he could run, throw, and hit. Well publicized before his arrival at the Flatbush Avenue ball yard, the Brooklyn faithful were expecting much more than they got in '47-48. Hard work by the unfinished California kid resulted in a good, but not super '49 season, although it must be considered the year he truly came into his own. In the World Series, he did little against the powerful Yankees except to tie Rogers Hornsby for the strikeout record for a five-game series. Determined to work even harder to improve himself, and with the prodding of owner Branch Rickey, Duke developed himself into a fine hitter. Three years later, he came back against the same Yankees in the World Series to bat .345 and hit four home runs, tying another World Series record, this time a positive one set years earlier by one Babe Ruth. Edwin Donald Snider entered the Baseball Hall of Fame in the summer of 1980.

The Dodger pitching crew in 1949 consisted of rookie Don Newcombe and veterans Carl Erskine, Ralph Branca, and Preacher Roe. Erskine, a little right-hander, had actually divided his '48 and '49 seasons between Brooklyn and their farm club in Ft. Worth of the Texas League, although he posted an 8-and-1 record for the '49 Brooks. Newcombe was selected by all reliable sources as the National League's rookie of the year for 1949. The big right-hander posted a very fine 17-and-8 won-lost record to lead the Dodger twirlers. He was not as successful in other endeavors, as he was tagged with the loss in the annual midsummer All-Star Game and dropped two games to the Yanks in the World Series, yet he was still by far the best newcomer of 1949. Moving up from Montreal of the International League in May, Newk put his 17 victories together before he opened the World Series, where he pitched one of the best losing efforts in the history of the classics. He suffered a 1-to-0 defeat in the opener when Yankee Tommy Henrich beat him with a home run in the last half of the ninth. His all-star outing was also creditable even though he got the loss.

Newcombe went on to ten years in the majors, pitched in a total of three World Series, and is still observed around the major league scene helping out where he can by pointing out the evils of alcohol. A former admitted alcoholic, since his cure he has done much to promote the cause of following a path away from the problems this affliction can cause. As a rookie, he had the firm backing of club owner Rickey, but manager Bert Shotton had his doubts and, as stated, Don was left behind with the Montreal Royals after spring training. As later events would prove, Rickey's faith would be justified, and Shotton would have a change of heart regarding his first opinion. Shotton never doubted Newcombe's ability, but he felt other factors outweighed the evident talent. Unjustifiably, Newcombe had gained a reputation as a troublemaker. Twice he had been released by teams in the Cuban Winter League, once by the Almendares Club managed by Fermin Guerra, who in 1949 was catching for the Philadelphia A's. When the A's and Dodgers met in a game at Vero Beach, Florida, during spring training, an incident developed that made the tag hung on Newcombe appear true. Guerra and Newk had been at each other during the contest, when Newk thumbed his nose at the Cuban and challenged him to a fight. There are conflicting reports whether the fight ever took place, but the result seemed evident as Newcombe was left with the Royals. With the '48 Royals he had been 17 and 6, and he opened the '49 campaign with two consecutive shutouts. Trouble arose again as a short while later he jumped the Montreal club, apparently dissatisfied with being forced to stay in the minors. Indicative of Don's character was the phone call Montreal general manager Buzzy Bavasi received, "Will you take a damn fool back?" Newcombe and the Dodgers never regretted that call, and Don learned what so many other rookies have had to learn, when the big club leaves you behind in the minors, they usually have a good reason for doing so, despite your belief that you should be in the majors.

When the call finally came from Brooklyn, it found Don with a sore arm. Determined not to miss his chance, he and his wife doctored the arm in the way he had seen his fellow pitchers do when he was with the Newark Eagles of the Negro League. All the rubbing and hot towels seemed to work, and he was finally ready for his chance. His first appearance was anything but a success. In relief against the Cardinals, he failed to get a man out. But three days later his determination came through, as he made his first start a success by pitching a five-hit shutout over the Cincinnati Reds.

Perhaps the one game which proved Newcombe was indeed the Dodgers' stopper, and the game which sent him on his way to rookie of the year honors, occurred on July 31 against the St. Louis Cardinals with whom the Brooks were battling for the pennant. Faced with dropping out of the race for the flag early, the Dodgers had seen the Cards win six of eight previous meetings, with two games ending in ties. It was a now or never situation for the Bums. Newcombe rose to the occasion with a 4-to-3 win, but there was more behind this triumph than Newcombe's ninth win of the season. The fans in St. Louis were probably unaware as they rode Newk unmercifully that day (while special details of police in the stands were guarding against possible incidents which might lead to a reoccurrence of that city's race riot problems), that they were actually making a better pitcher of Newcombe. Up until this game Newcombe had a tendency to get lazy on the mound, and it would take second baseman Jackie Robinson to get on his back to keep him in the game. No need that day, as the fans were doing what Robinson had had to do before. Jackie learned, that afternoon, that Newcombe could be effective if he bore down all the way, and never again did Robinson let his teammate forget it. It is strange how sometimes the hometown fans' well-intended reactions can work against their own club. In this case their taunts had a beneficial effect on a career as well. Before we leave the Dodger pitching picture, it should be mentioned that in that long-ago spring of 1949, they were looking over several other pitchers who were rated on a par with Newcombe according to early news releases. Only long-time Dodger faithfuls will remember Ezra McGlothin, Clarence Podbielan, Bob Austin, or Jack Banta. For the record, history of a sort was made on July 9, 1949, when for the first time in a major league game, the Giants' Hank Thompson stepped up to bat against Newcombe. It was the first time a black hitter had faced a black pitcher in a major league game.

The Dodgers and the Giants were not alone in being blessed with fine rookies during the 1949 National League season. Taking over for injured St.

Louis veteran third baseman, Whitey Kurowski, was Eddie Kazak, who clinched the job with his extra-base hitting. Kazak jumped up from the Rochester farm club and played well until on the eve of the All-Star Game he suffered an ankle injury that forced him out of the lineup for the last two months of the season. Kazak was joined in St. Louis by Tom Galaviano, who did a good job filling in for the injured Kazak. Both Kazak and Galaviano lasted five years in the majors. The Pittsburgh Pirates introduced a fine pair of rookies in hurler Bill Werle and outfielder Tom Saffell. In the southpaw hurling Werle, the Pirates had the third fine rookie hurler to reach the major leagues from San Francisco in as many years. Seals' manager Lefty O'Doul seemed to be turning them out on a yearly basis. In 1948, he sent along Bob Chesnes, and a year earlier he saw Larry Jansen make the transition. In the spring, the Bucs were dreaming of a team built on speed, as they were giving a look-see to a trio of youngsters up from Indianapolis, Ted Beard (13 steals) and Jack Cassini (33 steals) to go along with Saffel (22 steals). It was outfielder Saffell who survived and led National League rookies in batting at .322 to go along with his splendid fielding. Joining Saffell in the Buc outfield was another fine rookie, Dino Restelli.

In Philadelphia, which was rapidly becoming a paradise for rookies, a trio of youngsters, two of whom had been up for a cup of coffee before, came into their own; third baseman Willie "Puddinhead" Jones and catcher Stan Lopata had been up briefly, while second baseman Mike Goliat was new. The 24-year-old Lopata played 11 years for the Phillies and wound up his career with two years for the Milwaukee Braves. Jones, who was being compared to the great Pie Traynor, hit 19 homers, had 77 RBIs, and in one game hit four doubles. He spent 15 years in the majors, the bulk of which were in Philadelphia. Goliat remained for two years and part of a third before going to the St. Louis Browns. The Chicago Cubs picked up first baseman Herman Reich from the Cleveland Indians, who had gotten him from the Washington Senators. This probably qualified him for the all-time traveling rookie. Reich had played nine seasons for Portland of the Pacific Coast League before landing in Washington. He hit the long ball the Cubs were looking for and batted a fine .280 for them. Though he was chosen as the Cubs' rookie star, he was sold at the end of the season to the Chicago White Sox for the waiver price. It was the end of his very brief major league stay.

The Boston Braves had a dozen rookies trying to crash their 1949 lineup. Manager Billy Southworth was looking for big things from outfielder Don Thompson, who had hit .285 at Columbus, and pitcher Glenn Elliott, who had 14 wins at Milwaukee of the American Association. As fate would have it, it was a 19-year-old catcher who turned out to be the best of the dozen. Del

Crandall, an outstanding prospect, was called up from Evansville in June, and he quickly proved to be one of the greatest catching finds in years. He appeared in 67 games, batting .263 while working like a veteran.

Over in the American League, the St. Louis Browns were looking for big things from outfielder Ken Wood, former Cincinnati Red rookie pitcher Bill Malloy, second base hopeful Bill Summers, and a former Yankee hopeful, pitcher Dick Starr. Not mentioned in the spring was a young outfielder who in 1948 had played for Elmira of the Eastern League and Springfield of the Three I (Indiana, Illinois and Iowa) circuit. This hard-hitting rookie went on to take rookie of the year honors in the junior circuit and was one of the bright spots in the future book of the Brownies. Roy Sievers showed little promise when he started the season in left field, but once he was shifted to center field he batted and fielded brilliantly, earning the rookie award going away. After 17 years in the majors, he hung up his glove in 1965. The New York Yankees came up with a couple of good rookies. A real find was the agile, scrappy second sacker Jerry Coleman. He fielded so well that he forced the talented veteran George Stirnweiss into a bench role. To climax his great year, Coleman hit three doubles and fielded beautifully in the World Series. Outfielder Hank Bauer, who appeared in several games in '48, became a regular in '49. A powerful hitter and a good fielder, Hank put in 14 seasons and nine World Series before becoming a major league manager for eight years at K.C., Baltimore, and Oakland.

Philadelphia fans were holding their heads high in 1949 with all the fine rookies that the Phillies came up with. Their A's were boasting of Alex Kellner, a rookie left-hander who posted a 20-win season while losing 12—their first 20-game winner in 17 years. The Chicago White Sox had acquired rookie right-handed pitcher Bob Kuzava from the Cleveland Indians, for whom he had made several brief appearances. Kuzava's record was exactly half of Kellner;s, ten wins, six losses. Out for part of the season with injuries, the high point of his year was when he whiffed six Red Sox in succession to equal an AL record. A much-traveled player, he played for eight clubs in ten seasons. The Pale Hose also came up with a hard-hitting outfielder in Gus Zernial, who suffered a damaging shoulder injury, a broken collarbone, in May. Hitting .355 at the time, he came back after his injury mended to finish at a respectable .318.

The Detroit Tigers had the most widely publicized rookie, Johnny Groth. An outfielder, Groth had a brilliant schoolboy record in Chicago. He caught the attention of big league scouts while playing with a Navy team after entering the service. Upon his discharge from the service in 1946, he accepted a sizeable bonus and reported directly to the Tigers. After four games and nine plate appearances, he was sent to Williamsport of the Eastern League for the '47 season. After a two-game, four-at-bat appearance for Detroit that season, it was off to Buffalo in '48, only to be called up again at the season's end for another brief appearance. Arriving to stay in 1949, he had to overcome the handicap of too much advanced ballyhoo. Despite the experts saying he was the new Joe DiMaggio, he did a grand job at bat and in the field before a broken wrist forced him out of action after 102 games. He could well serve as an inspiration to all youngsters interested in a big league career, as living proof that there is always room at the top, even though the road may be rocky. Determination can always win out. Johnny had parts of 15 years in the big leagues. The Boston Red Sox, who got off to such a poor start but wound up battling the Yankees down to the final game of the season, had a club considered in many circles to be one of their best ever. Primarily made up of veterans, the Fenway crew did blend in two rookie pitchers of some promise. Maurice "Mickey" McDermott, a skinny, baby-faced left-hander, possessed one of the finest fastballs seen in years. At 21, Mickey showed definite signs of overcoming control problems and living up to his great promise. While with Louisville, before being summoned to Boston, he had set an American Association record by striking out 20 St. Paul batters in a single game. Joining McDermott was another southpaw, Chuck Stobbs. Only 20-years-old, this bonus baby became a regular starting pitcher at midseason with startling success, winning 11 games while losing only 6.

Cleveland also had two better-than-average rookies in 1949. Ray Boone was attempting to fill manager Lou Boudreau's shoes, and while he didn't fully replace his chief until 1950, he fielded well and quite often contributed hits when needed. Pitcher Mike Garcia, a big right-hander, by winning 14 games while losing only 5, was giving the Indians an inkling of what they could expect from him in the future. Strong and fast, the Mexican-American started out as a relief pitcher, but impressed Manager Boudreau so much he was soon getting starting assignments. Garcia's case illustrates a problem which confronts many rookies. Sometimes they have to wait for injuries to strike veteran members of the team before getting a chance to show their stuff. They must be ready when the opportunity arises. When spring injuries affected Cleveland veterans Bob Lemon, Gene Bearden, and Bob Feller, Mike was ready to step in, demonstrating the control and poise of a veteran. As we began our review of the '49 rookies with Don Newcombe, we close with a similar case in Garcia to end it. These two rookies were little thought of early on, but came along to show they had the necessary tools. Known as "The Big Bear," Garcia, like Newcombe, was in his mid-twenties. Like Brooklyn manager Shotton, Cleveland manager Boudreau was readily admitting he had misjudged his pitcher earlier in the year. Garcia, once too small to make his high school team, gained a never-quit-trying attitude. Unspoiled, he had the reputation of being a good guy with excellent habits, habits which gave him the element of consistency, a factor needed for success in the major leagues.

These then were the rookies who wound up the decade of the '40s and the heroes to be of the early '50s. Of them all it was Jackie Robinson who would emerge as the hero. The former football star accepted baseball's challenge and won, forever paving the way for his race and changing the caliber of baseball (and to some extent the face of this nation) for years to come. No matter how many black heroes arose, it was Jackie's example that was best known by the man on the street. If baseball could accept the change, certainly other areas would now be able to give it a try. Twice the Dodgers were forced to train outside of the continental United States because of Robinson's color, but by 1949 they were training in Florida again, and Jackie was being accepted for what he was and what he always wanted to be, a ballplayer. The public, as well as his fellow Dodgers, were accepting him. Football, boxing, track and field, and basketball had accepted Negroes, and now baseball could be added to the list. So ended the era when a man named Robinson arrived.

1950-55: A New York Era

To the careful observer of the baseball scene, there were cracks appearing in the armor during 1950 which would signal the many changes on the horizon for the game in the decade of the '50s. The owners, unhappy with several decisions made by Commissioner Chandler, openly rebelled against the man they had put in office. The iron hand with which Judge Landis had ruled the baseball world was gone forever. Without getting into details, the owners were upset at Chandler's handling of the case of the Pittsburgh Pirate bonus baby pitcher Paul Pettit, of slugger Dick Wakefield's dispute with the Yankees and the White Sox, and at a ruling he had made regarding a Dodger-Cardinal Sunday night game.

Another era ended with the startling announcement that the 87-year-old Connie Mack was retiring as manager of the Philadelphia Athletics, a post he had held since 1901. The 1950 season had been one of the most disappointing in Mack's career, as his A's stood at 52-102 as the season ended, with the brilliant rookie of 1949, Alex Kellner, losing 20 games after winning 20 in his rookie year. For Mack, a career dating back to 1894 came to an end. For 57 years he had been a manager, starting with Pittsburgh of the National League for whom he was catching when he was named their manager in September, 1894. Joining Mack in the retired ranks was the former managerial genius of the New York Yankees and Boston Red Sox, Joe McCarthy. Stricken with illness in mid-June, McCarthy left the Sox and returned to his upstate New York farm. Also disappearing from the major league scene was the playing manager, when at the season's conclusion the Cleveland Indians announced they were replacing Lou Boudreau with Al Lopez.

Signaling further changes were rumors out of the St. Louis Browns' front office that poor attendance might cause a shift of the franchise to Baltimore, an event in baseball which had not occurred since the early days of the American League. Before the Baltimore rumors could die down, Milwaukee and Houston got into the bidding for the Browns.

For years baseball clung to the white home, gray road uniforms, but in 1950 an innovation occurred in the Pacific Coast League which stirred up much comment, when the Hollywood Stars appeared in short pants and lightweight T-shirts. As if that weren't enough, the Cleveland Indians, fed up with customer complaints that games were too long, had a jeep bring in relief pitchers from the bullpens and had their pitchers take their place in the on-deck circle while waiting their turn at bat, instead of remaining in the dugout as was the tradition at the time. Another tradition was voted out when the National League decided to bar photographers from the playing field during the games.

New salary highs were reached when Boston's Ted Williams signed a contract for a reported $125,000, topping by $25,000 the pact given to the Yankees' Joe DiMaggio. I wonder what they would have commanded in today's market?

Prominent among the bonus babies in 1950 were the aforementioned Pettit at Pittsburgh, a 20-year-old Fordham University pitcher, Tom Casagrande, signed by the Phillies, and catcher-outfielder J. W. Porter, signed by the White Sox. The annual winter baseball meetings held in St. Petersburg, Florida, in December 1950 saw an end come to the controversial bonus rule. The rule had gone into effect in February 1947. A total of 65 players carrying the bonus designation had been listed on major league rosters during the four-year period that the rule was in effect. Of course, many of these rookies never worked out, probably because they were frozen to the major league rosters. Among those who enjoyed some success on the major league scene were Chuck Stobbs, Herman Reich, Paul Calvert, Bobby Avila, Luke Easter, Frank House, Lou Berberet, Jim Brideweser, Lew Burdette, Jackie Jensen, Hank Wyse, John Antonelli, Wayne Belardi, Billy Loes, Bill Serena, Ed Bailey, Harry Chiti, Bud Byerly, Bob Hazle, Lloyd Merriman, Rudy Minarcin, Stan Hollmig, Bob Miller, Robin Roberts, Curt Simmons, Bob Friend, Dale Long, and Paul Pettit. Long forgotten and less ballyhooed was the fact that there were some former major league players who had become free agents and re-signed under the bonus rule. They appeared as bonus babies. Remember Clem Dreisewerd, George Metkovich, Al Benton, Milo Candini, Satchel Paige, Paul Campbell, Tommy Fine, and Elbie Fletcher?

There were other more alarming signs of change in 1950. Attendance in both the majors and minors dropped sharply. The minors, after establishing new attendance highs for four years in a row, saw a seven million drop at their turnstiles. After reaching a peak of 59 leagues in 1949, the minors started to decline in 1950, a trend which would continue for some time. While only dropping down one league (the Colonial League, which operated in New York State and Connecticut), there were other signs of decline, as several leagues were forced to drop teams because of a worsening in the nation's economy and increased demands by the military for the induction of young men. By the conclusion of the season, a number of minor loops would vote to disband or shift franchises. Another issue raising its head into minor league territories was the rapid growth of television and the expanding radio coverage of major league games.

The New York Yankees opened the decade where they left off in the '40s by winning the second of five consecutive American League crowns. In the National League, the Philadelphia Phillies, who gambled more heavily on bonus youngsters than any other club, saw their efforts pay off when their Whiz Kids captured that loop's flag. It was not an easy task, however. Seemingly, the pennant race was locked up for the Phillies, when suddenly in September injuries riddled their starting pitchers, Bob Miller and Bubba Church, and their ace left-hander Curt Simmons was called to active military duty. Reversing the outcome of the 1949 National League race, the Phils squeezed out a 4-to-1 ten-inning victory over the Dodgers on a three-run homer by Dick Sisler on the final day of the season. A Dodger win would have resulted in a tie. In many ways it was a strange season. While the Phillies were winning 91 games, the top four American league clubs were all exceeding that victory total. New York had 98 wins, Detroit 95, Boston 94, and Cleveland 92. The World Series found the Yankees sweeping The Whiz Kids in four straight games, the first time that feat had been accomplished since the Yankees did it to the Cincinnati Reds in 1939. With a depleted and overworked pitching staff, the Phils were no match for the powerful New Yorkers. The Yanks allowed the Phillies but five runs, only three of which were earned.

The Phillies' best rookie was probably pitcher Bob Miller, who won eight straight games before he suffered his first defeat. His easy motion and cracking fastball gave him victories in his first two outings. His next two wins were shutouts, as he ran up a string of 22-2/3 consecutive scoreless innings. He was the victim of several mishaps, including a line drive which hit him in the face, all of which slowed his pace, and he finished with eleven wins and six defeats. After ten years with the Phils, he left the majors with an even 42-42 slate. Another rookie pitcher, Bubba Church, was used both in relief and as a starter while posting an 8-6 log. The Yankees, meanwhile, came up with a pitcher of their own who posted a 9-1 record. Future Hall of Famer (1974) Whitey Ford was *The Sporting News'* selection as major league Rookie of the Year. Called up from Kansas City on July 1, he won nine of ten starts and the fourth game of the World Series, a game in which Miller was the loser. Called into the military, he would not return to the Yanks until 1953. In 16 seasons he posted 236 wins for the Bronx Bombers, plus ten World Series wins in 11 series. Joining Ford in the service was a part-time second baseman named Billy Martin. He would return to the Yanks before Ford and in 1952 take over the regular second base chores. Gaining a reputation as a fighter, Martin enjoyed a stormy career with several clubs. Popular among Yankee followers, he returned to manage the Yankees on several occasions, before continuing troubles with Yankee owner George Steinbrenner and offseason battles with others led to his release by the Yanks. 1980 saw him take over the reigns of Charlie Finley's Oakland A's. Colorful and controversial, Martin has had fans everywhere wondering just what the next chapter in his stormy career will be. Known as a manager who can shake up a club, he is also respected for his baseball knowledge. Also joining the Yankees in 1950 was a bonus player for whom Manager Stengel was predicting a bright future. A former All-American football player, outfielder Jackie Jensen arrived from Oakland, but just where he would fit into things at Yankee Stadium was uncertain. Later sent to Washington and then on to the Boston Red Sox, he would later win the American League MVP and have the rare distinction of playing in the Rose Bowl game, the East-West Game, a World Series, and the major league All-Star Game. Fear of flying led to his retirement in 1961 after 11 campaigns. Taking over the first base chores was a rookie who had previously appeared in 12 games as a Yank. Up from Kansas City with a reputation as a slugger was Joe Collins. Occasionally used in the outfield, he turned out to be better defensively than offensively. One of the fastest men on the club, he remained a Yankee favorite until 1957. Making a token two-game appearance in Yankee pinstripes was a young right-hander who would surface later with the Boston Braves to become one of the better National League hurlers of the '50s and early '60s. Few today will remember that Lew Burdette first appeared as a Yankee in 1950.

While this book is concerned with major league rookies, an interesting story developed in the Pacific Coast League which deserves repeating. Perhaps it was the most sensational debut of any newcomer in 1950. Dave Melton was a 21-year-old shortstop signed off the Stanford campus for San Francisco. Joining the Seals in late June, he arrived too late for batting practice that first day. In the ninth inning of the game at Hollywood, Melton was called upon to pinch-hit. With a runner on base, he hit the first pitch to him in organized baseball over the left-field fence for a home run. Quite a feat. It did little good, however, as Hollywood won the game 8 to 6.

The baseball writers, in selecting their rookies of the year, had to look no further than the city of Boston to select the Braves' Sam Jethroe and the Red Sox' Walt Dropo. Jethroe had been sold to the Boston Braves by Branch Rickey of Brooklyn after a brilliant 1949 season at Montreal. Jethroe showed all the promise of becoming one of the most spectacular players in baseball. A switch-hitting outfielder, he gave the pitchers fits while at bat and drove them nuts on the base paths. He had established an International League record for stolen bases in 1949 at 89 thefts. He went on to lead the National League in pilfered bases in 1950 and 1951 with 35 each season. Popular with the fans, Sam had a way of drawing them to the ball park with his play. The early knock on him was that his arm was not up to major league par. The stock gag in the spring was that Sam could run in with the ball from the outfield faster than he could throw it. After three years with the Braves, Sam was back at Toledo in 1953 and then was traded off to the Pittsburgh Pirates in 1954 where he found his old boss Branch Rickey. Appearing in only two games for the Bucs in 1954, Sam found that his star had quickly faded and his career in the majors over.

Meanwhile the Braves' American League counterparts, the Red Sox, had been forced to recall first baseman Walt Dropo when their regular first sacker Billy Goodman suffered a chipped ankle bone. Dropo had been assigned to the Louisville farm club from the Sox spring training camp in Sarasota, Florida, without hardly a look at all. A year earlier, he had been the terror of the Sox camp, tearing apart the opposition during the training period. The big man from Moosup, Connecticut, via the University of Connecticut, arrived at Fenway Park in 1949 as the player who would lead the Bosox back to their former championship form. It didn't work that way, and once the play began for real, the rookie sensation fizzled in his first 11 games, managing only a .146 batting average. That earned him a ticket to Sacramento of the Pacific Coast League in a hurry. But in 1950 the temporary replacement for Goodman was determined to make good on his second chance. All he did was lead the Sox in home runs at 34 and fielding at .988, hit .322, knocked in a league leading 144 runs (tied with teammate Vern Stephens), led the league in slugging percentage, had 326 total bases, and scored 101 runs. After several seasons in which he never reached the same figures, the Sox traded him to Detroit in early June 1952, but he remained on the big league scene for 13 years with a variety of clubs. Think what might have been had Goodman not been injured. Would the "Moosup Mauler" have received a second chance?

It seemed that just about every club in the American League, except Detroit, came up with legitimate rookies in 1950. The Cleveland Indians had Al "Flip" Rosen who had been a perennial minor league leader and a yearly flop in the Indians' spring camps. Then Indians' general manager Hank Greenberg, cut loose the Tribe's veteran third sacker, Ken Keltner, over the objections of manager Lou Boudreau, opening the door for Rosen. Al responded by hitting home runs in bunches to become the league's home run champion as a freshman, with 37 round trippers. Except for a strange twist of fate, it might have been the Red Sox who he would have played for. Imagine the Sox 1950 infield anchored on both sides by slugging rookies? In 1942 Rosen had appealed to Red Sox farm director Herb Pennock for a job on one of his clubs. Rosen was sent to the Danville, Virginia, club for a look-see, but the manager there advised him to go home and forget about baseball. Instead, Rosen took up an earlier offer from Cleveland and joined their farm system. The Red Sox loss was Cleveland's gain. Of course, Rosen went on to a successful ten-year career and then got into the front office aspect of major league baseball. Even though Dropo and Rosen didn't get teamed up, Cleveland did have a rookie first baseman to go along with Rosen. Luke Easter, who like Dropo had a brief trial in 1949, arrived to stay in 1950. He would stay for six years, three as a regular. Arriving with a tag as the "greatest hitter since Babe Ruth," Luke never quite lived up to that advanced notice. Noted, however, for his long home runs, the former Negro National League legend was one of a few to hit a home run into the center-field stands at New York's old Polo Grounds. He also hit one of the longest home runs ever seen in Cleveland, 447 feet into the second tier in right field. Another drive went onto the roof of the right-field pavilion at St. Louis's old Sportsman's Park. He also hit one out of sight in Boston to the left of Fenway Park's center field bleachers.

Except for Easter, no American League rookie received as much notice during spring training as Washington's outfielder Irv Noren. Senator owner Clark Griffith had purchased the flyhawk from the Dodgers' Hollywood farm for $75,000 and groomed him to bat in the Senators' cleanup spot. Well worth the money, he led the Nats in many offensive categories and fielded well during the 1950 season. There were other surprises for Nats' fans, when Manager Bucky Harris uncovered two good pitchers in Sandy Consuegra and Connie Marrero, two right-hand-throwing Cubans. To catch the pair, along came Mickey Grasso, whose only previous fame was the amount of money he had contributed in fines while playing in the Pacific Coast League.

It seemed that every club was buying players from the Dodgers, and the

Chicago White Sox were no exception when they plucked a six-foot Venezue-lan from the Ft. Worth roster named Chico Carrasquel. Rated as a good glove man, Chico turned out to be a great one, as he plugged the shortstop hole left at Comiskey Park by Luke Appling. Chico, who also hit well, underwent a knee operation after the season which enabled him to stay around the American League for ten seasons. Chicago general manager Frank Lane also took a chance with Bob Cain, a pitcher the Giants had let go because of a record of wildness in the minors. Lane's judgement was correct, as the lefty Cain gave him 11 complete games. The Pale Hose also came up with a Cuban relief pitcher in Luis Aloma, who appeared in 42 games for them with 7-2 record and almost single-handedly kept the Sox out of the basement.

Despite their poor showing, the Philadelphia A's presented relief pitcher Bob Hooper, who was the only consistent pitcher on a staff full of inconsis-tencies. He broke no less than six disastrous losing streaks for Connie Mack's club. The St. Louis Browns carried more rookies than any other major league club, but it was first baseman Don Lenhardt who stood out for them in 1950. Don also demonstrated ability as a fly chaser, a spot where he spent the majority of his five big league seasons. Topping the Browns in most batting departments, the San Antonio product seemed certain for a first-string job for years to come.

The National League did not have as many outstanding rookies as the American League, but there were some of note. The Braves, in addition to Jethroe, had rookie second baseman Roy Hartsfield, who made it possible for GM John Quinn to risk disposal of the veteran Eddie Stanky before the season got underway. Roy took a firm hold on the keystone job, proving he had what it took to make the jump from Milwaukee. The Dodgers, who had been selling off farm players, came up with reliever Dan Bankhead, who had some control problems, and a fine-fielding shortstop in Bob Morgan, both from their Montreal Royals farm club. The Chicago Cubs came up with four freshmen in Bob Borkowski, Carmen Mauro, Bill Serena, and Wayne Ter-williger. Of the four, Terwilliger, a second baseman, turned out to be the best, as he banged out ten home runs and led the Cubs in stolen bases. Serena held down the hot corner, but Bill's weakness was his lack of hitting punch. Borkowski, an outfielder, hit well and fielded acceptably. Mauro, a left-hand-hitting outfielder, was never able to crack the starting outfield.

The Cincinnati Reds had a fine looking catcher in John Pramesa, who was expected to take over the number-one catching job, but couldn't move out the weak-hitting Dixie Howell. Used primarily in the Reds' outfield was Joe Adcock who arrived from Tulsa to play in 102 games. His work at both first base and the outfield was highly accomplished, and his bat added some much needed punch to the Reds' lineup. Joe later starred for the Milwaukee Braves and put in 17 seasons in the big time. The New York Giants had a good-looking first baseman in Tookie Gilbert until a late-season injury put him on the shelf. The St. Louis Cardinals had two decent rookies in Cloyd Boyer, a highly publicized pitcher (he won and lost seven games), and outfielder Bill Howerton, who decided he liked baseball better than cow-punching. Howerton was too good to be kept on the bench, as he fully lived up to his advanced promise, hitting .281 with 20 doubles, 8 triples, and 10 homers. The Pittsburgh Pirates had four rookies of note, three of whom became National League fixtures for years, right-handed pitchers Vernon Law and Bill MacDonald, infielder Danny O'Connell, and hard-hitting outfielder Gus Bell. MacDonald never enjoyed much success, but Law, a deeply religious man and a deacon in his church, pitched for 16 years for the Bucs. O'Connell showed little in the early going and was sent back to Indianapolis, where he starred and was recalled when Pirate shortstop Stan Rojek became injured. Returning to play shortstop, O'Connell was great on defense and batted a fine .292. It was a tough break for the Pirates when Danny was called into the service, from which he returned in 1953 for nine more seasons in the big time. Gus Bell spent 15 years in the majors, most of them with Cincinnati. In 1950 he was hitting .400 at Indianapolis when he received the Pirates' call, and after reporting to the Bucs he gained his first share of stardom.

1951 was an all-New York year in the major leagues, as the Giants and Yankees met in the World Series with the American Leaguers winning four games to two. The third New York team, the Brooklyn Dodgers, were also in the thick of things, tying the Giants at the end of the regular season. The two National League clubs were involved in a marvelous stretch drive which ended with a three-game playoff for the crown. It all ended in the third playoff game, when Giant Bobby Thomson hit his historic home run to send the Giants into the Series. The Giants, however, were unable to continue their "miracle" drive against Casey Stengel's Yankees in the World Series.

Organized baseball's jubilee year was marked by an off-the-field move of importance, as Commissioner Chandler resigned and was succeeded by National League President Ford Frick, who was in turn succeeded by Warren Giles. Giles had been the former head of the Cincinnati Reds. Down in Washington, Congress was probing into organized baseball chiefly to study the reserve clause, farm club agreements, expansion, and radio and TV agreements. Also at issue was the Pacific Coast League's request for major league status. Several cities were trying to interest the St. Louis Browns' new owner, Bill Veeck, into moving his team out of the Mound City. All met with failure. Veeck, the showman, provided many interesting innovations to try to hold fan interest in his Brownies. The most memorable was when he sent 26-year-old, three-foot, seven-inch Eddie Gaedel into a game as a pinch hitter. Batting for Frank Saucier, Gaedel drew a walk on four straight pitches by Detroit's Bob Cain. 1951 also saw eight more minor league loops fold up their tents, as there were now just 50 leagues in operation. Increased demands by the military, declining attendance, and inroads made by radio and TV resulted in more minor leagues voting not to operate in 1952. Blacks appeared in the lineups of clubs located in the South for the first time during the 1951 season, and another first occurred when the Southwest International League hired a Negro umpire, Emmett Ashford. Ashford later made it to the big leagues. Major league attendance was also down sharply. CBS presented the first color telecast when on August 11 they screened the Dodger-Braves game from Ebbets Field. The National League playoff and the following World Series were also telecast from coast to coast.

On the field, the Cardinals' Stan Musial won his fifth batting crown, while the A's Ferris Fain won the American League batting championship. Thirteen pitchers won 20 games, the most in 31 years, and Chet Nichols, a 20-year-old Boston Braves' rookie, won the National League's ERA championship. Long-time American League stars, Joe DiMaggio of the Yankees and Bobby Doerr of the Red Sox, announced their retirements. The baseball writers named Gil McDougald of the Yankees and Willie Mays of the Giants as rookies of the year, while *The Sporting News* named Mays and the Chicago White Sox' Minnie Minoso as their picks for the best newcomers of 1951.

The rookie story of the year may have been that of Bob Lightbody, a 20-year-old southpaw who showed enough promise during a spring trial to be signed by Great Falls of the Pioneer League. In his debut, he worked one inning in relief, striking out all three batters to face him. After two more relief chores, he got a starting assignment and shutout Boise on three hits 7 to 0. A few days later at cut down, he was sent to Eugene of the Far West League. In four games for Eugene, he went the route twice and had a 1-1 record, when he was returned to Great Falls in late June and released. Not an unusual career you say? Yes it was, you see Lightbody had only one hand.

While the two New York clubs dominated their leagues in 1951, they also shared an unusual rookie feat in 1951. Each would have in their lineups for the first time two rookies who would become the superstars of the '50s and '60s, and who would both enter the baseball Hall of Fame in the '70s. It was the year both Willie Mays and Mickey Mantle would arrive on the big league scene. In that first year it was Mays who was the better known of the pair. The

"Miracle Giants" were basically a club of experienced players, but it almost seemed their drive came from the 20-year-old outfielder from Fairfield, Alabama. After 35 games with Minneapolis, Mays was summoned to the Polo Grounds, where, by the season's conclusion, he had played 121 games. At the time of his recall in late May, Willie was hitting at an unbelievable .477 clip. Mays performed superbly for his manager, Leo Durocher, hitting for both power and average, running well, and throwing and fielding with such enthusiasm that it seemed to infect his teammates. A versatile player, he would often lead the league in power hitting or stolen bases during his 22 years as a member of the Giants and Mets. If he was considered fabulous at bat and on the bases, words would be hard to find to describe what he did in the field. He was in a class by himself. For anyone who ever saw him, the sight of him running out from under his hat to leap after a fly ball was something to remember for a lifetime. Not only did he and Mantle arrive in the same season, they both played center field. In 1979 "Say Hey" Willie Mays entered the baseball Hall of Fame.

Mickey Mantle divided his 1951 season between Yankee Stadium and the New York farm club at Kansas City, appearing in 96 games in New York and 40 in K.C. His full name was Mickey Charles Mantle, sometimes referred to as "The Commerce Comet" in reference to his home town in Oklahoma. His father gave him the name Mickey because of his admiration for the great catcher Gordon "Mickey" Cochrane. Mantle was a switch-hitting slugger who had equal power from either side of the plate. Bad legs prevented him from gaining the fame enjoyed by Mays in the field. He had a fine throwing arm and in his early years showed some good speed while running. Because of his devastating power at the plate, pitchers often walked him as a result of their careful pitching to him. His long home runs were hit in every ball park around the American League. One of his most famous blasts came in 1953 in Washington's Griffith Stadium, traveling an estimated 565 feet. Mickey played for 18 years in the Bronx ball yard and was voted into the Hall of Fame in 1974.

Despite all the talk about Mantle, it was his teammate, Gil McDougald, who was rated by the writers as the American League freshman of the year. Playing mostly at third base, Gil also saw considerable action at second base, as he was being groomed to eventually replace Jerry Coleman at the keystone sack. Surprisingly, he was the only member of the world champions to bat over .300, at .306. On May 3, the Yanks racked up 11 runs in the ninth inning at Sportsman's Park against the Browns, and among the records tied was that of six RBIs in one inning by young McDougald, as he hit a two-run triple and a grand-slam home run. It would be ten seasons before McDougald would leave the big league ranks. An aggressive player, he fit in well with the Yankee way of doing things. Right-handed pitcher Tom Morgan was another rookie who made good for Stengel's Yankees, turning in a 9-3 record. Losing his first start, he came back to pitch eight wins in a row. Demonstrating a number of pitches and great control, the New York faithful thought they had another Whitey Ford in tow. The durable Morgan pitched for a variety of American League clubs for 12 years, finishing with a 67-47 slate. Art Schallock, a reliever up from Hollywood, joined the Yank cast of rookies also.

Selected by *The Sporting News* as their Rookie of the Year was Saturnino Orestes Arrieta Armas Minoso, known for obvious reasons as Minnie. The flashy Cuban started the season with the Cleveland Indians, playing eight games before joining the Chicago White Sox for 138 more. The deal which brought him to Chicago was a three-way affair involving the Indians and A's and seven players. Performing both in the infield and the outfield, he showed great skill and in addition led the Chicago batters with a .326 average and the league in stolen bases with 31 and triples with 14. The bulk of his 16-year career was spent in the outfield, and he had a lifetime BA of .298. Rookie outfielder Jim Busby joined Minoso in the battle for base stealing honors and finished second with 26 thefts and a .283 BA. These two rookies helped Chicago lead the league in stolen bases and gain the nickname of the "Go-Go Sox"—based on their base running abilities, not the type of dancing so popular today.

The Cleveland Indians had a young right-handed hurler join them in May named Bob Chakales. Used primarily as a reliever, he did a good job handling the tough situations like a veteran. Appearing in 17 games, he had a 3-4 record. These were the days before the American League adopted the designated-hitter rule, and Bob took advantage of it by hitting a home run in his first big league at-bat. The Indians also had Harry "Suitcase" Simpson, a long lanky Negro outfielder who was tagged as a rookie sure-shot, but somehow failed to live up to those expectations. Somewhere along the line, the great hitting he displayed with San Diego in '50 deserted him, as he hit only .229. A post-season barnstorming tour saw his bat come alive, and in '52 he upped his batting mark to .266. The St. Louis Browns had Bob Young, a frail-looking second baseman up from Baltimore, and he proved to be a real find. Taking over as a regular, it appeared that he would be the star of the future. Not only highly skilled as a second baseman, he hit .260, which was 13 points better than the team average. Bob had had a three-game trial with the St. Louis Cardinals in 1948. A weak bat kept him from the promise he had shown in 1951; nevertheless he did put in eight seasons. Other Brownie hopefuls in '51 were infielder Bill Jennings, who was good defensively, poor offensively, and Frank Saucier, the Texas League batting champion in 1950, who refused to report to the Browns until Owner Bill Veeck stepped in to persuade him to. Frank got into only 18 games and batted .071 in his only big league season. Another Brown rookie was Bob Nieman, who came up from Tulsa late in the season, and looked like a sure-shot in the outfield. As long as baseball rookies are discussed, Nieman's name will be remembered, if for nothing else, for what he did in his first major league game. He established a major league record by hitting home runs in his first two appearances at the plate on September 14, 1951, against the Boston Red Sox.

The Washington Senators had three good youngsters. One was known as Jim Runnels, who was recalled from the Chattanooga farm club and was a steady fielder who hit .279. You will remember him today as Pete Runnels. Pete was a big leaguer for 14 years, traded to the Boston Red Sox prior to the 1958 season, and won the American League batting championships in 1960 and 1962. The Nats also had a pretty fair pitcher in Julio Moreno, who posted a 5-11 mark to go along with his nice fastball, and infielder Gene Verble, who failed to stick (both the batting and continuing kind). The Boston Red Sox were touting rookie pitcher Leo Kiely, who posted a 7-7 record and then entered military service and did not return to Fenway Park until 1954, never reaching the potential forecast for him in 1951. Fred Hatfield had a brief trial with the Bosox in 1950 after playing for seven minor league clubs starting back in 1942, and taking three years out for the service. Hatfield enjoyed moderate success in nine years with several clubs, although he did more against the Red Sox while with Detroit than he did for them during the 1951 season.

The 1951 National League rookie harvest was, of course, led by the previously mentioned Willie Mays, and while they may not have had the numbers that the Americans had, they did have some quality players, or at least some who turned out that way, although overshadowed by Mays in their initial year. Pitcher Bob Friend was handed a starting assignment with the Pirates and posted only a 6-10 record, but with a weak club that was outstanding. Bob was a premiere pitcher for 16 National League summers. Friend was joined at midseason by Paul LaPalme, a lefty who delivered some excellent relief pitching. The Brooklyn Dodgers brought up the colorful, speedy, sure-armed Rocky Bridges and outfielder Don Thompson. Although he only appeared in 23 games, the highly rated flyhawk, Dick Williams, was up from Ft. Worth. He really didn't live up to expectations, but in fairness to him, he was handicapped by injuries and faced a formidable task of making a club dominated by veteran ballplayers. Williams filled a major league utility role for 13 years, but he must have learned his lessons well, as he became a very successful manager with the Boston Red Sox, Oakland A's, and the Montreal Expos. He always made contenders out of the teams he managed.

The St. Louis Cardinals had a pair of highly rated pitchers in Tom Poholsky and Joe Presko. Both boosted the Redbirds' aging pitching staff. Presko had a sneaky fastball and good control, and Pololsky, who was being counted upon for '52, was called into the military. Joining Mays in New York was the Cuban catcher Ray Noble, who hit the long ball and showed a fine throwing arm. Pitcher George Spencer was also of immeasurable help out of the bullpen for the champion Giants. Chicago Cub manager Phil Cavarretta had little to boast about on his last place club except for first baseman Dee Fondy, who was being given a second chance, and Omar "Turk" Lown, a war-scarred hurler who was now fighting a different battle with something called control. The Reds had a fine shortstop in Roy McMillan, although his hitting was suspect. The Boston Braves had a big strapping rookie catcher in Ebba St. Claire, who did a good job as regular Walker Cooper's understudy, and an outfielder of some note in Bob Addis, and as previously mentioned, the NL earned run average champ in pitcher Chet Nichols. Nichols' father, Chet, Sr., had pitched in the National League from 1926 through 1932 with the Pirates, Giants, and Phillies, posting a 1-8 record in six seasons. Young Nichols lasted nine years with the Braves, Red Sox, and Reds, winning 34 while dropping 36 and is now a minor league executive with the Boston Red Sox farm club at Pawtucket, Rhode Island.

1952 saw the Cardinal veteran Stan Musial win his third consecutive batting crown and sixth overall and saw the Boston Red Sox' Ted Williams' bid farewell to baseball for the second time, in late April, as he was recalled into the Marine Corps for duty in Korea, a conflict which saw many diamond stars lost to Uncle Sam. The Yankees were hit hard by inductions when Jerry Coleman, Tom Morgan, and Bobby Brown were called up.

In addition to the nagging TV and radio problems, baseball had the problem of an increase in huge bonus payments to untried talent. Despite possible military service staring these bonus babies in the face, baseball clubs put out an estimated four-and-one-half million dollars to these untried high school and college players. Heaviest spenders were the Boston Red Sox, who inked 17 youngsters during one three-week period, and reportedly spent close to $500,000 of Tom Yawkey's fortune during the year. Most of the contracts called for payments over a three-to-five-year period. The Red Sox paid bonuses reported between 77 and 100 thousand dollars to four players. Pitcher-outfielder Marty Keough, pitchers Eddie Urness and Frank Baumann, and catcher Jerry Zimmerman. All except Urness eventually made Yawkey's Bostonians. There were two high-priced bonus stars who reached the majors in 1952, the year of their signing—Dick Groat with Pittsburgh and Harvey Kuenn with Detroit. Each were easily worth the cash they hauled away, as they starred for their clubs for years.

Like the National League, the American League had a repeat batting champion in the Athletics' Ferris Fain, the first time in 38 years that both leagues presented repeat batting champions. The pennant races found the Yankees winning their fourth straight flag, while the Brooklyn Dodgers picked up another National League bunting. A spectacular seven-game World Series found the Bronx Bombers again world champions, Casey Stengel's fourth straight world's title. There was a continuing trend of low attendance and reduced number of minor leagues in 1952. Organized base-ball's attendance was down 8.7 percent, while the number of minor loops dropped to 43, seven less than a year earlier. There were several notable rookies other than those selected as outstanding for the 1952 season. The Harrisburg club of the Inter-State League announced in June that it planned to sign a rookie, an announcement that caused quite a national incident. It seems the rookie was a female player, Mrs. Eleanor Engle, a 24-year-old stenographer. She worked out at shortstop with the club, but was not signed, and it became apparent that it was only a publicity stunt. The outcome was a ruling barring the signing of women as players. I wonder what problems such action would cause in our society of the 1980s.

The season's most talked about rookie was the 22-year-old shortstop-outfielder of the Boston Red Sox, Jim Piersall. The Connecticut native possessed a fine minor league record and showed signs of brilliance upon arrival at Fenway Park. He suddenly began attracting more attention with his on-the-field clowning than with his playing ability. In May he started a heckling exchange with the Yankee's Billy Martin, which wound up with an encounter under the stands before teammates could separate them. Hitting only .267 after 56 games, Piersall was sent to the Sox farm club at Birmingham, Alabama, after allegedly spanking the 4-year-old son of Red Sox shortstop Vern Stephens in the clubhouse. "I think they have farmed out the greatest outfielder in baseball. They better hurry to see me in Birmingham, because I'll be back in Boston before long," Piersall was quoted as saying. He continued his antics down South, resulting in four heave-hos in less than three weeks. On another occasion, after spraying home plate with a water pistol had resulted in his ejection from the game, he continued his heckling from the press box. All he received for his efforts was a three day suspension. Returning to Boston, he underwent a medical examination which showed him to be ill, and he was admitted to a hospital for treatment of a mental breakdown, spending the remainder of the season under medical care. He returned the following year and played good baseball for the Sox, until he was traded to Cleveland for the 1959 season. He remained in baseball for 17 years, retiring in 1967, but his antics during those seasons have become legend. Holding a variety of jobs since he left baseball, some in and some out of the game, he was still the center of controversy in 1980 while a broadcaster for the Chicago White Sox, for being too critical of Bill Veek's players. Colorful and likeable, Piersall remains in the thick of things in the baseball world.

Piersall wasn't the only story in Boston during 1952. Down the street from Fenway Park, where Jimmy was performing, stood Braves Field, home of the National League Boston entry. Long a doormat in the National League, the Braves had risen to become league champions in 1948, and it was hoped that the sudden boost they enjoyed at the gate would continue for the years ahead. For some reason it didn't work that way, and the Red Sox remained the darlings of the Boston crowd. The Braves' attendance continued to dwindle steadily until in 1952 they drew only 300,000 customers. This fact caused the owners to start looking westward toward Milwaukee, and sure enough it became the new home of the Braves in 1953. The last season on the banks of the Charles brought rookie Eddie Mathews in to play third base. The Braves top farm club was located in Milwaukee, so when the franchise shifted, it was back to Milwaukee for Eddie to star for most of his 17-year big league career. Jumping way ahead of our story, the Braves, of course, would shift to Atlanta in 1966, and Mathews would make that transition also. Interestingly, before Mathews played for the Milwaukee farm club, he had played at Atlanta, one of those strange quirks of fate that found him returning to the sites of his minor league days as a major leaguer. How many major leaguers can say they played with the same organization, yet found a home in three different cities during their career? In 1952 Ed Mathews was one of the brightest young stars in the organization. His long-ball power made him a sensation, as he banged out 25 homers. Rival pitchers said the youngster grew stronger in September and predicted big things for him in '53. They were right, as Ed hit better than 40 home runs for the next three seasons (47 in '53, 40 in '54, and 41 in '55) and repeated the feat again in 1959. When Mathews retired, he had connected for 512 round trippers. Johnny Logan, who had played some in 1951 for the Braves, finally arrived for good in '52 and proved to be a fine shortstop. The Braves were also holding high hopes for six-foot, eight-inch Gene Conley. The towering right-hander had taken a fling at professional basketball the previous winter with the Boston Celtics of the National Basketball Association. He had turned in a 20-9 record with Hartford of the Eastern League in 1951. So many rookies were trying out for the Braves that when the club hired a plane to cart the men of the press around, they dubbed it the "Boston Braves' Rookie Rocket." How many future stars can you find among those training with the 1952 Braves? Remember pitchers Lew Burdette, Dick Donovan, Bob Hall, Dick Hoover, Virgil Jester, Ernie Johnson, Don Liddle, Bert Thiel, and Murray Wall; remember infielders Harry Hanebrink, Jack Dittmer, and Billy Klaus, who would play only a few games with the Braves, but turned up with the Red Sox in 1955 to win the hearts of Boston fandom? Then there was first baseman George Crowe, who had sparked the Milwaukee Brewers all season long in 1951, and led his league in hits, total bases, doubles, and RBIs. In the outfield, rookies Jack Daniels and Bob Thorpe were being given a look-see. Seldom has any major league team presented such a large crop of top-notch rookies as the 1952 Braves.

While they didn't all make it in '52, the other gilt-edged rookies up for a look-see included quite a few who would lead the baseball parade of the '50s. Big Bob Alexander, who compiled a 15-8 record with Montreal, was highly regarded by Brooklyn. Despite an 11-14 record at Minneapolis, strong-armed Hoyt Wilhelm was expected to add depth to the New York Giants' mound corps. Wilhelm, of course, turned into a fine relief pitcher and spent many seasons in the majors. Jay Van Noy, a promising outfielder with speed and power, was up from Rochester with the Cardinals. He was paired with probably the most publicized rookie of the year, Wilmer "Vinegar Bend" Mizell, whose pitching with Houston was reminding everyone of Dizzy Dean. Mizell, who would put in two good years with the Cards before entering the service, crossed paths with the author on several occasions, while the Cardinal was pitching with the Ft. McPherson, Georgia, service team. One evening while sitting together between games of a twi-nighter and discussing our service experiences, I asked Mizell if he thought the Cardinals missed him. The Cards, at the time, were hot and doing quite well without their prize rookie. Looking me in the eye, the big likeable left-hander replied, "Not as much as I miss them," while giving the universal money sign of rubbing the first finger and thumb together. "Vinegar Bend" put in nine years in the majors before he took up politics, running successfully for Congress. Mizell's teammate at Houston was the hard-hitting Larry Miggins, who had belted 27 home runs for the Buffs. The Cardinals were hoping he would supply the desperately needed strong right-handed-batting punch for them.

The Chicago White Sox were hoping that Bob Boyd, a heavy-hitting first baseman with speed, would make the jump from Sacramento. They had also slated International League rookie of the year Hector Rodriguez for duty at third base. When Hector first reported to the Montreal Royals, the Cuban knew only three words of English, "I got it." There were many baseball observers who agreed that he had it, enough to make the Sox at the hot corner. The Cleveland Indians were counting on a San Diego graduate named Sam "Toothpick" Jones to bolster their already strong pitching staff. A fastball chucker, Sam had never played baseball until he went into the service in 1943. The St. Louis Browns claimed George Schmees in the minor league draft from Hollywood of the Pacific Coast League and were hoping his .328 average and 26 homers were no fluke. Joining George in St. Looie was a versatile Jim Dyck, who played infield and outfield at San Antonio and had won the Texas League's MVP honors. The New York Yankees were still coming up with talent from their vast farm system. Tops in the 1952 harvest were the International League's MVP outfielder Archie Wilson, and from Kansas City of the American Association, first baseman Don Bollweg. Bollweg had been hampered by a bad hand, but a successful winter operation boosted his chances. Down in Durham, North Carolina, at Duke University, they had an all-American basketball player who had closed out his career with a total of 1,783 points for an average of 23.2 per game. This basketball player could also play a pretty fair game of baseball. His hailing from the Pittsburgh area did not escape the eye of that smart old baseball man, Branch Rickey. He knew he had an instant box office success if the youngster could make the Pirates at shortstop. Well, Dick Groat made the jump from the campus to Forbes Field, and Rickey made a few bucks as a result. Groat was good enough for 14 seasons. Along with Conley, it seemed basketball players were invading the big league diamonds.

In 1952, there were many teams in a transition period, and the promise held by the large rookie crop had them running rookies in and out of their lineups on a regular basis. Red Sox manager Lou Boudreau even announced he was going to embark upon a program to rebuild his sagging Sox by playing rookies regularly. He opened the year by using the likes of Ted Lepcio, Faye Throneberry, Piersall, Ike Delock, Dick Gernert, Sammy White, Bill Henry, and Dick Brodowski. They could only carry him as far as sixth place, but it was one of the great rookie experiments of all time.

It seemed as if every team had a youngster of promise in 1952, as the roll call went on and on. The Cleveland Indians thought they had a dependable outfielder in Big Jim Fridley. Dependable he was, for his paycheck, on three different clubs in three years in the big time. The St. Louis Browns had a much publicized outfielder with the colorful name of "Jungle Jim" Rivera, who after 97 games was sent to the Chicago White Sox. Rivera, the Pacific Coast League MVP in 1951, came with excellent "stats." His first season was a disappointment, but he improved enough to spend 10 seasons in the majors. The Brownies also had Clint "Scrap Iron" Countney, a bespectacled backstop who had had a brief one-game trial with the Yankees in 1951. He was a fine receiver and a fiery competitor. Courtney was named by *The Sporting News* as their American League Rookie of the Year. Another catcher the Browns had in tow was a former Chicago White Sox bonus baby, J. W. Porter. The New York Yankees had two shortstops of note, Andy Carey, whom they were grooming to replace the aging Phil Rizzuto, and Jim Brideweser, a capable glove man who could also play second. Joining them were infielders Kal Segrist and Loren "Bee Bee" Babe, who had been summoned from Syracuse in August when regular Billy Martin became injured. The Yanks also had pitchers lefty Harry Schaeffer, Tom Gorman, who was called up from Kansas City and proved his worth with a 6-2 record and key wins over Cleveland and Boston, and Bill Miller who reminded veteran Yankee followers of Lefty Gomez. Detroit had picked up rookie pitcher Dave Madison, who earlier in the season had been 4-2 with the Browns, but broke even at 1-1 in Tigerland.

The Baseball Writers Association named Philadelphia Athletic right-handed pitcher Harry Byrd as their American League Rookie of the Year for 1952. The Darlington, South Carolina, native had spent most of his minor league career split between Martinsville of the Carolina League and Savannah of the Sally League, with one season at Buffalo of the International League. Byrd had had a six-game trial with the A's in 1950, during which he pitched only 11 innings with no decisions. In 1952 he had the best of his seven major league seasons and was by far the American League's best freshman pitcher. Teaming with little Bobby Schantz, they gave the A's a decent one-two punch on the mound. His 15-15 record failed to do justice to his effectiveness, as he lost several one-run and extra inning games. Among these was the 11-inning game in which the Yankees clinched the pennant. The A's were also looking at five others, all of whom contributed little in '52, but several of whom did spend a couple of more years in the big leagues: pitchers Marion Fricano, who had won 17 games for Ottawa, and Charlie Bishop, originally Cardinal property; outfielder-pinch hitter Kite Thomas, drafted out of the Yankee system; and infielder Everett "Skeeter" Kell, brother of Red Sox George Kell and Hal Bevan, a third baseman who played in one game for the Boston Red Sox before the A's obtained him on waivers in May of '52.

Speaking of the Red Sox, the group of youngsters being tried in the rebuilding effort in Boston all turned out to be decent major leaguers. When the Sox' regular third baseman, George Kell, became injured, the Sox called up Ted Lepcio, who had less than a full year's experience (90 games) to fill in. Lepcio's tenth-inning home run on September 13th against the Indians, who were neck and neck with the Yankees at the time, was a vital factor in the Tribe's bid to dethrone the New Yorkers. It should be interesting to note that it was on September 13, in 1946, that the Sox clinched their pennant with a win over the Indians, one of those little quirks of fate. Outfielder Faye Throneberry turned out to be a fair major leaguer, whose brother Marv was one of the early New York Mets. First baseman Dick Gernert socked 19 homers during two-thirds of the season once he had reported to Fenway Park. So impressive was Gernert in only three minor league seasons, the Sox felt safe in trading their regular sacker Walt Dropo to Detroit. Pitcher Ike Delock, whom a Red Sox scout spotted while Ike was pitching for a Marine Corps team, had been 20-4 with a fine 1.92 ERA at Scranton in 1951, and became a fixture for years on the Fenway Park mound. Pitchers Ralph Brickner, Dick Brodowski, and Bill Henry had only moderate success. Brodowski had a fine but short minor league record. He was 21-5 at Marion of the Ohio Indian League in 28 games, and in early '52 was 7-1 in 10 games in Louisville. Catcher Sammy White, who in 1949 as a Sox farmhand hit a home run at Seattle in his first time at bat as a professional, was an outstanding major league catcher for 11 years. Remembering those Red Sox pitchers reminds us of a great relief pitcher for them some years later, who was making his debut for the Washington Senators in '52, Mike Fornieles.

The other Sox team out in Chicago had a couple of players who were in their first season and also would play future roles with their brothers in Boston. Catcher Darrell Johnson, who would later manage the Red Sox, had started the season with the St. Louis Browns before being sent to Chicago, and pitcher Hector "Skinny" Brown later hurled in Boston. The Chisox also had two rookie Wilsons—catcher Red and outfielded Ted.

Chicago's National League entry turned over their catching job to Toby Atwell, after six fine minor league seasons, and he proceeded to make the National League all-star squad. Pitcher Steve Ridzik was the talk of Philadelphia. The Phillies right-hander hurled a spring training no-hitter on the way north against the St. Louis Cardinals and had allowed only two runs in 25 innings, including a string of 17 scoreless. Tobacco chewing Johnny Temple, a second baseman, led a trio of Cincinnati Reds' rookies. Temple didn't hit the long ball, but proved to be a good bunter and a speedy base runner. Few big leaguers have had the sensational start that Jim Greengrass had for the Reds. Purchased from the Yankee farm club at Beaumont late in the season, Jim reported in time to play in 18 games, during which he drove in 24 runs and hit five home runs, one a grand slam against John Rutherford of Brooklyn at Ebbets Field. An excellent curve-ball hitter, he also demonstrated good running speed. The third member of the Reds' trio was a pitcher who made an appearance in 1944. Eight years had elapsed since that appearance, and in the meantime, Joe Nuxhall had been learning his trade in such places as Birmingham, Syracuse, Lima, Muncie, Tulsa, Columbia, and Charleston. Forever the answer to trivia questions, Nuxhall was a 15-year-old kid when he made that first appearance. He retired two of the first three batters to face him in that 1944 game, but was unable to complete the inning. A good pitcher, Nuxhall played fifteen seasons. Temple lasted 15 years and Greengrass, who had the best start of the three, only five years.

The Brooklyn Dodgers had a number of newcomers, mostly pitchers, and one of these, Joe Black, was everyone's choice for the National League rookie of the year for 1952. Black arrived in Brooklyn with a so-so 11-12 record in two minor league seasons. Black earned his laurels because of the tremendous lift he gave the champion Dodgers as their most reliable relief hurler. Posting a fine 15-4 record, Joe also saved some 15 ball games and struck out 85 batters while walking only 41. Other Dodger mound hopefuls were Ron Negray, Jim Hughes, John Rutherford, Ben Wade, Ray Moore, Billy Loes, Ken Lehman, and Joe Landrum. Except for Billy Loes, who lasted for eleven years with a 80-63 lifetime record, none enjoyed much of a major league career. The St. Louis Cardinals finally saw the arrival of pitcher Harvey Haddix, who went to work without the benefit of spring training due to his late release from the service. Known as "The Kitten," he gained a place on manager Eddie Stanky's mound staff alongside veteran Harry "The Cat" Brecheen, which explains that unusual nickname. Haddix had a brilliant minor league career, posting a 19-5 record at Winston-Salem in 1947 and an 18-6 mark for the Columbus Red Birds in 1950. His 1952 mark of 2-2 was no indication of the 134 additional wins he would gain before retiring in 1965, after fourteen years on major league mounds. Joining Haddix was Stu Miller, a fine right-hander who after 16 years around the majors left with a 105-103 won-lost slate. They were joined by Willard Schmidt, who lasted seven years, and Eddie Yuhas. Strangely, it was Yuhas who had the best record of the rookies, 12-2, but he lasted only one more season, never winning or losing another major league game. After losing his first game, Yuhas relieved in 51 contests without losing and posted the League's longest winning streak at 10 straight.

At New York's Polo Grounds, James "Dusty" Rhodes was joining the Giants. He would become their pinch-hitting hero of the 1954 World Series. Dusty had a decent start, but gave no indication of future heroics, such as three successive home runs in 1953, and a 1954 twin bill in which he had two doubles, two triples, and two home runs. Joining Rhodes in the outfield was George "Teddy" Wilson, who had had a trial with the Red Sox and White Sox, the latter having traded him to New York. Interestingly, he got his nickname when the Red Sox returned him to the minors in 1951 and he, in all confidence, announced he would return and "hit better than Ted Williams." Infielder Daryl Spencer, who Leo Durocher said reminded him of Pee Wee Reese, also made his appearance for the Giants. Never matching Reese, he did, however, last for ten seasons. Catcher Ray Katt, with a reputation as a hitter, joined the Giants and left the majors seven years later with several records for passed balls and a .232 batting average. The Giants also had pitcher Jack Harshman, a converted first baseman who was 0-2 with a 14.21 ERA. After that poor start, Harshman recovered to post a 69-65 record during his stay in the big leagues. The Pittsburgh Pirates had a group of rookies up for a look-see. Third baseman Emanuel Senerchia, second baseman Clem Koshorek, pitchers Cal Hogue, Woody Main, and Jim Waugh, all never made much of a major league mark. Neither did Ron Necciai, who was 1-6, but what a minor league hero he was! With a poor record in two previous minor league seasons, Necciai started the 1952 season with Bristol of the Appalachian League, was promoted to Burlington of the Carolina League, and then to Pittsburgh. In his first 31 innings at Bristol, he fanned 77 batters, walked only 12, and allowed only two scratch hits. In his second game he struck out 19. In this third appearance, he came in in relief with the bases filled and none out in the seventh inning. He struck out three batters in a row, then eight more in succession, striking out 11 of the 12 batters he faced. In another game later, he struck out 11 consecutive batters, thus twice breaking the minor league record for consecutive strikeouts of 10 set by one Harry Ables of San Antonio of the Texas League in 1910. On May 13, 1952, Necciai known as "Rocket Ron," hurled a no-hit, no-run game against Welch, fanning 27 batters, only four runners reaching first base. Of the four, one was hit by a pitch, one walked, one reached when a strikeout pitch got by the catcher, and the fourth reached on an error by the shortstop. Quite a minor league campaign. Poor Ron lasted only that one partial season of 1952 with the Bucs. There they are, the class of 1952. In most cases, they showed little that season, and those that did didn't last long. But over the long run, there will be few years that produce as many future stars as 1952.

1953 found, for the second time in a decade, many GIs returning to the baseball wars, swapping khakis for baseball flannels. This time it was from the Korean conflict. It also found the New York Yankees of Casey Stengel winning an unbelievable fifth straight world championship, a feat never before accomplished, when they beat their old rivals, the Brooklyn Dodgers, four games to two in the fall classic. The series marked the 50th anniversary of the first World Series played in 1903 between Pittsburgh and Boston. For those of you who don't remember the hero of that 1953 series he is still around the big league scene. It was Billy Martin, who hit two homers, two triples, a double, wacked out seven singles, and drove in eight runs, including the game-winner in the final contest. The United States Supreme Court got around to ruling that baseball was a sport and not a business by a seven-to-two vote. Big news, but the story of the year had to be the shift of the St. Louis Browns to Baltimore for the 1954 season, and the Boston Braves' shift to Milwaukee for 1953. The Braves retained their name, but the Browns would become the Orioles, a name long associated with Baltimore baseball teams. The club transfers shattered a fifty-year precedent, as the last shift had occurred in 1903 when the New York Highlanders replaced Baltimore in the American League. The National League had not changed membership since 1900, when they reduced their clubs from twelve to eight. Strangely, it had been Milwaukee that bowed out of the American League in 1902, so that St. Louis could enter. In another move, the St. Louis Cardinals were sold to the Anheuser-Busch brewery. The players' and club owners' differences over the pension plan proposals led to the players' hiring of J. Norman Lewis as their attorney. Despite bonus rulings, large amounts were still being spent on untried young talent. The minor leagues continued to decline as thirty-eight were in operation, a reduction of five from 1952. The scene is now set; so let's look at the 1953 rookie crop.

Perhaps if you had teamed Detroit Tiger shortstop Harvey Kuenn and Brooklyn Dodger second baseman Junior Gilliam together, you might have the major league's most sparkling double play combination of 1953. The two infielders were hailed as the top rookies of the year. The Tiger shortstop led the majors in hits with 209 and was almost the first unanimous choice for the American League top rookie, with only Tom Umphlett of the Boston Red Sox receiving a vote for rookie honors preventing it. There was never any question about Kuenn's hitting ability, as he hit .308 in 1953. A brief 19 game, 80 at-bat trial in 1952 saw Harvey hit at a .325 clip. He tied the major league record by making 200 or more hits in his first full major league season, and broke a record set by Johnny Tobin of the St. Louis Browns in 1921 for the most times at bat in a season, when he went to the plate 679 times. Kuenn's hitting ability earned him a $55,000 bonus when he was signed off the University of Wisconsin campus. The 23-year-old Tiger, who had less than two years in organized ball, went the entire season without experiencing a real slump. When he first came up, Detroit officials were concerned about his fielding ability, but on that team was an old pro at picking up a ground ball or two named John Pesky. Pesky took the youngster in hand and taught him how to move in on slow rollers, how to cover the hole at deep short, and the fundamentals of a good double play. By the season's end, his range had improved and his moves were good. His strong accurate arm made him a sound shortstop. Harvey played 15 years in the big time with a fine .303 lifetime average.

The young Dodger keystoner worked his way to a record 100 walks. Gilliam was a switch hitter and an excellent leadoff man, with speed enough to steal 21 bases while batting .278. He also became one of the most popular Dodgers in the history of that club. In 1953 he was a big gamble, as manager Charlie Dressen benched his regular third baseman, Billy Cox, and moved his second baseman, Jackie Robinson, to third to make way for his 25-year-old rookie. Some of the Dodger players did not take kindly to the move, but Junior soon silenced them with his abilities as a leadoff man. Early on he went into a slump and on July 6 was benched. A week or so later, he was back in the lineup and proceeded to hit at a .320 pace for the remainder of the season, lifting his average from .236 to .278. In addition to his rookie record for walks, he also led his league in triples (17). Gilliam was in some pretty good company when he tied a World Series record for the most long hits (five) in a six-game series (three doubles and two home runs). The others who had done it were Babe Ruth ('23 Yankees), Chick Hafey ('30 Cardinals), and Billy Martin who also did it in the 1953 series. Gilliam played his entire career with the Dodgers, 14 years worth, appearing in seven World Series for them.

Scarcely noticed in the 30 games he appeared was another rookie on the Detroit Tiger squad. This youngster batted .250 and managed to play 20 times in the Detroit outfield. Quiet and reserved this 18-year-old showed definite signs that he had come to play. Remarkably, he had never played a game of minor league ball. As a youngster, he had suffered a bone-crippling bout with osteomyelitis, which left him with a couple of badly twisted toes on one foot. He never complained about them and never had to use them as an excuse. For 22 seasons, he pulled on a Detroit uniform, suffered a string of injuries, and never uttered a word in complaint. He gave the Tigers 2,834 games, 3,007 base hits, 399 home runs, appeared at bat over 10,000 times, and was one of the great outfielders of all time, a true champion, one of those guys who was always there making the needed catch and driving home the needed run. Not possessing the strength of the great sluggers, he did have what is described as a classic swing and excellent coordination. In 1980, the skinny kid off the sandlots of Baltimore entered baseball's Hall of Fame. Al Kaline was rewarded for all those years he was a fixture in right field for the Tigers. Yet in 1953 he was hardly noticed.

The St. Louis Browns marked their final year in the Mound City with a pitcher who stunned the baseball world. Alva "Bobo" Holloman pitched the majors' only no-hitter, when he set down the Philadelphia Athletics, 6 to 0, on May 6 in his first major league start. The 27-year-old chose a night game at Busch Stadium to turn in his gem. He fanned three and walked five, three of them in the ninth inning. A slim crowd, held down by a damp chilly evening, got another surprise when in the fifth inning, the St. Louis ownership announced it would honor rain checks at any future game. His no-hitter was the first in modern major league history by a rookie in his first start, and only the third ever, as two previous efforts had been turned in during the 1890s. Earlier in the season, Holloman had made four relief appearances. On July 23, Bobo was sold to Toronto of the International League, when his record dropped to 3-7. He never again appeared in the major leagues.

Giving Gilliam a run for his money as rookie of the year were two excellent St. Louis Cardinals, center fielder Rip Repulski and third baseman Ray Jablonski. Repulski had had several spring trials in past seasons, but always appeared to need more work. Up from Rochester, he had a tendency to strike out a bit too often, but possessed a good arm and had some power at the plate. After nine seasons, he closed out his career with the Boston Red Sox. The Cardinals had had their headaches at third base ever since Whitey Kurowski had retired, but it appeared Jablonski, a strong right-handed hitter, would end their search and his hitting ability would balance the middle of Manager Stanky's batting order. He lasted only two years in St. Louis, but eight overall.

The Boston Braves, now in their new home in Milwaukee, gave their new fans Bill Bruton, who covered the outfield like a tent, and a skillful bunter with tremendous speed, making an ideal leadoff man. In his first three seasons, he led the National League in stolen bases. Not a power hitter, he did spray the ball to all fields for the Braves for eight seasons and for the Detroit Tigers for four. The Braves also had high hopes for a little (no pun intended) left-hander named Don Liddle, one of their brightest prospects. He led the American Association hurlers in 1952 in strikeouts with 159 and a fine 17-4 record with a 2.70 ERA. Milwaukee was a Braves' farm club in 1952, so Liddle was no stranger to Brewer-Braves fans. He could only fashion a 7-6 record in '53.

Back in Boston, the city the Braves had deserted, the Red Sox were moving up from sixth to fourth place, mainly with the help of three rookies. Milt

Bolling had replaced Johnny Lipon at shortstop, center fielder Tom Umphlett had caught Manager Boudreau's eye with his fielding, solid line drives, and great throwing arm, and long, lean 20-year-old Gene Stephens was a serious contender for another outfield post. These three were the reason for the surprising Red Sox splurge. Umphlett, with Boudreau's help, replaced the long-time Boston favorite Dom DiMaggio in center field, while critics were saying Stephen's wrist action swing and long ball power reminded them of Ted Williams. None became great major leaguers, but Stephens lasted twelve years, Bolling seven, and Umphlett three, all with a variety of teams.

Shortstop Billy Hunter cost St. Louis Brown owner Bill Veeck $90,000, but he proved to be worth it. The New York Giants had a good pitcher in Ruben Gomez, who picked up the slack when his fellow pitchers faltered and became the mainstay of their staff.

The Cleveland Indians were glad to welcome back Jim Lemon from the service. He had hit 39 homers as a minor leaguer in 1950. The Tribe was also counting on ex-outfielder Dave Hoskins to bolster their already strong pitching staff. Hoskins, who had won 22 games for Dallas, responded with a 9-3 record, the only nine victories he posted in two seasons on the shores of Lake Erie. Another farmhand the Indians were looking to was Jose Santiago, a pitcher who didn't make it in 1953, was heard from in 1954, but never made it big.

There was another pitcher breaking in with the St. Louis Browns who one day would become a household word across this land. He had a rather undistinguished record in the minors, except for one season at Aberdeen of the Northern League where he was 17-11 in 1948. Arriving with little advanced notice, he compiled a 7-12 record for the 1953 Brownies. He gained more fame as a batter in that initial campaign, as he established a major league record for pitchers by getting seven consecutive hits over a three-game span. He went on to 14 major league seasons and appeared in five World Series. It was in the fifth game of the 1956 World Series, on October 8 at New York's Yankee Stadium, where he gained his everlasting place in baseball history. It was on that date that Don Larsen pitched a perfect game and the first World Series no-hitter. Winning by the score of 2 to 0 over the Brooklyn Dodgers, he retired 27 consecutive Dodger batters. It was the major league's first perfect game since April 30, 1922, when another rookie, Charlie Robertson of the Chicago White Sox, pitched his masterpiece against the Detroit Tigers, winning by the same 2 to 0 score. It was also the first no-hitter in 307 World Series games since the start of the classic in 1903.

Joining Gilliam and the other Dodger rookies previously mentioned were a number of young players who didn't make it in 1953, but would very soon appear for long major league stays. If they had been with an organization that did not have the talent the Dodgers possessed, they might easily have appeared in the 1953 big league box scores. Don Hoak, a sharp fielder who scored 109 runs for Montreal, was there. So was relief pitcher Ronnie Lee, a returning serviceman who was 14 and 4, with 2.20 ERA in 54 appearances for the 1950 Montreal Royals. Then there was a game shortstop up from Mobile, the Southern Association MVP, who was the Dodger choice as successor to Pee Wee Reese, named Don Zimmer, who most recently has been the Boston Red Sox manager. There was also a left-handed pitcher, who had been 5-5 at Montreal and who later would lead the Dodgers to a 1955 World Series victory over the arch-rival Yankees, named Johnny Podres. Podres stuck in '53 and was nine and four with the Bums. The 20-year-old Podres had been the sensation of the 1952 Vero Beach training camp a year earlier. He developed a friendship with Zimmer over the years and joined him in Boston as his pitching coach. In the New York Yankee camp at St. Petersburg, pitcher Whitey Ford (returning from service), outfielder Bill Skowron, first baseman Don Bollweg, and pitching Al Cicotte were giving it a go. Ford, of course, had had a partial season with the Yanks and of the rest only Bollweg stuck. He had previously had two tries with the Cardinals and had been the International League's MVP in 1952.

Others of note in the spring of 1953 were: Bob Marquis, a fine defensive outfielder with Cincinnati; Bill Taylor, a returning serviceman who had been an outfield sensation at Denver in 1950, now vying for Don Mueller's job in the Giants outfield; and Rance Pless, a slow third baseman but a natural hitter who looked like he might give the Giants some much needed right-handed-hitting strength. The Red Sox were still trying to find a spot for infielder Allen Richter and the Cubs for slugger Leon Brinkhopt, who they hoped to move from third base to the outfield. The Senators had in tow a shortstop with the colorful name of Pompeyo "Yo Yo" Davillio, who was supposed to play any infield spot and hit well, and Bucky Harris, Washington's manager, had his eyes on second baseman Leroy Dietzel. The "Yo Yo" saw action in nineteen games and Leroy had to wait for 1954 to appear in nine games. The Pirates had a young twirler who had pitched three no-hitters in the Appalachian League, named Bill Bell and nicknamed "Ding Dong," but he rung no chimes in '53. He appeared in a total of five big league games eventually (1952 and 1955) with an 0-1 record.

Mentioning the name of Boston Red Sox rookie, Al Richter, brings to mind an incident that happened to the author indirectly concerning Richter.

During the early Fifties, I was about the age of these up-and-coming rookies and traveled around to the ball parks of the East Coast watching the various ball teams, usually attending these games with my pals of the time. Being athletic ourselves, we were often mistaken for players by the hordes of young autograph seekers who hung around the ball parks. We had had incidents in Philadelphia and New York, but nothing like the one that happened to us late one season in Boston. Taking our time leaving Fenway Park one afternoon, and with no special place to go, we wandered from the ball park down to nearby Kenmore Square. Having decided to spend the weekend taking in the upcoming ball games at Fenway Park, we were looking for lodgings for the night, but in no special hurry to make these connections. Close by Kenmore Square was the old Kenmore Hotel, and passing by it we noticed a crowd outside the hotel. We decided to join them and wandered inside to check the room situation. You see, this was also the hotel where the ball clubs held up while in Boston. It was also the temporary home of the Red Sox rookies, who had been recalled from the Louisville farm club for the few remaining home games. After looking over the crowd of pushing, shoving humanity in the lobby, we decided to leave in quest of other quarters. Leaving the hotel required a walk from the main entrance down a short walk to the sidewalk, which ran in front of the Kenmore. This walk was lined with youngsters seeking those prized autographs, and we were immediately besieged by them. Their theory, I guess, was what would two young guys be doing coming out of the Kenmore if they weren't ballplayers. We seemed to fit the bill to a tee. The more we told them we were not ballplayers for the Red Sox, the more they disbelieved us. By now we had reached the sidewalk and began our retreat from the area. Well, the further we went, the larger the crowd of pleading youngsters grew, following us, pulling at us and begging. We spotted one of Boston's finest and asked what we should do to prevent being tugged apart and separated from out clothes. He sympathized with us and said our best plan would be to sign for these kids, and they would soon go away. Having earlier in the season had a similar group climb all over our car in Philadelphia, we decided we didn't want to go through that again, so it might be best to sign our autographs. We started signing our own names, which not being recognized by the group of youngsters only made them more antagonistic. At this point the officer, seeing our predicament, said to me, "Sign Allen Richter, he is new here, and they won't know him." At the same time, he came up with the name of some other now long-forgotten rookie for my friend to sign. His strategy worked, and we were soon on our way. Al Richter, wherever you are, I am sorry, but thankful. Surely your name is remembered by a group of youngsters who didn't mind chasing me for several blocks, and by me for getting me out of a jam. Some time ago you had a friend in the Boston Police Department.

Our rookie who didn't give up after being farmed out was George Wilson, who the New York Giants sent to their Minneapolis farm club. On June 28, he performed the rare feat of hitting home runs in three successive innings against Kansas City at Nicollet Park. And talk about turnarounds, consider pitcher Howie Judson, who was 0-1 with Cincinnati when they optioned him to Indianapolis where he was 1-4 when they sent him to Tulsa. Judson then turned in an 11-0 mark for Tulsa to equal a Texas League record. Then there was a Phoenix, Arizona, native George Aitken, a rookie pitcher hurling for Tucson, who tossed a no-hitter in his professional debut, beating Bisbee-Douglas 13 to 2. He walked nine and struck out ten, a start he will never forget. Speaking of Arizona, outfielder and rookie Bob Brown of Phoenix matched Wilson's rare three homers in three innings on June 4 against Mexicali. Topping those performances was outfielder Ted Beard of Hollywood, who in April had four consecutive home runs, and later in the month he had 12 consecutive hits.

In 1954 the New York Yankee string of American League championships came to an end at five, as the Cleveland Indians captured the crown. Cleveland had also been the last city to win it all in the American League, back in 1948. To find a winner other than New York or Cleveland, one had to journey back to 1946 when the Boston Red Sox were the champions. New York, however, was not without a World Series in 1954, as the Giants were the National League standard bearers. For the sixth year in a row, Gotham hosted half the games, and it was the sixth year in the last eight that a New York National League club was represented. The National League broke the string of seven straight series losses, as the Giants crushed the favored Indians in four straight games. Making it an unbelievable win was the fact that Cleveland had not only put down the mighty Yankees, but had set a league record with their 111 wins.

The great successes at the box office by the transplanted teams in Milwaukee and Baltimore spurred approval in November 1954 of the Philadelphia Athletics transfer to Kansas City for the 1955 season, thus ending the dynasty of the House of Mack. There was also talk of expanding the traditional eight-club major leagues to ten-club loops and toward the formation of a third major league, something the major leagues had not wanted since the demise of the ill-fated Federal League in the pre-World War I era.

It is interesting to note that the 1954 change of name and city worked the same wonder at the turnstiles for the Browns, now the Orioles, as it had a year earlier for the Braves. The Browns-Orioles went over the million mark for the first time. In 1953 at St. Louis, they could draw only some 297,000. The Braves had topped the million mark three years running in Boston, 1947–49. Then it was downhill until they arrived in Milwaukee when they packed County Stadium with 1,800,000 in 1953. 1954 saw them top the two million mark for the first time. Was it novelty that caused the rise in attendance? That certainly had to be a factor, but as we shall see, the quality of the product was on the upswing also. The Braves improved steadily for a period of time, only to move backward. But the Orioles made steady strides forward until the 70s when they were always in contention. Long forgotten by most fans today is the fact that the Baltimore Orioles were once the St. Louis Browns, a symbol of mediocrity.

In 1954, the plight of the minor leagues continued, as they now had a new adversary to contend with besides TV and radio expansion. Attendance continued to decline, and the National Association opened the season with 36 circuits, three of these failed to complete the year. 1954 became the first season since the wartime year of 1942 that more than one minor league failed during the season. There was, however, an outstanding accomplishment in the minors. The minors are traditionally the stronghold of the young rookie, but it was a 32-year-old minor league veteran who drew the attention of the baseball world in '54. First baseman Joe Bauman, playing with Roswell of the class C Longhorn League, established an all-time organized baseball record when he hit 72 home runs. Playing in each of his club's 138 games, the veteran batted an even .400 to lead the circuit, and set league records by scoring 188 runs, knocking in 224 runs, and amassing 456 total bases. Bauman's home run record still stands today as tops in baseball. His 72 topped the previous high of 69 set by Joe Hauser of Minneapolis of the American Association in 1933 and tied by Bob Crues of Amarillo of the West Texas-New Mexico League in 1948. His RBI record of 224 stands second all-time to Crues's 254 in 1948. His 188 runs scored stands as the fifth-highest minor league total of all time, tops being Tony Lazzeri's 202 while with Salt Lake City of the Pacific Coast League in 1925.

Manager Al Lopez of Cleveland had assembled a great ball club in 1954 with some fine hitters in Larry Doby, Vic Wertz, Al Rosen, Al Smith, and the American League batting champion, little Bobby Avila. He also had one of the all-time great pitching staffs featuring Bob Lemon, a converted out-fielder, and Early Wynn, each of whom won 23 games, and Mike Garcia (19 wins), Art Houtteman (15 wins), and the veteran fireballer Bob Feller. The relief specialists (that's right they had two) were rookies Don Mossi and Ray Narleski. Mossi was the left-hander and Narleski the righty. While their won-lost records weren't that great, it was the duo that seemed to slam the door in the face of the opposition time and time again. Mossi was 6-1 with seven saves and a fine 1.94 ERA in 93 innings. Mossi had been 12-12 in 201 innings for Tulsa the previous season. Narleski was 3-3 with 13 saves, third in the league behind the Yankees' John Sain (22) and the Red Sox' Ellis Kinder (15), appearing in 42 games, twirling 89 innings with a neat 2.22 earned run average. Narleski was a product of the Indianapolis farm club where he was 6-8 in 1953. Each wound up their big league stays with lifetime winning records. Don Mossi remained twice as long as Ray Narleski, putting in 12 seasons and winning 101 games while losing 80, not a poor record at all. In 1959, while pitching for Detroit, he had a 17-9 season and in 1961 showed a 15-7 slate for the same Tigers. Narleski had a 43-33 record to show for six years. In a rather strange deal, the duo were paired together with an infielder named Ozzie Alvarez and traded to the Detroit Tigers in November of 1958 for a couple of guys we have already met, pitcher Al Cicotte and second baseman Billy Martin. Mossi responded with 17 wins, as mentioned earlier, but Narleski fell to 4-12 and out of the league. Over one seven-game stretch in 1954, Don "Ears" Mossi retired 27 consecutive batters, the equivalent of a perfect game. The Indians also had a part-time rookie third baseman with the romantic name of Rudy Regalado, who played in 65 games of his three-year major league total of 91. The Indians, loaded as they were with pitching, were touting three more prospects down on the Indianapolis farm club. I wonder if anyone has ever considered how appropriate it was that the Indians had "Indian-apolis" as a farm team? One prospect was Herb Score, a 19-year-old bonus lefty who had won only two and lost five because of wildness in his debut at Indianapolis in 1952, but had been 7-2 at Reading in 1953. And there were a pair of 22-year-old right-handers—Howie Rodemeyer, 15-8 at Reading a year earlier, and Marion Murszewski, who was 16-9 at Spartanberg with a Tri-State League record 239 strikeouts. The former we will hear about again, the latter two did little except give the typesetter fits when he went to set the box score.

The world champion Giants saw rookie catcher Ray Katt finally assume their second-string catcher's job. Katt, up from Minneapolis, had blasted 28 homers, driven in 98 runs, and batted .326 for the Millers. They were also hoping for big things from Pete Modica, who had come up with a fine screwball at Nashville, and from utility infielder Billy "Shotgun" Gardner, who hit .308 at Nashville and was the Southern Association's All-Star shortstop.

At the Chicago Cub training camp in Mesa, Arizona, a number of rookies were trying to nail down jobs. There was one who had joined the Cubs in

1953 and appeared in ten games at shortstop after coming over from the Kansas City Monarchs of the old Negro League. Ernie Banks, the premier power hitter among shortstops, made the club and stayed for 19 seasons, switching to first base about halfway through his career. He was perhaps the most popular player in Cub history. He banged out 512 lifetime home runs and had well over 9000 at bats with 2583 hits. He won the National League's MVP Award twice—1958 and 1959. Playing alongside Banks at second base was another good black player up from the Los Angeles farm club, Gene Baker. He played seven games for the '53 Cubs, but stuck around for eight campaigns starting in 1954, although he called Chicago home for only three full seasons. The Banks-Baker duo replaced Roy Smalley and the one-time brilliant Dodger prospect Eddie Miksis, both of whom failed in the double-play department at Chicago. Among the other Cub rookies looking for jobs were: Outfielder Luis Marquez, a speedster out of the Braves' farm system; outfielder Bob Talbot from L.A.; catchers Hal Meek, Bob Murray and Elven Tappe; and pitchers Bob Zick, a stringy right-hander who had won 11 of his last 15 decisions at Des Moines, Joe Kunci 16-18 at Macon in the Sally League, and Bill Moisan, 10 and 11 at L.A.

The Brooklyn Dodgers entered 1954 hoping a few members of their vast farm system might prove helpful by breaking into their lineup of veterans. Foremost was a 23-year-old right-handed pitcher, Fred Bessent, who was 11 and 10 at St. Paul. He didn't make it in '54, but did return in late 1955 to post an 8-1 record. In Fred's first minor league season, he had tossed a no-hitter in the opening game of the Georgia-Alabama League playoffs against Carroll-ton for his LaGrange club, winning 14 to 0. The surprise for the Brooklyn club was another 23-year-old who was not listed on that '54 spring roster. Southpaw Carl Spooner was called up from Ft. Worth at the close of the Texas League season to make the most sensational debut of the 1954 major league season. He broke in against the champion New York Giants in late September by turning in a three-hit 3-to-0 victory, and established a record along the way by setting down 15 Giants via strikeouts. The strikeouts were a record for a pitcher in his first big league game. Spooner had been 21-9 at Ft. Worth despite losing part of the season to a knee injury. He also boasted 262 strikeouts. Spooner returned to the mound four days later to hurl the final game of the season for the Dodgers, beating Pittsburgh on another shutout 1 to 0, giving up four singles and fanning 12. Two games won, two shutouts, seven hits allowed, all singles, 27 strikeouts, not a bad start at all. At the time, there had been only two other rookie pitchers in National League history who had pitched shutouts in their first two games. Jim Hughes did it in 1898 for Baltimore, then in the National League, and Al Worthington did it for the 1953 New York Giants. The American League had had three rookies pitch successive shutouts in their first two starts: Joe Doyle for the New York Highlanders, now Yankees, in 1906; Johnny Marcum of the 1933 Philadelphia Athletics; and Dave Ferriss of the 1945 Boston Red Sox. Spooner pitched again for the 1955 Dodgers, posting an 8-6 record for his final season in the majors.

The Dodgers were also going to take a long look at Vic Marasco, a 25-year-old outfielder who had batted a .306 for Ft. Worth. Vic didn't make it, but a fairly good outfielder from the farms did. Remember Walt Moryn? Sandy Amoros was also back for a second try in the outfield. This young Cuban would supply some fine support for the Dodgers in the 1955 World Series. There were also a couple of rookies breaking in with the 1954 Dodgers who certainly were paying attention and learning their lessons well. One, an infielder up from St. Paul, had recovered from a serious brain concussion and was very highly rated was Don Zimmer, who later became a major league manager at San Diego, Boston, and Texas. A pitcher getting a look-see was a left-hander from Montreal named Tom LaSorda, who, of course, would become the Dodger manager in the late 70s. Remember Ed Roebuck, Glenn Mickens, Ray Moore, Ron Negray, Ken Lehman, and Bob Milliken? They were there too. Third base fill-in Don Hoak also made the Brooklyn club, and he gave the National League 11 years.

The Milwaukee Braves had the sleeper of all rookies of the National League in 1954, a 20-year-old infielder-outfielder who had batted a sensational .362 for Jacksonville of the Sally League. He was Hank Aaron who, of course, went on to become the home run king with 755 lifetime four baggers. He played for 23 National League seasons, followed the Braves to Atlanta in 1966, and finished his playing days with the Milwaukee Brewers in 1976. When he retired, he led all major leagues not only in home runs, but in games played (3298), at-bats (12,363), and RBIs (2297). He also had 3771 hits and a .305 lifetime batting average—one of baseball's all-time greats. Competing with Hank were the long forgotten Dick Sinovic, who had hit .342 and drove in 126 runs for Atlanta, and Bill Queen, a .281 swatter for Toledo. A pitcher of note up with the Braves for a second try was Gene Conley, the American Association MVP with 23 wins at Toledo. Gene, who also played basketball in the NBA, performed in 11 major league seasons. In '54, he was 14-9, traded to the Phillies, and then wound up his career with the Boston Red Sox. His trade to Boston was billed as one of the biggest trades of all time. You see, he was 6'8" and the guy he was traded for was pitcher Frank Sullivan who stood 6'6-1/2". Sullivan had also had a trial with the Bosox in 1953, but remained on the '54 squad posting a 15-12 record. Conley is better remembered in Boston for leaving a team bus one hot day in New York, along with an infielder named Pumpsie Green, stating they were headed for Israel. They never made it as world travelers. Conley had a hand in the '54 season's only no-hitter, when he suffered a back injury; it gave veteran Jim Wilson a start in his place, and Wilson no-hit the Phillies.

Aaron had 13 home runs in his first season to go along with a .280 batting average, but National League rookie of the year honors were gathered in by the St. Louis Cardinals' Wally Moon. Moon was up from the Rochester Red Wings, batted .304 with 12 home runs and 76 RBIs for his debut season. Moon joined that select group of rookies who had hit a home run in their first major league at bat when he made that debut on April 13. Batting second in the lineup, he tagged Chicago Cub southpaw Paul Minner for a first-inning homer at St. Louis's Busch Stadium. Strangely, Moon ended his season as he began it by clubbing a home run with a mate aboard in the final game of the season to give the Cards an 11-inning 2-to-0 win over the Braves at Milwaukee. It was quite a year for Cardinal rookies, as two other newcomers slugged homers for their initial hits in Red Bird uniforms, although not in their first at-bats. First Baseman Tom Alston, first Negro on the Card roster, went hitless in his first game, hit a homer in his second game, and Joe Cunningham, called up from Rochester in late June to replace Alston, socked a three-run homer in his third plate appearance. Pitcher Bob Greason became the first black pitcher to play for the Cardinals, but pitched in only three games with an 0-1 record. There were a couple of other pitchers the Cards were hoping would help them: Memo Luna, Pacific Coast ERA leader; Royce Lint, 22-10 at Portland; Floyd Woolridge, 15-13 at Houston; and Ellis "Cot" Deal, who had two tries with the Boston Red Sox and one with the 1950 Cards. Alex Grammas, a slick-fielding shortstop, took over that position from Solly Hemus. Grammas had hit .307 at the New York Yankee farm club in Kansas City where he was playing on option from the Cincinnati Reds, who later traded him to the Cardinals.

Rookie Bob Skinner took the Pittsburgh Pirate first base job away from Preston Ward, and Jerry Lynch saw considerable service in the outfield for the rebuilding Bucs. Ed Bailey, a Redleg bonus baby, saw some heavy duty behind the plate in Rheinland. The Phillies were hoping Ben Tomkins could make the jump from Terre Haute in the class B Three I League to second base. The ex-collegian from Texas University found the distance too far.

There were some outstanding performances by minor league rookies also. Consider Joe Blasco, a pitcher with Mt. Vernon, who whiffed 11 of 12 batters he faced in relief one day. Then there was Johnny Scroggs, who pitched a no-hitter in his first professional game for Waycross of the Georgia-Florida League, winning 3 to 0. He also hit a pair of doubles and drove in two runs. Gus Suhr, Jr., son of the former Pittsburgh Pirate first baseman, hit two home runs in the same inning for the Modesto Reds of the California League to tie a record. How about 53-year-old Bud Shaney, the groundskeeper for the Ashville Tourists, who took the mound to receive credit for a shutout win over Knoxville? He pitched only five innings, but got the win. He had retired after the 1942 season, rounding out a 22-year career with Hickory of the North Carolina State League. Twenty-one-year-old York shortstop Dave Mann swiped 88 bases to establish a new Piedmont League record. Speaking of the Piedmont League, Hagerstown of that league opened a game against Lancaster with nine successive hits. Bob Rivich, a catcher for Stockton of the California League, had 11 RBIs in five innings against Bakersfield. He had two homers and a pair of doubles. Suhr wasn't the only son of a former major leaguer to homer in his professional debut in 1954. Hal Trosky, Jr., son of the former Cleveland Indians and Chicago White Sox star, did it also. Just out of high school, young Trosky was playing with the Springs Sky Sox of the Western League. How about this for one of the greatest rookie stories of all time, a dream come true? At Columbus, Georgia, on April 24, 1954, a 21-year-old Joe Carolan purchased a ticket about an hour before game time to get into the Sally League park to see the Columbus Cardinals play Macon. Once inside the park, Joe purchased a scorecard to learn the name of the Cards general manager, with the purpose of asking for a tryout. Jim Grieves, the GM for some unknown reason agreed to give the youngster a trial. The big rookie impressed Manager George Kissell with three long drives over the fence during his tryout. He was signed to a contract one hour before game time and inserted into the starting lineup. As luck would have it, when he came to the plate for his first at-bat, the bases were loaded. You guessed it, he hit one out of the park for a grand-slam home run, giving the Cardinals a 4-to-3 lead. Macon eventually won the game in 13 innings 7 to 5, but how many rookies can claim such an unusual start? Joe's dream certainly came alive. Joe hit three more home runs that season, batted .231 in 33 games with 91 at bats. The author was a close observer of the Sally League that season and can attest that there were some pretty fair players in that league at the time, so it wasn't a case of making a talent-poor league.

The American League clubs seemed to come up with fewer rookies of lasting quality in 1954, but then for the past few years they perhaps had an overabundance of fine youngsters, and these things have a way of cycling out. When the ballots were in, the American League's rookie of the year was a fine right-handed pitcher who had worked his way up through the New York

Yankee farm system named Bob Grim. Signed in 1948, Grim started the 1951 season with Beaumont of the Texas League, but finished with Binghamton of the Eastern League where he was 16 and 5. Then along came Uncle Sam, and Bob spent the '52 and '53 seasons in the service of his country. Upon return from the service in 1954, he reported directly to the Yankees and posted a 20-win, 6-loss record, good enough to enable him to cop the rookie honors. He never again achieved the brilliance of his rookie campaign. He bounced around for seven more years with four different clubs, winning only 41 more games. Other young hurlers for the Yankees that spring were Wally Burnette, Bob Wiesler, Mel Wright, and an amateur named Ralph Terry. We will hear of Terry later. Bill Skowron also arrived to hold down the Yankee first base job for seven years and help them to a few more pennants.

The Philadelphia Athletics' third baseman Jim Finigan came the closest to challenging Grim for rookie honors. He had come to the A's from the Yankee affiliate at Binghampton. Hitting a career high of .302, Jim seemed like a solid fixture for the A's. Five years and three teams later he was a memory. The Athletics were in a state of reorganization, and the stress was on young players, most of whom did little to distinguish themselves. Their left fielder, Vic Power, came to them in a big trade with the Yankees. Actually billed as a first baseman, he had won the American Association batting crown in 1953 at Kansas City with a .349 average. A power hitter and a good versatile fielder, he could play infield also. He lasted for 12 years. Just to mention some of those newcomers who never made it with the A's, there was Forrest Jacobs, drafted from the Dodger chain, Tom Giordano, who hit 24 homers in the Sally League, catchers Al Robertson, Harry Minor, and Neal Watlington, and infielders Lou Limmer and John Littrell. On the mound, the A's were looking for big things from Bob Trice, who had been the International League's only 20-game winner in '53, and who in three games was 2-1 with the '53 A's. He could only produce a 7-8 record in 1954.

The Boston Red Sox had a rookie pitcher named Russ Kemmerer, who got off to an unusual beginning. His first major league start was a 4-to-0 one-hitter against the Baltimore Orioles. The lone hit coming off the bat of a former Red Sox, Sam Mele. The curious part of the affair was that an hour and a half before game time, Russ reported to Manager Boudreau's office expecting to be sent back to the bushes. Instead, he received his first starting assignment after five previous relief roles. The Red Sox also had high hopes for pitchers Tex Clevenger and Tom Herrin, but neither made much of an impression at Fenway Park. However, a Boston area native did arrive to capture the first base job. Harry Agganis, after one season in the minors, had the American League buzzing. Agganis had been a local high school hero and then went on to star in football at Boston University. Needless to say, he was an instant success at Fenway Park and was looked upon as the standard bearer in the Red Sox rebuilding efforts. A good rookie season seemed to point to a long career. During a June 1955 Western swing, the big first baseman took ill and was sent back to Boston. Several weeks later, after a brief return to action, he suddenly passed away, leaving Boston and the nation stunned. His death left a void at first base the Red Sox would spend years trying to fill. Harry's good friend and rival Norm Zauchin replaced him.

The Washington Senators had little in the way of production out of their rookies in 1954. One had the delightful name of Angel Scull, who was up from Charleston with a .286 batting average. Infielder Harmon Killebrew was signed for a $50,000 bonus and reported to the Nats immediately. He appeared in only three games that season, never going to the minors at all to sharpen his skills. He appeared in several games each year until he took over at third base in 1959. When Harmon retired in 1975, he had completed 22 seasons, splitting his time between the outfield and first and third bases. He was one of the premier players in the American League during the '60s and early '70s. A power hitter, he cracked out 573 home runs before ending his career. Yet in 1954, he was heard of only by the loyal Senator fans. It is one of those odd things that happen in baseball, but joining Killebrew was pitcher Camilo Pascual, another in the long line of skillful Cuban pitchers who toiled in shadow of our nation's capital. Like Killebrew, Pascual did little but lose games in his first five seasons (7, 12, 18, 17, 12). Following the pattern set by his teammate, the 1959 season saw him turn his large number of losses into wins (17, 12, 15, 20, 21, 15) for the next six years with not the best of Washington clubs. Pascual lasted 18 major league seasons and concluded with 174 wins against 170 losses.

The champion Indians had little in the way of rookies, and the only one of any note was a most promising pitcher, Dick Tomanek. Nicknamed "Bones," Tomanek put in a little better than three seasons in the Teepee and one and one half years at K.C. His final totals, 10-10.

The Baltimore Orioles had a fresh arrival in the most interesting Ryne Duren, a fireballing relief pitcher. He was promoted from San Antonio of the Texas League where he had won 12 and lost 12, pitched a no-hitter, a couple of one-hitters and led the circuit in strikeouts, with 212. He was robbed of a second no-hitter by a broken-bat bloop single in a game in which he fanned 11 batters. He, of course, was a mainstay in the New York Yankee bullpen for several years. The Orioles were loaded with rookie hopefuls. None made it big in the majors. Do you remember any of them? Pitcher Jim Post, a 10-game winner at Toronto; pitcher Jehosie Heard, up from Portland; second baseman Vincio Garcia, drafted from Shreveport; first baseman Ed Mikelson, a .294 hitter at San Antonio; third baseman Bob Caffrey, also up from the Missions; outfielders Bob Balenco, Jim Fridley, Karol Kwak, Jim Pisoni, and Bob Masser. The Detroit Tigers had a good rookie second baseman, Frank Bolling, to take over for the veteran Johnny Pesky. Frank's brother Milt was in his second full season as the Boston Red Sox shortstop. These then were the rookies of 1954.

As the decade approached the midway point of 1955, the New York clubs continued their dominance of the baseball world. The Brooklyn Dodgers not only reclaimed the National League flag, they finally, after seven appearances, captured a world's championship by besting their long time World Series tormentors, the New York Yankees. Casey Stengel's Bronx Bombers returned to the World Series as the American League's representative after a year's absence. It was Stengel's sixth triumph in seven seasons at the Yankee helm. Paced by Johnny Podres' two victories, the Dodgers won the series four games to three, as the Yanks' Whitey Ford won two games for the American Leaguers.

The Philadelphia Athletics became the Kansas City Athletics, a move which proved to be a gold mine at least for the first season. The Milwaukee Braves were leading the majors in attendance for the third year in a row, quite a switch from their Boston days. A bombshell was dropped in Brooklyn in mid-August when Dodger president Walter O'Malley said his club intended to abandon Ebbets Field as their home after the 1957 season, a move which did reach reality as we shall see later on.

Major league clubs continued their big spending for untried youngsters, a problem which was still causing some great concern. The Baltimore Orioles led the parade, spending $700,000 on raw talent. Five bonus players joined the Birds during the year: infielder Jim Ryburn, pitcher Bruce Swango, infielder Wayne Causey, first baseman-outfielder Bob Nelson, and catcher Tom Gastall. Causey was the only one of the five to nail down a full-time job, as he took over at third base, replacing Vern Stephens who was sent to the Chicago White Sox. Gastall, a highly rated receiver, met a tragic death in an airplane crash in September of 1956. Swango developed a sore arm shortly after signing and was released without making an appearance. The Yankees later signed Swango and assigned him to the minor leagues. Baltimore's youth movement seemed to be in continual trouble with baseball's bonus rules. They were also in trouble for their questionable maneuvers of putting players on disabled lists or in some way misrepresenting the contracts so that the players did not get the money they expected. In addition to the five bonus players already mentioned, Baltimore manager, general-manager Paul

Richards signed seven other rookies to major league contracts. They were pitchers Tom Borland, Vinnie Pignatello, Gordy Sundin, and Roger Marquis, infielder Brooks Robinson and outfielders Bill Lajoie and Angelo Dagres. All but Dagres and Marquis were farmed out after signing. The commissioner's office, after some investigation, made Pignatello and Borland free agents as a result of some Baltimore irregularities concerning those two players. The former later signed with the Yankees, the latter with the Boston Red Sox.

Borland's case was loaded with strange deeds. Signed off the Oklahoma A&M College campus for a substantial bonus, it was never reported to the baseball commissioner's office as required by baseball rules. Then Borland appeared on the mound for the Birds in a June exhibition game at York under a fictitious name (James Moreland), and the next day he appeared in uniform at Yankee Stadium as Tom Borland. When the Baltimore directors asked Richards not to sign Borland, it was arranged to have him sign with Oakland of the Pacific Coast League as a free agent, with the youngster getting the payments due him under the Oriole contract. Of course, if he proved himself in Oakland, the Birds were to have first choice for his contract. All this resulted in Commissioner Ford Frick making him a free agent and Borland signed on with the Red Sox. It is fairly well known that there was a period in baseball when, for one reason or another, young players would appear playing under various names, other than their own, only to pop up later with some big league club. I guess this was the early attempt at hiding players from the competition. There were also the college boys who summered in various minor leagues under assumed names to protect their personal eligibility and that of their schools. The colleges, of course, allowed only amateurs to compete on their squads.

Besides those Baltimore bonus players, there were others camping on the major league rosters in 1955. Some played briefly in '53 and '54, but none with much success. Long forgotten today is the fact that although some well-known players started out with bonus status, others were actually little known even to the fans of the day. A look at some of the names will either bring to your mind a puzzled "Who the heck was he?" or "Oh, yeah, I remember him, was he a bonus player?" Let's take a trip down Bonus Lane and look at some of the people who once lived there. Besides those Orioles already mentioned (surely you recalled Brooks Robinson), the Pittsburgh Pirates had the infield twins Eddie and Johnny O'Brien, pitcher Laurin Pepper (I suppose he was a hot prospect), catcher Nick Koback, and pitchers Paul Martin and Red Swanson. Other newcomers in 1955 were: catcher Jim Pagliaroni at Boston; outfielder Bob Powell in Comiskey Park; infielder

Clete Boyer at K.C.; infielder Ken Kuhn at Cleveland; pitcher Jim Brady and outfielder Jim Small at Detroit; shortstop Tommy Carroll with the Yankees; pitchers Lindy McDaniel at St. Louis; John Edelman at Milwaukee; Don Kaiser with the Cubs; outfielders Jerry Schoonmaker at Washington; Al Silvera at Cincinnati; and catcher Mack Burk with the Phillies. Of course, the pick of the litter (and I am not sure if I say that because most bonus boys turned out to be dogs) had to be the O'Brien twins, Jim Pagliaroni, who played more with Pittsburgh than Boston, Clete Boyer, who played for sixteen years, and Lindy McDaniel who pitched for 21 years, winding up with 141 wins against 119 losses.

Remember our highly touted rookie Richie Ashburn of the Phillies and Al Kaline, the youngster who joined the Detroit Tigers directly from the Baltimore sandlots with little ballyhoo, both of whom we met a few pages back? They were the major league batting champions of 1955.

For the first time in American League history there was no 20-game winner among the pitching staffs. The runaway selection for American League Rookie of the Year was left-handed pitcher Herb Score of the Cleveland Indians who would see that the negative record of '55 would not be repeated in 1956. His 16-and-10 record of 1955 turned to 20 and 9 in 1956. Score was signed to a bonus contract by the Tribe for a reported $60,000 in June of 1952 and was sent to their farm club at Indianapolis where he was 2 and 5. In 1953, he was sent down to the Reading club of the Eastern league where he improved his record to 7 and 3 with 105 strikeouts in 98 innings. The fireballer was back at Indianapolis in 1954, where he was 22 and 5 with an amazing 330 strikeouts in 251 innings, which set an American Association record and earned him the Minor League Player of the Year Award. On May 1, 1955, Herb set 16 Boston Red Sox batters down on strikes, nine of them in the first three innings. When the season ended, his record stood at 16 and 10, and he led the American League pitchers in strikeouts with 245. Truly, he was one of the most spectacular hurlers to come into the majors in many years.

There is a story they tell about Score, who was warming up on the sidelines prior to an exhibition at the Cleveland spring training site at Tucson, Arizona. There was this fan in attendance who kept begging the left-hander for an autograph. Score, busy preparing for the contest, explained he would be happy to sign for him after the game. The fan then began to get on Score's case by keeping up a line of chatter, primarily questioning the size of Score's head. Score tried to ignore the pest. Finally, his warm-ups completed, Score walked over to the stands, called over the loud-mouthed fan, and gave him the autograph. As he signed his name he said to the fan, "I'll say one thing, my head isn't nearly as big as your mouth." The story ends there, as I am sure that fan's taunts did.

The tall left-hander was to become the kingpin of the already fine Cleveland mound corps. Score possessed that blinding speed and wicked curve which made him an instant success. Then came a fateful game in his third season. On May 7, 1957, during the first inning of a game against New York, the 23-year-old pitcher was struck in the eye by a line drive off the bat of Yankee infielder Gil McDougald. Score was finished for the season. He returned the next year, but something was missing, and while Score pitched two more seasons for Cleveland and three more for the Chicago White Sox, he never regained the greatness he once showed. The man who Tom Yawkey, Boston Red Sox owner, once offered to buy for one million dollars, passed from the major league scene with a very brief career. For anyone who saw Herb pitch, you can't help but wonder what might have been for this likeable guy. He was by far the fastest pitcher I ever saw. Etched in my mind is his fluid motion, followed by that white blur headed toward home plate. Herb Score now does some radio work for the Cleveland Indians, one of the nicest people you could ever want to meet. Before we leave the Cleveland pitching staff, there was one other rookie in 1955 who started his career there, but it really didn't bloom until several years later when he was with Detroit. It was the first season for Hank Aguirre. Perhaps all those great Cleveland chuckers were wearing out their catchers, as the Tribe was giving a second look at catcher Hank Foiles, who had hit .332 at Indianapolis. A highly regarded 21-year-old got his first taste of the majors in the 1955 Indian outfield; his name was Rocco "Rocky" Colavito. Making the jump from A ball at Reading to triple A Indianapolis, this power hitter with a strong arm also hit for average. Spending 14 seasons in the majors, Rocky had 374 lifetime home runs and in three seasons hit better than 40 round trippers.

Up from Toronto to the New York Yankees was the first black to join that club, catcher Elston Howard. Howard had divided his time between the outfield and catching duties, was rated a good hitter with a strong arm, but a little slow in getting the ball away. The versatile, likeable Howard played first base and the outfield for the Yanks for 13 seasons, but was primarily their catcher during that period. He appeared in nine World Series for New York and one for the Boston Red Sox. His sale to Boston in early 1967 was the deciding factor in that youthful Bosox club's climb to the pennant. There was one bit of irony in the move. Earlier in the season, a young Boston pitcher named Billy Rohr was on his way to hurling a no-hit game against the Yankees in their Bronx ball yard, when Elston Howard's ninth-inning hit broke the back of the no-hitter. The Yankee hero of April became the Red Sox hero of October. After one final fling in 1968, Howard retired from the active ranks and returned to the base lines as a New York coach. A sad note is that Elston Howard died of cardiac arrest on December 14, 1980. He was always a class individual in every way. A veteran Yankee club had few rookies in 1955.

The Boston Red Sox were introducing an excellent third baseman in the tradition of Jimmy Collins and Larry Gardner when Frank Malzone made his debut. What a debut it was too! You could say he was off to a smashing start. It was September 20, with Baltimore at Fenway Park for a twin bill. In his first at-bat, he grounded out, but then reeled off four straight hits. He got hits in his first two trips to the plate in the second game, making it six straight hits. Six hits in ten tries, not bad! Malzone, and his ever-present cigar, is now one of the most respected scouts and troubleshooters in baseball. A super player, he was on the big league scene as an active player for 12 years. Joining Malzone in the continuing Red Sox youth movement were: catcher Haywood Sullivan, now one of the Red Sox owners; first baseman Norm Zauchin, who hit three home runs, including a grand slam and a double to drive in 10 runs in a 16-to-0 victory over Washington in May of his first season; three rookie catchers named Pete Daley, Guy Morton, and Eddie Buck; and pitcher George Susce. Susce and Morton were sons of former major leaguers. The Red Sox were the surprise of the league in '55 with their youngsters. Hero of many a game was their shortstop Billy Klaus, who had a brief trial with the Boston-Milwaukee Braves. Zauchin and Klaus were in the running for the rookie award with Score. Klaus was the runner-up in the voting with Zauchin right behind.

The American League also introduced a couple of other fairly decent catchers besides Howard. Hank Foiles was being given a second try with the Cleveland Indians. He stuck, and was much-traveled before leaving the majors 10 years later. The Chicago White Sox had Earl Battey, his .292 average and his 11 home runs up from Waterloo. After subbing for Chicago for five seasons, Earl moved on to Washington in 1960, moved with the franchise to Minnesota in 1961, and held down the first string receiving duties for seven seasons. Baltimore had catcher Hal Smith who lasted with a variety of teams for 10 years. He had been with Columbus, on option from the Yankees, who traded him to the Orioles in a blockbuster trade with pitchers Harry Byrd, Jim McDonald, and Bill Miller, catcher Gus Triandos, infielders Don Leppert, Kal Segrist, Willie Miranda, and outfielder Gene

Woodling for pitchers Mike Blyzka, Don Larsen, Bob Turley, catcher Darrell Johnson, infielders Dick Kryhoski, Billy Hunter, and outfielders Ted de Guercio and Jim Fridley. Seldom has such a large trade been made.

The Detroit Tigers found a young hurler at Buffalo, the right-handed Jim Bunning. Only 3 and 4 with the Bengals in 1955, he continued for 16 more seasons, winning 223 and losing 184, but along the way did some amazing things. Jim had only one 20-victory season in the major leagues, but consider that he had four 19-wins seasons, three of them in a row, 1964–66. After nine seasons with Detroit, he was suddenly traded to the Philadelphia Phillies. He owns a number of distinctions accumulated during his career, the most memorable of which was that he pitched a no-hitter in both major leagues. In July of 1958, he no-hit the Boston Red Sox 3 to 0, and in June 1964 he not only no-hit the New York Mets, but tossed a perfect game against them, winning 6 to 0. Add to these two gems the fact that he once struck out three batters on nine pitched balls, and you would think he had pretty good control of his pitches. Yet twice he allowed more homers than any other American League pitcher, and four times he led (tied once) the National League in hit batsmen. This makes you wonder if he was keeping those batters honest or not. In 1967, the Phillies had a hard time getting Jim any runs. He had a 17-15 record, but five of his losses were by 1-to-0 scores, which tied a major league record. He also led the National League in shutouts with six. To be involved in 11 shutouts in one season tells you something about the type of game you could expect when Bunning took the mound. Frank Lary also made the Tigers after a 15-11 season at Buffalo and went on to earn his nickname "The Yankee Killer" with his ability to defeat the New Yorkers. He would win 21 games in '56 and 23 in '61. Of all the American League rookies in 1955, the best over the long haul was a young third baseman named Brooks Robinson, who appeared in only six games at that position for the Baltimore Orioles. He had been playing with York of the Piedmont League when summoned for a late-season look-see. He spent part of three more seasons in the minors, but he became one of the all-time great third basemen putting in 23 years as a defensive genius at the hot corner. He led the Orioles to four World Series, made many All-Star squads, and was perhaps the most popular of all the Orioles. Nicknamed "The Head" by his teammates because of his receding hairline, he holds a whole host of fielding records, practically owning the third baseman's section in the record books. He has more Gold Gloves than any other third baseman and has been the standard by which other third basemen are rated today. His unbelievable fielding plays during World Series games thrilled the millions who were watching on national television and confirmed what Baltimore fans had known all along. It was a loss for baseball when Brooks retired in 1977 after 2,896 games in which he had appeared at bat 10,655 times. Both figures placed him fifth in the all-time listings for games and at-bats.

The Chicago White Sox were plugging a power-hitting, good-fielding first baseman in Jim Marshall, who had hit .285 in the Pacific Coast League with Oakland, while leading the league in home runs (31) and RBIs (123). They said he was still learning to hit and sent him back to Oakland to sharpen his skills. He continued his learning in Memphis and Vancouver before the Pale Hose gave up and traded him to Baltimore, a club he made in 1958. After 85 games, they shipped him off to the National League for the balance of his career.

The National League had some fine rookies of their own in 1955 and leading the parade was a bespectacled St. Louis Cardinal outfielder, Bill Virdon. Virdon had been touted for his great defense, speed, and fine arm while with Birmingham in the Yankee system. He came by trade to the Cardinals, along with several lesser lights in April 1954 for the popular St. Louis outfielder Enos "Country" Slaughter, who the Yankees felt, and rightly so, they needed to bolster their outer defense. Virdon was assigned to the Redbird farm club at Rochester for '54, but arrived in 1955 to take the rookie of the year honors with a .281 average to go along with 17 home runs. The Cards didn't keep him long, sending him to the Pirates in May of 1956, where he starred for nine more seasons before retiring, only to return for six games in 1968. Virdon returned to Forbes Field in 1972 to manage the Pirates to the National League East championship, only to lose an exciting play-off to the Cincinnati Reds, a play-off that wasn't decided until the last inning of the fifth game. Virdon has also managed the New York Yankees and the Houston Astros.

The old Chicago Cub-Brooklyn Dodger infielder Billy Herman, now a Dodger scout, had found a shortstop down in Cuba who he proclaimed was, "Ready for the majors, best kid shortstop around. Great glove and arm." Chico Fernandez actually had been in the Dodger system for years prior to Herman's evaluation and remained in Montreal for 1955 and most of 1956 before he arrived at Ebbets Field, only to be traded to the Phillies. He stayed up for eight years, most of which was with Philadelphia and Detroit. Twenty-three-year-old pitcher Ray Crone, who was up briefly in 1954, arrived in Milwaukee after tossing a no-hitter for the Toledo Mud Hens against the St. Paul Saints. He put in four more seasons, going out with an even 30-30 record. The Cincinnati Reds had high hopes for a great competitor with a natural sinker in pitcher Rudy Minarcin, the former Phillie bonus baby who had been 12-2 with Toronto. He wound up 5 and 9, and was traded to the Boston Red Sox in 1956, where in two seasons he won one game before ending his career.

The Cardinals, in addition to Virdon, had some other pretty good rookies in 1955. Third baseman Ken Boyer belted 18 homers, while driving in 62 runs. Pitcher Luis Arroyo, who later starred for the New York Yankees, was 11 and 8. In 65 games for the Yanks in 1961, Arroyo was 15-5, and who can ever forget his arriving at Yankee Stadium one day and popping out of a huge replica pack of Lifesavers. He certainly was the lifesaver in many games for the '61 champion Yankees. Second baseman Don Blasingame also made his big league debut in the Card youth movement. While he only appeared in four games, Lindy McDaniel spent the year in the Cardinal bullpen. Never appearing in the minors, Lindy was on the major league scene for 21 years. His brother Von also played for the Cardinals in 1957 and 1958. Pitcher Tony Jacobs was also rated a Card to watch.

The New York Giants looked to Bob Lennon, a 27-year-old outfielder and nine year minor league veteran, for outfield help. He had hit .345 at Nashville, his first time above the .300 mark. Noted as a slow fielder, he impressed as the batting champ, home run king at a fantastic 64, RBI leader (161), leader in hits (210) and in runs (139). His record earned him only three partial major league seasons. He returned to play in the minors until 1961, but never again approached his 1954 records. The Cubs were delighted with Bob Thorpe, a 19-year-old right-handed pitcher who was 28-4 at Stockton (class C) for the top minor league mark in 1954. His live fastball, good curve, change-up, and pinpoint control could not help him make the big jump to the majors, and his only trial in 1955 led to a grand total of two appearances, with a total of three innings pitched. The Cubs also hoped for results from John Andre, 21-9 at Shreveport, while the Phillies were looking at pitcher Jim Owens and first baseman Marv Blaylock. The Dodgers looked at Ken Lehman, 18-10 at Montreal, and the Redlegs, as Cincinnati decided to be called in 1955, had hopes for pitcher Jerry Lane, 13-8 with Chattanooga.,

The Milwaukee Braves also had a nine-year minor league veteran in outfielder Chuck Tanner, who had hit .323 at Atlanta. For eight seasons he patroled major league outfields and pinch-hit his way around for the Braves, Cubs, Indians, and Angels. He learned his lessons well and returned in 1970 to manage the Chicago White Sox for six years, Oakland one season, and in 1977 joined Pittsburgh as their manager and led them to a pennant and world's championship in 1979.

The Pirates meanwhile were coming up with brother infielders Gene and George Freese. George had had a one-game trial with Detroit in 1953. Each were third basemen, and George got into 50 games while Gene played 65 at third and 57 at second base. George played nine games with the Cubs in 1961 for his only three seasons in the bigs. Gene, tabbed as a firebrand who hit with power and displayed quick hands in the field, lasted twelve seasons. The Pirates, like the Orioles and their Brooks Robinson, were blessed with the sleeper of National League rookies in 1955. The previous winter they had drafted a young player from Montreal, who in 87 games had batted 257 with five doubles, three triples, two home runs and twelve RBIs. Young outfielder Roberto Clemente had nothing to make anyone looking at his record assume he would be headed for stardom. Record books do not always tell about the desire and undeveloped talent which resides inside a player's mind and body. Clemente had it all, and in 18 years he amassed 3000 hits and a .317 lifetime batting average. An outstanding fielder with many Gold Gloves to his credit, he hit safely in every game of the 1960 World Series, hit three home runs in a game twice, and in another game he had three triples and was the National League's MVP in 1966. He led his league a record setting number of times (five) in outfield assists. A member of the National League All-Star squad 15 times, he also appeared in two World Series. No telling what further records might have come his way had he not been killed in an airplane crash on December 31, 1972, while on a mercy mission out of his native Puerto Rico. Bob Clemente was named to baseball's Hall of Fame in 1973.

There were a few other rookie feats of note in 1956 worth recounting even though they occurred on the minor league diamonds. Sid Harvey, a rookie catcher with the Muskogee Giants hit grand-slam home runs on successive at-bats. Rookie third sacker Bill Dennis of the Lawton Braves had a seven-for-seven day at bat, including three singles, a triple, and three home runs. Eighteen-year-old pitcher Stan Williams, who was with Newport News, struck out 20 Lynchburg batters. Stan, current pitching coach with the New York Yankees, made the big league in 1958 with the Los Angeles Dodgers and pitched for 14 years in the big time. Another pitcher, Bob Theiss, pitched a no-hitter in his first game in organized baseball for Quebec. Ron Owen, a towering southpaw hurler at Hornell matched Williams in his debut by fanning 20 batters. He struck out 13 of the first 15 Olean batters he faced. Two Texas City players accomplished the rare feat of smashing back-to-back homers in consecutive innings against Corpus Christie. In the eighth inning, Ed Kneuper and Les Witherspoon connected in succession and followed up their act again in the ninth inning. Charley Beamon, a young black right-hander, won 16 consecutive games with the Stockton Ports of the California League for a perfect 16-0 mark. Recalled by Oakland of the PCL, he won his first game for the Oaks 1 to 0 for 19 straight wins, as he had won his last two decisions with Wenatchee of the Western International League in 1954. The Seattle Rainiers of the PCL had a pitcher named Bob Fesler who, believe it or not, had pitched 55 no-hit games—that's right 55! An underhander, he made his debut against San Francisco and in two-thirds of an inning allowed five runs, two hits, five walks, a balk, and two wild pitches before he was relieved. Subsequent chances proved him to be no better. You say how come after all those no-hitters? Well, you see, they were with a softball team. Don Minnick, who had a two-game trial with Washington in 1957, won his first 16 pitching decisions with Reading of the Eastern League, setting a league record for the most successive wins at the start of the season. He finished with a 20-4 slate. Tommy Fine, who had a shot with the Red Sox, had set the Eastern loop mark of 17 straight wins for Scranton in 1952.

A strange year, that of 1955, as the two rookies who were hardly noticed, Brooks Robinson and Roberto Clemente, turned out to be the best of the crop. A lesson which has often been repeated in baseball through the years, those with immediate success are not always those who endure over the long haul.

1956-59: "Go West, Young Man"

The 1956-59 half of the decade of the '50s was an exciting one for baseball, as we shall see. It was marked by the continued change in the face of the baseball map, as changes were taking place that were only dreams ten years earlier. It saw many new names arrive to make their mark, and it saw many who had arrived in the early days of the decade blossom into genuine heroes. The never ending stream of rookies continued their advance, displacing the aging veterans, winning places on the rosters and in the hearts of the fans of the nation.

Interest in baseball was growing to an all-time peak. This was due in a large degree to the fact that television was bringing the game into the living rooms of the nation to a greater degree than had its predecessor, the radio. the swing away from a game played in the sunshine to a game played under the arcs was making baseball available to millions who had to work during the daylight hours.

At one time baseball's problems had come from within the game itself. The owners with strong clubs had drawn fans to their ball yards and made money, while the weaker clubs told fans "Wait until next year." Now they had TV to contend with. Players were contending with a series of problems, the most serious of which was the increase in night games. Television sponsors were demanding that more night games be played. Oh, how the players squawked at first about night play! Complaints that the cold and damp nights were hurting their arms and shortening their careers were commonplace. The older players were concerned over the bonuses given to green kids and the effect it was having on salary levels.

The advanced thinkers were well aware that for the game to survive, night baseball would continue to grow until day games might only become realities on Sundays and holidays. Slowly the players began to forget their complaining, as salary levels began to rise. A long way from today's standards, in the mid-Fifties the 15 to 20 thousand dollar salary was becoming more common. The players knew that to maintain these standards, the owners must have night games and television. As is true today, by 1956 every ball park except the Chicago Cubs' Wrigley Field had lights.

The rookies coming up from the minors were used to night ball and adapted themselves easily. Still there were complaints about physical tensions, the upsetting of eating and sleeping schedules, and the generally jumbled life due to the mix of day and night games. There was growing sentiment among players to play all night games, thus keeping a fairly standard routine in their life style. Despite the problems and gripes, baseball moved on.

I suppose the biggest event of 1956, at least the most remembered, has to be New York Yankee pitcher Don Larsen's perfect no-hitter in the fifth game of the World Series against the Dodgers, a series which New York won in seven games. The Yanks had an easy time winning Casey Stengel his seventh pennant in eight years by finishing nine games in front of the second place Cleveland Indians. The Brooklyn Dodgers didn't have it so easy, however, winning the flag on the final day of the race by nosing out the Milwaukee Braves by one game and the Cincinnati Reds by two games. An interesting sidelight to the 1956 season is that it was the first season in major league history where there was no player-manager on any club. A second interesting incident occurred when a well established Ted Williams was fined $5,000, equalling a fine once slapped on Babe Ruth. The Babe had broken training rules once too often for his manager Miller Huggins, and Ted had spit in the direction of a Fenway Park crowd for the third time in as many weeks, which proved to be too much for Red Sox owner Tom Yawkey, who levied the fine. Mickey Mantle, the newest Yankee hero, won the triple crown in the American League, while Don Newcombe was winning 27 games and losing only 7 for the Flatbush nine of Brooklyn. The minor leagues were still decreasing and had now dropped to 28 loops, a decrease of five over 1955. The proving ground for our rookies was slowly drying up. A new award for pitchers was inaugurated and called the Cy Young Award in honor of the famous pitcher of the same name.

For the first time since the Rookie of the Year Award was established, a player was unanimously voted the winner. Cincinnati Red outfielder Frank Robinson was the player so honored. The long-ball hitting Redleg slugger had tied the all-time record for a first year player by hitting 38 home runs.

Before Robinson's 21-year major league playing career would end, he would establish another first by becoming the first player to win the Most Valuable Player Award in both leagues, the National in 1961 and the American in 1966 when he also won a triple crown. In October of 1974, he became the first black to be hired as a major league manager, a career which lasted until 1977 when he became the first black to be fired from a manager's job. Robinson spent the bulk of his career with the Reds and the Baltimore Orioles, although toward the twilight he performed with the Dodgers, Angels, and Indians. Nine times at the height of his career he hit over .300, but had to settle for a .294 lifetime figure when he hung up his cleats. Frank had three minor league seasons under his belt when he arrived at Crosley Field in 1956. The author had a number of opportunities to see Robinson perform during his two seasons at the Reds' Columbia, South Carolina, farm in the Sally League. Robinson, a favorite with the fans, was easily spotted as a future major leaguer, as he seemed to do everything well, even giving it his all when hurt. As hard as it may be for today's younger fans to realize, these were still the days of segregation in the minors, and the ball parks in the Sally League still had special sections far down the foul lines for black seating only. The segregation did not end there, however, as the Columbia Reds' ball club boarded across the street from me, that is, all except for Robinson and a handful of other blacks, who had to find living quarters elsewhere in the city, in areas predominantly black. These were but a few of the obstacles to be overcome by players of Robinson's caliber and race.

Finding a left fielder had been a headache for several years in Cincinnati, with the likes of Joe Adcock, Jim Greengrass, and Stan Palys attempting to hold down the job before Robinson arrived amid words of praise from Manager Birdie Tebbetts. Robinson and his big bat fit in well with the great hitters already in Cincinnati like Ted Kluszewski, Johnny Temple, Ray Jablonski, Gus Bell, Ed Bailey, and Wally Post. Pitching was the Achilles heel of the fine Redleg team that was then performing at Crosley Field. Robinson's inexperience is what Tebbetts feared the most, but Robbie proved him wrong as he banged out 38 homers and knocked in 83 runs to go along with 6 triples, 27 doubles, and a league leading 122 runs scored and a .290 batting average. The right-handed-hitting Robinson broke in with two hits on opening day and soon demonstrated his long ball power. For a couple of months he was among the home run leaders while maintaining a respectable average. His questionable arm turned out to be strong enough to keep base runners honest and to carry him to rookie honors as an all-around player.

Each season seemed to bring its critical position, and 1956 seemed to be the year of the shortstop, especially in the American League. The Yankees introduced Jerry Lumpe, who was touted as the Yank shortstop for years to come. Brilliant in the spring, he faded quickly when his marked weakness on ground balls and double plays became apparent. After three seasons he was sent to the Kansas City A's. To go along with Lumpe, the New Yorkers had Bobby Richardson, who was sent back to Denver before his cup of coffee got cold. The Boston Red Sox had Don Buddin at shortstop. A favorite of Boston manager Mike Higgins, this seemed to be the only factor which kept him around Fenway Park for five seasons. Despite his small size, Buddin's strong wrists gave him good power at the plate, but his fielding failed to improve. Erratic in the field, he found a knack of messing up easy as well as tough chances. While Buddin had accumulated 16 errors by June 1, Manager Higgins kept his shortstop hero of 1955, Billy Klaus, and one-time regular Milt Bolling on the bench, much to the dismay of the Fenway faithful.

The Chicago White Sox had such confidence in their 1955 shortstop at Memphis that they traded away their regular shortstop Chico Carrasquel to make room for the newcomer. The Chisox manager was a former star shortstop himself, Marty Marion. Perhaps he knew something to justify taking such a chance on Luis Aparicio who had only two seasons of minor league experience. The scrappy 22-year-old Venezuelan did, however, justify Marion's confidence. Early scouting reports said that all he could do was run; others credited him with being a slick fielder, but with no prospect of hitting big league pitching. Marion was not worried saying, "He can field so well he won't have to hit much." When he did hit, he banged out line drives sprayed to all fields, and his great speed enabled him to stretch many a single into a double. Small (5'8", 157 lbs.) and agile with a strong throwing arm and good range, his glove permitted him to make some exciting plays which made up for his light bat. That speed allowed him to lead the league in stolen bases, which he did for his first nine consecutive seasons, and earned him American League rookie of the year honors. Eighteen years later, he retired as an active player, in ninth position on the all-time list of base stealers. Oddly, the man he replaced, Chico Carrasquel, was his neighbor back in Venezuela, and it was he whom Aparicio credited with teaching him the game.

We previously have mentioned the Cardinal's shortstop of five games in 1955, Don Blasingame, but he was another shortstop who came into his own in 1956, giving the St. Louis club an outstanding rookie for the third year running—Wally Moon in 1954 and Bill Virdon in 1955. Don took the shortstop post away from Alex Grammas until a June trade brought Al Dark to the Mound City and Blasingame moved to second base in the hustling Redbird infield.

The 1956 season wasn't a month old when the New York Giants summoned big Bill White from their Minneapolis farm club to fill in for incumbent first baseman Gail Harris, who was having his problems. White broke in with a homer in his first time up and added a double and single later in the game. Big and powerful, White was extremely fast for a man of his size, and while it worked out that he was rushed along too fast, the Giants felt he was the best they had had at first since Whitey Lockman, and their most promising rookie since Daryl Spencer. White later starred with the St. Louis Cardinals and the Philadelphia Phillies during his thirteen-year career. Today he is with the New York Yankees as a radio-TV broadcaster.

The Baltimore Orioles had a left-handed pitcher in Don Ferrarese that they said could throw as hard as Herb Score. In his first major league win, he held the New York Yankees hitless for eight innings until they got two scratch hits in the ninth. A week earlier he had struck out 13 Cleveland Indians in a 2-to-1 loss. Eight years and three clubs later, he concluded his big league stay with a 19-36 record. Baltimore also had outfielder Tito Francona, who made nine other stops on the big league trail in fifteen years. The much-traded outfielder gained a good record as a pinch hitter over the period. The Detroit Tigers dug down and came up with right-hander Paul Foytack and his hopping fastball when Billy Hoeft, Ned Garver, and Virgil Trucks complained of sore arms. Improved control and slider helped Foytack to a 15-13 record for fifth-place Detroit. Lou Berberet, a good but not spectacular catcher and a fair hitter, finally made a contribution with Washington after his trade by the Yankees to the Senators. His major drawback was his lack of running speed. Other Senator imports, outfielders Dick Tettleback and Whitey Herzog, experienced mixed fates.

There were other American League rookies of note. At Baltimore, beside Ferrarese, there were left hurler Lloyd Gosney and right-handers Mel Hill and Bob Harrison. They also had amateur pitcher Roger Marquis, signed out of a Holyoke, Massachusetts, high school. The Red Sox were hoping pitchers Joe Albanese, Roy Tinney, Al Schroll, Dave Sisler, or Jerry Casale would improve their pitching staff, but none of them did. Casale returned in 1958, but he never set any records for his pitching. Sisler's 9-8 record was the best of the bunch. At Detroit, a young catcher named Charlie Lau appeared in three games in his first of eleven years. Never making much of a mark as a catcher, he surfaced years later as a successful and much sought after batting instructor. His lifetime BA? .255. A journeyman, Rance Pless, appeared briefly with Kansas City as did pitcher George Brunet. The Yankees brought up pitcher Jim Coates from Binghamton where he was rated fast but hitable. The Senators had a weak-hitting, highly rated substitute first baseman in the

Cuban Julio Becquer. Appearing in three games for the Boston Red Sox was outfielder Marty Keough, who later became fairly successful with the Sox. Keough had two claims to fame, as his brother Joe Keough would arrive in the American League with Oakland in 1968, and his son Matt would arrive with the same club in 1977.

In the National League, some other pretty fair rookies were breaking in, none spectacularly, although some of them made quite a name for themselves in the years to come. The Cardinals had outfielder Jackie Brandt for 27 games, before they traded him in a multi-player deal to the New York Giants. He spent 11 years in the big leagues, most of them with the American League Orioles. Curt Flood was up for a second brief trial with the Cincinnati Reds as an infielder. He later switched to the outfield after his trade to the Cardinals, where he starred for 12 years. The Chicago Cubs had bonus baby Moe Drabowsky, who was 2-4 without benefit of any minor league experience. He spent 17 major league seasons with numerous clubs. They also had pitcher Jim Brosnan, who posted a 5-9 record. Outfielder-third baseman Lee Walls was up for a second try with Pittsburgh after a good year at Hollywood. Walls was joined by a fine infielder named Bill Mazeroski, who spent 17 years at second base in Forbes Field, where he led the Pirates into several World Series. They were joined by part-time catcher Danny Kravitz, who the Pirates felt would be better than Yogi Berra. The Giants were working out a good shortstop in Ed Bressoud and a mediocre pitcher named Jim Constable. The arch-rival Brooklyn Dodgers had a good-looking right-handed pitcher who posted a 5-5 record. His name was Don Drysdale, and he went on to become one of the great National League pitchers for 14 years. He won 209 games lifetime, while losing 166, and was a key figure in five Dodger World Series. His start was only so-so but, oh brother, how he finished up. He won 25 in 1962 and 23 in 1965. The 1956 Dodgers were one of those few clubs who had all right-handers as starters. Brooklyn also had an infielder who would help bring in the pennants for them named Charlie Neal. Neal was characterized as temperamental, no hustler, and needing to pull the ball to hit over .250, but was rated as a good fielder. Joining them was outfielder Gino Cimoli, who played with six other major league clubs over the next ten years. The Milwaukee Braves had first baseman Frank Torre (Joe's brother), a fine prospect up from Toledo where manager George Selkirk called him the best fielding first baseman he had ever seen. Frank seldom struck out, and in seven big league seasons he was set down on strikes only 64 times. The advanced book on Torre, however, said he was a risk, as he was slow and appeared to lack hustle at times. One of the most versatile infielders ever to play in the majors was making a 35-game appearance with the Braves.

That was Felix "The Cat" Mantilla. They said he was a good field, no hit player, but after 11 seasons this appeared to be only half correct. He fielded and hit well. Matching Mantilla's 11 seasons was a fairly decent outfielder up with a .326 BA at Jacksonville for his first trial, Wes Covington. The Braves actually were loaded with rookies on their roster, many of whom will be remembered by fans of that era as genuine prospects. Remember pitchers Paul Cave, Dick Grabowski, Joey Jay, Don McMahon, Red Murff, Humberto Robinson, Bob Trowbridge, and Carlton Willey; catcher Mike Roarke; infielders Ed Charles, Joe Koppe and Bob Malkmus; and outfielders Jim Pendleton and Al Spangler? All were soon to play roles in National League history.

Down on the farm clubs along the minor league trail, rookie right-hander John Herbert was hurling Erie to a 7-to-0 no-hit perfect game win over Hornell. It was the first perfect game ever hurled in the Pony League. Tony Komisar, a left-hander with the Leesburg Braves, had the rare thrill of retiring three Daytona Beach batters on one pitch. In the Florida State League game, Tony came in to pitch relief in the seventh frame with the bases loaded. His first pitch was lined to the third baseman, who stepped on third and tossed to second to catch a runner and retire the side. Three minor leaguers, one of whom will be remembered for his exploits later on in the majors, joined the exclusive 60 home run club in 1956. Dick Stuart hit 66 round trippers for Lincoln of the Western League. Stuart will be remembered not only for this feat, but for his slugging and fielding adventures with the Pirates and Red Sox. Ken Guettler of Shreveport of the Texas League hit 62 home runs, breaking the record for that loop. Frosty Kennedy knocked out an even 60 for Plainview of the Southwestern League. One of Stuart's teammates, right-hander Jackie Brown, also established a league record when he fanned 21 Amarillo batters while pitching the Chiefs to an 8-to-2 playoff victory. Brown had been brought up to Lincoln late in the season from Williamsport of the Eastern League. Speaking of the Eastern League, pitchers on the Reading Indians tossed 49 straight scoreless innings, five successive shutouts. Pitchers involved in the record performance included: Wally Seward, Bobby Locke, Tom Herrera, Charlie Kolakowski, Vic Lapiner, and Gary Bell. Seward was a reliever, and one of the wins he preserved, at the start of the skein, was for Jim "Mud Cat" Grant. Of course, Grant and Bell will be remembered by major league fans. Not exactly a rookie, unless you believe in a second life, was a 59-year-old Pacific Coast Leaguer. Frank "Lefty" O'Doul, who had won the National League batting crown in 1929 and 1932 and who had broken in with the New York Yankees in 1919, demonstrated that he could still hit by tripling off Sacramento pitcher Gene Bearden, who we met earlier in this book. O'Doul, at the time, was managing the Vancouver Mounties and put his reputation on the line in a meaningless season-ending game as a pinch hitter. In fairness, the Sacramento manager, Tommy Heath, had called his outfielders in to play just behind the infield grass. Lefty's hit, of course, went over the infield and took itself a long roll.

The 1957 season found the New York Yankees winning their third straight crown and eighth in the last nine years. It marked the twenty-third league championship in the history of the team. In the National League, the Milwaukee Braves, who had a near miss at that league's crown in 1956, rewarded their faithful fans with a pennant. The win ended a ten year domination by the league's Eastern clubs, as they became the first Western club to cop the laurels since the St. Louis Cardinals' victory in 1946. Like the Cardinals, the Braves not only won the league crown, but claimed the world's championship by besting the Yankees in the World Series, winning four games to three. The hero of the series for Milwaukee was Lew Burdette, a former Yankee farmhand, who won three games and hurled 24 consecutive scoreless innings.

While the Braves' Series win was big news, perhaps even bigger was the news that Brooklyn would win no more pennants. The Dodgers, deep in National League tradition, announced that they were making good on their threat of several seasons earlier to shift their franchise to Los Angeles. This became official after the 1957 season, the most startling of all franchise shifts. As if that news was not hard enough on New York area fans, the other local National League team, the New York Giants, announced that they would resume their long time rivalry with the Dodgers on the West Coast. "Go West young man," seemed to be the trend, as the Giants decided to settle in San Francisco. When the Boston Braves shifted to Milwaukee and the St. Louis Browns journied to Baltimore and the Philadelphia Athletics became the Kansas City Athletics, lack of fan interest was the underlying cause. This was not entirely the compelling factor in the Dodger-Giant shifts for 1958. In both cases, these clubs maintained their fan interest, but outmoded ball parks and deteriorating neighborhoods coupled with the tempting new dollars to be made in the virgin Western territory were just too much not to take advantage of. The moves left New York without a National League representative for the first time since the League was formed, and it would remain so until 1962, when the New York Mets would be born to be led by the same man who was managing the 1957 champion New York Yankees, Casey Stengel.

There was one important change adopted in 1957 for the 1958 season which affected our rookies and probably bears some explanation. It may even have been confusing to those who lived through the era of the bonus rule and the bonus babies and certainly may be confusing to the fans today who were too young to remember it. A little history of the bonus rule may be appropriate at this juncture, especially considering that it applied exclusively to rookies. Its abolishment in late 1957 and the institution of an unrestricted draft of four-year players to replace it was a welcomed addition to organized baseball's structure. Charges of under-the-table payments and the lack of an enforceable way to police the rule were the major factors in its repeal. When the regulation went into effect, it was designed to halt the wild spending for untried youngsters just entering professional baseball. The rule was first adopted in 1946, but was abandoned in 1950 only to be adopted in a revised form in 1952. The last regulation provided that any free agent (a player not under a professional contract) who was given or promised more than $4000 when he signed his first organized baseball contract became a bonus player. Any major league team signing such a youngster was forced to keep him on its roster for two years before he could be sent to the minor leagues. We have spoken of many of these youngsters in previous chapters, and at the time of the repeal of the rule there were 21 of these players on the major league rosters, including a dozen who were signed in 1957.

The 1957 crop included a few who would develop into pretty fair big leaguers. There were also some who would not. Among those signed in '57 were catcher Bob "Hawk" Taylor and outfielder John DeMerit at Milwaukee; pitchers Von McDaniel and Bob Miller with St. Louis; infielder Steve Boros and infielder-outfielder George Thomas at Detroit; catcher Frank Zupo and pitcher Jerry Walker at Baltimore; infielder Buddy Pritchard at Pittsburgh; pitcher Dave Hill at K.C.; pitcher Jay Hook at Cincinnati; and pitcher Ralph Lumenti at Washington. There were also nine players remaining on the major league rosters carrying bonus designation, the most prominent of whom were pitcher Billy O'Dell (Baltimore), catcher Jim Pagliaroni (Boston), outfielder Jerry Schoonmaker (Washington), infielder Jerry Kindall (Chicago Cubs) and pitchers Paul Giel and Mike McCormick (San Francisco).

There were a number of tragic incidents during the 1957 season involving some of the rookies we have aleredy spoken about. It was the season that saw Cleveland's ace pitcher Herb Score struck down by a line drive. The New York Giant catcher Bill Sarni suffered a heart attack in his first workout of the spring, and after the season the Dodger's great catcher Roy Campanella suffered a fracture of the spine in an auto accident, which left him paralyzed. The Cardinals had a promising young rookie outfielder named Charlie

Peete, who was killed in a plane crash in Venezuela while on his way there to play winter ball. Peete had been counted upon to be the Redbirds center fielder in 1957 and his untimely death forced the Birds to move their fine third baseman of 1956, Ken Boyer, to center field. The move of Boyer to center field was a good one for the Cards, as he ranked ahead of such greats as Willie Mays, Richie Ashburn, and Duke Snider as a glove man during his one season in the outer garden. The emergence of rookie center fielder Curt Flood in 1958 allowed Boyer to return to third base in 1958, and forced the fine 1957 rookie third sacker Eddie Kasko to move over to shortstop, replacing the veteran Al Dark.

It was the St. Louis Cardinals who gave the eventual winners, the Braves, their biggest competition in the early going in 1957. The Cards, paced by an aging Stan Musial, Boyer, and a pair of pitching brothers, 21-year-old Lindy and 18-year-old Von McDaniel, led the National League in the early summer. The young McDaniel brothers were being favorably compared to the Dean brothers, Dizzy and Paul, who had led the Cardinals to pennants in the 1930s. Von McDaniel had been signed as a bonus player, and when arm trouble finished him, the Cardinals dropped out of first place and Milwaukee took over to capture the flag. This left the Cards to struggle to hold on to second place over the Dodgers. Lindy McDaniel finished at 15 and 9 and Von at 7 and 5. As related previously, Lindy went on to pitch for 21 years, while Brother Von, after two appearances in 1958, was all done.

The National League rookie of the year was the Philadelphia Phillies' 19-game winner, right-hander Jack Sanford. Sanford had appeared in three games for the 1956 Phils (after his release from the service), having won one game. Sanford had a fine seven-year record in the minors before arriving in the City of Brotherly Love. Sanford's 188 strikeouts was tops for the league. Traded to San Francisco late in 1958, Jack starred for the Giants for better than six seasons, winning 24 games in 1962. He was later traded to the California Angels in 1965. He closed out his career with Kansas City in 1967 for a total of twelve big league seasons.

While the National League had selected a pitcher for rookie of the year, the American League was selecting an all-around player from the New York Yankees. Versatile Tony Kubek had a trial at several positions, and while plans called for him to be the Yankee shortstop, he had been impressive in the outfield, which many baseball experts felt was his best position. In his first two minor league seasons in the Yankee system, Kubek had been employed strictly as a shortstop. Then in 1956 while at Denver of the American Association, he played some third base and outfield to go along with his shortstopping. Not a long ball hitter Kubek was consistently hitting for averge, being well over the .300 mark during his formative years. His first season with the club from the Bronx found him appearing in the outfield, where he was splitting the left field duties with Enos Slaughter. Kubek's outfield mates were a couple of pretty fair outfielders named Mantle and Bauer. In 1958 the Yankees shifted him to the shortstop position, while their 1957 shortstop, Gil McDougald, went to second base to replace rookie Bobby Richardson. Richardson had had several tries at second base for the Yankees and still qualified as a rookie in 1957. Richardson was known for his fast hands, and was excellent on the pivot for the double play. Like Kubek, he was not a power hitter, but was a slash hitter who poked the ball up the middle well. Kubek spent nine seasons in New York mostly at shortstop, while Richardson, also a shortstop, spent most of his twelve Yankee years at second base. Kubek, known today to millions for his TV work on "The Game of the Week" and World Series telecasts, is also remembered by many who were watching the seventh game of the 1960 World Series against Pittsburgh. The Pirates went into the bottom half of the eighth inning down 7 to 4. Gino Cimoli, batting for pitcher Elroy Face, singled off Yankee Bobby Shantz to open the inning. Then came the big play of the Series. Bill Virdon, the Pirate center fielder, rapped a ground ball to shortstop that took a bad hop and struck Kubek in the throat, going for a hit. Immediately, it appeared that Kubek was seriously hurt, and he had to be taken out of the game in favor of Joe DeMaestri. The play opened the gates for the Pirates, who went on to score five runs to take the lead 9 to 7. The Yankees came back with two runs in the top of the ninth to tie the game. In the last of the ninth with the fifth Yankee pitcher of the day, Ralph Terry, on the mound, the Pirate second baseman Bill Mazeroski stepped to the plate. Maz took the first pitch for a ball and then homered to give the Bucs the championship.

Speaking of Ralph Terry, he, like Richardson, had had a cup of coffee with the Yankees in 1956, but arrived in 1957 only to find himself in a multi-player trade with Kansas City, where he pitched for a while before K.C. traded him back to New York in another multi-player trade in May of 1959. Going along with Terry to K.C. was a little infielder-outfielder who had developed into a good big league prospect, Woodie Held.

Promoted to the Milwaukee Braves from their Wichita farm club in mid July '57 was one Bob "Hurricane" Hazle. He finished the season by hitting .403 with seven home runs and 27 RBIs in 41 games. Bob had had a brief try with the Reds in 1955. In late May 1958, he was batting .179 in 20 games, when he was traded to Detroit, where he hit .241 in 43 games and was released, ending forever his big league career. That interesting nickname came about when a hurricane named Hazel struck the U.S. in 1953 causing extensive damage. Hazle at the time was with the Tulsa club in the Texas League, and because of the similarity of Bob's last name and the hurricane's name, it is easy to see why it stuck with him. Actually, the name was little used until he started his batting spree in 1957.

The Braves also had pitcher Juan Pizarro, probably the top hurler in the minor leagues in 1956. In only his first year in organized baseball the 20-year-old left-hander had a 23-6 record with the Jacksonville Braves. Juan at times had some control problems, but his blazing fastball and major league curve was good enough for him to strike out 318 Sally League batters. He did not make the Braves in spring training, but was farmed out to Wichita of the American Association, where he quickly ran up a 4-0 record, earning him a return trip to the teepee in Milwaukee. Turning in only a 5-6 record with the Braves, he was not the immediate success that was predicted for him. He did gain the poise he needed by spending several more seasons jumping between the minors and majors. When it was all over for Juan in 1974, he had spent 18 years in the big leagues with eight different clubs. The Braves management was hoping that 1957 would see Pizarro or one or two of the other fine rookie hurlers match the 1956 performance of rookies Taylor Phillips and Bob Trowbidge. They boasted of Dick Grabowski, Charlie Wrinn, Corky Valentine, Humberto Robinson, Don McMahon, and Joey Jay. Of course, the best of this group turned out to be the big right-hander, Don McMahon. He matched Pizarro's 18 big league seasons. Used almost exclusively as a reliever in those 18 seasons, Don started only two games and both of them were in the same year, 1963, when he was with Houston. He was as well-traveled as Pizarro, spending his time with nine different clubs.

There is one interesting little story about the Braves' rookie Taylor Phillips, who had been pitching with that great Fort McPherson army team mentioned earlier. Phillips was known as somewhat of a character among those of us who knew him. I was up for discharge before Taylor, and when he learned that I was getting out after the end of the season, he said, "Hey, where are you from?" I said, "Connecticut," explaining I would quite likely see the Milwaukee Braves, to whom he was under contract, at either New York or Brooklyn. He replied, "Listen, when you get up there, go see Spahnie (Warren Spahn) and the boys and tell them not to worry, Ole Taylor is on his way." And certainly he was. I had no doubt that one of them would have to move over for Ole Tay.

The 1957 Pittsburgh Pirates where hoping outfielder Johnny Powers, a strong power hitter, would be able to make the conversion to first base for them. The requirement of hitting for average was the missing ingredient for Powers as he fell by the wayside.

The Philadelphia Phillies came up with a first baseman in Ed Bouchee, a move which allowed the Phils to keep catcher Stan Lopata behind the plate instead of a dual role as a fill-in first baseman. Bouchee was a good fielder who hit with some power. His biggest challenge was in keeping his weight down. He was selected by *The Sporting News* as the non-pitching National League Rookie of the Year. In addition to their National League rookie of the year, the Phils were talking of pitchers Dick Farrell, who had a good fastball to go along with fine control, and another hard thrower in Seth Morehead. Despite the fine future predicted for these two, the Phils had rookie Don Cardwell post a 4-8 record.

The Dodgers in their final season in Brooklyn nominated rookie John Roseboro, a fine catcher with good credentials in Montreal for rookie honors. It was Roseboro who took over the catching chores for the Dodgers after Campanella's unfortunate accident. Johnny spent 14 seasons handling big league pitching. Backing up Roseboro was catcher Joe Pignatano, who spent most of his career doing exactly what he did in 1957, backing up in the catching department. They also hoped outfielder Don Demeter could cut down on his strikeouts and make it but he couldn't. Knuckleballing lefty Fred Kipp also failed. There was also a big powerful first baseman up from Ft. Worth named Jim Gentile. They said Gentile could be pitched to, and he wound up only appearing in four games in Brooklyn, and after five more in L.A. he moved on to Baltimore. There he developed the power that was predicted of him and became the Orioles' regular first sacker during the '60s.

The New York Giants, who were joining the Dodgers in moving to the Coast for the 1958 season, were high on a young third baseman named Ossie Virgil, who in '56 got off to a slow start at Minneapolis, but straightened out to bat .265. Virgil, a line drive hitter, was known as a good hit-and-run man who could come through in the clutch. He also had a strong, accurate arm. To play alongside Virgil, the Giants came up with a shortstop from the Bahamas in Andre Rodgers. Rodgers, a former cricket star, seemed to have all the tools to make it big, and the Giants, realizing this, were in no hurry to move him along too fast. The Giants, who were in a limited youth movement, had seen the military draft take away rookies Brandt, White, and their top prospect Willie Kirkland, and seemed in no hurry to make player moves in their final season at the Polo Grounds. It was as if they were waiting to capture the hearts of the fans who waited their arrival in San Francisco's Bay area.

The Chicago Cubs introduced a switch-hitting infielder in Casey Wise. Wise, an excellent fielder, was also a pesty hitter with runners on base during his brief four year major league stay. Dick Drott, a 20-year-old rookie right-hander, set a modern record for Cub pitchers by whiffing 15 Milwaukee Braves as he won 15 games for the Cubs. Frank Ernaga, an outfielder, homered in his first at bat and tripled in his next time up. As if to prove this was no lucky performance, he hit a homer, double, and triple for his next three hits, giving him five extra base hits in his first eight at-bats. The Cubs also had a catcher who was noted for his handling of pitchers, Cal Neeman, who they drafted out of the Yankee system. His weak hitting was all that stood between him and a first-string job during his seven campaigns in the big show. The Cincinnati Reds had a pitching hopeful, who never really arrived until 1962 with the American League Washington Senators, in Claude Osteen. Appearing in only three games with no record, it was Osteen's first of 18 big league seasons. Curt Flood, an outfielder, was back for a very brief second try. He made it big in 1958 and by then had been traded to the St. Louis Cardinals for whom he starred for 12 years. The Cardinals had two rookie shortstops to battle the veteran Al Dark—Dick Schofield and Eddie Kasko. Kasko, a bespectacled guy with a .303 batting average at Rochester, was the more experienced of the two. The sure-fielding Kasko won the post over Dark and the erratic fielding Schofield. Kasko managed the Boston Red Sox for three years (1970–72) before moving into his present job in their front office as director of scouting. The Cards were also hoping outfielder Bobby Gene Smith, a good hitter with running speed and a fine arm, and pitcher Tom Cheney might make the squad.

Over in the American League, the Boston Red Sox were still singing the praises of Kasko's present boss, catcher Haywood Sullivan. The second coming of Bill Dickey, they said. It was still not Sullivan's year. Center fielder Marty Keough still couldn't move out Jimmy Piersall, despite his great speed and steady hitting, as his arm was letting him down. The Sox did introduce second baseman Ken Aspromonte, who was relegated to a utility role by Sox vets Bolling, Lepcio, and Klaus. Aspromonte is better remembered today as the Cleveland Indian manager of 1972–74. Jim Landis, a good fielder, finally hit well enough to crack the Chicago White Sox outfield. The Pale Hose hoped Tom Flanigan, Bill Fischer, Jerry Dahlke, or Fred Rudolf would bolster their pitching staff. They did not. The outstanding rookie in the Kansas City Athletic camp was outfielder Jim Pisoni, the former Oriole prospect. Former and future Yankee hurler Ralph Terry won a regular job at K.C. with a 4-11 record for the next-to-last place A's. Fastballing Gene Host, purchased from the Tigers, was the A's big rookie hope for 1957.

The Detroit Tigers, meanwhile, were expecting that lefty Hal Woodeschick would help them. He didn't. He did show up in '58 with the Indians for his second season in an eleven-year tour. The Indians had as their number one prospect an excellent power-hitting outfielder who had the reputation of driving in the big runs. This speedy outfielder made it and was traded to K.C. in '58. The A's in turn sent him to the Yankees for the 1960 season. It was there that Roger Maris gained his greatest stardom in 1961, as he hit 61 home runs to break Babe Ruth's home run record of 60 round trippers. The Tribe also came up with a good catcher in Russ Nixon and looked to pitchers John Gray, Bill Daley, and Stan Pitula to strengthen an already sound mound staff. Rangy and fast, the 19-year-old Brooks Robinson was getting his third and most successful try with Baltimore. Pitcher Charlie Beamon, on the strength of a late season shutout of the New York Yankees in 1956, was just as highly rated. He had been 13-6 at Vancouver. Two other highly thought of young Birds were pitcher Bob Harrison and outfielder Carl Powis. The last place Washington Senators were hoping former Red Sox farmhand Neil Chrisley, a .298 hitter with 24 home runs at Louisville, could bring that beautiful sweep stroke of his to the plate in Griffith Stadium. Hoping to join the long line of Cubans who had played for the Senators was right-hander Evilio Hernandez, the owner of a fine fastball.

There were a couple of minor league rookie pitchers who had fancy records in 1957. Bob Riesener, a Yankee farmhand, established an all-time organized baseball record when he was 20-0 with the class C Alexandria Club of the Evangeline League, and Don Nichols, another Yankee farm clubber, was 22-3 in relief for Peoria of the Three I League for one of the fanciest relief records ever. Minor league life is always considered a tough grind for the rookies working their way up. The bus trips are long, living conditions often poor, but it is the price they must pay before getting a major league trial. As bad as minor league life could be, seldom does it compare to the bizarre incident that took place in Ponca City of the Sooner State League in early August 1957. In the second inning of a game with Ardmore, a spectator pulled out a pistol and fired several shots at a member of the Ardmore team. The shots missed the player they were intended for and hit player-manager J. C. Dunn of the Cardinals, one in the ribs, another in the leg. The game was suspended, and Dunn was rushed to the hospital. Dunn recovered and hit a phenomenal .502 to lead his team in a postseason playoff. Although it is jumping ahead of our story a bit, this incident brings to mind the case of Boston Red Sox rookie Bobby Sprowl, who while lying in his bed one evening at the Sox 1978 spring base in Winter Haven, Florida, was shot in the arm, the bullet coming through the wall from the room next door where a guest was cleaning the weapon. Sprowl recovered and advanced through the Red Sox chain from A ball to Fenway Park that same season.

As the Milwaukee Braves repeated their 1957 National League championship in almost the same manner in 1958, the city was being proclaimed the new capital of baseball. The National League's geography was transformed for the 1958 season with the transplanting of the New York Giants to San Francisco and the Brooklyn Dodgers to Los Angeles.

Meanwhile, the American League champions were, for the fourth successive season, the New York Yankees and for the ninth time during Manager Casey Stengel's ten years at the helm. Opening the season with seven wins in their first eight games, they left the second place White Sox and the third place Red Sox at the starting gate. In the World Series, the Yankees gained one of their finest hours, making a courageous comeback to win after being down 3 games to 1. Only once before, in a seven-game series, had a team come back from such a deficit, and that was way back in 1925 when the Pittsburgh Pirates achieved it against the Washington Senators. The win gave the Yankees the distinction of beating every National League club in at least one World Series.

The switch to the West Coast did nothing for the Dodgers, as they slipped to a lowly seventh place in the National League. It did, however, seem to work for the Giants, as they climbed from sixth place to third in the standings. Actually, the pennant races were uneventful, and there was little for the fans to do but wait for the Series or to follow the struggles of Philadelphia's Richie Ashburn and Boston's Ted Williams in the race for the batting titles. Pirate fans saw their Bucs move up to second place after finishing last in 1957. Actually, Pittsburgh had finished no higher than seventh since 1949. The Pirates were led by a pair of fine outfielders, shortstop Dick Groat, and second baseman Bill Mazeroski. While their regular first baseman was Ted Kluszewski, they had as a back-up rookie Dick Stuart, who shattered home run records on every stop he made along the minor league trail. In his first year as a Pirate, he hit 16 in 67 games, but also led the league in errors.

The American League was unveiling a rookie of sorts of their own in late 1958. Actually, mention of the Pittsburgh Pirates brings to mind this rookie, as it was with them that he broke in as an infielder in 1926. Joe Cronin had moved over to the American League Washington Senators in 1928 and was named their manager in 1933, one of the youngest ever to take a major league helm. He brought the Senators home in first place in his rookie year as manager, but lost the World Series to the New York Giants and Bill Terry, who was in his second year as the Giant leader. Cronin moved on to manage Tom Yawkey's Boston Red Sox in 1935, a post he held until he stepped down in 1947. Now he was again in a rookie post in late 1958 as American League president, replacing Will Harridge, the distinguished 72-year-old American league czar, who suddenly retired after almost 28 years as head of that League. Cronin was a real success story. Coming off the streets of San Francisco and advancing from player, to manager, to front office (Red Sox general manager), to league president. Actually, Cronin was not officially named to the post until January 31, 1959, although he was preparing for the job in 1958.

Rumors bounded around the major league scene that Cronin's old club, the Washington Senators, might move on to greener pastures. There were also reports that the Cleveland Indians, Philadelphia Phillies, and Cincinnati Reds were looking westward also. Hearing the rumors grow louder, the cities of Minneapolis and Houston took steps to prepare for such possible moves. 1958 was not the year for the moves, but it would not be long before clubs would be located in those cities, as we shall see later on.

The rookie awards for 1958 saw outfielder Albie Pearson of Washington, one of the smallest players in major league history at five feet-six inches, and first baseman Orlando Cepeda of San Francisco capture the baseball writers' honors. Cepeda was a unanimous selection. *The Sporting News* selected Pearson and Cepeda, but also singled out rookie members of the pitching fraternity for honors—Ryne Duren of the New York Yankees in the American League and Carlton Willey of Milwaukee in the senior circuit.

Pearson was a product of the Boston Red Sox farm chain and was traded to the Senators in January 1958 along with first baseman Norm Zauchin for infielder Pete Runnels. He won over fans everywhere with his charm and hustle. The 22-year-old Californian was left-handed all the way and hit with fair power for a little man. A good runner, he possessed a great arm, all factors which won him the regular center field post for the Nats. Albie spent nine seasons with several American League clubs, in eight of which he enjoyed some fairly moderate success.

The larger Orlando Cepeda, 6'2" and 205 pounds, known as "The Baby Bull," enjoyed a much more illustrious major league career. A first baseman in his rookie year, he later divided his playing time between first base and the outfield. For 17 years, Cepeda played on major league diamonds. The Giants sent him to the St. Louis Cardinals, and they in turn traded him to Atlanta. He moved to the American League at the end of his career and enjoyed great success in Boston in 1973 as their first designated hitter, a factor which undoubtedly prolonged his major league career. The hard-hitting Puerto Rican rookie drove in 96 runs, hit 25 home runs, and batted .312 to gain the unanimous vote of the scribes as their National League rookie in 1958. Plagued with personal problems once his career ended, the popular big guy appears to be making a successful comeback in the big leagues today as a coach.

Ryne Duren had been bouncing around the minor league trail since 1949, with cups of coffee at Baltimore and Kansas City, before landing in the New York Yankee bullpen to grab his share of rookie honors. The bespectacled right-hander possessed a blazing fastball, and his occasional wildness was enough to keep American League batters off guard and insure his success. He lasted ten years on the big league scene, traveling from club to club and winding up with a poor 27-44 log. Of the 311 regular season games he appeared in all but 32 were in relief. Like Cepeda, Duren had personal problems (although his appeared during his major league stay), but he also has now overcome them and is helping to steer youngsters into better lives.

Rated as the best young pitcher in a well-stocked Milwaukee Brave farm system was the slender right-hander Carlton Willey, who had won 21 games and struck out 174 for Wichita with his steaming fastball. He won a job on the talented Braves' staff, and while posting a 9-7 record, he led the National League in shutouts with four. The Maine native spent nine years in the big time with the Braves and Mets, posting 38 wins while dropping 58 decisions.

The Detroit Tigers were singing the praises of the star of the 1957 Cuban Winter League, right-handed pitcher Bob Shaw. The well-educated 24-year-old from the Bronx was a control pitcher with a good slider, curve, and fastball. In eleven seasons, he posted two good seasons with the Chicago White Sox to whom Detroit had traded him, 18-6 in 1959 and 13-13 in 1960. He was 15-9 with the 1960 Milwaukee Braves and 16-9 with the 1965 San Francisco Giants. The Motor City club also came up with a slick-fielding shortstop in Orville Inman "Coot" Veal. A long-time minor leaguer, he was one of the best fielders this author has ever seen. While living in the Sally League area, the chance arose to see the Augusta Club play. I could always count on a good-size-group to venture to the nearest ball park. The attraction was the fielding of Coot Veal. He was a picture fielder, worth the price of admission just to watch him gobble up ground balls. Unfortunately, as so often happens, he was no puzzle to opposing pitchers. Six seasons were all he could manage in the big leagues. But Inman Veal, wherever you are, thanks for those wonderful fielding exhibitions! Many fans will forget that a Detroit hero, who made his initial big league bow in 1958 as a pinch hitter, was in the uniform of the Chicago White Sox. The White Sox, much to their regret, gave up on Norm Cash and sent him in a multi-player deal to Cleveland, who in turn peddled him to Detroit before he could appear in a game at the teepee. He was a 15-year fixture in Detroit. A power hitter, he was a key figure in the Detroit attack for years.

The Indians, however, had another Georgian like Veal in infielder Billy Moran. Not a top-flight hitter, Moran was quick with great speed on the bases and had an outstanding glove. Noted as the type of player who could keep a club on its toes, he paralleled Veal again, as his bat did him in after seven seasons.

Joining Pearson in Washington was Bob Allison, a fine all-around outfielder who lasted 13 seasons in the American League. Cepeda was joined by four other outstanding rookies in San Francisco, third baseman Jim Davenport and outfielders Leon Wagner, Willie Kirkland, and Felipe Alou. Just imagine those guys along with Willie Mays in your outfield, and you can see how awesome the Giants could be. Alou, Mays, and Kirkland were the starting outfield. Felipe was the first of three Alou brothers to make their major league bows with the Giants. All were fine ballplayers. Matty came along in 1960 and Jesus in 1963. All were outfielders. Felipe lasted the longest at 17 years, Jesus 14 years, and Matty 15 years. Leon "Daddy Wags" Wagner, always a threat at the plate, played for 12 years and gained stardom as a member of the American Leagues' Los Angeles Angels and Cleveland Indians. The big hitter the Giants were looking for to join Mays was Willie Kirkland. He had a terrific minor league record before a service hitch. A big strong left-handed slugger with real power, he had much to learn about playing the outfield, but with his power, speed, and strong arm, he made the Club. Like Wagner, he also was traded eventually to Cleveland midway through his nine year career.

The Giants' long-time rivals, the Dodgers, had outfielder Don Demeter on hand again after a brief three-game trial in 1957. Kept around mainly for insurance against the aging Los Angeles outfield of Carl Furillo, Duke Snider, and Gino Cimoli, the big Oklahoman was noted for his fielding and power hitting. He had missed out on spring training because of military service, but the Dodger brass was well aware that he could be a capable outfield replacement if needed. Don lasted for 11 major league seasons, split between the Dodgers and Phillies in the National League and Detroit, Boston, and Cleveland in the American League. The Dodgers also introduced another rookie outfielder in Ron Fairly. Fairly later switched to first base, a familiar procedure for aging veterans to help them prolong their careers, and played in 21 major league seasons and four World Series during which he hit an even .300 in the fall classic. A big right-handed pitcher, Stan Williams compiled a 9-7 record for L.A., but spent nine of his fourteen major league campaigns in the American League. A giant of an outfielder, 6'7", 250 lbs., made an eight game appearance with L.A. Remember Frank Howard? He jumped up from Green Bay of the Three I League, but the jump was a bit too much for him to handle, and he summered in the Texas and Pacific Coast Leagues in 1959. He arrived to stay in 1960 with the bulk of his playing time in the outer garden, with several appearances at first base. In 1964 he went over to the American League Senators and finished up his career with Detroit in 1973. Like Fairly, he also spent time at first base. We will meet him when we discuss the 1960 season.

The Chicago Cubs introduced a couple of rookies who would be around for a while. The Cubs had hopes of sewing things up with a couple of Taylors. Sammy was a catcher breaking in with the '58 club. He lasted six seasons with several clubs, and Tony (no relation), a fine infielder, would be traded to the Phillies in May 1960 in a deal which brought our former rookie of the year Ed Bouchee to Chicago. Tony starred in Philadelphia, and when he retired in 1976, he had 19 seasons behind him. Tony tied an unusual major league record in 1960, when in a twin bill he had no put-outs while playing second base. The other Chicago team, the White Sox, had outfielder Johnny Callison, who like so many of the other rookies of '58 would wind up with and star for the Philadelphia Phillies. Callison, a highly regarded flyhawk played for 16 years and was remembered more for his play in Philadelphia than Chicago.

The other National League Ohio entry, the Cincinnati Reds, had a most sensational youngster in 19-year-old outfielder Vada Pinson. He not only hit with left-handed power, but could really move down the line to first base. He had hit .367 and stole 53 bases in 1957 with Visalia of the class C California League, a loop he led in hits (209), runs (163), doubles (40), and triples (20). Red Manager Birdie Tebbetts was sure he was ready. He came to stay in 1959, for 18 years with four clubs. The St. Louis Cardinals were looking to a tobacco-chewing Georgian named Phil Clark to develop into a badly needed relief pitcher. Clark had good control and a fine sinkerball and appeared to be strong enough to handle the job. He had 63 appearances for Houston's Dixie Series champions, winning 16 and losing only 6 with a brilliant earned run average of 1.83. After two seasons and 14 games for the Cardinals, Clark had only an 0-2 record to show for his final big league mark.

The Cleveland Indians came up with a big right-hander in pitcher Jim "Mudcat" Grant, who lasted 14 years and had a 145-119 record when he bowed out. Heir apparent to the Baltimore Oriole shortstop job, held by a weak-hitting Willie Miranda, was Ronnie Hansen, a tall rangy 19-year-old with only one season of professional experience. He was coming off a year on Vancouver's disabled list. A fluid, graceful fielder, Hansen was not yet a good hitter and after twelve games was sent to Knoxville to sharpen his batting eye. A short two-game look-see in 1959 proved little, but the determined worker returned in 1960 to win the regular job. He played for 15 years in the

American circuit, mostly for the Orioles and White Sox. For the third year in a row, the Boston Red Sox were looking for handsome Haywood Sullivan, the former Florida football star, to become a big league catcher. Now 27 years old, they were sure he had learned to catch and pretty sure he could hit. Intelligent and confident, the 6'4", 210 pounder summered on the disabled list in 1958. The New York Yankees came up with a first baseman-outfielder with the colorful name of "Marvelous Marv" Throneberry. Marv's brother Faye was an outfielder with the Red Sox (1952-57), Senators (1957-60), and Angels (1961). Marv played for three seasons with the Yankees and several with Kansas City and Baltimore before moving on to the New York Mets. Known today for his beer commercials on television and as a symbol of the early inept Mets, his earlier career, which was much longer than his stay in New York, is largely forgotten. The Yankees also had a hard-luck kid, who had for two years been trying to crack their lineup as an outfielder, in Norm Siebern. Tall and graceful, Norm appeared in 57 games in 1956, but was farmed to Denver in 1957 where he proceeded to lead the American Association in runs (124), hits (191), doubles (45), triples (15), and batting (.349). He made it in 1958 as Casey Stengel's left fielder, joining Mickey Mantle and Hank Bauer in the American League champions' outfield. There were two National League rookies who it appeared might have brilliant futures, but it did not turn out that way. They deserve mention here, outfielder-catcher Gene Green with the Cardinals and pitcher Geoge "Red" Witt with the Pirates.

Philadelphia Phillie rookie Chuck Essegian will never forget how his double turned into a double play. In a game against the Reds at Connie Mack Stadium in Philadelphia, he came to bat with Richie Ashburn on second base and Chico Fernandez on first base, and sent a long drive to center field which bounced off Gus Bell's glove for a double. Ashburn, thinking Bell might catch up with the drive, held up at second for a moment and was only steps ahead of Fernandez, when they both rounded third base. Having no choice but to head for home, Ashburn was nailed at the plate by Roy McMillan's relay throw to catcher Smoky Burgess. Burgess then threw to George Crowe, who had Essegian trapped between second and third and Fernandez caught between third and home. The Reds then went for and nabbed Fernandez, to complete the double play, while Essegian pulled into third,

An 18-year-old Dick Ellsworth, signed by the Chicago Cubs out of a Fresno, California, high school, was used in a charity game in June against their crosstown rivals, the White Sox, and he responded with a four-hit 1-to-0 win. His first National League start resulted in a shelling by the Cincinnati Reds and his option to Ft. Worth of the Texas League. He returned in 1960 to stay for twelve more big league seasons.

The decade of the Fifties closed out amid continual news centering on the expansion byword that had so characteristically marked the entire era. 1959 was just one more eventful chapter in the westward movement, or at least of the continued discussion of the movement, by the major league powers to be. The more prominent developments included the proposed formation of a third major league, to be known as the Continental League, a dream which never reached fulfillment. Joe Cronin assumed the reins of the American League, and the majors took a big step in helping rookies along when they took action to allot nearly one million dollars to finance player development and promotional programs in the minor leagues. The clubs which had shifted cities over the past six years showed great financial success, a fact which did not escape notice by those older franchises which were struggling in the money market. The tremendous population explosion taking place in many minor league cities, as the war babies were coming of age, coupled with shifts of industry from the Eastern United States to the South and West were resulting in formerly unheard of cries for expansion. Some cities, Minneapolis and Houston as previously noted, were already taking steps to attract major league clubs. When New York failed to regain a spot in the National League, hurried plans were drawn up for the third major league.

The 1959 club owners fought the third major league by drawing up plans to expand their circuits, first to ten clubs, and later to twelve teams with an eventual division into three loops. Though neither league took any positive action to implement the plan, it is interesting to see how the tide was running. This was really the forerunner of the current talk of inter-league play and additional splitting of the present divisions. A tough set of rules for major league classification were set up by the owners, perhaps in fear of having a repeat of the Federal League (1914–15), which had raised havoc at the time with the American and National Leagues. By late July, plans were announced for the new league under the guidance of William A. Shea of New York, the man who had led the unsuccessful effort to obtain a franchise for New York to replace the departed Dodgers and Giants. April 1961 was set for the opening day for the league, which was never to field a team. Interestingly, some of the areas considered by the new league are today on the major league map, Atlanta in the National League and the Dallas-Ft. Worth area (Texas Rangers) in the American League.

The player development plan met with great success and was again promised to the minor leagues for 1960. The second time around, more emphasis was placed on promotional plans, however.

The pennant races of 1959 were dramatic, with the Chicago White Sox breaking the long reign of the New York Yankees in the American League. The Pale Hose were the first club other than New York to cop an American League crown since the Cleveland Indians' victory of 1954, and it would be the last win until the mid '60s when the Minnesota Twins would prevail. In the National League, the dominance of the transplanted teams continued, as the Los Angeles Dodgers and the Milwaukee Braves finished in a first place tie. The Dodgers, who had finished seventh in 1958, captured the flag by defeating the Braves in a playoff, 3 to 2 and 6 to 5, the second contest going 12 innings in their best-of-three playoff series. The win continued the Dodger supremacy which had begun in 1952 and was interrupted only by the New York Giants in 1954 and the Braves in 1957-58. The White Sox, whose win was their first in 40 years, fell to the Dodgers in the World Series. It took the Bums 65 years to win a world's championship in Brooklyn and only two to come up champions after their move to L.A.

Manager Al Lopez's White Sox featured strong pitching backed up by a tight defense, and they exhibited such good speed they were being called the "Go-Go" Sox. they appeared to be a formidable task to overcome for the West Coast Dodgers. The hero of the series, which was won by the Dodgers, was a rookie right-hander named Larry Sherry. Sherry had had an unsuccessful brief five-game trial with the 1958 Dodgers, in which he was credited with only four innings pitched. He began the 1959 season with St. Paul of the American Association, where in fifteen games he had gained six wins against seven setbacks. He did, however, have 109 strikeouts and only 53 walks in 115 innings pitched. Promoted to the Dodgers, the Los Angeles native had appeared in 23 games and posted a 7-2 record before the regular season ended. In the World Series, he stood out above all the other players. The 24-year-old rookie relieved in all four games. The Dodgers won, winning two of them and saving the other two—quite a feat for a rookie hurler under the pressures of World Series play. In the first World Series where neither clubs pitching staff would record a complete game pitched, Sherry's work would prove to be the difference. In the 12-2/3 innings he pitched, he allowed only eight hits and one run. While 1959 would be the only World Series for Sherry, he did put in eleven major league seasons equally split between both leagues.

The Dodgers also had a rookie at shortstop in 1959 in young Maury Wills, a smooth fielding, speed demon. This base-stealing wiz led the National League in stolen bases for six consecutive seasons (1960–65) with 104 thefts to his credit in 1962. Overall, when Wills hung his spikes in 1972, he was seventh on the all-time list of base stealers. In 1980, he gained a lifetime ambition of becoming a big league manager by being named manager of the Seattle Mariners and becoming only the third black to manage a big league club (preceded only by Frank Robinson and Larry Doby).

While the Dodgers were boasting of Sherry and Wills, their old rivals from the days on the East Coast, the Giants, had come up with a pretty good rookie of their own. Good enough to become everyone's National League Rookie of the Year was San Francisco's Willie McCovey. When Willie received the call to report to the Giants, he was in the shower after playing in a game for the Giants' farm club in Phoenix, Arizona. Told to report the next day, he began his packing chores. Always a first baseman, thoughts ran through his head as to where he might play once he reached San Francisco. You see, he knew the Giants had an excellent first baseman in Orlando Cepeda, the rookie of the year in 1958. Willie knew his league-leading batting average of .372, 29 home runs, and 92 RBIs looked good, but he hoped he wasn't being called up just to sit on the bench. After being up all night, he reported to Seals Stadium, where the Giants were playing before Candlestick Park was complete, and was greeted by Manager Bill Rigney. Rig wasted no time in getting the big rookie into the lineup against the Phillies and Robin Roberts, the ace of the Philadelphia staff. The Giants had just dropped four straight, and Rigney was desperate to find someone to shake up his club. He couldn't have found anyone better. Tired as he was from his all-night trip, Willie got two singles and two triples and started the Giants on their way to a modest four-game winning streak. Cepeda made way by moving to the outfield. In his first seven games, McCovey hit three home runs, scored nine runs, knocked in nine more, and hit at a .467 clip. The start of his 22-year major league career was off to a grand beginning. When the season ended, Willie had hit .354 with 68 hits, including nine doubles, five triples, and thirteen homers. All of this led Manager Rigney to predict that he had found baseball's next .400 hitter. Willie never made it to .400, and except for a .320 season in 1969, never hit .300 again, although he remained a feared hitter, one who could "put it out of the park" at any time. His fielding often left much to be desired, especially on easy ground balls. Lefty all the way, he did, however, gain a reputation as a hard and willing worker. He remained at first base in 20 of his 22 seasons, although he underwent a three-year experiment (1962–64) in the outfield. San Francisco fell in love with the big guy, and he, in turn, with San Francisco. "It's not like the minors, here you can see a different movie every night," he was quoted as saying. It was a long way from that late July start until Willie hung "them" up in 1980. His 18 grand slams are a National

League record and second only to Lou Gehrig's 23. He was only the second player ever to lead his league two years in a row in RBIs and slugging. The "comeback player of the year" 18 years after his start, his early promise bloomed in full and now his smooth and dangerous swing is gone.

While McCovey was being selected for the National League's rookie honors, the last-place Washington Senators of the American League saw their rookie center fielder Bob Allison gain that league's laurels. Allison had had a 25-at-bat, 11-game trial in 1958, as previously mentioned, but he arrived in 1959 to stay, ending his career with the same Senators in Minnesota in 1970. Like McCovey, Allison topped both the six-foot and 200-pound mark although he did his hitting and throwing from the right side. Another hard worker, if one word could describe Allison, it would be desire. Wonderfully well built, he reminded one more of a professional football player. The handsome, mild-mannered guy seldom got anyone mad, as he displayed a boyish charm which made him one of the most popular of the Senators' and later Twins' ballplayers. Often on the receiving end of rival players' kidding, he was called Mr. America, and he would have no part of wearing his uniform pants down around his ankles as was becoming the fad. "Wear your pants long and the umpires have to guess where your knees are," was his answer to his critics. It was his desire to excel which carried him. A batter who could swing with power, he hit 256 lifetime home runs, 30 of them in his rookie year. Four unimpressive minor league seasons only made him work harder to achieve success in the big leagues. Attending Kansas University on a football scholarship, he turned his attention to baseball after his sophomore year. With offers from five teams, including the New York Yankees, he chose the Senators because of the possibilities of quick advancement. His first three years were unimpressive, hitting .256, .233, and .246. Then it was hard work and desire in 1958 and a rewarding .307 average and a chance at the majors. Allison joined his roommate Harmon Killebrew and youngsters Rich Rollins, Bernie Allen, Tony Oliva, and Jimmy Hall with the Twins, as the Senators became known after their move in 1961, to turn Calvin Griffith's club from a doormat to a contender. That also sums up the special attitude that was the dominant trait of young Bob Allison.

There were other good rookies in 1959. The Cleveland Indians brought up a pitcher with a 16-8 record at their Reading Eastern League farm club named Jim Perry. He posted a fine 12-10 record and dispelled any question of a sophomore jinx when he was 18-10 in 1960, tops in the American League. He showed a lot of confidence, as he announced that he was there to stay when he arrived at the Indian camp for the first time. Traded to Minnesota in 1963, the big right-hander won 20 for the Twins in 1969 and 24 in 1970 and closed out his career in 1975 with 215 wins against 174 setbacks. He is the brother of another great hurler, Gaylord Perry, who we will meet later on. Another right-hander who had raised the stock of the Boston Red Sox by leading their pitching staff was Jerry Casale at 13-8. Jerry disappeared after three more seasons during which he only won four games while losing sixteen. Joining Casale was another hurler of great promise named Earl Wilson. Earl pitched excellently for Boston over six-and-a-half seasons before going over to Detroit where he won 22 in 1967. Earl pitched for 11 seasons and realized every pitcher's dream by tossing a no-hitter among his 121 major league wins. Righty Barry Latman, after logging only 59 innings in two previous trips to Comiskey Park, finally earned a permanent spot on the White Sox roster with an 8-5 record and put in portions of 11 seasons. Also, the Pale Hose let Gary Peters into two games and kept letting him into a few games in each of the next four years until he rewarded them handsomely in 1963—but that is getting ahead of our story. Baltimore had 6'2", 215-pound chucker Jack Fisher with a poor 1-6 record, but he improved that to 12-11 in '60. "Fat Jack" was one of those guys who seemed to be on the big league scene for years, in his case 11, but never making much of a mark. Perhaps the most memorable seasons Jack suffered through were spent with the inept New York Mets. In 1965 he was 8-24 to lead his league in losses, and he repeated his performance with a 9-18 record for the same club in 1967. Equally as big, but doomed to spend his career with poor clubs was Ken Johnson who was 1-1 with the Kansas City Athletics.

Of all these fine pitchers to arrive in 1959, the one who turned out the best was a St. Louis Cardinal right-hander named Bob Gibson. A former Harlem Globetrotter basketball player, he was competing for a spot on the Card staff with the likes of long-gone Bill Smith, Bob Miller, Dick Ricketts, Dick Luebke, Frank Barnes, the Blaylocks—Bob and Gary, Phil Clark, and Ernie Broglio. Broglio actually posted a 7-12 record while Gibson was 3-5. The others were forgotten. Broglio lasted eight years, but Gibson stayed for 17 to become one of the all-time National League greats. Gibson never had a great minor league record, as he was 6-4 in 1957, 8-9 in 1958, and 9-9 in 1959, but a close look at his strikeout record will show that he had some promise. The majors worked wonders for him, as he won 251 contests while losing only 174. He had five 20-win seasons, struck out 3,117 batters, to place second on the all-time list, and he hurled 56 shutouts, including 13 in 1968. In World Series play he was even more dominant, winning seven while losing two in three World Series. He was 3-0 in the '67 series against the Red Sox, during which he put on one of the greatest of all World Series exhibitions.

While the pitchers appeared to lead the way among newcomers in 1959, there were others who were making the rookie harvest a good one. Two catchers of note were the Yankees' Johnny Blanchard and the Cardinals' Tim McCarver. Blanchard summered for eight years in Yankee Stadium as a very capable backup backstop for Yogi Berra and Elston Howard before putting in a few career-ending games with K.C. (where many Yankees seemed to wind up), and several games for Milwaukee. McCarver, however, spent 20 years behind the plate for a number of teams, but primarily the Cardinals. A good handler of pitchers, he gained a reputation as a good team man, one who could bolster the spirits of a club, a leader, always popular among his teammates. Tim also played some first base and outfield, and while with the Red Sox in 1974 he appeared as a designated hitter. In 1980 he was quoted as stating that he would attempt a comeback if needed, and when he was activated by the Phillies in September of 1980, he became a four-decade major leaguer.

The Chicago Cubs introduced a fine, highly rated outfielder in Billy Williams from the town with the interesting name of Whistler, Alabama. He was a regular Cub outfielder for 13 of his 18 seasons before switching to first base in his final years. The long line of Cuban players in Washington continued as the Senators introduced the speedy, slick-fielding Zoilo Versalles. This little shortstop put in twelve major league seasons. Kansas City had a .313 hitter in outfielder Russ Snyder. Russ hung around for 12 seasons, most of which were with Baltimore.

Dodger rookie Frank Howard, farmed out to the Victoria Rosebuds of the Texas League, put on one of his power-hitting displays by homering in three innings in a row against Austin. They were all gigantic blasts coming in the fifth, sixth, and seventh innings. Not to be outdone, a rookie for Auburn of the New York-Pennsylvania League, Bob Kaczynski, socked two grand slams in successive at-bats to spark his team to a 9-to-1 win over Erie. Quite a feat for any player to accomplish.

Then there was a farmed-out Washington Senator rookie named Jim Kaat. Only 0-2 with the Nats, he whiffed 18 batters in one game for the Chattanooga farm club, as the Lookouts took a 7-4 win over Nashville. His chief victim was one Ultis "Chico" Alvarez, who was set down five times. Kaat had trials in the nation's capital in '59 and '60 before sticking with the Senators in 1961 after Washington had moved to Minneapolis and become the Twins. Still in the majors in 1980, Kaat has had a marvelous career lasting 22 years through the '80 season. Consider how many pitches that left arm had tossed! He won 25 games in 1966, 21 in 1974, and 20 in 1975. Truly, he is one of the most remarkable players ever to grace the major league scene, another four decade major leaguer. I can't help but be reminded of my stay in

Columbia, South Carolina, during the summer of 1955 when I hear of Chico Alvarez. Columbia was in the Sally League in those days as a Cincinnati Reds' farm team. We have already met Frank Robinson of that club and Inman Veal of the Agusta club in the same loop. As good at fielding as shortstop Veal was, Alvarez was in the Reds' outfield. Chico never made it to the majors, although he had several trials with Cincinnati, but he was a favorite of Columbia fans in '55 mainly for his fielding gems. I will always remember Chico for another reason. The Reds' club lived in a rooming house directly across the street from the house I was boarding in. The house that was home for the Reds had large windows across the front on the second floor and a long stone wall running in front of the house along the sidewalk. On many a hot Southern night, I would be awakened by voices outside, and as my bed was near the window, which faced the Reds' home away from home, I would raise up and peer out to see who in the world would be out there in the middle of the night. There would be Chico sitting on the wall, quite often with company, discussing that evening's game, I suppose! Or I might hear a soft "Chico, Chico" riding on the gentle night air and see one of those big windows light up and Alvarez appear to find what sweet thing might be calling his name. Since the Reds played most of their games at night, you might often find Chico sitting in one of those windows in the daytime, a rookie passing the time of day. Such is the life of a rookie working his way up to the "bigs." I often wonder what Chico was doing the night before he ran into Kaat and sat down five times. Or maybe what he did that night. I don't know if they have walls in Nashville, but I'll bet Chico found some place to reflect upon his performance of that day.

It had been twelve years since Jackie Robinson made his debut with the Brooklyn Dodgers, and it took that long before the cycle of each major league club using their first black player would be completed. The cycle was completed on July 21, 1959, when the Boston Red Sox recalled infielder Elijah "Pumpsie" Green from their American Association club at Minneapolis. He made his bow that evening at Chicago, entering the game in the eighth inning as a pinch runner and finishing up as the shortstop. Pumpsie played for four seasons with the Red Sox with little success and wound up in 17 games with the 1963 New York Mets. Except for being the first Red Sox black player and completing the cycle of each club having a black, he might little be remembered today. Oh, there was the time he and pitcher Gene Conley jumped the team bus on a hot day in New York after a defeat at Yankee Stadium and disappeared for several days, stating their intentions were to go to Israel, for reasons known only to them. "Pumpsie" returned to the Sox from his ill-fated trip after a couple of days, with Conley reappearing several days later.

There they are, the decade-ending crop of the '50s, not a bad group at all. It marked the second consecutive year that rookies from the Senators and Dodgers captured the rookie awards—East Coast, West Coast, old team, transplanted team—strange contrasts. As the era ended, the minor league loops dropped from 24 to 21. Attendance, surprisingly, was up along the minor league trail, not much, but nevertheless up. As we shall soon see, things were up in the majors for the '60s, despite the disappearance of the farm clubs, the rookie breeding grounds.

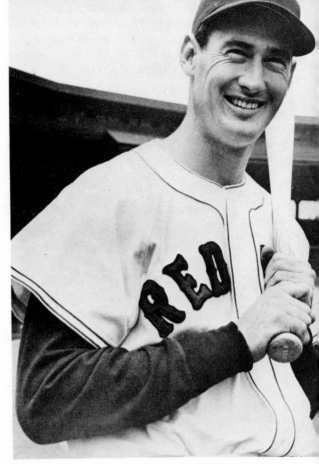

TED WILLIAMS
A brash rookie in the Boston
Red Sox Camp of 1938. He re-
turned in 1939 to make good his
boasts for 19 seasons at Fenway
Park.

JACKIE ROBINSON
Brooklyn Dodger and everyone's
Rookie of 1947, the Hall of Famer
changed the course of baseball and
is seen here in Brooklyn's Ebbets
Field.

PHIL RIZZUTO
New York Yankee shortstop
the 40's and 50's is seen he
in the classic pose of his er
He hit .307 in his rookie ye
of 1941 and was A.L. MVP
1950. A Yankee broadcaster
recent years his last big leagu
season was 1956.

AL KALINE
Detroit Tiger rookie outfielder arrived in 1953 with no minor league
experience and stayed for twenty two
seasons and wound up in baseball's
Hall of Fame.

KEN BOYER

One of three Boyer brothers to perform in the majors, he had a solid rookie season for the St. Louis Cardinals and remained a major league third baseman for fifteen years.

▲ DICK GROAT

A mainstay of the Pittsburgh Pirates and St. Louis Cardinals, he teamed up with Bill Mazeroski to form the national league's best keystone pair in the late 50's and early 60's. Pirates offensive leader in 1960, he won the batting title and was the league's MVP.

◀ TOMMY DAVIS

Hard hitting Dodger outfielder won back to back batting titles in '62 and '63. He was a star on the great Dodger teams of the 60's, always seeming to come through in the clutch.

GEORGE FOSTER

Cincinnati Red outfielder has had some great seasons on his way to becoming one of the top power hitters in baseball. His N.L. MVP award in 1977 made him the fourth of the big Red Machine operatives to cop the award in the decade of the 70's. His home run feats have become legend in the NL.

SATCHEL PAIGE

Seen here in a St. Louis Brown uniform. Was one of the oldest rookies to appear in the major leagues when he posted a 6-1 record pitching for the 1948 Cleveland Indians.

BILL RUSSELL

Durable Los Angeles Dodger shor stop had a memorable debut as Dodger in 1969 when he went 4 fc 4 and hit for the cycle.

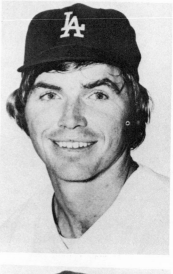

DON SUTTON

Former Los Angeles Dodger righ handed pitcher captured rookie honors in 1966 with a 12-12 record. The all time L.A. strikeout leader, he is the Dodger all time leader in five other pitching departments. Has averaged better than 15 wins per season for 15 years. Declared free agency in 1980 and signed with Houston for 1981.

MICKEY MANTLE
Isn't this a wonderful shot of the New York Yankee Rookie
in 1951?

RON CEY
Power packed Los Angeles third baseman is L.A.'s all time home run leader. His advice is "never be satisfied. Team accomplishments are more important than anything you can do as an individual," he has said. Good advice to young ball players.

▲BROOKS ROBINSON
Appeared at third base for the Baltimore Orioles in his first year in pro ball and stayed around for 23 years. Became a national hero in the 1970 World Series with his fielding and hitting heroics. The finest fielding third baseman of his time and maybe of all time.

◄PEE WEE REESE
One of the most popular Dodgers of all time. His appearance as a rookie triggered a new Dodger era.

DUKE SNIDER

A much heralded rookie outfielder when he arrived at Brooklyn's Ebbets Field in 1947. A product of Branch Rickey's talent hunts he was at his best when New York teams peaked during the 50's. The Giants had their Mays, the Yanks Mantle, but the Bums had their Duke of Flatbush.

LARRY BOWA

Philadelphia shortstop arrived in 1970 and has given the Phillies a decade of excellence defensively. A little guy, 5'10'', 155 lbs., he has had some good seasons at the plate also. In his first ten seasons he committed only 128 errors in 7,087 total chances.

ERNIE BANKS

For nine years a shortstop and for ten more a first baseman Ernie was Mr. Chicago Cub. A fine example for young players, he'd hit with power and was a fine fielder, one of the most popular Cubs of all time. Now a Hall of Famer, he was N.L. MVP in '58 and '59. Strangely he and Ed Mathews each hit 512 lifetime home runs.

GIL McDOUGALD

An infielder with the New York Yankees who won rookie honors in 1951 and led the Yanks into a new era of successes. It was Gil's line drive which struck Herb Score, the great young Cleveland Indian Pitcher.

BILLY WILLIAMS

Muscular Chicago Cub outfielder was the N.L. Rookie of the Year in 1961. One of the top sluggers in Cub history, his 42 home-runs in 1970 set a club record for left handed hitters. Played in 1117 consecutive games, a N.L. record, and hit over 400 home runs.

▲ SANDY KOUFAX

Joined the Brooklyn Dodgers in 1955 at 19. Did little on the mound (36-40 for six years), then put it all together: 4 no hitters (one perfect game), 382 strikeouts in one season, 25 game or better winner three times, three Cy Young awards, five consecutive seasons ERA leader etc., etc., all of which goes to prove rookie seasons do not always indicate what will follow.

◄ ROBERTO CLEMENTE

With only one season of minor league experience, Roberto arrived in 1955 as a Pittsburgh Pirate outfielder and started a career that led to the Hall of Fame, the first of a new breed of Latins to achieve that honor. Died in a plane crash while on a mission of mercy on December 31, 1972.

JUNIOR GILLIAM
National league rookie of the year in 1953 with the Brooklyn Dodgers, he made the switch to L.A. and remained a valuable and most popular Dodger for years.

ROY CAMPANELLA
Brooklyn Dodger catcher from 1948-1957. Did not have a sensational rookie year, but developed into a durable Dodger star until an accident tragically ended his career. His determination in recent years can serve as an inspiration to us all.

DON DRYSDALE
A 5-5 rookie season on the mound hardly indicated what was ahead for this Brooklyn L.A. right hander. 14 seasons, 209 wins and in 1968 he pitched 58 consecutive scoreless innings topping Walter Johnson's 1913 record.

BOB GIBSON
A two time Cy Young award winner for the St. Louis Cardinals and one of the greatest pitchers in their history. His 3-5 record as a rookie in 1959 was no indication of what would follow.

EDDIE MATHEWS
One of the better rookies in Boston National League history, he was a crack third baseman for the Braves in Boston, Milwaukee and Atlanta during the period of franchise shifts. Eddie hit 512 lifetime home runs.

BILLY ROHR
Made a sensational debut with the Boston Red Sox in 1967 by pitching 8 2/3 hitless innings against New York and did little else.

JIM RICE
Teamed up with Fred Lynn in 1975 to form one of the most sensational rookie duos in major league and Boston Red Sox history.

TOM TRESH
Highly touted as New York Yankee rookie, he won rookie honors in 1962 but he never seemed to regain his rookie touch. His father, Mike, was a major leaguer for twelve seasons.

GEORGE BRETT
Kansas City Royal pride and joy hit .125 in a brief major league trial in 1973. Determination in 1980 led to a crack at the magic .400 mark and a MVP award.

THURMAN MUNSON
One of a long line of good rookie catchers to come up with the New York Yankees. He won rookie honors in 1970.

RICK PETERS
Stepped into the Detroit Tiger outfield in 1980 and paid unexpected dividends to the Tiger cause.

MOOKIE WILSON
Popular outfielder of the New York Mets arrived at Shea Stadium in 1980 with an excellent minor league background. The speedster is a prime candidate to be a full fledged major leaguer in the 80's.

MARK FIDRYCH
Talk of the baseball world in 1976 when he won rookie honors. His unusual mannerisms on the mound put new life back into the game.

WALLY BACKMAN
This switch hitting infielder is the New York Mets number one prospect for future stardom. Hit .293 at Tidewater and .323 for the New Yorkers in 1980.

FRED LYNN
His 1975 rookie season with the Boston Red Sox earned him unheard of dual awards as American League MVP and Rookie of the Year.

FRED MARTINEZ
Rookie pitcher for the California Angels in 1980 was one of the bright spots in an otherwise dismal Angel season.

DOUG CORBETT
Doug slipped through the Cincinnati Reds and Kansas City Royals organizations to become a top rookie reliever with the Minnesota Twins in 1980.

HUBIE BROOKS
A New York Met infielder, Hubie is another in the long line of Arizona State ball players to reach the majors. Major league stardom appears to be in his future.

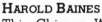

HAROLD BAINES

This Chicago White Sox out-fielder caught the attention of Chisox owner Bill Veeck while a twelve year old in Little League. Has the potential to become a really great hitter.

BRITT BURNS

A fine year with fifteen wins earned rookie honors for this young Chicago White Sox left hander. He credits his father for his pitching successes.

BILL GULLICKSON

His 10-5 won-lost record for the 1980 Montreal Expos combined with a 3.00 ERA earned him Rookie honors.

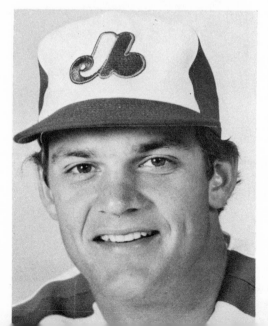

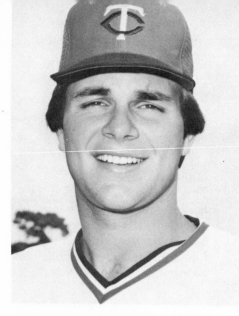

RICK SOFIELD
Rick passed up a football scholarship to Michigan, where he might have been the starting quarterback, to become a Minnesota Twins outfielder and a good one at that.

RENIE MARTIN
Kansas City Royal rookie right hander could manage only a 0-3 record in 1979 but responded in 1980 to win ten games and help K.C. to the A.L. pennant.

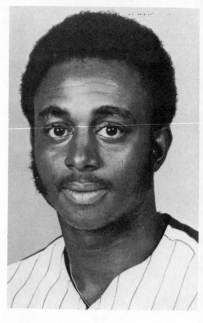

LONNIE SMITH
Gave the Philadelphia Phillies some fine outfielding in 1980 on his way to capturing rookie honors.

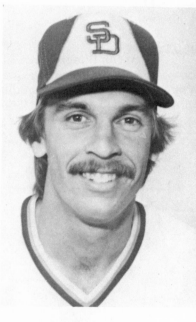

GARY LUCAS
A sinker ball pitcher, Gary recovered from a 1979 broken wrist on his pitching arm to become a top San Diego Padres rookie in 1980.

DAVE SMITH
Houston Astro rookie right hander arrived suddenly in 1980 and posted a neat 1.92 ERA. He should play an important role in future Astro pennant hopes.

AL HOLLAND
Responded well as a San Francisco Giant relief pitcher in 1980 and he should remain a key reliever for the Giants. His team leading ERA was an excellent 1.76.

◀ **DAMASO GARCIA**
Toronto Blue Jay ace rookie second baseman of 1980 teamed up with Alfredo Griffin to form one of the American League's top D.P. combinations.

MARK BOMBACK ▶
New York Met right hander star his career in the minors in 1971. 2 at Vancouver in '79 led him to S Stadium to become the Mets w ningest pitcher in 1980 as a rooki

STEVE HOWE
Lefty pitcher who operated out of the 1980 Los Angeles Dodger bullpen to give them a team leading 17 saves. Named BWAA National League Rookie of the Year.

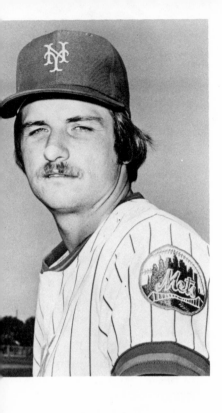

CHARLIE LIEBRANDT
Cincinnati Red pitcher who sky-rocketed on to the Reds mound in 1980 to keep them in contention for the N.L. West title.

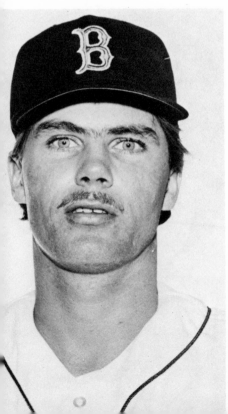

WIN REMMERSWAAL
The Boston Red Sox rookie pitcher was the first native born and trained European to make it in the Major Leagues.

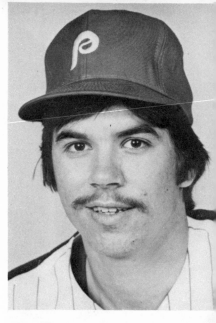

BOB WALK
Philadelphia Phillie right hander made the jump from Double A to the majors in 1980. Started and won the opening game of the World Series. Quite a feat for a rookie.

DAVE STAPLETON
His 1980 rookie season with the Boston Red Sox may be his first as an American League star of the 80's.

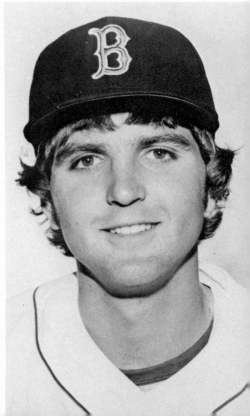

GLENN HOFFMAN
It would seem the Boston Red Sox will have to find a spot for him after his fine rookie season of 1980.

Jim Spencer
The top fielding first baseman in American League history, signing autographs at the Barnes and Noble store in Farmington, Connecticut (photo by Art Ballant).

Joe Charboneau
1980 American League Rookie of the Year and a big hero in Cleveland, relaxing with son Tyson. (photo by Art Ballant)

1960–63: A
New Era

Along with the dawn of a new decade came a new era to the world of baseball. Before the decade would end, changes would take place on the baseball map that would break the old order of things. Gone would be the traditional two eight-club leagues, lost to expansion. Gone from some of the original major league cities would be certain league representation; gone would be a slice of Americana which the traditionalists had lived by for a good portion of their lives. Old rivalries would be replaced by new ones. Despite what some fans would believe, baseball would continue into an era marked by asterisks, but one which would see more fans than ever flocking to new ball parks, parks which lacked the character of their predecessors, but which seated more and not so consequently brought more of the green into the coffers. With ever-rising salaries and costs of doing business the new had to be. How else could a club survive?

Perhaps significant of the ties that bound the beginning of the '60s to the decades past was the rare feat which occurred on September 2, 1960, between a young Washington Senator rookie pitcher, a right-hander named Don Lee and the Boston Red Sox veteran left fielder and slugger Ted Williams. Unusual, indeed, was the Red Sox slugger's home run that evening off the Senator youngster. Williams had completed the rare feat of hitting home runs against a father-son combination. Don Lee's father was the former southpaw hurler with the Cleveland Indians, Chicago White Sox, and the New York Giants (1933–48), Thornton Lee. Williams over the years had hit several homers off Thornton. Neither father nor son was any real slouch, as the elder Lee played sixteen years with a 117-124 record, while son Don played for five clubs over a nine-year career and would wind up in 1966 with a 40-44 slate.

157

There was another family relationship making history on the West Coast when Larry Sherry pitched and his catcher brother, Norm, caught. We have already mentioned Larry, but Norm was a rookie catcher with the Los Angeles Dodgers in 1960. May 7 marked the first time they had teamed up with the Dodgers and also the date they became the tenth such brother act to ever perform in the majors. Norm never really caught that many games during his five major league seasons during which he saw service in 194 contests, 186 of them as a receiver. As we have previously stated, brother Larry was around for eleven seasons.

1960, however, was not all a family affair. In an unprecedented move, the major leagues talked of, and voted for expansion during a year that must be remembered for these startling changes and historic developments. There was a series of events which led up to the expansion. Without going into the long details, there was a continuing, so it seemed, congressional hearing again investigating baseball's status as a sport. The collapse of the proposed Continental League had the major league powers looking toward several of the cities that appeared ready to establish franchises in that new league. These events were followed by the decisions of the American and National Leagues to expand their membership to ten clubs and the actual formation of those new teams. A new era had started for the game.

It was a year of strange events, as a first was accomplished when the Detroit Tigers and the Cleveland Indians pulled off a trade of managers. Joe Gordon went to Detroit and Jimmy Dykes moved to Cleveland. As if that wasn't enough, the Chicago Cubs swapped their manager and their radio announcer, Charlie Grimm and Lou Boudreau.

The National League voted first to expand to ten clubs for the 1962 season. The American League not to be outdone, countered by voting to expand to ten clubs for 1961. The Nationals chose Houston, where preparations had been underway for several years, and realizing how they had missed the New York market since the departure of the Giants and Dodgers, they decided to place a club back in Gotham. The Americans, looking toward the Minneapolis-St. Paul area, voted to transfer the Washington Senators to that area and place a new club in the nation's capital, and after a battle for territorial rights with the National League, add a club in the Los Angeles area. Thus were born the Minnesota Twins and the Los Angeles Angels. The Angels, of course, became the California Angels in later years. Skipping ahead of our story a bit, but so the reader will get things straight, the expansion Washington Senators were moved to Arlington, Texas, for the 1972 season to become known as the Texas Rangers. Of course, the major factor in these moves was the congressional lawmakers' close look at the organized baseball structure and baseball's hopes to shake them from their backs before Congress would dictate its wishes to baseball.

The San Francisco Giants were moving into their new ball park, Candlestick Park, while the American League was attempting to work out a plan to stock their new Washington and L.A. teams. The stocking was worked out so the players would come, on an equal basis, from the eight clubs, with a player to be picked from each farm system all with suitable monetary compensation. A few of our rookies will, of course, come from this pool as we shall see.

1960 would become the final year for Casey Stengel to manage the New York Yankees and would also be the last active season for their long-time general manager, George Weiss, to whom most of the credit goes for building the mighty Yankee clubs of the '30s, '40s and '50s. It might also seem that it was Ted Williams' year to pick on rookies. Not only did he homer off Don Lee, he cracked his 500th career homer off a young Cleveland Indian rookie, Wynn Hawkins. Ted would also join Weiss and Stengel in announcing his retirement at the conclusion of the 1960 season. Before he would leave the major league scene as an active player, he would take advantage of one more rookie hurler. Williams made his farewell appearance at the Red Sox final home contest of the season, a game against the Baltimore Orioles. To celebrate the occasion on his final at bat, he blasted a Jack Fisher pitch into the right field stands for his 29th home run of the season and the 521st of his career. Actually, Fisher, a right-handed chucker, had appeared in 27 games for the Orioles in 1959, but 1960 was the first year he had come into his own. He completed 11 major league seasons before retiring.

Selected as rookies of the year for 1960 were shortstop Ron Hansen of the Baltimore Orioles in the American League and big Frank Howard, an outfielder with the Los Angeles Dodgers in the National League.

The Orioles were in the midst of a youth movement in 1960, and under the guidance of Manager Paul Richards, had climbed from sixth place to second in the standings, as the New York Yankees were winning another American League crown. Blending his kids—pitchers Steve Barber, Chuck Estrada, Jack Fisher, Jerry Walker, and Milt Pappas; infielders Brooks Robinson, Marv Breeding, Jim Gentile, and Ron Hansen—with a veteran cast Richards started Baltimore on a rise to respectability they have continued until today. Of the group, Barber, Breeding, and Estrada were joined by first baseman Buddy Barker and outfielder Dave Nicholson in their major league debuts, while the others had had brief previous trials. Hansen had appeared in twelve games in 1958 and two in 1959 and was the biggest prize in the Baltimore youth program. In his first season, he was the only rookie named by either league to start in the All-Star Game. Pitcher Steve Barber had been signed for a $500 bonus in 1956 and spent three seasons in class D ball before he suddenly developed his control and made the jump straight to the majors. Fifteen years later, he left the majors with a 121-106 record, winning 20 in 1963. First baseman Jim Gentile had been a forgotten man with the Dodgers when he moved over to Baltimore, where he became an immediate star, leading all American League hitters at midseason. In his nine seasons he banged out 179 homers. The Birds traded two top pitchers to the Giants to get outfielder Jackie Brandt. Not a genuine rookie in 1960, he was nevertheless a youngster who played for eleven years in the bigs. Second baseman Marv Breeding was a product of the Baltimore farm system. Brooks Robinson was only 23-years-old and a veteran of five big league seasons. He stayed for 23 seasons while Breeding lasted only four. While Robinson turned out to be the best third baseman for many years in the junior circuit, 1960 was Hansen's year. Shortstop Hansen was signed for a $4000 bonus right out of high school as a slugging third baseman. At the Oriole farm in Stockton, California, he was shifted to shortstop to replace an injured regular. Bird management was not in favor of the move and dispatched a scout out there to shift him back to third. That winter, still a shortstop in the Veracruz League, Hansen worked tirelessly to perfect his skills, having been warned of what a great third baseman Robinson had become. As an 18-year-old in 1957, Hansen was the talk of the Oriole spring camp, but before it ended he ruptured a disc in his back, and a subsequent operation idled him for the year. Returning in 1958, he appeared slower, and with his height and long arms had difficulty in the hitting department. By 1960 he had adjusted his batting style and regained his speed, all of which led him to rookie honors. Hansen was noted for his tremendous range and ability to get the ball away quickly. Of his fifteen big league seasons, five were with Baltimore and the rest with four other American league teams.

Like Hansen, Frank Howard had had a look-see with Los Angeles in 1958 and 1959. Standing six-foot-seven and weighing in at 245 pounds, Howard had been known as the big man with the big ballyhoo. They were speaking of him as "the next Babe Ruth," and he was trying to live up to that billing. The Dodgers thought so highly of him that the L.A. general manager, Buzzie Bavasi, issued orders for no one to discuss batting with him lest he should become confused. The rookie at 23 was hitting the ball with as much power as anyone in the game. Signed for a bonus reported to be $108,000, the former All-American basketball player at Ohio State had put in two seasons of professional baseball, hitting 82 homers and knocking in 235 runs in 285 games, when he finally arrived in L.A. It was agreed that he could become the games' next superstar. The man whose locker was next to Howard's at Dodgertown in that 1960 spring was five foot-nine inch Don Zimmer, current manager of the Texas Rangers, but then a Dodger infielder. Zim liked Howard and decided it would be best they become pals, because as he said, "If Frank doesn't like you he may just pick you up and throw you over the grandstand." Optioned to Spokane, Howard returned to capture the rookie honors, retaining the award on the West Coast among the transplanted New York teams. For 16 seasons, Howard's big bat boomed across the major league scene, first with L.A. and later with Washington. He also had very brief stays with Texas and Detroit. He led the American League in homers in 1968 and 1970 with 44, but in between, in 1969, he hit 48, having to settle for second place as Minnesota's Harmon Killebrew hit 49.

Hansen and his fellow Baltimore rookies and the giant Howard were not the only rookies of note to arrive in 1960. The Dodgers also introduced a young catcher named Doug Camilli whose Dad, Dolph, had been a star first baseman with the old Brooklyn Dodgers. Young Camilli had alternated between catching and the outfield while working his way up through the Dodger farm chain and had spent most of 1960 with the Atlanta club of the Southern Association. Rated as an excellent defensive catcher, Doug played in nine major league seasons with L.A. and Washington, but never gained regular status due mainly to his weak hitting. In recent years, he had coached with several major league clubs. The Dodgers also gave right-handed pitcher Jim Golden a brief look. He had two tries with them and two with Houston and left a 9-13 mark in the major league record books for his efforts. L.A. also introduced three other pitchers in 1960: righty Phil Ortega, who played for ten seasons in the majors and enjoyed some fair success with Washington in the late 60s; Ed Palmquist, another righty who enjoyed very little success in two partial seasons; and Ed Rakow, a right-hander who was fairly well rated. Traded to Kansas City, Rakow enjoyed moderate success for five American League seasons, but never fulfilled his promise and returned to the National League in 1967 for a final fling with Atlanta. After seven seasons, he showed a total 36-47 record.

Of the crowd of rookies who pulled on Dodger blue, perhaps the best over the long haul were a couple of guys with the same last name, Davis. While the rookie of the year in the National League was Frank Howard, the Davis boys appeared on the major league scene for longer periods of time. When the final returns were in, Tommy Davis, an outfielder who occasionally appeared at third or first bases, lasted 18 major league seasons with a fine .294 lifetime batting average. Tommy's namesake, also a Dodger outfielder, was Willie Davis, and he lasted for 17 years with a .279 lifetime BA. While

Tommy led in average, it was Willie who led the duo in power hitting. Howard, by the way, finished up with a .273 lifetime average over 16 seasons, but way outslugging the Davises in home runs with 382 circuit clouts. The Davises were not brothers. Tommy was right-handed all the way, Willie swung from the port side. Tommy had made one appearance with the '59 Dodgers, but arrived to stay in '60, batting a .276, which prompted long-time Dodger outfielder Duke Snider to predict Davis would someday be a cinch to win the league batting crown. Davis fulfilled the prediction by winning the National League crown in 1962 with a .346 mark and repeating the feat a year later with a .326 average. Willie, meanwhile, appeared in only 22 games for L.A. in 1960 after demolishing opposition pitching while with Spokane of the Pacific Coast League. He led the West Coast loop in hits, doubles, and set a league record with 16 triples. On top of that, he drove in 90 runs and stole 33 bases. 1961 found Willie in the Dodger dugout to stay.

The Dodgers' West Coast neighbors, the San Francisco Giants, also had a good crop of youngsters in 1960. Matty Alou, the middle of the three Alou brothers, arrived for four games in the outfield alongside of older brother Felipe. Matty was an off-again on-again outfielder for the Giants until he gained a regular job in 1964. Younger brother Jesus would not come along until 1963. All three brothers were natives of the Dominican Republic, an area from which more big leaguers seemed to be arriving. The Giants were also boasting of three pitchers who were making their first appearances in 1960. A right-hander from Canada with an interesting name, Georges Henri Maranda, a Braves' system castoff who was around long enough to win only one game while dropping four and later appearing with the Minnesota Twins in 1962 with a 1-3 record. A fascinating name, it was a mixture of French and Spanish. The second of the trio definitely has a Spanish name, Juan Marichal, another product of the Dominican Republic. A right-hander, Marichal produced a 6-2 record in only his third season in organized baseball. He had an excellent minor league record with a 21-8 slate with Michigan City of the Midwest League in 1958 and a fine 1.87 ERA. Duplicating his 1959 season with Springfield of the Eastern League in 1959, he led that pitcher's league with an 18-13 record and a 2.39 ERA. Juan was 11-5 at Tacoma when he received the call to report to San Francisco. From then on, it was all glory for the likeable pitcher. He was around for 16 big league seasons during which he posted 18 wins in 1962 and 1971 and had 20-plus-win seasons six times—26 in 1968, 25 in 1963 and 1966, 22 in 1965, and 21 in 1964 and 1969. His final record was 243 wins against 142 losses and a reputation as an all-time great moundsman. The third pitcher of the trio also had a colorful name, Sherman "Roadblock" Jones, a big right-hander.

Roadblock was not too successful as a big leaguer as he boasted a three-year 2-6 record with three clubs. He was 1-1 with the Giants in 1960, matched that record in 1961 with Cincinnati, and was 0-4 with the 1962 New York Mets.

Actually, it is interesting to note that the Giants were making little mention of Marichal as they were preparing for the 1960 season. Giant farm team director Carl Hubbell was sure it would be Maranda, who was 18-6 at Louisville, who would be the potential star. Hubbell was boasting of a Puerto Rican sinkerballer, Julio Navarro, Joe Shipley, a Cardinal discard with a no-windup delivery, and two others with promise, Verle Tiefenthaler and Charlie Davis. Consigned to also-rans were farmhands Gaylord Perry, sidearmer Bob Bolin, bonus boy Ron Herbel, and Marichal. How often it happens that the headlines are grabbed by those who never make it big, while the future stars are not that highly rated.

The Milwaukee Braves introduced their own trio of pitchers in Terry Fox, Don Nottebart, and Ken MacKenzie. To catch them, they gave a two-game trial to the brother of their first baseman Frank Torre, the 18-year-old Joe Torre. The Braves were deep in catchers with Del Crandell, Charley Lau, and bonus beauty Bob "Hawk" Taylor. Torre returned to catch in 112 games in 1961 and remained for 16 more seasons. He gained stardom not only in Milwaukee, but in Atlanta and St. Louis, where he switched to first and third bases, and then wound up with the New York Mets, a team he eventually managed.

The Philadelphia Phillies introduced catcher Clay Dalrymple, shortstop Bobby Wine, and pitchers Dallas Green and Art Mahaffey. Green and Mahaffey were up from the International League champion Buffalo Bisons. Mahaffey was the most successful of the two, going 7-3 while Green was 3-6. A Philadelphia hero in 1962, Art turned in 19 wins for his best of seven big league seasons. Green, of course, returned as the Phillies' manager to lead them to victory in the 1980 World Series.

The St. Louis Cardinals had a large harvest of rookies in 1960, a couple of whom helped them out. Left-handed pitcher Ray Sadecki was 9-9, but won 20 games for the '64 Redbirds. He pitched for 18 seasons for a variety of clubs, ending his career with an almost identical 135-131 won-lost record. The Dominican Republic continued to send major leaguers, as a tall, skinny second baseman named Julian Javier arrived to hold down that position for 12 seasons for the Cards before closing out his career with a year at Cincinnati. Another Latin American made his first appearance at shortstop for the 1960 Cards; he was Julio Gotay. He enjoyed ten partial big league seasons. The other first-time Cardinals were outfielders John Glenn (not the famous astronaut), Doug Clemens, and Gary Kolb. They were joined by catcher

Chris Cannizzaro, who would gain greater fame with the New York Mets and the San Diego Padres, and infielder Bob Sadowski.

The Chicago Cubs had seven rookies in their dugout who were of some note: Catcher Dick Bertell; outfielders Dan Murphy, Al Heist, and Nelson Mathews; and two fair pitchers in John Goetz and Jim Brewer. Brewer spent 17 years in the big time, mostly as a relief pitcher with the Cubs and Dodgers. Pitcher Dick Ellsworth, who had a brief trial in 1958, also arrived to stay. The premier rookie for the Cubs was third baseman Ron Santo. The youngster did the Cub third base chores for 16 seasons before winding up for one season with their American League counterparts, the White Sox. Santo had played only one-and-a-half minor league seasons before he arrived at Wrigley Field where he was a Chicago favorite. Before long, Santo was being compared to the Cubs' former great third baseman, Stan Hack. Actually, in the end, Hack had played one more season and wound up with a lifetime BA of .301 to Santo's .277. Santo was the better power hitter of the two, however. Santo possessed that important ingredient needed to be a successful major leaguer, desire. As a youngster in his native Seattle, Washington, he announced to all who would listen that, "I'm going to be a big leaguer some day." Santo gained a reputation as being cocky, but was eager and dedicated to improvement as a player. Cub manager Lou Boudreau handed the third base chores to Santo immediately upon Ron's arrival from Houston. The Cubs, mired in a losing streak, were to face the Pittsburgh Pirates at Forbes Field against the Buc aces Bob Friend and Vernon Law that day. Singling off a Friend fastball in his first trip to the plate, Santo later produced two more hits—a double and a home run—as the Cubs snapped a nine-game losing streak. Later that season in a twin bill against the Phillies, he homered to give the Cubs a 2-to-1 victory in the opener and returned to hit a grand-slam home run to win the nightcap 7 to 3.

Speaking of Pittsburgh, they had rookie pitcher Joe Gibbon and a highly rated shortstop in Tony Barone, neither of whom turned out to be any threats to be enshrined at Cooperstown.

Completing this bumper crop of National League rookies were the crew which made their debuts with the Cincinnati Reds. A couple of this group turned out to be pretty fair major leaguers for a few years. How many recall first baseman Rogelio Alvarez, outfielder Tony Gonzalez, shortstop Chico Cardenas, and catcher Joe Azcue, all from the island of Cuba? To go along with this Cuban invasion was a second baseman from Venezuela, Elio Chacon. The Reds certainly had a Latin flavor to match some of the clubs the Washington Senators had during the '40s. The Reds also had rookie outfielder Joe Gaines and pitchers Jim Maloney and Duane Richards. Maloney pitched for the Reds for 11 seasons, winning 23 in 1963 and 20 in 1965, and called it a career after an 0-3 record with the 1971 California Angels. Of the others, Azcue caught for five American League clubs for 11 seasons. Gonzalez was traded to the Phillies before the season was over for a variety of players, including the former Cincinnati favorite, Wally Post. Shortstop Cardenas played for 16 seasons split between the two big leagues. The others accomplished little except for Chacon, who will be remembered as the New York Mets' first shortstop in 1962 before bidding goodbye to the majors.

The 1960 harvest in the American League could not match the National League newcomers. Except for those previously mentioned at Baltimore, the Boston Red Sox presented the largest group, as they struggled along with their youth movement under manager Pinky Higgins. Three journeymen pitchers saw their names added to the list of major leaguers—Tom Borland, Arnold Earley, and Tracy Stallard. Stallard gained the most notoriety of the trio, even if it was of a negative nature. The record books recorded one Evan Tracy Stallard as giving up home run number 61 to New York's Roger Maris on October 1, 1961, to live forever in the annals of the trivia quizzes generated by baseball buffs. An outfielder of some note was Lou Clinton, and an infielder of little note was Marlin Coughtry. Behind the plate for 36 Bosox games was Ed Sadowski, breaking in the same season as his brother Bob of the St. Louis Cardinals. It would seem that the major leagues have had their share of three-brother acts. There were the three DiMaggios, the three Alous, and the three Boyers, but how many remember the three Sadowskis? Ed was the oldest and performed in parts of five seasons; brother Bob, a pitcher, would break in with the 1963 Milwaukee Braves and wind up with the Boston Red Sox in 1966; and brother Ted was a pitcher with the Washington Senators, also breaking in in 1960. Add to them infielder Bob Sadowski, who broke in with the Cardinals in 1960 as previously mentioned, and you have a totally confusing picture. Who said it was a SAD situation?

Speaking of Washington, they produced outfielder Lamar Jacobs, hard-hitting first baseman Don Mincher, who lasted 13 years, and pitcher Rudy Hernandez. Detroit contributed a couple of good rookies in infielder Dick McAuliffe, an American League steady for 16 seasons, and a pitcher with a lot of promise in righty Phil Regan. After six decent American League summers, Regan spent seven more in the National League with his final season split between Chicago's White Sox and Cubs. The White Sox had a good outfielder in Floyd Robinson, and Kansas City produced outfielder Lee Posada and pitcher Dave Wickersham, who they traded to the Detroit Tigers after the '63 season. Dave proceeded to hang up 19 wins for the 1964 Motor City nine. The New York Yankees came up with little in 1960, though there was Deron Johnson, who came up as a third baseman, switched to the outfield, and followed the familiar path to first base and designated hitter before retiring 15 years later. They also had a couple of pitchers of promise in Bill Short and Bill Stafford, neither—to make a play on words—filled the bill. Short pitched for six seasons, each with a different club, and Stafford pitched for eight years, his best being 1961 and 1962 when he produced identical 14-and-9 records for the New Yorkers. Before we leave Short, the Philadelphia Phillies had a no-relation pitcher named Chris Short, who had made three appearances with them in 1959, coming into his own in 1960. He enjoyed four good seasons in his total of 15, when he won 17, 18, 20, and 19.

The Cleveland Indians hoped for big things from outfielders Walt Bond and Ty Cline. Bond enjoyed two successful years at Houston during his six seasons, and Cline, never living up to another famous Ty named Cobb, drifted around the bigs for twelve years. The Cuban influence made itself known in the Cleveland infield in the person of Mike de la Hoz, who was a utility infielder for nine years, five of which were in the National League. Left-handed pitcher Dick Stigman made his bow with a 5-11 record in the Teepee, where he remained for two seasons before moving on for four with Minnesota and one in Boston.

1960 also brought some short-lived glory to several minor league rookies. Eighteen-year-old Bob Sprout, a left-handed pitcher with Decatur, turned in a spectacular pitching performance when he struck out 22 Waterloo batters on his way to hurling a no-hitter. Sprout was a budding Detroit Tiger farmhand. Then there was 19-year-old Rudy Tretter of Fresno of the California League. He got a victory without throwing a pitch. With his team behind 5 to 4 in the top of the ninth against Bakersfield, he came into the game in relief and picked a runner off first base for the third out. Fresno rallied in the bottom of the inning to take a 6-to-5 win. Rudy got credit for the win without having thrown a pitch. Then there was Dave Nidiffer of Modesto, who hit a three-run homer over the fence and failed to touch home plate, a fact that was not overlooked by the Fresno club. Dave not only lost the homer, but his club lost the game 11 to 10 when he was retired at home while sitting on the dugout bench.

1961 was a year long to be remembered by American League followers as the junior circuit expanded from eight to ten teams and replaced the traditional 154-game schedule with a new 162-game slate. The National League would not adopt the 162-game format until 1962. The American League installed teams in Los Angeles and Washington, the latter to placate Senator fans who had seen their original Senators move on to Minnesota to become the Twins. The astute follower of baseball could begin to see a trend developing in the early Sixties, as the line became more evident between the two major leagues in their recruitment of black and Latin players. We have already mentioned the large number of Latins entering the National League. Leading hitters in the National League were increasingly coming from the black and Latin ranks, while the whites still prevailed in the American League, despite expansion. American League pitching depth was certainly weakened by expansion and hitting overall seemed to drop, a fact which escaped most when covered up by Detroit's Norm Cash with a .361 average and the Yankees' Roger Maris and Mickey Mantle assaulting Babe Ruth's home run mark. In fact, Cash's batting mark would be the highest for the first nine years of the decade in the American League, and the only above .330 until Tony Oliva hit .332 in 1969. Cash led the Tigers to 101 wins, good enough to finish second, eight wins below New York's 109. The Yankees were on their way to another five-year dominance under new manager Ralph Houk. Pitcher Whitey Ford's 25 wins coupled with excellent relief work by Luis Arroyo, the late season hitting of catcher Elston Howard, and the home run antics of Maris and Mantle assured the Yanks of their second consecutive pennant and an easy World Series win over the Cincinnati Reds.

The new American League schedule suddenly produced an unexpected problem for the baseball record keepers. With Maris and Mantle challenging Babe Ruth's record 60 home runs, controversy mounted about what would happen should one of them top the Babe's 60. Would it really be a new record if it took the additional eight games to surpass the Babe? Commissioner Ford Frick ruled that it would indeed be a new record if Ruth's total was surpassed in 154 games. If it were broken in a later game, it would be a new record but an asterisk would be placed in the record books to indicate that it had required more than 154 games. Mantle, due to injuries, dropped off the pace, but Maris continued, hit number 59 in his 154th game, number 60 in his 158th game, and 61 in his 162nd game. He hit number 60 off Baltimore's Jack Fisher, who we met earlier when he gave up Ted Williams' last homer, and number 61 came at Yankee Stadium in the fourth inning of the 162nd game off the Red Sox' Tracy Stallard. Thus Maris, who played in 161 of the Yankees' 163 games (they had an early season tie), gained himself an asterisk.

In the National League, the Cincinnati Reds of manager Fred Hutchinson surprised everyone by copping the crown, jumping from sixth place to do it. The Rhinelanders were the fourth different club in as many years to take the flag, showing the baseball public just how balanced that league was. To show you what a strange club the Reds were, they suffered eight straight losses in the early season, only to follow that up with nine consecutive wins. Forty-year-old Warren Spahn won his 300th major league game, and the

Chicago Cubs tried a system of rotating coaches in the manager's seat, an experiment which resulted in no significant improvement in their club. When your favorite team suffers tough going, consider what manager Gene Mauch and his Philadelphia Phillies went through in 1961. In early May they had a ten-game losing streak, and if you don't consider that bad enough, starting in late July they lost 28 out of 29 games, including a modern day record of 23 setbacks in a row.

With expansion opening additional spots in the majors, more recruits than usual were receiving their baptism on the major league diamonds. Of 114 new players, the American League introduced 75. While they came in numbers, it didn't seem that they necessarily came in quality. Two of the most brilliant entries were made by rookies with Kansas City and Milwaukee. Kansas City signed an 18-year-old pitcher, the son of a former major leaguer, right out of high school. Young Lew Krausse banked a reported $125,000 bonus and reported directly to manager Hank Bauer of the Athletics. Lew's dad, Lew senior, had pitched for Connie Mack's 1931–32 Philadelphia Athletics with a combined 5-1 record. The much-heralded appearance of young Krausse was set for mid-June against the Los Angeles Angels at K.C. The right-hander just out of high school blanked the Heavenly Ones 4 to 0 on three singles. "Lord, what is the league coming to when a high schooler can step in and accomplish this?" was the cry heard across the land. Finishing with a 2-5 record, Lew went to the minors to polish his skills and did not return until 1964. After 12 seasons, he had a 68-91 slate to go along with his memory of that June night in 1961 under the lights in Kansas City, when the world was his. The Milwaukee Braves called up Mack "The Knife" Jones from their Louisville farm club in mid-July and put him in the lineup against the St. Louis Cardinals. He responded with four consecutive hits in the game at St. Louis' Busch Stadium to tie the National League record for hits at the start of a career. Two other National Leaguers got off to good starts, as each hit a home run in their initial plate appearance, Don Leppert of the Pittsburgh Pirates and Cuno Barragan of the Chicago Cubs; both were catchers. Neither did much in the majors and soon disappeared. For Barragan, it was his only major league home run. Leppert hit 14 more over a four-season period.

The baseball writers and *The Sporting News* both selected Boston Red Sox right-handed pitcher Don Schwall as their Rookie of the Year in the American League. *The Sporting News* also chose a player in a dual rookie award format, and he was Kansas City shortstop Dick Howser. The two groups also agreed on Chicago Cub outfielder Billy Williams in the National League and *TSN* added Cincinnati Red hurler Ken Hunt, a right-hander, to their selections. While these players were selected as tops for 1961, a special tip of the baseball cap should be awarded to a rookie second baseman for the Cincinnati Reds. Few fans today will remember the unique accomplishment of Jim Baumer. Jim appeared in only ten games for the '61 Reds, nine of them at second base. Jim had made a previous eight-game appearance with the Chicago White Sox, seven games of which were at shortstop. What is unique about that? Many players enjoy only brief stays in the major leagues. Well you see, Jim's appearance with the White Sox was in 1949—better than a decade separated his appearances, and he still met rookie qualifications in his second try.

Right-hander Don Schwall was brought up by the Red Sox from their Seattle farm club in mid-May. He defeated every club in the league at least once, except Detroit, whom he did not face. He turned in a 15-7 record overall and had a sensational 10-2 record at Fenway Park. The sinkerball pitcher had attended Oklahoma University, where he was much better known for his basketball ability before being signed by the Bosox. The 6'6", 200 pounder had outrebounded and outscored basketball great Wilt Chamberlain in a game against Kansas while performing on the court for Oklahoma University. He was 7-6 with Waterloo in his first season and was tied as the top minor league winner of the year at 23-6 for Alpine in his second season. A 16-9 record at Minneapolis in 1960 and a 3-1 card at Seattle in early 1961, after an impressive spring training stint, earned him his promotion to the Red Sox. He represented the Bosox in the second All-Star Game of 1961 played at Fenway Park, the only Red Sox to appear in the rain-shortened 1 to 1 tie. He did, however, give up all five hits that the National Leaguers made in the contest during his three-inning mound appearance. A graduate of Oklahoma, Schwall was a teacher of typing and shorthand. Schwall remained in the majors for seven seasons, but never enjoyed the success of his rookie year. The Sox traded him off to Pittsburgh in November, 1962, along with catcher Jim Pagliaroni for pitcher Jack Lamabe and slugger Dick Stuart.

Joining Schwall for American League rookie honors was Kansas City shortstop Dick Howser. Heady, gutsy, and an excellent student of the game, Howser batted .280, stole 37 bases and represented the Athletics in the All-Star Game. During eight seasons, he went from the A's to the Cleveland Indians in 1963 and then to the New York Yankees in 1967, never again repeating the great rookie year he had at K.C. Following his retirement as an active player in 1968, he became the Yankees' third base coach, replacing the legendary Frank Crosetti, and remained there for ten seasons. He left the New Yorkers after the 1978 season to coach the baseball team at Florida State University but the call of the major leagues was too great, and he returned to the Yankees as their manager in 1980 to lead them to a division champion-ship. Only an average player, he developed skills which he utilized to carve out a fine baseball career.

The National League selection for rookie pitching honors was right-handed pitcher Ken Hunt of the Cincinnati Reds. Ken posted a 9-10 record with the National League champions and a 3.96 ERA. A prime prospect in the Reds' system, he had been slated to play in Indianapolis after a 16-6 log at Columbia where the bonus beauty had led the circuit in strikeouts with 221 and apparently had overcome his tendency toward wildness. He had been an unanimous choice to the Sally League All-Star team. At Cincy, he managed 75 strikeouts in 136 innings while walking 66. Ken was in the fight for the fourth spot on the Reds' 1962 pitching staff, but wound up with San Diego where he was 1-2 and Macon where he was 1-6, never again to return to the majors.

The best of the rookies to receive official honors in 1961 was the Chicago Cubs' outfielder Billy Williams. It was Bill's third try at the Cub outfield, as he had been up for cups of coffee in 1959 and 1960. Billy put in all or parts of 16 seasons with the Cubs and two more with the Oakland A's before he put away his bats in 1976. In those eighteen years he compiled a lifetime batting average of .290. A slender man with great strength, he could really snap the bat. A good power hitter, he banged out 426 home runs, 88 triples, and 434 doubles during his career. In his early career, he looked at fly balls as a threat and grounders as an adventure, but slowly he developed into a good out-fielder. No less an authority than Reds manager Fred Hutchinson predicted in 1961 that Williams would become a great hitter. Only once in his Cub career did he dip below his rookie average of .277 and then by only one point. Five times he hit over .300 and in 1972 led the National League in batting with a .333 mark. His 37 home runs that year has been the most by any National League batting leader since Hank Aaron hit 39 in 1959. In 1970 Billy hit 42 round trippers. A traditionally slow starter, Williams found himself benched in early '61 because he was hitting only .143, but he rebounded as the season progressed. With that short compact swing he was able to wait on a pitch until the last second, one of the classic swings in baseball. A careful observer of opposing pitchers, he made it a habit which paid handsome dividends. Signed for a free bus ticket to tryout camp and a 15¢ cigar for his dad, he was one of the best bargains the Cubs ever had. From his first spring training camp with them in Mesa, Arizona, to Wrigley Field, it was obvious that the Cubs had to find a spot for Billy. He came to play and overcame early batting and fielding problems.

There were other good rookies making the move into the big leagues in 1961. The Boston Red Sox, in addition to pitcher Schwall, had several. Joining Schwall on the mound was Galen Cisco, a former football player who had starred in the 1958 Rose Bowl as a linebacker for Ohio State. He had started the 1961 season at Seattle, where he had a 6-1 record and in his last four outings there had allowed only one run. All of his outings were complete games. His seven-year major league stint netted only 25 wins against 56 losses. Joining Cisco and Schwall was a young twirler who had grown up in the shadow of Fenway Park, Wilbur Wood. A southpaw, he was rated the best prospect to come out of New England in years, as most major league teams expressed interest in him. Noted for his remarkable control, he jumped directly from Winston-Salem of the Carolina League to the Sox. In a little better than three seasons he produced an 0-5 record in Boston. The Sox traded him to Pittsburgh, where he faired no better, and the Pirates sent him to the Chicago White Sox where he was a hero for twelve years. During one four-year stretch he won twenty or more games each year. For seventeen years, he pulled on a major league uniform and took the mound. The Red Sox also had a pair of roommate rookies on that 1961 outfit. One was a decent second baseman, the other an outfielder and a sure-bet Hall of Famer. Chuck Schilling was the brilliant young infielder who ranged far and wide around the keystone base. He led the league with 854 fielding chances, and his eight errors set a new league low for second basemen. Of the eight errors only two were on ground balls; two were on missed throws while covering second, and four were on throws he made. Schilling played five seasons for Boston before weak hitting did him in. The future Hall of Famer was Carl Yastrzemski who was still playing for the Red Sox in 1980. Completing his 20th season for the Sox, he surpassed Ted Williams (the man he replaced in left field) in all-time service to the Bosox. He has done just about everything for the Sox in those twenty years, has led them to two pennants, won a triple crown, an MVP award, batting championships (1963, 67, 68), was the first American Leaguer to get 400 home runs and 3000 hits, played several positions, won awards by the carload, and appeared in numerous All-Star Games. In 1961, he joined the Sox with only two years of professional experience and under great pressure to live up to his advanced notices. A graduate of Merrimack College, he must be rated as an all-time baseball great, something that was hoped for back in 1961; but little did anyone realize the durability he possessed would carry him as far as the 1981 season. Many a youngster could learn a valuable lesson from Yaz as to the benefits of clean living and strenuous training programs. Again, we can see that the rookie of the year awards, as chosen by the experts, do not always insure the winner the greatest fame over the long haul.

With expansion, the Americana League crop of rookies was understandably greater than the National League's. The Kansas City Athletics led the way with 14 newcomers, including the previously mentioned Howser and Krausse. None of the 14 made much of an impression. Among the group was a pitcher who lasted only three seasons and left the major league active ranks with a 6-6 record. Strangely, however, he is still active in the American League and completed his twelfth season as an umpire in 1980. Bill Kunkel is now one of the American League's umpire crew chiefs. Another rookie pitcher on the A's staff was John Wyatt, who put in seven seasons including several with the Boston Red Sox, for whom he won the sixth game of the 1967 World Series. Wyatt's final season in the majors saw him return to the A's, this time, however, in Oakland. Perhaps the most successful, at least in his first season, was left-hander Jim Archer who was 9-15; 0-1 in '62, he faded from the major league scene.

The Detroit Tigers welcomed ten rookies, several of whom were pretty good. There was Jake Wood, a second baseman who showed the poise of a veteran despite setting several strikeout records. While a minor leaguer, Wood was a consistent .300-plus hitter. Like Wyatt, Wood also lasted for seven seasons, but could only average .250 against big league pitching. Catchers always seemed to do well in Detroit, and newcomers Mike Roarke and Bill Freehan were no exceptions. Roarke, a former Brave farmhand, was expected to make a strong bid for the first-string job in his first solid big league trial. At 30 years of age, he had spent four years in triple A ball. Mike never became more than a backup catcher in his four seasons in the big time. Freehan spent most of his '61 season with Knoxville with a late-season four-game trial. Denver was his home port in 1962 where he divided his time catching and first basing, something he would also do after he won the Tiger catching assignment in 1963, replacing vet Dick Brown. For 14 more seasons Freehan proved to be one of the American League's top catchers, both offensively and defensively. Wycliff "Bubba" Morton, an erratic outfielder, arrived and he, like several other of his '61 classmates, lasted seven seasons. Pitchers Fred Gladding, 13 years in the big time, and Howie Koplitz were the only other young Tigers of note.

Baltimore had two kid pitchers, Jim Lehew and Johnny Papa, who were highly rated but accomplished little. Papa only did more to confuse people into thinking he was Oriole's pitcher Milt Pappas than he did on the mound. The Birds did call up a young giant of an outfielder for a late season look-see by the name of John "Boog" Powell. He returned in 1962 and was an

American League fixture for fifteen seasons before a final fling with the L.A. Dodgers. Finishing his career batting .266, he also banged out 330 lifetime home runs and was one of the majors' most feared hitters. Among the five new White Sox pitchers, Joel Horlen turned out to be the best. Former manager Al Lopez was calling him potentially the league's best right-hander. With highly impressive ERAs in the minors, he was often troubled by a scarcity of runs by his teammates, rather than poor pitching on his part. Twelve seasons brought him an almost identical 116-117 record. Outfielder Mike Hershberger had a look-see for the first of his eleven American League seasons. The top New York Yankee prospects were all pitchers, Al Downing, Hal Reniff, and Rollie Sheldon. Downing never reached the potential anticipated by the Yankees, although he did have five moderately successful seasons in the pinstripes. After splitting the 1970 season between Oakland and Milwaukee, he enjoyed his best season in 1971 by winning 20 games for the Los Angeles Dodgers, in one of baseball's all-time great comebacks. From then on, until his retirement in 1977, it was mostly downhill. Reniff, with a strong arm, good control, and a sharp breaking ball, later did some good relief work for the Yanks. Like Reniff, Sheldon was also regarded as a Yank top prospect, but he also was plagued with arm problems.

Among the top prospects with the expansion Los Angeles Angels were pitcher Dean Chance, shortstop Jim Fregosi, catcher Bob Rodgers, and third baseman Tom Satriano. Chance lasted eleven seasons in the American League and was regarded as one of the top hurlers despite his 1961 0-2 record. He had pitched a sensational 18 no-hitters in high school before he was signed by the Oriole organization. The Angels took him in the expansion draft from Baltimore. He did pitch a no-hitter as a major leaguer while with the Twins in 1967, a season in which he also won twenty games for the second time in the majors. Fregosi, a one-time Red Sox farmhand, was a fine shortstop before shifting to third and first bases in the last eight of 18 seasons in the majors. He recently has been a highly regarded manager of these same Angels, a team he took to their first division title in nineteen years in 1979 despite their high rate of injuries. Rodgers' career spanned nine seasons during which he was noted for his fine handling of the Angel pitching staffs. Originally an outfielder, Bob shifted to catching during his minor league career. His first major league home run was a grand slam, hit in late 1961.

The other expansion club, the Washington Senators, came up with little among nine new rookies. Catcher Ken Retzer and outfielder Chuck Hinton were decent hitters, with Hinton enjoying a .310 season in 1962, his second of eleven. Retzer lasted only four years. Tops in the long haul was Ed Brinkman who was at third base for three games, but shifted to shortstop in 1962 where he was a fixture in the majors for fourteen more seasons. Always a fine defensive player, it was at the plate where Brinkman fell down. Great range and a fine arm, developed while a high school pitcher, were Ed's strong points. The original Senators, who had moved on to become the Minnesota Twins, tried a number of rookies in '61. Tops among them were pitchers Jerry Arrigo and Lee Stange and third sacker Rich Rollins. After four tries with the Twins, the lefty Arrigo moved on to Cincinnati where he spent the bulk of his ten major league seasons. Strange, a gutsy little right-hander also lasted ten seasons and enjoyed success during the later part with the Boston Red Sox as a starter as well as a reliever. A pitching coach for the Red Sox today, he is popular and respected by Sox hurlers wherever he goes. To know Lee is to like him. Rollins, like his fellow rookies, lasted ten seasons, primarily as a good fielding and hitting third baseman. Rollins had less than a full season's experience in the minors. The Cleveland Indians came up with outfielder Al Luplow, who had a spotty seven-year career, perhaps best remembered by fans in Boston for a fantastic catch he made falling over the center field bullpen wall to take a home run away from the Sox' Dick Williams. It was one of the all-time great Fenway Park catches. Steve Hamilton, a relief pitcher, made his debut, but he enjoyed more successes on diamonds away from the shores of Lake Erie. "Sudden Sam" McDowell, a left-handed fireballer, pitched his first big league game. In 15 seasons, Sam set down 2453 batters on strikes, leading the American League in that area five times while winning 141 games against 134 defeats.

The National League had far fewer quality rookies in 1961; as a matter of fact, they had very "slim pickins." Pittsburgh had an outfielder who would switch to first base in '62 and become a decent player, often flirting with a .300 average, in Donn Clendenon. Donn had great speed on the bases for a big man and was a skilled operative in the field. Donn had had a football offer from the Cleveland Browns and a basketball bid from the Harlem Globetrotters before turning to baseball. The St. Louis Cardinals came up with pitcher Ray Washburn who hurled for ten seasons. The Milwaukee Braves had a rookie battery in pitcher Tony Cloninger, who won 24 for the 1965 edition of the Braves and left after twelve seasons in the senior circuit with a neat 113-97 slate, and catcher Phil Roof. Roof was a decent defensive, weak-hitting receiver for fifteen seasons with a variety of clubs. The Reds also had two good catchers to go along with the previously mentioned rookie pitcher Ken Hunt. Jerry Zimmerman, after a nine-season minor league career in the Boston Red Sox organization from whom he had reportedly received a $77,000 bonus, had a 76-game rookie season with the Reds. The Reds then traded him to the Minnesota Twins where he spent seven seasons.

John Edwards went on to be a National League catcher for thirteen more seasons after his rookie year of 1961 in the Rhineland.

The Los Angeles Dodgers introduced Ron Perranoski out of Michigan State, a good major league reliever for fourteen years, Tim Harkness, a so-so first baseman, and outfielders Carl Warwick, who they wound up sending to St. Louis, and Gordon Windhorn, who had had a seven-game trial with the New York Yankees in 1959. Gordie, who had demonstrated a great potential for years after leaving Arizona State University, never lived up to his promise in three partial major league seasons. The Phillies gave a trial to catcher Clarence "Choo Choo" Coleman, who would become more endeared to New York Met fans in 1962 and '63. The Mets had selected him in the draft from the Phils. Relief pitcher Jack Baldschun also got his start in Philly in '61, the first of nine seasons. The Chicago Cubs gave a four-game trial to a young outfielder named Lou Brock. In 1964 the Cubs traded Brock to the St. Louis Cardinals and he immediately developed into a base-stealing whiz. Ten years later, Brock would steal 118 bases to break Maury Wills' record of 104, to establish a major league single-season high, and to vault into the lead as the all-time leader in stolen bases. When our decade of the '60s began, Brock was still a student at Southern University in New Orleans, Louisiana, and had yet to break into pro ball. He spent most of the 1961 season at St. Cloud of the Northern League. Brock played for nineteen years, retiring in 1979, with an excellent chance to enter baseball's Hall of Fame. Left-handed pitcher Jack Curtis was 10-13, but was gone two seasons later. The San Francisco Giants had eight rookies break in, the most of any National League club. Pitcher Bob Bolin was the best of three hurlers, lasting 13 seasons with a final 88-75 record. He was joined by Jim Duffalo and Dick LeMay. Catchers Tom Haller and John Orsino were aboard the Giant club also. Haller, a former University of Illinois football quarterback, was a regular catcher for most of his twelve major league seasons and a decent hitter. Orsino, who was once billed as a long-ball hitter, never lived up to his advanced billing, although he was the regular Oriole backstop in 1963, and did hit nineteen home runs while batting .272. Others included first baseman-outfielder Bob Farley, infielder Ernie Bowman, and second baseman Chuck Hiller. Hiller had eight years in the majors to become the best of this trio.

A banner total of 147 rookies made their first major league appearances in 1962. One would believe that the expansion of the National League to ten teams would have contributed greatly to this high of newcomers, but strangely, the senior circuit had only one more neophyte than the American League. Making their debuts were some of the highest priced bonus players of all time. Third baseman Bob Bailey of the Pittsburgh Pirates got into fourteen games at the tail end of the season after a fine year at Columbus that saw him being named the minor league player of the year. It was the first of 17 years that Bob, who received a reported $175,000 to sign, played in the major leagues. A couple of bonus boys from Santa Clara University got their first taste of the big time—pitcher Bob Garibaldi at San Francisco and shortstop Ernie Fazio at Houston. Denis Menke, an infielder who signed back in 1958 with the Milwaukee Braves, made his debut. Former University of Mississippi football star Jake Gibbs got into a couple of games with the New York Yankees at third base. He returned in 1963 as a catcher, where he remained until his retirement in 1971. Tom Fletcher, a bonus boy pitcher with the Detroit Tigers, made it into one game for two innings, his only major league outing after pocketing an estimated $60,000. Another bonus baby was the popular hero of the New York Mets, Ed Kranepool, who spent his entire major league career of seventeen years with the New Yorkers. Then there was Dave DeBusschere, the bonus pitcher of the Chicago White Sox, who was a baseball and basketball star from Detroit University. Dave spent only parts of two seasons with the Pale Hose, compiling a 3-4 record before he decided his future was in the NBA, where he starred for several years. Infielder Cap Peterson, who later converted to the outfield, played four games for San Francisco, the first of eight years. Most successful of all the bonus boys who arrived in 1962 was left-handed pitcher Dave McNally of Baltimore. He came up late in September from Elmira of the Eastern League to toss a two-hit shutout against Kansas City, winning 3 to 0. Dave stayed around for 14 seasons, winning 22, 20, 24, and 21 four years in a row (1968–71). His final totals were 184-119.

There were two other rookies who broke in with unusual rookie seasons in 1962. Kansas City had an outfielder from the Dominican Republic named Manny Jimenez, who had been a great minor league hitter. When he broke in, it appeared that major league pitching would also pose no mystery to him either, as he was leading the American League in batting with a .350 average halfway through the season. He wound up hitting .301, and from then on went downhill for his remaining six seasons in the big leagues. Then there was one of the most colorful players to come upon the major league scene, Robert "Bo" Belinsky. Bo had been in the minors for six seasons, and in one year, 1959, he played for four different clubs. He broke in with the Los Angeles Angels in '62, winning 10 and dropping 11. This represented highs in both categories for him in his eight seasons. Among those ten wins, however, was a no-hitter, a 2-to-0 victory over the Baltimore Orioles in early May. He struck out nine batters on the way to his gem. There were times when it appeared various Hollywood starlets were more important than the

Angels or the four other clubs Bo appeared for. Nevertheless, not many rookies even came close to no-hitters in their rookie year, but then again there are very few as colorful as Bo Belinsky.

1962 was again a year which featured expansion, this time in the National League, following a similar move by the American League in 1961. It certainly heralded the beginning of a new era in baseball. With the Nationals moving to Houston, a new territory was opened for the first time to major league baseball—Texas, long a hotbed of minor league baseball and birthplace of many former major leaguers. The new Texas entry was known as the Houston Colt .45s. Today they are the Houston Astros. After a four-year absence, the senior circuit returned to their old stomping grounds, New York City. They reopened the Giants' old home in the famed Polo Grounds and unveiled something known as the New York Mets, hoping to attract old Giant and Dodger National League fans. The major leagues now had twenty clubs with enlarged 162-game seasons. Boosted by these new clubs, attendance hit an all-time high as better than 21 million fans pushed their way into the ballparks. Both new clubs announced that they had plans for new ball parks within a few years. The Colts had begun work on a new domed stadium, another first for the majors. The Mets, playing in the refurbished Polo Grounds, were waiting completion of their new facility in Flushing Meadows, not yet named Shea Stadium. For the record and the benefit of Mets' fans, they opened their season on the jinx of all days, Friday, April 13th. They lost to the Pirates 5 to 3.

There were other new ball parks in 1962 also, as the Dodgers moved into their new baseball showplace, Chavez Ravine. The Washington Senators moved from Griffith Stadium to the ultra-modern stadium called District of Columbia Stadium, now known as Robert F. Kennedy Memorial Stadium. Not to be outdone, St. Louis, Pittsburgh, and Philadelphia were planning new stadiums. In Boston a stadium commission was announcing plans for a stadium with a retractable roof. Red Sox owner, Tom Yawkey, was delaying any decision of moving his club in, however.

An unusual deal took place between the Los Angeles Angels and the Kansas City Athletics involving a couple of rookies, in which Commissioner Ford Frick had to get involved. The Angels acquired rookie forkball relief pitcher Dan Osinski from the A's Portland farm club in late July. Actually, Osinski had made his debut in April with the A's. He eventually pitched for eight years in the majors with fair success. A short time after the deal, rumors cropped up that the A's in addition to a cash consideration would receive southpaw Bob Belinsky from the Angels to complete the deal. When the Washington Senators heard about the deal, they put in a waiver claim for

Belinsky, which caused the Angels to say Bo would be sent after the season to the A's when waivers were not needed. Frick then stepped in saying he would not approve such a deal. The Angels finally completed the deal in November by sending their lefty hurler Ted Bowsfield to K.C.

When it came to picking rookies of the year, the choices boiled down to two infielders, one of whom moved to the outfield to make room for a returning serviceman. Selected were second baseman Ken Hubbs of the Chicago Cubs and Tom Tresh of the New York Yankees.

Tresh, the American League's top rookie for 1962, was the son of the long-time Chicago White Sox catcher Mike Tresh. Tom had appeared in nine games for the 1961 Yankees, but in '62 he gained the shortstop job as a replacement for Tony Kubek who had been away in the service. When Kubek returned, the switch-hitting Tresh moved to left field. It was there that he tied a World Series record for the most putouts in a six-game series as he helped the Yankees defeat San Francisco in the fall classic. Not only did Tom hit .286, drive in 93 runs, and smash 20 home runs, he held down the two key positions for the New Yorkers. In some circles Tresh was considered the best of the young Yankees, which included such heroes as Moose Skowron, Bobby Richardson, Elston Howard, and Mickey Mantle. Except for his final two major league seasons (1968–69) when he returned to shortstop. Tom spent his playing days in the outfield. He really never equalled his first year, and as his hitting slipped away, so did his nine-year career. The Yankees also introduced several other decent rookies along with Tresh and the aforementioned Jake Gibbs. There was infielder Phil Linz, who gained more notoriety during his seven-year career as a harmonica player than between the foul lines, and Joe Pepitone, a first baseman and sometime outfielder who made his mark by being one of the first players of the modern era to wear long hair and a beard. It may have been that Joe was more concerned with his hair dryer than his first baseman's mitt. Then there was pitcher Jim Bouton, a right-hander who won 21 for the '63 Yankees, 18 the following year, and then went rapidly downhill. He became a best-selling author with the original publication of *Ball Four* in 1970. Then he entered the broadcasting field while continually threatening to make a comeback. He retired in 1970, but eight years later his comeback attempts chronicled in *The Greatest Summer*, led to a month with the Atlanta Braves. The updated *Ball Four Plus Ball Five* was published in April of 1981. Not all the Yankee rookies of '62 were memorable, as probably only the most die-hard will remember pitcher Jack Cullen. Yes, he actually was with the team for parts of three seasons.

The National League rookie of the year was Ken Hubbs, the second baseman of the Chicago Cubs. Like Tresh, he also had previous experience, a ten-game stay in Wrigley Field in 1961. While he hit only .260, it was his fielding at second base which earned him the rookie of the year designation. He made big news in the National League, not so much with his bat but by going through 78 straight games (418 chances) without committing an error, thus breaking the old record for second sackers set in 1948 by Bobby Doerr of the Boston Red Sox. A very popular and likeable addition to the Cubs, he had replaced Don Zimmer in the Cub infield. With first baseman Ernie Banks and third baseman Ron Santo, hopes for the future looked bright for the Cub infield and the team's future, but tragedy waited around the corner. Hubbs followed up his '62 season with another good one in '63. The baseball world and Hubbs's teammates were shocked, however, when the likeable youngster, who appeared to be headed for a brilliant career, met his death in the crash of his own airplane into a Utah lake during a February snowstorm in 1964. The extremely popular Ken Hubbs was only 22-years-old at the time of his death. The Cubs brought in eleven other rookies in 1962 in hopes of bolstering their sagging fortunes; none among the group left any marks upon the big league scene except Hubbs and pitcher Cal Koonce, who enjoyed a 10-10 rookie year, but actually accomplished little in nine more seasons.

It was actually a great season for newcomers in the American League. Perhaps next best to Tresh were the Minnesota Twin third baseman Rich Rollins and the Boston Red Sox surprise of the year, relief pitcher Dick Radatz. Rollins played in a few games in '61, but in '62 he batted .298 for the Twins and started for the American League All-Star team at third base. The 24-year-old redhead made that All-Star squad by garnering more votes than any American Leaguer, including the Yankees' popular Mickey Mantle. He also hit 16 home runs and drove in 96 runs. Richie put in ten major league seasons. The second-place Twins also had a rookie at second base, making half of their infield rookies. Bernie Allen, an ex-quarterback from Purdue, starred at the keystone. Bernie had pocketed a $50,000 bonus from the Twins and had put in only 80 games in organized baseball, all with Charlotte of the Sally League. Before reporting to Minnesota the left-handed-hitting Allen made such an impressive showing in spring training that he not only made the team, but shoved former second baseman Billy Martin right out of baseball. He displayed a strong arm in the field and was noted for his excellent range while flashing power and consistency at the bat. The Minnesota Twins had several other rookies in 1962, all of whom did little. There was one, however, a young Cuban, called up in early September for nine games but returned to the Dallas-Ft. Worth farm club for 1963, who would be destined for fame. He did return in late 1963 for seven more games. We will meet him in 1964. You remember Tony Oliva.

Getting back to the Boston Red Sox, Dick Radatz was a great pitcher who compiled an amazing relief record for the Sox. He was the league's relief king, appearing in 62 games with a 2.23 ERA while striking out 144 in 125 innings. Four good, but not outstanding, minor league seasons gave no indication of what the giant of a man would accomplish once he set foot on a major league mound. For anyone who ever saw him sew up a Red Sox victory, hands and arms extended high above his head in a victory salute as he strode off the mound, the sight will be one long cherished. One of the league's top relievers for his first four seasons, he showed 144, 162, 181, and 121 strikeouts. For five-and-one-half seasons, Fenway's faithful enjoyed seeing that blazing fastball of the "Monster's." His tireless work (62, 66, 79, and 63 games) is all that held up the sagging Sox during his stay there. His arm worn out, Dick appeared with four other teams before he left his seven-season career for other work. Who would have thought that the Michigan State graduate, who signed into the Red Sox system and was assigned to Raleigh where he won his first start and then proceeded to drop six in a row, would make it so big in the majors? The Red Sox were heavy in pitching rookies in 1962. They brought up seven promising newcomers, and six were hurlers. That should tell you what the needs were at Fenway Park, a familiar story. The lone non-pitcher was a catcher, probably needed to handle all those new arms, named Bob Tillman. He was a promising long-ball hitter who had been shifted to first base in the minors, but injuries to others forced him to return to catching. He played for nine big league seasons. The pitchers had such forgetable names as Kolstad, Smith, Nippert, MacLeod, and one memorable addition, Dave Morehead. Dave had practically every major league club after him when he finished high school before signing with the Red Sox. In the early going, Dave was compared to Robin Roberts, displaying a real fastball and an excellent curve. His major league career, while good, was not outstanding. It lasted eight seasons and included a no-hitter over the Cleveland Indians in 1965.

In addition to pitcher Bo Belinsky, the Los Angeles Angels, who were sharing the Dodgers' new stadium at Chavez Ravine, had the rookie battery of pitcher Dean Chance and catcher Bob Rodgers that helped power them to a surprising third place finish. Also making a three game appearance for them was catcher Ed Kirkpatrick, who performed at various positions for several teams over a 16-year period, and some good advanced notices were out on pitcher Fred Newman, who left five years later with a 33-39 mark. Pitcher

Bobby Darwin pitched one game, which he lost, and seven seasons later (1969) popped up again in L.A., this time to make three appearances with the Dodgers. He may have been the first pitcher to hurl for both an American and National League California club. The Cleveland Indians had two rookies who would later in their careers play for the New York Mets, where they would be better remembered than in Cleveland—a good hitting outfielder Tommy Agee and relief pitcher Ron Taylor. Taylor put in eleven years, Agee twelve. Max Alvis, Cleveland's third baseman for seven seasons, bowed in along with catcher Hank Edwards.

It may have seemed like a year for future Mets to break into the American League, as the White Sox were looking over Al Weis, an infielder who they kept around until 1968, when they shipped him off to Shea Stadium. Al joined nine other Chicago rookies, none of whom proved much except outfielder Ken Berry, who won a regular spot with the '65 Pale Hose and put in parts or all of fourteen seasons. Detroit had such forgetable youngsters as pitchers Bill Faul, Tom Fletcher, Doug Gallagher, and Bob Humphries and outfielders Purnal Goldy and Frank Kastro. Another future Met broke the ice with Kansas City, third baseman Ed Charles, who joined nine other K.C. hopefuls—the previously mentioned Osinski and Jimenez along with only two others of any note, pitcher Diego Segui and outfielder Jose Tartabull. Breaking in with Washington were infielder John "JK" Kennedy, later to gain a reputation as a "super sub" with the Red Sox, outfielder Don Lock, and pitcher Dave Stenhouse who was 11-12. Washington's neighbors, the Baltimore Orioles, had pitcher John Miller, third baseman Pete Ward, and a pretty good catcher in Andy Etchenbarren, who put in fifteen years in the American League.

The National League had a number of rookies in 1962, but not too many of lasting quality. The Cincinnati Reds introduced only three, but they were all good: infielder Cookie Rojas, who gained his fame during sixteen seasons mainly with the Phillies and Kansas City; outfielder Tommy Harper, a speedster and a most likeable guy who stayed around for 15 seasons; and a very decent pitcher in Doc Ellis. The New York Mets, with the already mentioned Kranepool, also had infielder Rod Kanehl and pitcher Al Jackson, up for coffee previously with Pittsburgh. In '62, Al was 8-20. The Phillies' crop produced pitchers Dennis Bennett, who seemed always to have a sore arm and whose brother Dave would join him in the City of Brotherly Love in 1964; Jack Hamilton, who would appear in many cities but never for long; and outfielder Ted Savage, who for nine years bounced around the National and American Leagues never to exceed the 127 games he gave the '62 Phillies. San Francisco had among their rookies outfielder Manny Mota, who played for 16 more seasons in the outfields of Pittsburgh, Montreal, and Los Angeles. There was also a young pitcher, a right-hander, who posted a modest 3-1 record. Reported to have received a $90,000 bonus from the Giants, this guy was still taking the mound in 1980. Gaylord Perry, whose brother Jim pitched for four American League teams, was his name. Gaylord has at one time or another led his league or been near the lead in most every pitching area. A Cy Young Memorial Award winner in both major leagues, he has seen duty with the Giants, Cleveland, Texas, San Diego, and the New York Yankees. Perry, a Hall of Fame candidate, had 279 victories entering the 1980 season against 217 defeats. He got his big break in 1964 when a rash of ailments hit the Giant staff, and he moved into a starting assignment.

The Giants' West Coast pals, the Dodgers, were high on righty Joe Moeller, who gave them eight seasons, and right-hander Pete Richert, who pitched for them until '65 when he was sent to Washington, then Baltimore, and finally back to L.A. for 1972-73 before calling it quits in 1974 with the Cards and Phils. Young infielder Dick Tracewski started the first of eight big league seasons, but in 1966 the Dodgers sold him to Detroit, where he completed his career in 1969. Bob Burda, an outfielder-first baseman, infielder Dal Maxvill, and first baseman Fred Whitfield all were rookies with St. Louis.

The Milwaukee Braves had two Aarons in their lineup, as Hank Aaron's younger brother Tommie joined the club and appeared at several positions, but primarily at first base as a fill-in for Joe Adcock, who was putting in his final season for the Braves. Tommie remained with the Braves for seven seasons before calling it a game, never reaching the heights his older brother attained. A colorful young catcher named Bob Uecker made his first appearance in mid-April, the first of six seasons in the majors. Uecker is better known to today's fans as a color man on telecasts of ballgames and as a frequent guest on TV talk shows. Joining Aaron, Uecker, and Menke were a number of youngsters who did little, although two pitchers, Denny Lemaster and Hank Fischer, did put in a number of seasons, with little success. Lemaster, billed as the new Spahn, did top Spahn's Milwaukee strikeout record with 190 whiffs in 1963. The Houston Colt .45's, known today as the Astros, welcomed nine new rookies, none of whom set the league afire. They did have a decent rookie battery in catcher Matt Ranew and pitcher Dave Giusti. Ranew was with five clubs in five seasons and the right-handed Giusti, after six seasons in Houston, spent one in St. Louis and then it was on to Pittsburgh where he performed well for eight years. One more season, for a total of fifteen, saw him retire. Giusti actually went back to the minors in 1963 and after successful surgery on his elbow between seasons came back to lead the Pacific Coast League in shutouts. Returning to Houston in 1964, he shuttled back and forth between starting assignments and relief roles.

The Pittsburgh Pirates, still rebuilding and polishing up a machine that would stay in the thick of things in the National League, paraded more rookies in and out of their lineups than any other club. Most passed into obscurity, but those that stayed were good ones. One still listed on the Pirates 1981 roster arrived in Pittsburgh after four minor league seasons. Willie Stargell made his initial appearance in mid-September. A power hitter, Willie today ranks high in the all-time Pirate offensive categories—runs, hits, doubles, total bases, and is the all-time Pirate leader in home runs, RBIs, and extra base hits. He holds, or is tied for, a host of National and major league records. He was named the major league player of the year in 1979 and was named co-most valuable player of the year in 1979 with St. Louis Cardinal Keith Hernandez. Willie was signed as a free agent by the Bucs in 1958 and in addition to his Pirate records also holds several World Series records. His career has been marked by surgery and injuries on several occasions. In 1978 he was named as his league's comeback player of the year. The big first baseman is the only player to ever hit a home run completely out of Dodger Stadium, a feat he has accomplished twice. On the negative side, but for a feat associated with big sluggers, he holds the major league record for the most seasons with 100-plus strikeouts. The Pirates also came up with a good left-hander in pitcher Bob Veale. A strikeout artist, he later became the first Buc hurler ever to get 200 whiffs in one season. Veale stood in at 6'6", and while he came up tabbed as a relief hurler, he switched to a starter until late in his 13-season career. He once fanned sixteen Phillie batters in a game. The Pirates did have a rookie reliever, however, in Jack Lamabe, a right-hander who bounced around the majors for seven seasons. He also made the switch from reliever to starter and back again. The Boston Red Sox were after him when he was attending the University of Vermont, and finally got him when he was a "throw-in" in the Dick Stuart for Don Schwall deal with the Pirates. These then, along with Bob Bailey who we met earlier, were the tops among the Pirate rookies standing far ahead of the others who bore such names as Sisk, Priddy, Plaskett, Butters, Ellis, Elliott, Goss, and McFarlane.

1963 saw the New York Yankee dynasty begin to crack, and while the Yanks did win the pennant in '63 and again in '64, it was the National League's Los Angeles Dodgers and St. Louis Cardinals who came away from the series as winners. It was one or the other of these two clubs who won the pennant from 1963 through 1968, including four of six World Series. It was an era dominated by the pitching of Sandy Koufax and Bob Gibson. In '63 it was the Dodgers of Koufax, Drysdale, Davis, and Wills who humiliated the once mighty Yankees by beating them four straight games in the series. As we shall see, the demise of the Yankees opened the way for the Minnesota Twins, the Baltimore Orioles, the Boston Red Sox, and the Detroit Tigers to rise to the top of the American League. In Milwaukee and Kansas City there were rumors that these clubs might again be seeking to shift their base of operations. They stayed put for '63, although the names Atlanta, San Diego, and Oakland kept popping up. Problems with park leases and declining attendance were at the root of the rumors. New ball parks were becoming the order of the day as the Mets, Phillies, Cardinals, and Colts were all waiting for construction to be complete on new stadiums. The Polo Grounds, Connie Mack Stadium (Shibe Park), Busch Stadium (Sportsman Park), and Colt Stadium would become a part of baseball's past. Six-figure salaries, so common in today's major leagues, were gained by Willie Mays and Mickey Mantle as they became the fourth and fifth major leaguers to reach that exclusive club, joining Ted Williams, Joe DiMaggio, and Stan Musial who had preceeded them.

Rookies were again plentiful in 1963, and while some fifteen fewer made their debuts than had in 1962, there were several who went on to leave their marks on the major league record books. The National League outdistanced the American League in youngsters, led by the Houston Colt .45's who presented 20 newcomers. Twelve of these rookies arrived at the tail end of the season as the club called up numerous players to protect them from the first-year draft. There was even one late-season game where Houston gave four of the youngsters a taste of National League ball all at the same time. While it is not unusual for a club to make numerous recalls during the closing weeks of a season, it is rare when they are not blended into the lineups along with the veterans. In that one game, the .45's introduced pitchers Dan Coombs, Jay Dahl, and Joe Hoerner and shortstop Sonny Jackson. Dahl was the starter and loser in that game, his only in the majors. The others faired better, however, as lefty Joe Hoerner lasted for 14 seasons, Danny Coombs for nine, and shortstop Jackson for twelve years, although he did perform on occasion in the outfield after he was traded to Atlanta halfway through his career. While on the subject of rookies making the lineup at the end of the season, it may not have been noticed by many, but the 1980 Boston Red Sox presented a nearly all-rookie lineup in the closing stages of that season. While it may be jumping ahead of our story, this might be a good place to bring to mind what the Bosox did. They were using an all-rookie infield anchored at either end by rookies who had played most of the season as regulars due to injuries to veterans Butch Hobson and Jerry Remy. Glenn Hoffman was at third base, and Dave Stapleton had moved from second to first base. They were using newcomers Chico Walker at second base and Julio Valdez at shortstop. The catcher at times was Rich Gedman, and with Sam Bowen, Garry Hancock, and Reid Nichols in the outfield and pitchers Bruce Hurst, Steve Crawford, or Keith MacWhorter or relief pitcher Luis Aponte on the mound, you had an all-rookie lineup. An unusual fact which has slipped past many baseball buffs—seldom has a team gone so completely with rookies. We will meet and assess some of these youngsters later on in this book.

Getting back to 1963 and Houston, you may recall a few of the remaining twenty. There was Dave Adlesh, who was their backup catcher for six years, some of those years behind John Bateman who was a regular at Houston and Montreal for ten years. A third rookie catcher was Jerry Grote, who was later sent to the New York Mets where he was the catcher for eleven-and-one-half of his fifteen big league seasons. All Mets fans who remember that Jerry started out with Houston may raise their hand. And why is it that so many remember that little pepper-pot Joe Morgan only in a Cincinnati Red uniform when Joe was among the '63 twenty and appeared in nine seasons for Houston before moving to the Reds in November of 1971? Of course, this All-Star second baseman has reaped awards by the carload. Joe holds the record for consecutive errorless games by a second baseman at 91, is tied for several other records, has led his league in many categories, was his league's MVP, and although he broke in with twenty, he maintained his rookie status until 1965 when we will meet him again. Of course, he went the free-agent route in 1979 and was re-signed by the Houston Astros, thus completing the cycle by returning to the city where he first faced National League pitching. The .45's also had two other shortstops in the group of twenty—Glenn Vaughn and Jimmy Wynn. Yes, that is the same Wynn who starred in the Astro outfield for eleven years, before closing out his 15 big league seasons with L.A., Atlanta, and the Yankees and Brewers. The outfielders who were among the twenty didn't gain as much notoriety: Brock Davis; Ivan Murrell (ten years, three of which he started for San Diego); John Paciorek, who went three for three in his first game at only 18-years-old; and Aaron Pointer. There were also hurlers Chris Zachary, Larry Yellen, and Jim Dickson. Mike White was at second base for a couple of games, and the rookie first baseman who also saw action in the outfield, was a young redhead who at the end of 1980 had just signed a new three-year contract with the New York Mets. Do you remember Rusty Staub? He was one of the twenty. Perhaps you recall him starring in the outfield for Montreal, the Mets, the Detroit Tigers, or the Texas Rangers?

This then was the story of the 1963 Houston club. Plagued with problems but soothed by thoughts of the future, they had signed more prospects than any other club, and they were waiting for them to develop. It was a long wait, as nothing really good happened until 1980 for Houston. By then the .45's, Colts, or whatever, had long been forgotten as they had become the Astros. That 1963 training camp under Manager Harry Craft was one where the youngsters were put through their paces by a team of veteran coaches. While jokes abounded about their pennant chances, none were made concerning the long-range plans. Since joining the National League, the Colts had invested more money in young players than any other club. More than 300 scouts had signed better than 230 players in the 1961–62 period alone. More than two million was spent in signing them, money which such authorities as Branch Rickey would say was well spent. In 1962 alone the Colts signed 120 players to Rickey's Cardinal 14. Houston had cornered the free agent market. One of the rookies snared in this huge dragnet was a pitcher who never made it with Houston, but in 1980 was one of the premier pitchers in the American League, Boston's Tom Burgmeier. Houston general manager Paul Richards was quoted as saying, "We think we have the greatest bunch of hot prospects in either league." And perhaps he did.

In contrast to Houston's twenty newcomers, the Cincinnati Reds had only one rookie break in 1963, but he turned out to be the best of all of them to start out that season. Still playing in the National League and an apparent future Hall of Famer is Pete Rose. Pete appeared in 157 games at second base and one in the outfield, a position he starred in for many years. He eventually shifted to third base and first base. For 16 seasons Pete performed for the Reds accomplishing enough and gaining enough honors, including his league's MVP Award, that it would take a book all by itself to recount his illustrious career. A great hitter with a better than .300 lifetime average, a star in the field and terror on the base paths, Pete went the free-agent route and was signed by the Philadelphia Phillies for the 1979 season and proceeded to lead them to the 1980 world championship. His talent was easily recognizable back in 1963 and led to his being named rookie of the year in the National League. Pete was known as "Charlie Hustle," a name put on him by the Yankees' Whitey Ford when he saw Rose race to first base after a walk. When quizzed as to why he did that, Rose explained how he had once seen Enos Slaughter do it and had done it ever since. Hustle became Pete Rose's way of life, a virtue instilled in him by his father. Like so many others who excel in the big leagues, a baseball player was all Pete ever wanted to be. A native of Cincinnati, Pete is also one of a rare breed that was able to play before the home folk most of his career. Always a good hitter, he had to work at his fielding, but no matter what, it would seem baseball has always been number one with Pete

Rose. His former roommate, Art Shamsky, once told how Pete arrived at spring training one year at eleven o'clock at night only to beg Shamsky to get his glove so they could get in a little early work. When told it was too dark and that sleep would serve them better, Pete sulked but accepted the decision.

The L.A. Dodgers had a crop of rookies, none of whom ever did much, but one started off pretty well. First baseman Dick Nen was just up from Spokane when he was called upon to pinch-hit late in a game against the St. Louis Cardinals, who the Dodgers were battling for the pennant. Nen struck out, but in the next inning socked a crucial game-tying home run. The Dodgers went on to win the game and sweep the three game series from the Redbirds, just about knocking them out of the pennant race. The importance of Nen's blow was recognized by his teammates when they voted him a $1000 share of the World Series money. Young pitcher Nick Willhite broke in sensationally by tossing a five-hit, 2-0 shutout at the Chicago Cubs. The old Dodger rivals, the San Francisco Giants, had a rookie, who later proved to be a good one, but got off to a rough start. Third baseman Jim Ray Hart collected two hits in the first game of a twin bill with the St. Louis Cardinals, but in the second game he got plunked by a Bob Gibson fastball that fractured his collarbone. He recovered to appear in six more Giant games before the season ended, his first of twelve. Two decent outfielders got their start in '63 with the Giants— Jesus Alou, one of the Alou brothers we spoke about earlier, and Jose Cardenal, a young Cuban. The youngest Alou was around through 1979 when he was granted free agency, much of his career having been spent with Houston. Cardenal, who also played some infield, played for California and Cleveland in the American League before returning to the senior circuit with St. Louis, Chicago, Philadelphia, and New York with a half-season at Milwaukee sandwiched in between. He was with the Phils and Mets in 1979, and the K.C. Royals in 1980. Pitcher Ron Herbel made his debut in '63, his first of nine National League summers.

The Pittsburgh Pirates had three decent rookies in shortstop Gene Alley, catcher Ron Brand, and pitcher Tom Parsons. Among others the Chicago Cubs had first baseman, later an outfielder and catcher, John Boccabella and outfielder and sometimes infielder Billy Cowan. The New York Mets were boasting of second baseman Ron Hunt, outfielder Cleon Jones, and pitcher Larry Bearnarth. Then there were others at Shea Stadium remembered only by the most faithful of Met fans—pitchers Don Rowe, Steve Dillon, and Grover Powell, who perhaps was known as Groover, shortstop Dick Moran, second sacker Ted Schreiber, and outfielder Dick Smith. Milwaukee had two good pitchers—Bob Sadowski, one of three brothers to appear in the major leagues, and lefty Wade Blasingame, who hurled for parts of ten years in the league before winding up for half a season with the New York Yankees. Pitcher Dan Schneider and shortstop Bill "Woody" Woodward were other hopefuls. Woody, cousin of actress Joanne Woodward, lasted for nine years. The best, in the long run, of the new Braves was a converted catcher who made only two pinch-hitting appearances, but returned in 1964 as an outfielder, his primary position, although he did play some first base. From the Dominican Republic came Rico Carty. Rico had a rough time in the big show, as he was stricken at the height of his career with tuberculosis, causing him to miss the entire 1968 season. He did return and played on through 1979, when he was the DH for the Toronto Blue Jays. Off and on disabled lists for various reasons, he spent the bulk of the 1974 season in the Mexican League while working his way back to the bigs with Cleveland. Of the St. Louis Cardinals' rookies, the most memorable would include catcher Dave Ricketts, first baseman Jeff Long, outfielder Jim Beauchamp, and second baseman Phil Gagliano.

The Philadelphia Phillies, still trying to regain the magic of their 1950 Whiz Kids, had six rookies, half of whom developed into good players. Forgotten today are first baseman Cal Emery and outfielders Wayne Graham and Charlie Harrington. Remembered are pitchers Marcelino Lopez, another product of Cuba, Ray Culp, and outfielder Dick Allen. Lopez, other than having a catchy name, played with several clubs over an eight-year stretch finishing with a combined 31-40 slate. Culp, however, posted a 14-11 record in '63 and 176 strikeouts to earn *The Sporting News'* National League Rookie Pitcher of the Year Award. He remained with the Phillies until 1967, when he was traded to the Chicago Cubs who later sold him to the Boston Red Sox for delivery in 1968. He enjoyed four of his best seasons with the Red Sox, becoming one of the American League's best hurlers. Arm problems plagued Ray in '72 and '73, after which he retired. A control pitcher, he posted 122 wins against 101 losses with a fine 1411 strikeouts against 752 walks. One of the few players to be selected an All-Star in both leagues, Culp was one of the best acquisitions Boston ever got, as they gave up only a questionable outfielder, Bill Schlesinger, to obtain him. Ray was the mainstay of the Sox hill corps in the years following their "Impossible Dream" season of 1967. Allen, variously known as Dick or Richie during his hectic fifteen-year career, was one of the top power hitters of his era. Like most power hitters, he also piled up a long string of strikeouts. While Allen broke in as an outfielder, he spent more time at first and third bases. Always in the middle of some controversy, he was sent to St. Louis in '70, L.A. in '71, to the Chicago White Sox in '72, back to the Phils in '75, and to Oakland in '77. He led the American League in home runs in '72 and '74. Strangely, he like the

Alous and Sadowskis, was one of three brothers (Hank and Ron) to appear in the major leagues.

The smaller crop of the American League rookies had a couple with sensational starts. The aforementioned Boston Red Sox right-hander Dave Morehead shut out the Washington Senators 3 to 0 on five hits in his April 13 bow. Another pitcher, Buster Narum of Baltimore, hit a home run on his first time at bat, although it was his fifth game in the majors. Gates Brown, an outfielder with Detroit, socked a pinch-hit home run in his first at-bat, only the seventh player in major league history to hit a pinch homer in his first trip to the plate. Of the trio, Narum did the bulk of his pitching in four seasons with Washington. Brown continued to pinch-hit for 13 seasons with the Tigers, and is today ranked among the all-time top pinch-hitters.

In addition to Morehead, the Red Sox introduced pitchers Bob Heffner and Jerry Stephenson. Heffner is long forgotten and Stephenson, whose father Joe Stephenson is the successful West Coast scout for the Red Sox, is better remembered in the Hub for the pictures of his attractive wife which were forever appearing in the Boston dailies, than for his pitching. Joining them were outfielder Jim Gosger, who played backup roles for most of ten seasons with a variety of teams, and a fine shortstop, Rico Petrocelli. A good hitter as well as a fielder, Rico established a home run record for shortstops in 1969 with 40. Often outspoken and involved in controversy, Rico moved to third base in the later stages of his 13-year Boston career. He then moved into the radio booth for the 1979 season and is still active in radio circles in Boston.

The New York Yankees, Los Angeles Angels, and Washington Senators contributed little in the way of rookies in 1963; that is, unless your favorite was among such names as Gonzalez, Metcalf, Dees, Gatewood, Perry (Mel), Brown, or Duckworth.

The Chicago White Sox could only add an infielder named Don Buford who they traded to Baltimore in 1968. They converted him to an outfielder. He really was a decent player who lasted ten years. They also had pitchers Fred Talbot and Bruce Howard, and a first baseman named Tom McGraw who put in thirteen American League seasons, but not all in the Windy City. Chicago had two players who, while not making their major league debuts, still enjoyed rookie status—pitcher Gary Peters and third baseman Pete Ward. These two walked away with American League rookie honors in 1963. Peters was a lefty all the way, while Ward batted from the left side but threw right-handed. Ward had appeared with the 1962 Baltimore Orioles, while Peters saw limited service with the White Sox in '59, '60, '61, and '62. Ward was rated a "can't miss" rookie prospect by most observers. An excellent hitter, he still lacked the polished fielding skills to rate as a future great. They said that the nicest thing you could say about Pete's fielding was that he catches the ball sometimes. Ward, nevertheless, was a hitter, banging out 177 hits, including 22 homers with 84 RBIs. His .295 average might easily have risen to well over .300 had he been able to run. So there he was, he couldn't field and he couldn't run, but all he could do was bang baseballs all over the field, a trait which often leads to success at the bank and the ball park. They said Pete Ward used to sleep in a tent while in the minors, but if his success could continue, he might be making his home in a palace. Sadly, it was mostly downhill for Ward, traded to the Yankees in 1970. It was his final season. His teammate on the White Sox, Gary Peters, as we said, had been up from the bushes for four cups of coffee once in each of four seasons. He had appeared in just 12 games for a total of 21-1/3 innings and with one loss and no wins. Gary arrived off a mediocre 8-11 record with Indianapolis and very little fanfare. Peters' star burst dramatically on the major league scene, as he posted an excellent 19-8 for the second-place Pale Hose. His success coupled with another good performance by the young Joel Horlen, who had been slowed by arm trouble during his rookie season, seemed to bode well for the baseball fortunes at Comiskey Park. Peters was also a good hitter, a trait pitchers were not necessarily known to possess. Gary didn't get to start a game until early May in 1963, but when he did his five-hitter was good for a 5 to 1 Sox victory over K.C. In one stretch he won 11 successive games, and of his 19 wins, three were shutouts and 10 complete games. He beat every team in the league except Washington, who knocked him out on the final day of the season, preventing him from becoming the first rookie to post 20 wins since New York's Bob Grim did it in 1954. Peters topped his '63 performance in '64 with a fine 20-8 record and was in the double win figures until 1969 when he dropped to 4-15 and was subsequently traded to the Boston Red Sox. The change of Sox seemed to work wonders for him, as he became one the aces of the Bosox staff along with Ray Culp. His first year in the Hub he posted sixteen wins. That '70 season was a rather unusual one for any pitcher. After a sensational spring, where he allowed no earned runs in 32 innings, he was 3-1 in April. Then he ran into all kinds of early-inning problems in May and finished that month 0-5. Then from June 16th on he turned around and posted a 13-4 record. An All-Star pitcher on several occasions, he tied a White Sox record with 11 straight wins in 1963. As has been mentioned, he was one of the best hitting pitchers in the game and was strictly a first baseman before turning pro.

The Baltimore Orioles gave a one-game shot to a right-handed pitcher named Wally Bunker, whom we will meet later on, and a look-see at a fair outfielder, Wally Bowens. The Cleveland Indians had a good sprinkling of rookies. Infielder Larry Brown, who wound up an American Leaguer for 12 years, was joined by Tony Martinez, who had a fine minor league record and great natural talent, with exceptional range to either side to go along with some good hitting. Outfielder Bob Chance was there, but he was converted to first base for five more American League seasons. Joining Chance in the outer garden was a fine outfielder named Vic Davalillo, a native of Venezuela. Vic was a popular player for several teams for 14 years. The Tribe also had catchers Jim Lawrence and Bob Lipski, but neither could move aside regular receiver Joe Azcue. Pitcher Gordon Seyfried had the first of two unsuccessful tries, but he was joined by a lefty with an unsensational minor league record named Tommy John. John went on to star for the White Sox and the L.A. Dodgers before going the free-agent route in 1979 and joining the New York Yankees. The Yanks were willing to chance their hopes on John who had, by then, a history of arm problems. Their faith was justified as John turned in a 21-9 record in his first season in the Bronx. Still pitching in 1980, he bettered his '79 record by posting a 22-8 record at age 37 in his 17th major league season.

The Minnesota Twins brought up Jimmie Hall, who had languished in the minors for seven seasons. Hall, who had twice hit a high of 15 home runs in the minors, teed off on major league pitching for 33 homers, after hitting just 62 in seven minor league seasons. The 33 round trippers established a new high for first year players, breaking Ted Williams's rookie mark of 31 set in 1939. The remarkable thing about this record is that Twins' manager Sam Mele used Hall as a late-inning defensive replacement for Harmon Killebrew, and Jimmie never started a game until June 8. Hall had a fine arm, and it appeared that he was headed to become an exceptional outfielder. While upping his average during his next two seasons, Hall never matched his rookie output in home runs, and after four seasons with the Twins wound up on a variety of teams before passing from the majors after eight seasons. Joining Hall with Minnesota as rookies of note were pitchers Fred Lasher and Gary Roggenburk, and catcher Paul Ratliff. Joining Minnesota as rookies of little note were third baseman Jay Ward, and pitchers Dwight Siebler and Don Williams.

The Kansas City Athletics had a large contingent of youngsters, a few of whom would leave their mark on the baseball world. A shortstop named Tony LaRussa, who spent a spotted career in and out of both major leagues but primarily in the minors, returned to the majors in 1979 as the manager of the Chicago White Sox. Then there was first baseman Ken "Hawk" Harrelson, who had a few good years in K.C. before being traded to Washington in

1966 and then back to K.C. in 1967. It was at K.C. in 1967 that he had a run-in with K.C. owner Charlie Finley, who became exasperated and released the Hawk, by now a part-time outfielder in addition to a first baseman. Free to deal with any club, an unusual occurrence in those days, the Hawk flew over to Boston, a team in the middle of a fight for the pennant. An immediate hero to the good folk of New England, he helped their "Impossible Dream" come true as the Red Sox captured the American League crown. Harrelson enjoyed a popularity in Boston that was greater than many a player could ever hope for. His surprise trade to Cleveland in early 1969 touched off many a demonstration in the Massachusetts capital. The popular Hawk, after a try at the professional golf tour, returned to Boston in 1975 as a TV announcer. At shortstop with LaRussa was a slick-fielding, but weak-hitting Dick Green. Green showed signs of developing into the League's top shortstop. Among the best, he played twelve years for the Athletics, but never lived up to that early great promise. Except for outfielder Tom Reynolds, the other A's rookies were all pitchers. Of the seven, the tops were Bill Landis, John O'Donoghue, and Jose Santiago. The remainder included Dale Willis, Dave Thies, Pete Lovrich, and Aurelio Monteagudo.

The Detroit Tigers had the largest number of new players, and there were some good ones among the lot. Third baseman Don Wert, outfielders Gates Brown and Willie Horton, catcher John Sullivan, and second baseman George Smith rounded out the fielders. Pitchers included Bob Dustal, Larry Foster, Al Koch, and Willie Smith. They were joined by two who will long be remembered by Tiger fans. Denny McLain was a big right-hander who would win 16 in '65, 20 in '66, 17 in '67, compile an amazing 31-and-6 record in '68, and win 24 in '69 before the controversial big guy would start a rapid downhill slide from 1970 to 1972. In 1971, he dropped 22 games for Washington. While McLain was suffering through bad times, his rookie teammate Mickey Lolich would continue hurling in the majors until 1979. He wore the Tiger uniform until 1975, pitching Detroit to a championship in 1968 and posting a 3-0 record in the World Series that year against the St. Louis Cardinals. The winner of the other game in the Tiger Series victory over the Redbirds that fall was McLain. Lolich was a steady winner for Detroit from 1964 until he was traded to the New York Mets after the '75 season. In 1971 he won a high of 25 games and followed that up with 22 wins in '72. Only 5-9 in his rookie year, he never again dropped below 12 wins for Detroit and certainly must be considered among the all-time greats of the Motor City hill corps. He struck out more batters than any left-handed pitcher to ever pitch in the major leagues (2,832). He holds the left-handed lifetime American league strikeout record (2,679), in seven seasons struck out 200 or more batters, and for 13 consecutive years struck out 100 or more batters. As late in his career as 1971, he led his league in complete games with 29.

Before we leave the 1963 story altogether, let's go back for a second to that large crop of twenty rookies that were in the Houston camp. We spoke of John Paciorek, who as an 18-year-old went 3 for 3 in his first game. Well, John also had two walks in that game and scored four of the five times he was on base as the Colts were defeating the New York Mets 13 to 4 in the final game of the season. Of the better than twenty batters to achieve perfect 1.000 lifetime batting averages, most, of course, went 1 for 1, but not John with his 3 for 3. As Casey Stengel would say, "You could look it up."

John's performance led to talk of, "A cinch to make it as a big leaguer," "Promises to be a great hitter," "Swings with authority and demonstrates speed in the outfield and on the bases, too." The rosy predictions, as so often happens, found John back in the minors in 1964 where he remained until a back operation in 1967 ended any hopes he may have had of returning to the majors for another try. His younger brother Tom broke in with the 1970 Dodgers and was with Seattle in 1980, a postscript to the career of one of the major league's 1.000 hitters.

1964-66:
Something Old—
Something New

The New York Yankees won the American League pennant again in 1964; but for the second straight year they lost the World Series and it was obvious that the demise of another Yankee era was taking place. It would not be until 1976 that the Yankee pinstripe would again appear in the fall classic. The demise opened the way for a new set of teams to rise to the top of the American League. A one-year effort mounted by the Minnesota Twins was followed by a Baltimore Oriole win, as this new breed began to run championship pennants up their flag poles. As we shall see in future chapters, Detroit and Boston would also get into the act.

There were also changes in the National League. The Milwaukee Braves became the Atlanta Braves in 1966, bringing major league baseball to the South for the first time. The St. Louis Cardinals returned to the top of the league in 1964, and the Los Angeles Dodgers, while winning pennants in 1965-66, were also coming to the end of a winning era.

Observers close to the baseball scene were noticing some very unusual and strange things happening on the big league scene during the '60s. Several years had passed since Roger Maris had hit his 61 home runs, yet many youngsters were beginning to struggle at the plate, losing their timing trying to emulate him. What made this even more unusual was the fact that they had started off with fairly decent years and appeared headed for stardom and long careers. Tom Tresh of the New York Yankees and Peter Ward of the Chicago White Sox might stand out as the prime examples, although a close check of the record books will reveal more. It seems there was a period through the early '60s when few rookies, especially those singled out for awards, would continue to live up to their promise.

Players snared up in the home run craze were everywhere, and about all their wild swinging was accomplishing was to improve the strikeout records of the pitchers. I suppose this would naturally go hand in hand, and so it was that while there were some truly great pitchers on hand, there were others whose strikeout records would not have been so high had they appeared in some other era of baseball history. Interestingly, one of the better pitchers during the sixties was the St. Louis Cardinal Bob Gibson. He only led the National League once in strikeouts, yet by pitching in this free-swinging era, he amassed more career strikeouts than any other pitcher in history, except the great Washington Senator, Walter Johnson. Perhaps it was no accident that the leading hitters during this period were two Latins who consistently were up at the plate to make good contact and not swing for the fence. Remember the Pirates' Roberto Clemente and the Twins' Tony Oliva?

1964 saw a great pennant race in the National League with the Philadelphia Phillies making their first serious effort for a league crown since 1950. The Phillies had a six-and-one-half game lead heading into the final weeks of the season when suddenly they lost ten in a row. The Cardinals emerged as the champions, but only after the Phillies had regained their winning ways to defeat the Cincinnati Reds, giving the Cards the crown. The Reds were in the thick of the pennant race until their manager, Fred Hutchinson, suffering a bout with a fatal case of cancer, had to leave the club in September. The Cardinals were also having managerial problems, and even before their victory it was rumored that Manager John Keane would be gone. A similar situation was occurring in the American League, where rookie New York Yankee manager Yogi Berra was having dissension problems with that team. He rallied his club to a 22-6 record over the final weeks and nosed out Chicago by a game to capture the crown. However, it would appear the second straight World Series loss was too much for General Manager Ralph Houk and he fired Berra. To complete the surprise, Keane resigned his post with the Redbirds after the Series and was named to replace Berra.

Other events were taking place in 1964. As previously mentioned, the Milwaukee Braves received permission to move to Atlanta in 1966, and the Los Angeles Angels received word that they would be allowed to pull out of L.A. and move to Anaheim to become the California Angels, also in 1966. It was a year which saw the Phillies' Jim Bunning pitch a perfect game and Sandy Koufax pitch his third no-hitter in as many seasons. The big news in player signings was the Angels inking the University of Wisconsin flash, Rick Reichardt, for a bonus estimated at over $200,000. It was also a year of new stadiums, as the Mets unveiled their Shea Stadium showplace, while Houston's indoor arena, the Astrodome, was just about completed. The

Astros did not move in until 1965. New stadium plans were announced for St. Louis, Philadelphia, and Pittsburgh, leaving only Cincinnati and Chicago among National League clubs in their old parks. Not to be outdone, the cities of Oakland and Arlington, Texas, announced that they were embarking on building new stadiums. The face of the big leagues was changing rapidly from old to new. Fans were put to the test in '64 when a Met doubleheader on May 31 with San Francisco went on for almost ten hours. Almost 15,000 of the original 57,000 were still on hand as the second game ended after 23 innings in an 8-to-6 Giant victory at 11:25 P.M. It was the longest doubleheader in major league history.

The number of new rookies entering the majors in 1964 was slightly under what it had been in the previous two seasons. Looking back now, the crop was rather slim. There were some good ones, but many more fell by the wayside, despite great advanced ballyhoo. The crop was just about evenly split between the two leagues.

The Boston Red Sox unveiled the largest number of newcomers with ten, followed closely by Philadelphia and the Chicago Cubs at nine. Of the Red Sox ten, only one really worked out to any degree and he was struck down by a fastball one night at Fenway Park in 1967 and never regained the skills which had made it appear that certain stardom would be his. Remember Tony Conigliaro? Then there was Dalton Jones, who was a decent utility man for nine seasons; but how many except the most die-hard Red Sox fan will remember catcher Mike Ryan, pitchers Ed Connolly, Pete Charton, Bill Spanswick, Jay Ritchie, Dave Gray, outfielder, later to turn first baseman, Tony Horton and first baseman Bob Guindon?

Perhaps the most sensational performance was turned in by the Minnesota Twins' rookie Tony Oliva. Young Pedro Oliva had had cups of coffee with the Twins in 1962 and 1963, but still qualified as a rookie in 1964. And what a year the young right fielder had, a year which earned him American League rookie of the year honors. As the season was approaching, Oliva was faced with the task of breaking into the veteran outfield of Killebrew, Allison, and Hall. Oliva was always a good hitter as his minor league stats show. His first year in pro ball he led all pro hitters with a .410 average at Wytheville. In 1964 by hitting .323 he won the American League batting championship, the first rookie to ever do so. Quite a feat for the young Cuban. Tony stayed with the Twins through the 1976 season and became one of the most feared hitters in the American League, winning the batting championship again in 1965 and 1971. The power-hitting Twins were always on the lookout for decent pitching, as reflected in the rookie pitchers they tried, Bill Whitley, Gerry Fosnow, and Charlie Nieson, none of whom solved the problem. Rookie right-hander Dave Boswell helped and in 1969 won 20, but that was his last hurrah and he was soon gone. Joe Nossek, a much-traveled outfielder before he was out of the majors, made it, along with a decent first baseman in Rich Reese, who played for ten seasons. Of the three rookies Washington had, none made any significant contribution except for pitcher Don Loun's 1-to-0 win over Boston in his first game, his only major league victory.

Consider now for a minute the plight of the fading New York Yankees. Usually their farm system was loaded with talented youngsters, but in 1964 it produced a below-average crop. There was first baseman Mike Hegan, son of the former Cleveland Indians' great catcher, Jim. Mike put in 12 American League seasons with a variety of clubs. There was the highly regarded outfielder Roger Repoz, who spent nine years in the big time, most of it on the West Coast with the Angels. And there were first baseman Archie Moore, not the boxer, outfielder Elvio Jimenez, Manny's brother, and pitchers Pete Mikkelsen, Bob Meyer, and the most successful of the bunch, Mel Stottle-myre, who was called up in early August and helped the Yanks to the flag. It was "Stot" who gave the Yankees any respectability they had during their down years. For some reason, it seems to me, he is never given the credit he deserves by Yankee faithful. Mel won 20 in '65, 21 in '68, 20 in '69, and was in double figures in wins for 9 straight years. Pitching in 11 seasons, he won 164 and lost 139.

Out on the West Coast, the Angels introduced the bonus baby Reichardt who didn't play much in his first three seasons, but did gain some slight prominence during an eleven-season stay. Rich started his career in the minors and was called up by the Angels on September 1st. Other Angels of note were outfielder Paul Schaal, catcher Bob Lee, and second sacker Bobby Knoop. Chicago had little to present, except for catcher Jerry McNertney.

Detroit and Cleveland each had some good youngsters. It seems that Detroit would come up with at least one a year, and this 1964 season was no exception. Mickey Stanley arrived for the first of his 15 years which were spent mostly in Detroit's outfield. He was joined by outfielder Jim Northrup. They would be teammates for ten years. Pitcher Joe Sparma arrived, and left the majors after seven seasons with an identical 52-52 mark. First baseman Bill Roman hit his only major league home run in his first time up with the Tigers. The Indians had catcher Duke Sims for a look-see. He returned in 1965 for ten seasons. Vern Fuller, an infielder, was aboard as were a couple of good pitchers, Sonny Siebert and Luis Tiant. The latter, a young Cuban, broke in with a sensational four-hit 3-to-0 victory over the New York Yankees on July 26. "Looie," of course, is now an American League legend for his marvelous comeback after being considered finished. It was the Boston Red

Sox who gave him a second life in 1971, but who let him go to the New York Yankees as a free agent in 1979. He was of great help to Boston, three times winning 20 or more games. Strangely, Siebert, who like Tiant, was a winner with Cleveland, also wound up hurling for the Red Sox before they sent him to Texas. Sonny enjoyed his way through twelve seasons with 140-114 record. Looie is still pitching, rolling on with his bobs, weaves, head fakes, and strange moves.

Kansas City had a few good ones, but it was Bert Campaneris who enjoyed the most sensational start. When regular shortstop Wayne Causey was injured in mid-July, the call went out to the A's farm club at Birmingham of the Southern League. The 21-year-old shortstop, a native of Cuba, caught a late plane and arrived bleary-eyed after the trip to Minnesota where K.C. was playing. Placed into the game, he came alive and slammed a Jim Kaat pitch over the left field fence. Later he singled and grounded out, but in the seventh inning he hit his second home run of the game. His two homers equaled the major league record for home runs in a first game. The only other player to do it was Bob Nieman of the old St. Louis Browns back in 1951. Joining "Campy" as rookies with K.C. were pitchers Jack Aker, Ken Sanders, and the very excellent Johnny "Blue Moon" Odom. To catch this trio the A's brought along Dave Duncan. Another pitcher, Vern Handrahan, lost his first of two major league games. First baseman Rick Joseph played in 17 games, but he wound up playing more with the Phillies during his career, like outfielder Larry Stahl, who spent most of his ten major league seasons in the National League.

The Baltimore Orioles only had four new rookies in 1964, but a returning pitcher, Wally Bunker, qualified for rookie status and was chosen the American League rookie pitcher of the year, based on his 19-5 record. Not bad for a 19-year-old! Bunker appeared to be a complex person, one hard for all concerned to figure out. The Bunkers, in a bidding war for their son's services, asked a high price for the boy, but when Minnesota scout Billy Martin said he felt Wally was lazy, the price dropped. True or not, it is a tag which was hung on this young man with a world of promise. In one game that he was scouted, Bunker struck out every batter for some four innings, and when his team got a big lead he just let the other club hit the ball. The bidding war for his services never really materialized, as no other club would match Baltimore's offer. Nineteen wins as a 19-year-old in '64, a sore arm in '66, and except for a World Series shutout, nothing of note thereafter. Pitchers Frank Bertaina and Dave Vineyard joined Bunker as mound hopefuls in Baltimore. There were two decent outfielders in the Oriole camp who are still around the major league scene, Paul Blair and Lou Piniella. Blair gained his fame with the Orioles, but went to the New York Yankees in later years. Sweet Lou, of course, gained his fame in K.C., but has really starred with the Yankees.

While the National League had a few more rookies in number, their quality was far below what had been produced for the past several seasons in the senior circuit. The New York Mets' right-handed pitcher Dennis Ribant was the only worthwhile rookie they produced from among people named Hinsley, Locke, Sutherland, Wakefield, and Stephenson. The St. Louis Cardinals were in the same boat with such forgettables as Spiezio, Dowling, Lewis, Richardson, and Bakenhaster. The Pittsburgh Pirates had a decent catcher in Jerry May to catch the slants of right-hander Steve Blass; both put in ten big league seasons, but that was about it among other Buc hopefuls. Blass was a strange case. After eight good seasons for the Pirates, in the last of which, 1972, he won 19 games, he suddenly lost his control and could not find the plate. Comeback attempts in 1973 and 1974 only resulted in a 3-9 record. So strange and unusual was Blass's case that since then when pitchers experience the same problem they are referred to as having the Steve Blass disease. It was really a shame how this fine Connecticut native with so much talent should lose it overnight and never regain his form. Joining the Pirates with very little were the Houston Colts, who had a hustling outfielder named Walt "No-Neck" Williams for only ten games. He disappeared, only to pop up three years later with the Chicago White Sox, for whom he was a popular player for six seasons. No one seeing him could forget the way he hustled at every opportunity. He actually appeared to have no neck, as if his head were right on his shoulders. Right-hander Larry Dierker was an 0-1 chucker for the Colts, but he returned in 1965 and was a mainstay of their staff for twelve seasons, winning 20 in 1969.

The Milwaukee Braves listed six rookie pitchers on their list of those making debuts in 1964; Braun, Eilers, Kelley, and Umbach are probably names quickly forgotten. Not forgotten, however, would be Clay Carroll, who would gain some renown as a good relief pitcher primarily for the Cincinnati Reds and put in fifteen major league seasons. Joining Carroll was Phil Niekro, who showed little in 1964 but developed into a great hurler for the Braves after their move in 1966 to Atlanta. Phil showed 23 wins in 1969, 20 in 1974, and 21 in 1979 and had wins in double figures for each season since 1967. Phil holds a host of major league records, some of a negative nature, especially in the area of wild pitches. He has been known to have control problems. In 1979 Phil established a National League record for starts with 44. He has led his league in complete games several times. In 1973 he hurled a no-hitter against San Diego, winning 9 to 0. A good fielding pitcher, he and his brother Joe are the only brothers in National League history to achieve twenty pitching victories each in the same season. Joe was 21-11 with Houston in 1979, while Phil was 21-20 with Atlanta. Joe arrived with the Chicago Cubs in 1967, and we will encounter him later in our story. Joining Niekro and Carroll on the Braves was a journeyman infielder, Sandy Alomar, who traveled from team to team, seven in all (some more than once), during 15 big league summers.

The San Francisco Giants had an interesting cast of rookies, including Randy Hundley, a catcher, and Hal Lanier, an infielder, both of some note. It was also the first season of a two-year experiment with the Japanese hurler Masanori Murakami, who in those two seasons won five and lost one for the Giants. I can't help but mention Giant pitcher Dick Estelle who I am sure is long forgotten by most baseball fans. Dick broke in in 1964 with a 1-2 record, his final record for two seasons; but I remember him not for what he did on the mound but for the fact that a friend of his, whose name I have long since forgotten, was one of the most attractive girls I have ever worked with. I wonder what happened to her? Down at Wrigley Field in Chicago, the Cubs put nine rookies into their lineup at various times during the '64 season. Eight of them would mean little to today's fans, Campbell, Flavin, Gregory, Jaeckel, Popovich, Roznousky, Schurr, and Slaughter. The ninth, a tall lanky switch-hitter, arrived in early September from the Texas League. In Don Kessinger, the Cubs picked up a record-breaking fielder, an All-Star, and a fixture at their shortstop position until they traded him to the Cardinals in late 1975. After two seasons in St. Louis, he was traded back to the Windy City, not to the Cubs but to the White Sox for whom he played through the 1979 season.

Out in the far West, the Dodgers had two young outfielders break into their lineup, Willie Crawford and Wes Parker. Parker won a first-string job after only one minor league season split between Santa Barbara and Albuquerque. Switched to a full-time first baseman in 1965, he played nine seasons for the Dodgers. Like Wes, Willie had had very little minor league experience, having started the '64 season at Santa Barbara. Seems the Dodgers were rushing their young players along pretty rapidly. Willie put in 14 full or partial big league seasons. Hometown pitcher Bill Singer made his first start for L.A. after an 11-10 year at Spokane. He turned out to be a winner, pitching for L.A. until 1973 when he joined the California Angels where he promptly won 20 games, repeating his twenty wins of 1969. He hung up his pitchers' toeplate after a 2-8 season with the Toronto Blue Jays in 1977. A backup catcher for ten seasons in the majors, Jeff Torborg joined the Dodgers in 1964 with only one minor league season under his belt. After seven seasons with the Dodgers, he followed Singer over to the California Angels in 1971. It was amazing how the Dodgers were bringing up those players with so little experience.

The Philadelphia Phillies were leading the National League by 6½ games with just two weeks to go in 1964, when they had a disastrous ten-game losing streak that put them behind for keeps. They finished in a second place tie with the Cincinnati Reds, both one game behind the champion St. Louis Cardinals. The loss was no fault of the National League rookie of the year, third baseman Richie Allen. He had hit .318, got 201 hits, including 29 home runs and a league-leading 13 triples. Richie always has claimed he was fortunate during his rookie season to never have had a really poor day. There was one day, however, at midseason when the Phillies were in St. Louis for a doubleheader with the Cardinals, when he may have found himself wondering. In the opening game, Allen struck out five times in a row and then came right back in the second game to get three hits. To give you some idea how popular Allen was with the Philadelphia fans that rookie season of 1964, in late September they gave him a night. Imagine a rookie getting a night when some players go through long careers without ever getting one. Like so many successful major leaguers, from the time he was born he could be found on a baseball diamond, bat and ball in hand. A good long-ball hitter, the bespectacled Allen, like so many sluggers, also had a very high ratio of strikeouts to at-bats. Another of the three brother combos to make it in the majors, Richie's brother Hank arrived with Washington in 1966 and brother Ron with St. Louis in 1972. The way this Phillies' prize rookie started his career, with home runs and flashy fielding plays, he figured to have a long career ahead of him. He stayed with the Phils until 1969, when in successive years he appeared with St. Louis, L.A., and the Chicago White Sox. After three American League seasons, during which he won the American League MVP Award, he returned to the Phillies for a couple of years before winding up his career with Oakland in 1977. While Richie Allen was the top National League rookie, the Phillies were also looking over the likes of pitchers Gary Kroll, Dave Bennett (Dennis's brother), and Rick Wise. Wise was not as highly touted as the others, yet he turned out to be the best. He was still pitching in the majors with the San Diego Padres in 1980. Others getting a look-see with the Phils included highly rated catcher Pat Corrales, recently the Texas Ranger manager, first baseman Costen Shockley, and four hard-hitting outfielders—John Briggs, Alex Johnson, Danny Cater, and the highly rated Adolfo Phillips.

Named National League rookie pitcher of the year was a big Cincinnati Red left-hander named Billy McCool. Billy was primarily a relief hurler, and while his overall record was just 6-5, he was 5-2 with seven saves in relief. He also whiffed 87 batters in 89 innings and posted 2.42 ERA. Appearing for five seasons with the Reds as a reliever, he recorded 21 saves in 1965 and 18 in 1966. A season at San Diego followed by one in St. Louis in 1970 ended his career. The Reds also were introducing: Tommy Helms, a shortstop who we will meet later on; infielder Bobby Klaus (Billy's brother), who was soon traded to the New York Mets; third baseman Chico Ruiz, a speedy and capable glove man; outfielder Mel Queen, up from the San Diego farm club and rated the top Red prospect; and first baseman Tony Perez. Perez at 22 led the Pacific Coast League in RBIs at 107 and was second in homers. While he only spent a month with the '64 Reds, being used only sparingly, he would return later to become a Redleg hero. It was decided that he should play every day, so he was sent back to San Diego where he proved to be outstanding. The young Cuban, originally a third baseman, was moved to first base in 1964 and turned in an adequate job. In five years of pro ball, Tony had already recorded such impressive figures as a .348 season, 27 homers, and 132 RBIs. The Reds traded Tony to Montreal in 1977, and in 1979 he entered the free-agent draft and was signed by the Boston Red Sox. At 38 years of age, he is still hitting home runs, driving in over 100 runs, and playing first base for the Bosox.

1965 saw the Minnesota Twins win the American League pennant with ease, while the long reign of the New York Yankees ended as that club tumbled all the way down to sixth place. The Griffith family, who moved from Washington to Minnesota just five seasons before, had waited for a pennant since 1933, when Twins' owner Calvin Griffith's uncle, the late Clark Griffith's Senators had won a pennant with rookie manager Joe Cronin.

An equally interesting story was taking place in the National League, where the Los Angeles Dodgers were jumping up from a sixth-place finish in 1964 to capture the pennant in '65. It seemed that it was becoming a tradition to stage a multi-club dogfight down to the wire in the senior circuit; this time it was the Dodgers, the San Francisco Giants, and the Cincinnati Reds who were battling away until the final days of the season. Other events of importance were William D. Eckert being selected and elected as baseball's new commissioner, the first free-agent player draft, and the opening of the first air-conditioned stadium, Houston's Astrodome.

It might be well to pause here a moment and reflect upon the free-agent draft, which as we mentioned, was first held in 1965. What actually takes place is that all the clubs meet (in 1965 they gathered in New York City, while today it is often done by nationwide telephone hookup), and select the right to negotiate with amateur players who are called free agents because they are not affiliated with any team. The teams select in reverse order of their finish the previous season; thus the last place team in the league which lost the previous fall's World Series has the first choice, with turns switching from league to league until finally the world's championship club selects. Once all of the teams of each league have selected, that constitutes round one, and then it's on to round two, repeating the process for several days until all the prospective players are selected. These rookies are then able to negotiate with the team who selected them in the draft and are bound to sign with that club if they decide to sign a professional contract for that season. Should they decide, for one reason or another, not to sign, they will be eligible to go back into the draft the next year and are available for any team to select. It is not uncommon to find players on some of the nation's better college teams who have been selected on several occasions but have decided to continue with their college careers before turning professional. The draft was professional baseball's attempt at distributing the better upcoming players around the leagues, and it is hoped that eventually it will tend to balance the leagues by equalizing the teams.

Some of the players selected in that first draft are recognizable to today's baseball fans, but at the time they were known only to the scouts and fans in the areas from which they came. Most spent time in the minor leagues sharpening their skills. Among those players selected in the first round and signed were: the very first player selected, Rick Monday, a highly touted 19-year-old outfielder from Arizona State University; Les Rohr; Joe Coleman, son of a former major leaguer; Billy Conigliaro, brother of Tony; Ray Fosse; Eddie Leon; Jim Spencer; Alan Gallagher; Bernie Carbo; and Bill Burbach.

Before moving on, I must mention Alan Gallagher again. Alan was the first choice of the San Francisco Giants, and at 19 was a third baseman at Santa Clara University. He had, like Monday, also attended Arizona State. Signing with the Giants, he was assigned to their Tacoma, Pacific Coast League farm club, but after 33 games he was sent to Springfield, Massachusetts, of the Eastern League. From his first season he worked his way up through the Giant system with stops at Fresno, Phoenix, Tacoma (again), and Amarillo before reaching the Giants in 1970. There he remained until early 1973 when he was traded to the California Angels, where his career ended after the '73 season. It was an average career for Gallagher, nothing great, just a few good years to prove he could make it. What then is unusual about Alan Gallagher? "Come on," you say. "Just a good Irish name." Wrong! Good yes, but get a look at his complete name and hope when he signed autographs that he didn't sign his full name—Alan Mitchell Edward George Patrick Henry Gallagher. He was the only child born to his parents, who had been waiting eight years to have a baby. They gave their son all the names they had thought about for all those years when he was born on that October 19 in 1945. They say there were times when he was known as Patrick Henry Gallagher and he had a nickname of "Dirty Al," but no matter he certainly must go down in baseball annals as a player with one of the longest names.

1965 also marked the first time in baseball history that the pennant winners of one season (1964) failed to play at least .500 ball the next year. The Yankees dropped to sixth place and the Cardinals fell to seventh in their league. The rookie batting champion of 1964 in the American League, Tony Oliva, retained his championship in 1965, proving his 1964 season was no fluke. 1965 was also the year for an unusually large number of managerial changes. Five clubs made changes during the year, in addition to the announced retirements of long-time managers Casey Stengel and Al Lopez. Stengel, in an unusual move, was later named to the baseball Hall of Fame. Without getting into all the details of the changes, there was one managerial change that may have or has had an effect indirectly upon a number of young rookies. In mid-May the Kansas City Athletics dismissed their manager, Mel McGaha, and replaced him with the 1965 majors' youngest skipper, 34-year-old Haywood Sullivan. He became Charlie Finley's fifth manager in as many years of ownership. In late November, Sullivan resigned to take a position as vice-president and director of player personnel for the Boston Red Sox. Sullivan, of course, has risen to the chief in the Red Sox front office and has influenced or will bring to bear influence on many a player's career.

There was an interesting game pitched by a rookie hurler at Toronto, then of the International League, in late June. The youngster's name was Bill Rohr, who we will meet again in 1967. Bill had a no-hitter going in the first game of two at Toledo—as a matter of fact he was down to his final pitch—when he saw his no-hit bid and the game slip away from him. As we shall see, he had a similar experience in his big league bow in '67, but with different results. In that last inning Mud Hen batter Roger Repoz led off with a walk and was sacrificed to second base; then an intentional walk put a runner on first base. Bob Schmidt then ended the no-hitter and the game with a single that scored a run, and Toledo had a 1-to-0 victory. The Eastern League, long known as a pitchers' league, saw Elmira rookie right-hander Ed Watt toss no-hitters in two of his first three starts. In his first start he no-hit Williamsport 4 to 0, and then failed to get a decision in his second start, this time against Pittsfield. His third start against Reading saw him hurl his second no-hitter, winning 5 to 0. Watt's teammate Ed Barnowski also tossed a no-hitter that season and almost had another no-hitter on his next outing when he hurled 12 innings of one-hit ball, whiffing a league record of 19 batters before being removed for a pinch hitter. Another pitcher, Billy MacLeod, had a perfect 18-0 record for Pittsfield, another all-time Eastern League record. His 18 consecutive wins broke the previous record of 17 set by Tommy Fine in 1946. Actually, lefty MacLeod had won his last four decisions with Reading in 1964, giving him a string of 22 wins in a row. How would you like to have been a batter in the Eastern League in 1965? Just for the record, Pittsfield's George Scott with a .319 mark led the league. We will meet George in 1966.

1965 produced a number of standout major league rookies, some of whom enjoyed some fairly long careers in the big leagues. Two rookies took part in some high drama in mid-September. Brant Alyea, a rookie outfielder up from Hawaii with Washington in his first major league at-bat, hit the first pitch by rookie pitcher Rudy May of the California Angels for a three-run homer. A spectacular debut. May, who hailed from the same town as the great Walter Johnson, came to the Angels from the Philadelphia Phillies in the Bo Belinsky trade and became a regular starter for them early in the season. In his first start the rookie left-hander almost hurled a no-hitter. Facing Detroit on April 18, he permitted just one hit in nine innings and that coming in the eighth inning by pinch hitter Jake Wood. Although May had fanned ten and walked only five, he was relieved by Bob Lee. Manager Bill Rigney was impressed with his 21-year-old southpaw, despite the big rookie's occasional bursts of wildness. A shutout of the Orioles in June was May's first in the big time, and it also marked the first game he had gone through without issuing a walk. Originally the property of the Chicago White Sox, May had been traded to the Phillies in October and then to L.A. in December. In two minor league seasons he had a 28-19 record, with 173 strikeouts in '63 and 235 in '64. Alyea, an outfielder drafted by Washington from San Diego, had spent three seasons in the minors playing some first base and making a couple of appearances on the mound in his first season. In 1962, at Geneva of the New York-Pennsylvania League, he had hit 32 home runs. Brant spent six years in the majors, while Rudy May was still pitching in 1980 with the New York Yankees. May actually went back to the minors after the '65 season for three years before he arrived with California to stay. In his 10th big league season in 1977 he won 18 games for Baltimore. Speaking of names, Brant was short for Garrabrant.

Rudy wasn't the only rookie named May to appear in 1965. The Cincinnati Reds had a top prospect in first baseman Lee May up from the Macon farm club where he had hit .303 with 25 home runs to go along with a league leading 110 RBIs. Lee caused some confusion in the National League as the Milwaukee Braves had a veteran player who they traded in the early season to Houston named Lee Maye. Rookie Lee May has enjoyed sixteen years in the majors, the last six of which have been with Baltimore as a combination first baseman-DH. He was still a feared batter in 1980. Lee's brother Carlos appeared in 1968 with the Chicago White Sox as an outfielder-first baseman and spent most of his ten major league years with the Pale Hose.

The Baltimore Orioles, making their way up in the American League standings, had a bumper crop of rookies in 1965, including their present ace right-hander Jim Palmer, shortstop Mark Belanger, infielder Davy Johnson and the American League rookie of the year, outfielder Curt Blefary. Of this talented group, Jim Palmer has certainly turned out to be the best and most durable. In 1980 he was still the big man, the stopper on the mound for the Orioles. He arrived in Baltimore with just one season of professional baseball under his belt, that at Aberdeen of the Northern League where he was 11-3 in just 19 games, one of which was a no-hitter. The no-hitter is a feat he repeated in the majors in 1969 against the Oakland A's. Palmer pitched his first professional game at age 18, and while he didn't get the win, he did return one week later to pitch a ten-inning three-hit shutout for his first victory. He is the holder of numerous records, both in American League, World Series and Championship Series competition. He is one of three pitchers who have won the Cy Young Award three times, and he has appeared in numerous All-Star Games. Back and shoulder injuries nearly ruined his career in 1967-68, a period which saw him pitch in Rochester, Elmira, and Miami, trying to shake the ailments; it took a winter of pitching in the Puerto Rican League (1968) for him to overcome these problems, Palmer also suffered serious arm problems in 1969, '74, and '79 that for long periods found him on the disabled list. In 1974 he spent nearly eight weeks on the disabled list with a sore elbow and had his only losing season. Jim has had eight seasons in which he has won twenty or more games. Truly one of the all-time great pitchers, he has appeared as a color man for several years on the ABC network television coverage of American League playoffs and has been active as national sports chairman for the Cystic Fibrosis Research Foundation. To give you an idea of how important he has been on the Baltimore scene, he is that team's all-time leader in most all major pitching categories: strikeouts, games, wins, innings pitched, shutouts, losses, and won-lost percentage, and he stands third in ERA for pitchers with 500 or more innings pitched.

The shortstop in that first game that pitcher Jim Palmer started for the

Aberdeen Pheasants back in 1964 was a young Mark Belanger, who by the way had two triples and three RBIs. Belanger had actually started in the Oriole system in 1962, but had been called into the military where he spent the 1963 season. He was with Aberdeen in '64 where he was named rookie of the year and at Elmira for '65 with a late season recall to Baltimore where he managed to appear in eleven games. Mark spent most of 1966 with Rochester, returning to Baltimore for eight games at the end of the season. He made the club in 1967 and has played for the Birds ever since as their regular shortstop. In 1965 the Birds were chirping about this great infield prospect because of his great glove, his strong accurate arm, great range, his excellent pair of hands and his running ability, skills he has more than lived up to during his career. Hitting, or lack of it, was the only thing holding Mark back, but he was showing signs of coming around with the bat. Today Mark has played more games than any other Oriole in history except Brooks Robinson, has a trophy case full of Gold Glove Awards, and has only hit nineteen career home runs. I guess young players could well learn from Mark that you don't have to hit home runs to survive in the majors, but you better know how to field. Mark, by the way, while still in high school at Pittsfield, Massachusetts, was offered a basketball scholarship to Notre Dame.

Infielder Dave Johnson had impressive minor league stats before his arrival for part of the 1965 season. On board at the start of the year, he went back to Rochester for some polish but returned to stay in '66. He was rated as an outstanding competitor with excellent offensive ability; a right-handed batter, he had the power Belanger lacked. With Baltimore until 1972, he was traded in the off-season to Atlanta, where in 1973 he established a record for home runs by a second baseman with 43. He holds several records and several Gold Gloves and was often an All-Star player appearing in the midsummer dream game for both leagues. In his first season with Atlanta he was named comeback player of the year. In April of 1975 the Braves released Dave, and he went to Japan where for two seasons he played with the Yomiuri Giants, before returning to the states and joining the Philadelphia Phillies. After a couple of seasons, they traded him to the Chicago Cubs from whom he retired in 1979.

Of all of these great Baltimore rookies of 1965, it was outfielder Curt Blefary who captured the honors by being named the American League rookie of the year. Oriole farm director Harry Dalton named Blefary as one who would make the jump from the minors to the bigs. The sensation of the International League, the 21-year-old lefty swinger had hit 31 homers, driven in 80 runs, and received 102 walks while batting .287 with Rochester. He had been plucked from the New York Yankee farm system on first-year waivers.

Rated an excellent competitor with good power, he was thought of as having a chance to become one of the outstanding sluggers in baseball in several years. As the spring training season moved along, Curt, upset because he wasn't playing more, popped off at Manager Hank Bauer. But he soon learned that he could not talk his way into the lineup and might only talk his way into a return trip ticket to Rochester. Less than two weeks after his indirect criticizing of his manager, the Orioles' right fielder Sam Bowens pulled a leg muscle, and Blefary took over and remained for the season. Manager Bauer grew to admire his rookie, especially for his hustling attitude, a characteristic which had to remind Bauer of the way he had played the game in his day. It is an interesting story of how Curt became an Oriole. As stated, he was in the New York Yankee system as a "protected player." The Yanks needed a spot on their roster, and since Blefary had a minor injury at the time, they decided to put him on waivers and told him to keep his mouth shut for the 72-hour waiver period after which they could reclaim him. Deep in the minors, they reasoned that he would be overlooked. Not being able to keep quiet, he approached Ray Scarborough, a scout for Baltimore, and told him he was okay and the injury was not serious. Needless to say, the Orioles claimed him for $8000. With a reputation of being a bit flaky, it was said that he liked clam chowder and french fries for breakfast. Curt once remarked, "I do everything right-handed, except swing a bat and think." Known for his bad temper during his early minor league days, he took the advice of older coaches and curbed his outbursts, a fact which also led to his advancement. Blefary's first major league game was nothing special, but he will long remember his second game, as he equalled an American League record with two homers to tie Bob Nieman and Bert Campaneris for the most home runs in first two games. Oddly, or perhaps as so often happens, it was Blefary who had the shortest major league career of this fine crop of 1965 Oriole rookies. It was only eight seasons long.

Out in Kansas City, the A's took a number of rookies to spring camp with them but only one really made it big. While they were inviting twenty pitchers to camp, they really only touted two, Jim Dickson and Ron Tompkins. It was, however, a rookie who in 1964 had been on the disabled list at Daytona Beach and arrived in camp with no minor league experience who would steal the spotlight. What would you say his chances of making it would be? Well, this outstanding pitcher not only made it but turned in an 8-8 record. He went on to win 224 games, while losing only 166 in 15 big league seasons. He won 21 games three years in a row, 1971-73, in 1974 he won 25, and in 1975 he captured 23. Declared a free agent in December 1974, he left Oakland (Kansas City had moved there by then) and signed on with the New York Yankees for a reported $2.85 million. You remember Jim "Catfish" Hunter, I am sure.

Speaking of the New York Yankees, they had a bright prospect up from Greensboro, a shortstop named Bobby Murcer. The Yanks, of course, converted him to an outfielder in 1969, traded him to San Francisco in '75, and after a two-and-a-half year stint with the Cubs, he returned to the Yankees in 1979. Joining in the Yankee infield was a switch-hitter with the speed of lightning, quick hands, and good range in the field. Horace Clark was regarded as the finest infielder in the Yankee organization. Horace, who hailed from the Virgin Islands, had ten big league years. Joining the other Yankee newcomers was an outfielder who was perhaps their steadiest player over the next fourteen seasons, although he rarely received the credit due him. Roy White gave more than his share to the Yankee cause. Little mentioned in preseason '65, White had been a second baseman for four seasons in the Yankee system. Like Clarke, he was also a switch-hitter, and on five occasions hit homers from opposite sides of the plate in one game. An excellent base stealer, he swiped 232 bases in his career. Roy tied or set a number of major league records.

The New York National League entry, the Mets, introduced big-time baseball to a trio of good rookies—Ron Swoboda, Frank "Tug" McGraw, and Cleon Jones. Jones had had a six-game trial in 1963, his first year in professional baseball, but had then spent 1964 playing for Buffalo. He also spent most of 1965 with Buffalo, being recalled by the Mets at the end of the season. For 11 seasons he remained a fixture in the Met outfield before a 12-game finale with the Chicago White Sox in 1976. Cleon came from the same Mobile, Alabama, suburb which produced Hank Aaron, Billy Williams, and Willie McCovey. Spending the 1965 winter season in the Puerto Rico League, he developed into a good pull hitter and into a fine defensive outfielder. A former all-state football player, he possessed some extraordinary speed.

Ron Swoboda was one of the most popular of the early Mets and arrived in 1965 to capture the regular left field spot after only one minor league season. Not only did he gain a first-string spot, but he led the Mets in home runs with 19, a club record for rookies. His first major league hit was a pinch-hit homer off Houston's Dick Farrell in his second major league at-bat. Ron remained a Met for six seasons before he was traded to Montreal and then on to the New York Yankees for two-and-one-half seasons before he put away his bats after the 1973 season.

"Tug" McGraw has been one of the National League's ace relief pitchers from the day he joined the Mets in 1965 with only one minor league season behind him. In 1980 he was one of the World Series heroes for the Philadelphia Phillies. Brought along slowly by Manager Casey Stengel, he did get a chance as a starter under interim Met manager West Westrum, although he faired much better in relief roles. McGraw joined the Marines after the 1964 season, but was back in time for the '65 season. He credited his leatherneck experience with helping him "gain maturity and a positive approach." He holds the National League record for the most saves lifetime and was a prime contributor to the Mets' World Series appearances in 1969 and 1973 in addition to what he did to put the Phillies in a similar spot in 1980. He was also the winning pitcher for the Nationals in the 1972 All-Star Game. Always colorful and popular, McGraw tied the National League for the most grand-slam home runs allowed lifetime (four) in 1979 and then was quoted as saying, "I had a chance to set a record against Houston when they loaded the bases on me. However, I put the team ahead of my personal records and got Terry Puhl to hit into a double play." Back in 1965, the Mets were calling him the most promising lefty to arrive in the National League in a long time. It would appear they knew what they were talking about.

The mention of McGraw and the Philadelphia Phillies brings to mind that another of the 1980 Phillie pitching staff—the ace as a matter of fact—Steve Carlton, was making his debut in 1965. Like McGraw, he was with another club back then also, the St. Louis Cardinals, and also had only had one year in the minors. With the Cards that season he appeared in 15 games without a decision. At 24-9 for the 1980 season, it marked the fifth time in Steve's career that he has won twenty or more games. He won 27 games for the 1972 Phillies, the first season pitched for them after his trade from St. Louis for pitcher Rick Wise. Carlton has set or tied a number of major league records, has been an All-Star pitcher, and is a three-time winner of the Cy Young Award ('72, '77, '80).

The Cincinnati Reds, after a number of seasons introducing top rookie prospects gave us only outfielder Art Shamsky in 1965, and he did more pinch hitting than outfielding. He was a good hitter and had thumped out 43 homers in two minor league seasons. Shamsky moved on to the New York Mets in 1968, where he was a regular flyhawk for several years. Although the pickings were poor in Cincinnati, a player who would eventually wind up with the Reds, star for them, and become more associated with them than any other club was breaking in with Houston and gaining *The Sporting News'* National League rookie of the year honors. Second baseman Joe Morgan, who we briefly mentioned before, was up after short trials in 1963 and 1964. Little Joe, 5'7", 155 pounds was a fixture with the Houston club until his trade to the Reds in 1972. His national exposure with the Reds came mainly in All-Star Games and three World Series. In 1979 he was granted free agency and returned to the Houston Astros, where he led them into a Championship Series, which they lost to the Phillies. This little pepper pot has records, awards, honors, and league leaderships by the carload, most prominent of which are his two National League MVP Awards (1975 and 1976). Luman Harris, Houston's field boss, was very high on his 21-year-old left-handed hitter saying, "This youngster has all the equipment to become an outstanding major leaguer for a long time." How right he was. Joe had been the Texas League MVP and possessed the baseball instinct to make the right play at the right time. At San Antonio in 1964 he had hit .323, with 42 doubles, 12 homers, 90 RBIs, and 47 stolen bases. For a little guy he showed a remarkable total of 30 home runs in just two professional seasons. He was a graduate of the same High School in Oakland, California, that sent Vada Pinson, Willie Stargell, Tommy Harper, Bill Russell, Marty Keough, Jesse Gonder, Ernie Broglio, Eddie Lake, and Frank Robinson to the majors. He followed the Giants' 1964 rookie Jesus Alou into the exclusive 6-for-6 major league club, the only rookie of 1965 to do so. In a twelve-inning game at Milwaukee, Joe had two homers, a double, and three singles. Unfortunately, his team lost the contest 9 to 8. The fine defensive ability, good speed, and consistent hitting have remained with Morgan throughout his career. Only two clubs, the Astros and the Mets, expressed any interest in Joe as a youngster, and only the Astros promised him a bonus and a chance. The Mets insisted they would only offer him a tryout. What was Joe's secret to success in the majors? Clean living (a typical all-American boy) and his byword, confidence.

The Boston Red Sox had a big gangling rookie right-hander named Jim Lonborg, who found the only club he could consistently beat was the Yankees. He beat them for three of his nine rookie-season wins. He moved into Boston's regular lineup after only one minor league campaign. Signed off the Stanford University campus, he had planned to study medicine until a huge bonus lured him away. "Gentleman" Jim progressed steadily and led Boston into its first World Series since 1946 in 1967, when he won 22 games against 9 defeats. A postseason skiing accident tore up a knee and all but ended a most promising career. The Sox gave him four seasons to regain his old magic, but finally traded him to Milwaukee, who in turn sent him to the Phillies where in 1976 he was 18-10. He retired after fourteen seasons in 1978. How marvelous he was for the "Impossible Dream" Red Sox, and he came within a whisker of winning three games in the 1967 World Series for them. But fatigue finally took its toll, and that combined with the fantastic pitching of Bob Gibson gave St. Louis the world's championship.

Pitchers seemed to be dominant among the 1965 rookies; at least a number of those who made their big league starts developed into pretty decent hurlers over the long run. The Philadelphia Phillies gave a late-season trial to the young Canadian who they had had under tow for four years. His name was Ferguson Jenkins, and he is still pitching in the big leagues. Fergie was a 6'5", 200 pounder. Actually, you might say it was a "big" year for Phillie rookie pitchers, as in addition to Jenkins, they had two others with equally imposing physical characteristics—Dave Bennett, younger brother of pitcher Dennis, and Len Clendenin. All were flame-throwers with decent minor league credentials. Jenkins, however, turned out to be the best of the group by far. Starting out as a reliever, he posted only a 2-1 record in his brief stay in Philly. They soon traded him along with highly regarded outfielders Adolpho Phillips and John Herrnstein to the Chicago Cubs, where he became a starter. In his second season in Chicago, Jenkins became a 20-game winner, repeated the feat again the following year, and then won 21, 22, 24, and 20. But when he slipped to 14 in 1973, the Cubs traded him to the Texas Rangers. 1974, his first season with Texas, saw him post 25 victories, an American League high for that season. He thus became one of a very few pitchers to win 20 games in both leagues. The Rangers traded him to the Boston Red Sox, who two seasons later traded him back to Texas. A control pitcher, he has averaged fewer than two walks per nine innings during his career. He is also approaching 3000 career strikeouts. In his 16 major league seasons, he has 259 wins against 194 defeats. The 1971 Cy Young Award winner in the National League, he has often been the center of controversy during his career. He stands second to Baltimore's Jim Palmer among active pitchers for seasons with twenty or more wins, with seven to Palmer's eight.

The Sporting News also named rookie pitchers for the 1965 season, and while their selections appeared wise at the time, as we have so often seen, they were not the better hurlers over the years that followed. The selections were Frank Linzy of the San Francisco Giants and Marcelino Lopez of the California Angels. Linzy was a righty, Lopez a lefty. Linzy, who had a brief trial in 1963, was up from Tacoma and turned in a remarkable job for the Giants considering the pennant pressure and poise that was required to fill a relief role. His fastball, sinker, and slider saved a dozen games to go along with his nine wins. He lost only three contests. Originally an outfielder, he was later converted to the mound. He had an outstanding season with Springfield of the Eastern League in 1963 with eighteen complete games, a 16-6 record, seven shutouts and a 1.55 ERA. Frank put in eleven big league seasons. Lopez also had had a brief trial in 1963 with the Philadelphia Phillies. He was assigned to the Angels in October of 1964 to complete the deal that saw Vic Power sold to the Phillies. Perhaps the best freshman flinger in the American League in 1965, he posted a 14-13 record for the seventh-place Angels. His win total matched teammate Fred Newman and was one less than Angel ace Dean Chance's 15. There was little in Lopez's minor league record to indicate that he might have a bright major league future. He pitched for four American League clubs over a seven year period, never again coming close to his fourteen wins as a rookie.

Joining Frank Linzy on the Giants was a Cuban infielder named Tito Fuentes. A second baseman most of his career, he played nine years for the Giants before putting in time with San Diego, Detroit, and Oakland. Fuentes was called up late in the season after hitting .302 and 20 homers with Tacoma of the Coast League. Early in his career there were indications that he would be a big league prospect, especially when he hit .347 with El Paso of the Texas loop. His teammates pinned the nickname of "Parakeet" on him because of his habit of talking to everyone while he was on base. Tito tried his hand at managing for a while. We are not sure how it turned out as it was at the Little League level.

The Baseball Writers Association did not agree that Joe Morgan should be their rookie of the year in the National League and selected Jim Lefebvre, a second baseman with the Los Angeles Dodgers. Jim was a surprise member of the Dodgers in '65, taking over the keystone chores from Nate Oliver. He was added to the L.A. roster during spring training, and he went on to cop the rookie honors. His .250 average failed to show that he hit at a .333 clip during the Dodgers' 13-game September winning streak. A switch hitter, he showed good power from both sides of the plate. "Frenchy" was hardly mentioned when Dodger rookies were extolled prior to the season, perhaps because he put in only a partial minor league season in 1964 due to his being in military service. The Dodgers were listing as untouchables the likes of Willie Crawford, Tommy Dean, John Purdin, and Al Ferrara. Jim played infield for L.A. for eight years before he hung up his glove.

Other rookies of 1965 would include a 29-year-old first baseman, Ray Barker, of the Yankees, a travel-worn minor leaguer who was convinced he would never reach the big leagues after a decade of the bushes. Fellow first basemen were Tony Horton at Boston, a former shortstop and Los Angeles area scholastic basketball great who was a good power hitter, and Dick Nen of the Washington Senators, a former Dodger who appeared to have a big future in the nation's capital city. The Chicago Cubs hoped a converted shortstop named Glenn Beckert would develop into a successor to Ken Hubbs at second base. The Minnesota Twins were hoping that the aggressive chatterbox, but weak-hitting Frank Quilici would solve their keystone problems. A fine fielder with a good arm was the California Angel third baseman Paul Schaal, but his batting was suspect. The Detroit Tigers faced a similar problem with shortstop Ray Oyler, excellent defensively but his bat was short of expectations. The Chicago Cubs had a capable reserve shortstop in Jimmy Stewart, but he couldnd't move Beckert and Kessinger and found himself backing up both of them in the Cub infield. The Twins were finally getting some dividends from long-time minor leaguer Sandy Valdespino in their outfield. His eight-year minor league career ended in Atlanta when he led the International League with a .337 average; aggressive, speedy, and with a good arm, he looked like a comer. Bob Locker, on the strength of a good sinker moved into the Chicago White Sox bullpen early in the season. In 21 winning games he had a 5-2 record in relief. Nelson Briles was carried by the St. Louis Cardinals to protect him from the draft, but to their surprise he turned in some sparkling efforts with his powerful fastball. Ted Davidson, a lefty, showed remarkable poise on the mound for the Cincinnati Reds, mainly in relief roles. Larry Jaster was recalled toward the end of the season from the Texas League and gave the St. Louis Cardinals three victories and three complete games. He had 219 strikeouts in 210 innings with Tulsa. After a brief trial with Baltimore, Darold Knowles was traded to the Phillies to make his debut. Believed to be too small by most scouts, Dick Selma was 2-1 with the New York Mets after successful shoulder surgery during the previous winter. And Rene Lachemann showed unusual defensive ability as a catcher for the Kansas City Athletics, who were hoping he might also do something unusual as a hitter.

The story of 1966 had to be the World Series. The Los Angeles Dodgers were repeat winners in the National League, while the Baltimore Orioles replaced the Minnesota Twins at the top of the American League. The Dodgers went into the Series the favorites over the Orioles, who were seeing the youth movement we have spoken of earlier finally bear a pennant. The Dodgers had pitching, they thought, with Sandy Koufax winning 27 games, in what would be his final season, and Phil Regan who logged 21 saves and a 14-1 record. Tossed in for good measure was Claude Osteen with 17 wins, Don Drysdale with 13, and Don Sutton with 12. The Orioles, on the other hand, won their championship on the hitting of Boog Powell, the Robinson boys—Brooks, and triple crown winner Frank—and a pitching staff that had set a record for the fewest complete games by a pennant winner. It was expected that the Dodgers, despite not having a .300 hitter in their regular lineup, would defeat the Birds. Instead the baseball world saw the Oriole pitching staff give up two runs in a 5-to-2 win in the opener and then slam the door for the remaining 33 innings of the Series. To add insult to injury the three pitchers, Palmer, Bunker, and McNally, who shut-out the Dodgers in the final three games, had among them only tossed one shutout all season. Admittedly, the Dodgers were no powerhouse, but again the Birds' pitchers struggled all year and seemed to survive on hitting and outstanding defense. The Dodgers' pitchers did hold the Orioles to a combined .200 average, the lowest for a winner in a four game series, but the Oriole staff proved to be phenomenal as they held the Dodgers to just two runs, 17 hits, and an extremely low .142 batting average. The Orioles won the last three games 6-0, 1-0, and 1-0. One would have to journey all the way back to 1915 to find a World Series with such low scores. That year the Boston Red Sox dropped a 3-to-1 opener to the Philadelphia Phillies and then won four straight one-run games, 2-1, 2-1, 2-1, and 5-4.

In New York other strange things were happening. The Mets were celebrating their very first season out of the National League cellar, while their American League counterparts, the Yankees, were finishing last, one half game behind the Boston Red Sox. It was the first time the Yankees had found themselves holding up the league since 1912. I mention the Red Sox finish only because it will play an important role in 1967, as we shall see.

The Orioles, as we mentioned, won mainly because of their bullpen, as they had a hand in no less than 81 of the club's 97 wins, picking up 37 wins, while registering 44 saves. That crew consisted of Stu Miller, Ed Fisher, Moe Drabowsky, Dick Hall, Gene Brabender, and Eddie Watt. Of the group Brabender and Watt were rookies. Brabender, a powerfully built 6'6", 220-pound rookie had spent three years in the minors and then two years in the service where an Oriole scout saw him and recommended that the Birds draft the fastball whiz. He started his career slowly and in trouble when he overslept one morning in spring training and missed the team plane. His major league debut was even more embarrassing as he relieved against the Chicago White Sox with the bases loaded and balked home the winning run. On one other occasion, he reversed his form and pitched five-and-two-thirds innings of relief against the A's to gain a win. He did it, too, on an empty stomach. Seems he overslept again and missed breakfast. He spent five years in the big time with a 35-43 lifetime mark.

Eddie Watt had spent four good minor league seasons and had distinguished himself with Elmira of the Eastern League in 1965 by pitching two consecutive no-hit shutouts, the first Eastern League pitcher in the history of that loop to hurl two nine-inning no-hitters. By late July, Watt had a 6-1 record with four saves in 27 appearances when Manager Hank Bauer made him a starter only to have the Oriole starter jinx hit his arm. He finished the season at 9-7, the most wins he would have in a single season during his ten-year career. Watt had exceptional control of his emotions as well as his pitches, a characteristic that fits a relief pitcher well. When spring training got underway, it appeared the top rookie hurlers for the Orioles would be John Miller and Frank Bertaina, but by the season's end they had a combined 6-13 record.

The Birds gave a six-game trial to first baseman Mike Epstein, a one-time college All-American first baseman at the University of California and a powerful fullback on the football squad. He was rated a good fielder with a fair arm and was a decent runner for a big man. Mike had won MVP and rookie of the year awards in both the California and International Leagues and in 1966 was the minor league player of the year, while with Rochester. Catcher Andy Etchebarren, who had two previous shots, became the number one catcher. You must wonder what part a rookie first-string catcher played in the performance of the pitching staff?

Other events in the world of baseball found the Milwaukee Braves become the Atlanta Braves despite court action by the Wisconsin city in an attempt to keep them, as big league baseball moved south into Dixie. The California Angels moved to Anaheim, and the St. Louis Cardinals unveiled their new home, Busch Memorial Stadium, thus becoming the sixth senior circuit club to move into a new home in seven years. There was a sad note concerning the Detroit Tigers. Their manager, Chuck Dressen, suffered his second heart attack in as many years. He was replaced by coach Bob Swift, and almost two months from the day Dressen was stricken, Swift was hospitalized with suspected food poisoning. Coach Frank Skaff took over the club. Further tests on Swift revealed a malignant tumor on his lung. Dressen meanwhile was making a fine recovery, but in early August entered the hospital again for what was diagnosed as a kidney infection. He died three days later of heart failure. Swift remained in the hospital, but succumbed to cancer on October 17th. Marvin Miller was elected executive director of the Players' Association. It was also the year Dodger pitchers Sandy Koufax and Don Drysdale teamed up on a joint salary demand and remained holdouts until March 30.

There was an interesting twin bill in mid-May in Greensboro, North Carolina, as the Carolina League class A Rocky Mount Leafs took the measure of the Greensboro Yankees in both games, 5 to 0 and 2 to 0. Two seven-inning no-hitters were hurled by Rocky Mount rookies Dick Drago and Darrell Clark that day. The two were roommates, and when Clark was congratulating Drago after the first game he jokingly remarked, "Now I guess I'll have to go out and pitch one too." A doubleheader no-hitter, it has not been heard of before and represented a fantastic feat.

Perhaps the best group of rookies to join a team in 1966 were those who arrived in Boston's Fenway Park. While it might not have been recognized as a banner group at the time, they would all play a role in future events at that old ball yard on Yawkey Way. Three quarters of Boston's future infield arrived during that season. The regular Sox first baseman was a long-ball-hitting, fancy-fielding guy named George Scott. Scotty arrived as a third baseman, a position he had spent a great deal of time at in the minor leagues. In 1965 Scott was the Eastern League's MVP while playing at Pittsfield, and all he did to earn that prestigious award was lead his league in hits, doubles, home runs, RBIs, and batting average. He was also a leader in such defensive areas as putouts, assists, and negatively, errors. Known as the "Boomer" because of the long "Taters" (home runs) he hit, George was an instant success with Boston fans who were hungry for a new star. He remained in the Hub until after the 1971 season when he was traded to Milwaukee.

Rookies continued to play a role in George's career. In 1976 he returned to Boston in a trade along with Bernie Carbo for a promising young first baseman named Cecil Cooper. It certainly must have been a difficult trade for the Sox to make. A young man who was showing all the signs of a brilliant future for a veteran with a limited future. As so often happens, a team will decide it has a chance to win a pennant with perhaps one additional player, a situation we might call "going for broke" or "shooting for all the marbles." At any rate, it appeared that the Red Sox were willing to gamble, trading away a future for the present, and let the future develop as it might. Now stop for a second and remember that in Scott the Red Sox were getting a Gold Glove first baseman with proven hitting abilities and giving up a yet to be proven rookie. Now to this reasoning add the fact that perhaps the Sox best outfielder, Carl Yastrzemski, was being employed at first base in 1976. Then realize that two rookie infielders, third baseman Butch Hobson and shortstop Rick Burleson, were breaking in at those positions and that many of their tosses to first base were off-target, a fact which would call for a good-fielding first baseman. Consider all this and you have developed the thinking behind getting the veteran George Scott and his fielding genius back to Fenway Park. Many Boston fans fail to realize what Scott's fielding meant to Boston's young left side of the infield in 1977. We use this as an example that despite what many fans believe when trades are made, there may sometimes be reasons that are not evident on the surface.

In the case of the Cooper-Scott trade, it gave both clubs what they needed. Cooper was allowed to develop more slowly without being under the pressure of a pennant contender on a club with a nice blend of youngsters and veterans. As we know now, it was a move which paid handsome dividends to the Milwaukee Brewers, as Cooper has developed into one of the bright young stars in the American League. Now as for Boston, they lost the gamble with Scott, as they did not win the pennant and they wound up trading him to the Kansas City Royals in June of 1979 for a young utility outfielder named Tom Poquette. Hold it, look a little closer before you write the original deal off as a bad one, however. Sure, Boston lost the gamble for the 1977 pennant, but perhaps it gained more when it bought a year in the development of Hobson and Burleson by having a first baseman who could handle their sometimes erratic throws, a first baseman who could build the confidence of the youngsters. Remember what happened in 1978. In the early season, Boston appeared to be running away with the pennant, a good share of the credit going to Hobson, Burleson, and Scott, plus allowing Yastrzemski to return to his outfield post, a move which also helped. Of course, there were other dramatics in 1978 which led to a playoff and a New York Yankee victory, but I think by now you understand that sometimes trades made by major league clubs need to be analyzed a little deeper to catch the real reasons for being made. Often rookies play important roles in the reasoning behind the trades which are not apparent to the average fan at the time the moves are made.

Getting back to our 1966 story, in addition to Scott, the Red Sox had Joe Foy at third base. Joe had been the International League's MVP and rookie of the year at Toronto in 1965 in addition to being named *The Sporting News'* Minor League Player of the Year. The Sox sent Foy to K.C. in 1969 when he began to slow down from a weight problem, and after two more seasons he had eaten his way out of the majors. The third member of the Sox infield was Mike Andrews who was a back-up second baseman to George Smith at the tail end of the season. In 1967 he would take over the regular job at second. Andrews would stay with the Sox through 1970, after which he went to the Chicago White Sox for several years. Joining this trio was another Toronto product, outfielder Reggie Smith, who had been drafted by the Red Sox out of the Minnesota Twins organization. Smith returned in 1967 as the Sox second baseman, but with the development of Andrews moved to the center field position where he remained for seven years before being traded to St. Louis and from there to Los Angeles where he was still playing in 1980. Arriving by a trade of minor leaguers to Houston was right-hander Darrell "Bucky" Brandon, who posted an 8-8 record with the ninth-place Sox, but pitched some important games for them in 1967. Two other rookie hurlers were Guido Grilli and Pete Magrini, both highly rated, but neither contributed much. Grilli was sent to Kansas City before the season ended while Magrini was returned to Toronto.

The plight of those forgettable Red Sox pitchers seemed to be typical of the major league rookie pitchers for 1966. They came in great numbers and in most cases left in great numbers. Other than those already mentioned as being at Baltimore, there were very few quality hurlers to arrive. You could count the good ones on the fingers of both hands. Houston had Mike Cuellar, who would go on to star at Baltimore, winning 20 or more in four of his eight seasons with the Orioles. Houston also had Don Wilson, an effective right-hander who died tragically at the height of his career in 1975. Then there was Woody Fryman at Pittsburgh, Pat Jarvis at Atlanta, Chuck Dobson at Kansas City, Bill Hands, Chuck Hartenstein and Rich Nye with the Chicago Cubs, Jim McGlothlin at California, Dick Hughes at St. Louis, who had spent eight minor league seasons with eleven teams, some of which he was with more than once, and the pitcher who turned out to be the best of the bunch, Nolan Ryan with the New York Mets. Nolan was traded by the Mets to the California Angels, where he developed into a great strikeout pitcher, recording better than 300 strikeouts on five occasions, leading the American League in many pitching areas for years, hurling four no-hitters, establishing and tying records by the carload, and gaining many awards and honors—the prime right-hander of his era. Becoming a free agent in 1979, he was signed by the Houston Astros and led them to the 1980 Western Division title in the senior circuit.

Selected as rookie pitchers of the year were Jim Nash, who was 12-1 with Kansas City, and Don Sutton, 12-12 with Los Angeles. Nash, after that impressive, start did little for the A's, Braves, and Phillies in seven seasons. Nash was being heralded as the best right-hander to come along in quite a while and such knowledgeable people as Manager Al Dark and pitching coach Cot Deal were saying he was the most mature 21-year-old they had ever seen. "He handles himself like he has been around forever." With a little help from the bullpen, Nash might easily have been 16-1, and his 2.06 ERA was second only to Chicago's Gary Peters at 2.03. The A's were building a pretty good team, and Nash was considered their top pitcher among such others as Lew Krausse, Catfish Hunter, Chuck Dobson, Paul Lindblad, Gil Blanco, and Blue Moon Odom. "Jumbo Jim" was in fast company, but as we have seen, the best rated do not always turn out to be the best over the long haul.

Don Sutton was still with the Dodgers in 1980 after 15 seasons, and while often controversial, he has been one of the National League's top pitchers for most of that span. With only one season in professional baseball, he joined Los Angeles in 1966 rated as a brilliant prospect. He had a reputation as a control pitcher, and his minor league record showed 23 wins, 7 losses, 24 complete games in 31 starts, and 247 strikeouts in 258 innings. His freshman season saw him walk only 52 batters in 226 innings. These then were the best of the large crop of pitchers.

You may wonder who some of the others were. If you remember half of them you are truly a loyal baseball fan: Stan Bahnsen, who we will meet later, Fritz Peterson, Bill Henry, and Dooley Womack with the Yankees; Skeeter Wright and Bill Kelso with California; Dick Kelley, Ron Reed, Charlie Vaughan, and Cecil Upshaw with Atlanta; Greg Bollo and Fred Klags with the White Sox. Washington had a decent pitcher in Dick Bosman, but they also had Casey Cox, Dennis Higgins, and Dick Lines. Dave Dowling and Bill Connors were joining others already mentioned with the Cubs. The St. Louis Cardinals had Jim Cosman and Ron Willis. The Minnesota Twins were hoping for good results from Ron Keller and Jim Ollom. And there was Danny Coombs at Houston, George Culver at Cleveland, Mike Davison and Rich Robertson at San Francisco, Jim Shellenback with the Pirates, Rich Rusteck with the Mets and Bill Edgerton at K.C. Do you remember any of these hopefuls? Before we leave the pitchers, the Chicago Cubs gave left-hander Ken Holtzman a three-game trial in 1965, and he returned to post an 11-16 record in '66, which I suppose you could consider his rookie year. He was on major league rosters for fifteen years, enjoying success at Chicago as well as Oakland.

Named as rookies of the year for 1966 were Tommie Agee, an outfielder with the Chicago White Sox, and Tommy Helms, an infielder with the Cincinnati Reds. I suppose you could say the major leagues were beating their tom-toms. Both of these players had previous big league experience but still met the rookie qualifications. Agee had trials with the Cleveland Indians in 1962, '63, '64, and with the White Sox in '65, and Helms as a pinch-hitter with the Reds in 1964 and as an infielder in 1965.

The White Sox were one of baseball's weakest hitting teams, but Manager Eddie Stanky had built an offense that thrived on speed and stolen bases. The likes of Agee, Don Buford, Tommy McGraw, Al Weis, Ken Berry, and even such slowpokes as Pete Ward and Wayne Causey were turned loose in hopes of stealing a pennant. Agee perhaps typified the spirit of the Sox on the base paths. Not a stylish base stealer, he would manage one way or another to get to the bag before the throw. Yankee catcher Elston Howard felt Agee was the fastest runner in the league. Agee had stolen a career high 35 bases at Portland in 1964 before his 44 at Chicago in '66. Agee, after a couple of seasons with the White Sox, moved on to the New York Mets to star for five seasons. The White Sox were also claiming top rookies in catcher Duane Josephson, and outfielders Buddy Bradford, Jim Hicks, and Bill Voss.

When the 1965 season opened, the Cincinnati Reds were considered the favorites to win the flag, but they flopped to fourth and this caused a mild shuffle in the Ohio city for '66. Among the changes was at third base where Tommy Helms replaced Deron Johnson who was moved to the outfield. Rave notices were out on Helms, who had hit .319 with San Diego of the Pacific Coast League and .381 in a late-season showing with the Reds. Helms had been used mostly at shortstop in the minors and had teamed exceptionally well with Pete Rose at Macon in 1962, making a great double-play combination. He was juggled around the Reds' infield in '66, but put in most of his time at third base. Not a power hitter, he batted .284 with 154 hits. Tommy played for fourteen seasons, mostly with the Reds and Houston. Lee May, the only other Red rookie of note, was back for 25 games at first base before the Reds sent him to summer with Buffalo.

Kansas City had rookie outfielder Rick Monday, one of the mostly highly rated youngsters. Rick, the first player selected in the 1965 draft, had led the Arizona State Sun Devils to the NCAA College World Series championship in the summer of 1965, and had hit well with Lewiston in the A's farm system. Joining him was another Arizona State product, third baseman Sal Bando. Bando, of course, has been an American League star for years. Joining them was another product of the Minnesota Twins' farm system, second baseman John Donaldson.

The New York Mets were presenting catcher Jerry Grote, and shortstop Bud Harrelson was up for a second try. Both became popular and good additions to the Mets. The last-place Yankees had third baseman Mike Ferraro, who did little during his career, but gained fame at third base as a coach during the 1980 playoffs with Kansas City by incurring the wrath of Yankee owner George Steinbrenner when he sent home a runner who was thrown out on a crucial play. Joining Ferraro was outfielder Steve Whitaker.

Other notable American League rookies of 1966 were outfielder Hank Allen at Washington, another of the major league's three-brother acts, he was the brother of Richie and Ron Allen. The Senators had a decent catcher in Paul Casanova and an infielder of some note, Tim Cullen. The Minnesota Twins also had a good catcher in George Mitterwald, called up from St. Cloud late in the year, and Don Clark, a third baseman. From Caracas, Venezuela, to the Twin Cities came a combination infielder-outfielder Cesar Tovar, who during his 12-year career was continually performing at a variety of positions. Another catcher was making a start with Detroit; Orlando McFarlane, one more in the long line of Cubans to appear in the majors. He was joined by Arlo Brunsberg, another backstop who enjoyed a two-game major league career. The Cleveland Indians had third baseman Vern Fuller and catcher Buddy Booker; the Orioles had catcher Larry Haney; and the Angels had outfielder Jay Johnstone.

In the National League the better of the rookies included outfielder Bill Robinson, infielder Lee Bales, and second baseman Felix Millan at Atlanta. Millan, from Puerto Rico, was the best of the group and starred for the Braves and New York Mets for his 12 major league seasons. Another infielder who got his start in 1966 also played for 12 seasons; Sonny Jackson started with Houston and wound up with Atlanta.

Actually, Jackson had cups of coffee in Houston in '63, '64, and '65. It was shortstop Jackson who teamed up with second baseman Joe Morgan in the minor leagues to become the Texas League all-star DP combination. Jackson was joined by a big first baseman out of the Cardinals' system, Nate Colbert, outfielders Ron Davis, a long-time minor leaguer who had a six-game whirl in the Houston outfield in 1962, and Norm Miller, back for a second try. Getting a one-game trial was another big rookie up from Cocoa of the Florida State League named Bob Watson. Sent to Amarillo and Oklahoma City in '67, he was back for six games at the end of the season. 1968 and '69 found him again up and down, but in 1970 he arrived to stay. After spending 1979 in Boston, he became a free agent and signed with the New York Yankees and became a big factor in their 1980 American League East championship. Not associated with the Pittsburgh Pirates by many fans today was a skinny infielder named Gene Michael. He is more likely to be thought of as being with the New York Yankees, but "You could look it up." He was in 30 games for the Pirates in 1966. How many remember that he was with Los Angeles in '67 or Detroit in '75 or had a spring training trial with the Boston Red Sox in 1976? Outfielder Don Bosch, also better remembered in New York by Mets' fans, first appeared with the '66 Bucs. The Cardinals had infielder-outfielder Bobby Tolan. The Dodgers gave catcher Jim "Junior" Campanis his first taste of major league life. His father had a seven-game trial at second base with the 1943 Brooklyn Dodgers, but you may remember him as the present vice president, player personnel, for the L.A. Dodgers, Al Campanis. Another of the many new catchers in 1966 was Dick Dietz with the Giants. Still another catcher, Randy Hundley with the Chicago Cubs, had two previous short tries with San Frncisco, while second baseman Paul Popovich was up with the Cubs for a second time.

These then were the rookies of 1966.

1967-69: Cardiac Kids and Miracle Mets

The short era of 1967 to 1969 was, for those of us who lived through it, an unbelievable segment in the passing parade of baseball. The period started with a most unexpected event. Never in modern major league history has a team climbed from a last-place finish to win a pennant the next season. The Miracle Boston Braves of 1914, despite what many believe, were in fifth place in 1913, and they were last as late as July 18, 1914, before recovering to take the National League pennant that year. When another Boston club, the 1967 Red Sox, climbed from ninth place to win the flag, it marked the first time a team had made such a reversal in form. Remember, the 1966 Red Sox were just one half game ahead of the tenth place New York Yankees. One would have to go way back to 1890 to find a parallel, when Louisville of the American Association won the flag by ten games over Columbus after finishing eighth, 66½ games behind Brooklyn, who won the 1889 crown. As the 1967 pennant race entered its final stages, the Red Sox, Detroit Tigers, Chicago White Sox, and the Minnesota Twins were in a virtual tie for the league lead. Kansas City finally eliminated the White Sox while the Twins and Red Sox were meeting for a two-game series in Boston on the final weekend of the season, with the Twins holding a one-game lead. Boston fans surely remembered the feeling of those tail end series with New York in 1948 and 1949. Those earlier Boston clubs, however, did not have Carl Yastrzemski or Jim Lonborg. It was Carl who put on one of the greatest displays of clutch hitting that any player has ever put on to almost single-handedly help the Sox sweep the series from the Twins. The great pitching of Lonborg on the final Sunday of the season didn't hurt any either. After that win of the final game, the race was still not over for Tom Yawkey's club, as all Boston had to wait for was a Detroit Tigers-California Angels twin bill to finish up on the West Coast. The Tigers still had a chance to tie for the pennant. When the Angels won the second game of the doubleheader, it was all over, the Red Sox were the champions.

The World Series promised to feature the bats of Yaz and St. Louis' Orlando Cepeda and the pitching of Lonborg and Cardinal ace Bob Gibson. After four games, the Redbirds were up three games to one. The Sox rallied to make it 3 to 3, and it all came down to the final game with pitching aces Lonborg and Gibson scheduled to face each other, the winner to have won three games for his club. Gibson and St. Louis won out over a worn-out Lonborg, who still captured the Cy Young Award in his league. Yastrzemski starred for Boston, but Cepeda's bat went silent and it was Lou Brock who emerged to carry the Cardinals by hitting .414 and stealing a record seven bases. Boston skipper Dick Williams won manager of the year honors, Yaz a triple crown—.326, 44 home runs and 121 RBIs—and the season that started with the Sox being rated 100-to-1 shots at winning the pennant was history, a glorious page in baseball lore. It will be ever remembered as "The Impossible Dream" year after a popular song of the day, or to the youngsters who made it possible, the year of the "Cardiac Kids."

The Red Sox did it mainly with a cast of young players, most of whom had arrived within the previous couple of years, and they took these youngsters and blended in a few veterans to make a pennant-winning mix. They introduced only six new players in 1967, most of whom contributed to the victory. Perhaps more than any one thing that set the Red Sox machine in motion was the performance of rookie left-hander Billy Rohr in an early April game at Yankee Stadium. Whenever New York and Boston get together anything can happen. In his first major league start, Billy pitched 8-2/3 innings of no-hit ball against the Yankees before Yank Elston Howard singled, the only Yankee hit of the game. Boston's spirits soared; something different was happening. Their tempo seemed to move upward, and it lasted until October. As for Billy Rohr, he was not the second coming of Cy Young. He won only one more game for Boston, was sold to Cleveland, and quickly faded from view. Red Sox shortstop Ken Poulsen faded just as fast. One of the Boston catchers was Russ Gibson, and he could serve as an inspiration to any up-and-coming rookie who might become discouraged. You see, Russ had toiled for ten seasons in the Sox farm system. Not many young players today have that kind of patience. Russ stayed seven seasons in the majors with Boston and San Francisco. The three remaining pitchers were lefty Ken Brett, who became the youngest pitcher ever to appear in a World Series when he was called upon to relieve in game four. If he keeps going, he may become the oldest pitcher to appear in a fall classic, as in 1980 he was still pitching for the Kansas City Athletics. Ken is the brother of the Kansas City hero and third baseman George Brett. Another relief pitcher, also a left-hander, who was making his big league start with Boston, was Sparky Lyle. A colorful and effective reliever with the Red Sox, he went on to the Yankees, the Texas Rangers, and finished the 1980 season with the Phillies, with no plans of retirement. Sparky holds a number of pitching records, has led his league in saves many times, was the American League fireman of the year in 1972, and the Cy Young Award winner in 1977. Boston had drafted him from the Baltimore Oriole system. Joining the others was pitcher Gary Waslewski, a right-hander with seven years of minor league experience, his best years being 13-5 at Reno in 1963, 12-1 at Kinston in 1964, and 18-11 at Toronto in 1966 when he was named the International League Pitcher of the Year.

Meanwhile, the world champion St. Louis Cardinals were only breaking in two rookies, a shortstop named Steve Huntz, who appeared in only three games and seemed to change teams every year during a five-season 237-game career. The other new Cardinal was a big right-handed pitcher, who strangely in 1978 wound up with the Red Sox and was still with them in 1980, Mike Torrez. A journeyman pitcher, Mike has moved from club to club over the years with moderate success along the way. He won twenty games for Baltimore in 1975, and after a 1977 trade brought him from Oakland to the New York Yankees, he proceeded to lead them brilliantly down the stretch and gave them two complete-game World Series triumphs. As scarce as rookies were in St. Louis, they were even more so in Washington as the Senators introduced only reserve second baseman Frank Coggins and pitcher Dick Nold.

Other events were occurring in 1967 throughout the baseball world. In October the American League approved the transfer of the Kansas City A's to Oakland for the 1968 season and approved expansion franchises for Kansas City and Seattle for the 1969 season. Thus, the Athletics completed the shift from Philadelphia via K.C. to Oakland. One rookie made big news. Mike Epstein, a first baseman with Baltimore (6 games in 1966), rejected his demotion to the minors, an unprecedented move, and staged a 19-day sit-down strike, which led to his trade to Washington. He had appeared in 19 games for the Orioles, hitting .154. In 96 games with Washington he hit .229, but hung on for seven more big league years. Los Angeles Dodger rookies experienced a first for L.A. rookies, as a game was actually rained out in L.A. for the first time since the Dodgers moved from Brooklyn in 1958. The National League announced that they too would expand at some future date, and franchise applications were received for consideration from Dallas-Ft.

Worth, Milwaukee, Buffalo, San Diego, Toronto, and Montreal. Milwaukee welcomed back big league baseball when the Chicago White Sox announced they would play nine home games there in 1968. In another change affecting rookies, the majors decided to trim their opening day rosters from 28 to 25 players. This was an attempt to solidify minor league rosters before the opening of their seasons. It was also the first year that separate Cy Young Awards for outstanding pitchers were instigated. It had been a single award since its inception in 1956.

While the number of rookies began to dwindle, the New York Mets set a major league record in 1967 by calling on 27 different pitchers. The Mets led all clubs in the number of rookies given a trial with 12, and as might be expected, eight of them were pitchers. They included Billy Wynne, who couldn't, Al Schmelz and Jerry Koosman, who couldn't either, and Danny Frisella and Bill Denehy, both of whom each won a game, Les Rohr (not related to Billy and born in England) who won two, Don Shaw who won four games, and the best rookie of all and the Mets' top pitcher, Tom Seaver, who led the club with sixteen wins. Seaver was selected by the baseball writers as their National League rookie of the year. Tom had been originally selected by the Dodgers in the June 1965 free-agent draft, but chose to stay in school at the University of Southern California. Eligible for the special draft in January, he was selected by the Atlanta Braves and signed to a $50,000 bonus contract. However, the baseball commissioner's office voided the contract, ruling that Seaver had signed after USC had started its college season, and that any other club could bid for his services by matching the Atlanta offer. The Mets, Phillies, and Indians all submitted bids, with the Mets winning in a special drawing. Seaver had been a high school teammate of Met pitcher Dick Selma and his dad was a one-time Walker Cup golfer. Tom, of course, developed into one of the premier National League pitchers, hurling for the Mets until his trade to the Cincinnati Reds in 1977. He is the holder of many records and awards and pitched a no-hitter in 1978. He was 10-8 with the 1980 Reds. The other new Mets of '67 were a pair of second basemen, Ken Boswell and Bob Heise, third sacker Joe Moock, and outfielder Amos Otis, who is a cousin of teammate Cleon Jones. Originally selected by Pittsburgh, Otis was drafted by the Mets from the Boston Red Sox system and traded to the Kansas City Royals in December 1969 with pitcher Bob Johnson for Joe Foy, a third baseman, in a move the Mets hoped would solve their jinx in finding an acceptable third baseman. Foy was not the answer, and while the search goes on today, Amos Otis continues to star in the Royal outfield as he did in the 1980 World Series against Philadelphia.

The Cincinnati Reds had only three new rookies in 1967, two of whom would become household words for years—pitcher Gary Nolan, who summered for ten years on the banks of the Ohio, and catcher Johnny Bench, perhaps the best catcher in baseball during his prime with the Reds and still with them in 1980, although he has requested only part-time duty in 1981. The third rookie was Len Boehmer, who appeared only twice and later made a few appearances with the New York Yankees. The majors' other Ohio team, the Cleveland Indians, had four rookies but only catcher Ray Fosse would be remembered today. He did well until put out of commission by Pete Rose in the 1970 All-Star Game. Fosse has never been quite the same since, but give him credit, he was still around in 1979. Pitcher Steve Bailey and infielders Gus Gil and Gordon Lund were all forgettable.

The *Sporting News* selected as their 1967 National League rookies two players we have already spoken of. Their pitching selection was Dick Hughes of St. Louis, who had been 2-1 in 1966, but came up with a fine 16-6 record in 1967 with a 2.67 ERA. In 1968 he dropped to 2-2 and disappeared from the majors. Their rookie player was Lee May of Cincinnati, a first baseman, although in 1967 he appeared in 48 games in the outfield and 81 at first base. May batted .265 with twelve home runs and has played with Houston and Baltimore, being with the Orioles in 1980. For eleven years, 1968 to 1978, May hit better than twenty home runs per season. In May of 1969, Lee knocked out six home runs in three games, and in late April 1974 he hit two round trippers in one inning.

In the American League, *The Sporting News* agreed with the baseball writers as both selected the fine Minnesota Twin second baseman Rod Carew. The rookie from Panama made the jump from Wilson of the Carolina League to the majors and by July had been named to a starting role on the American League All-Star Team. Carew's .292 average was tops among the Twins' regulars despite the pressures put upon the youngster in the pennant race. Rod has become one of the best and most consistent players in the American League. Little mention was made of the left-handed hitter in preseason publicity, but it wasn't long before fans around the league were singing his praises. The Twins were finally becoming a harmonious club again. Gone were the squabbles between players, coaches, and the manager that prevailed when Sam Mele was in charge, which is not meant to be a rap on Mele. It was just that some players didn't like him. Carew seemed to be a standard-bearer of this new atmosphere. Rod has become a great base stealer, has had 200 or more hits four times, has led the American League in batting seven times, was the 1977 MVP and would appear headed for the Baseball Hall of Fame. Traded to the California Angels in early 1979, he was still with them in 1980. The American League rookie pitcher was Tom Phoebus of

Baltimore who had a 2-1 record with the 1966 Birds. In '67 he was 14-9, tops among the Oriole pitchers, and was undoubtedly the best rookie pitcher in the league, as he saved the Baltimore staff from a complete collapse by pacing them in almost every category. At one point, he hurled three straight shut-outs, only to have an unearned run end the string. Hailing from Baltimore, he was called up from Rochester in 1966 and broke in before the hometown fans with two consecutive shutouts. In 1968 Tom won 15 games and in '69, 14 games, but from then on it was all downhill, and he passed from the majors after the 1972 season.

Joining Carew in Minnesota were outfielder Pat Kelly, a left-handed batter who has spent 14 seasons in the American League and has played with Baltimore for four seasons. At third base was a rookie who is now more familiar to folks at Yankee Stadium, Graig Nettles, and there was a catcher named Hank Izquierdo, a Cuban who got into 16 games. He is one of the few major league players whose last name starts with an I. You will also notice with the 1967 rookies how many with Spanish surnames begin to appear on the major league rosters.

The Chicago clubs both had quite a few rookies in 1967, none of whom left much of an impression upon the majors, except perhaps Joe Niekro, who is now pitching for the Houston Astros but was then with the Cubs. Others with the Cubs were outfielders Joe Campbell and Clarence Jones, pitchers Jim Ellis, Dick James, Bill Stoneman, and John Upham, and second baseman-outfielder Norm Gigon. The White Sox were ballyhooing Charles "Cotton" Nash but in three seasons, two with Minnesota, he played only thirteen games. They also brought up pitchers Roger Nelson, Steve Jones, and Cisco Carlos. They had a decent catcher in Ed Herrmann and had a shortstop named Rich Morales.

Baltimore, with a weak pitching staff, was trying to find a winner among Bill Dillman, Jim Hardin (who came the closest at 8-3), Tom Fisher, Dave Leonhard, Paul Gilliford, and John Adamson. None really panned out. Then there were outfielders Curt Motton and Dave May. The left-hand-hitting May bounced around the majors for twelve years.

The Yankees paraded a crowd of rookies for whom they had high hopes. None were of any help in raising them from the unaccustomed depths to which they had fallen. For the record they were pitchers Thad Tillotson, Dale Roberts and Cecil Perkins, catchers Frank Fernandez and Charlie Sands, shortstop Jerry Kenney, and outfielders Tom Shopay and Frank Tepedino.

Out West, Detroit had two good pitchers in starter Pat Dobson, who developed into a winner in the early '70s with San Diego, Baltimore, and the Yankees, and reliever Mike Marshall. Marshall holds a number of relief records established with Montreal, L.A., Atlanta, Texas, and Minnesota, a well-traveled pitcher who, as you can see, did not make all his trips from the bullpen to the mound. The Tigers also brought along catcher Jimmie Price, shortstop Tom Matchick, second baseman Dave Campbell, and outfielder Wayne Comer. The Kansas City A's had two excellent outfielders, both of whom are still in the majors and will be easily recognized, Reggie Jackson and Joe Rudi. Both were important members of Oakland's championship clubs of the '70s and Jackson, of course, led the Yankees to greater heights in the late '70s and in 1980. First baseman Ramon Webster and shortstop Ted Kubiak may bring memories to some die-hard baseball fans, but the remaining A's were soon forgotten: Roberto Rodriguez, Tony Pierce, Al Lewis, Lois Bowlin (known as Hoss), and George Lauzerique, another Cuban who had pitched a perfect game earlier for Birmingham and had another near miss a bit later. The California Angels had a decent third baseman in Mexican Aurelio Rodriguez who has starred for years with Detroit and in 1980 was with San Diego and the Yankees. His brother Francisco was once in the Cardinal chain. Others with the Angels were pitchers Jim Weaver, Ken Turner, Rich Clark, catcher Jim Hibbs, outfielder Don Wallace, and first baseman Larry Stubling.

The National League Dodgers had nothing in rookies Al Foster, John Duffie, Tommy Dean, Bruce Brubaker, and Angel Alcaraz. The Cardinals were little better with Ron Bryant, Nestor Chavez, Bob Etheridge, Cesar Gutierrez, and Dave Marshall. The Atlanta Braves joined them with Angel Hermosa, Ramon Hernandez, Jim Britton, George Stone, Mike Lum, Clarence Gaston, and Glen Clark.

The Pittsburgh Pirates were building, in an attempt to win the flag which had eluded them because of pitching inadequacies in recent years. Bruce Dal Canton and Bob Moose helped some, but not enough. Bob Robertson was a rookie first baseman, and a catcher who would be of future help was Manny Sanguillen. The Astros had borderline rookies in pitchers Tom Dukes and Pat House, catcher Hal King, third baseman Doug Rader, and outfielders Al Harris and Jose Herrera. The Phillies had little of help to them in pitchers Dick Thoenen and Larry Loughlin or shortstop Terry Harmon.

One of the weakest hitting teams in professional baseball in 1967 were the Eastern League York White Roses. They were shut out 29 times and no-hit four times and had a team batting average of only .217. Consider for a minute the hard luck of their pitcher Dick Such. The rookie righty had an excellent

2.80 ERA, but he lost 16 straight games, failing to register one victory for the season. In eleven of his defeats Such allowed no more than two runs. Such was the luck of the White Rose pitcher!

1968 found the Detroit Tigers replacing the Red Sox at the top of the American League and defeating the St. Louis Cardinals four games to three in the World Series. Detroit had pitching ace Denny McLain, who had won 31 games, the first pitcher to win 30-plus games since Dizzy Dean in 1934. With a hard-hitting team, Detroit would have to stop St. Louis' Bob Gibson, the ace of their staff, and the speedy Lou Brock. When it was all over, the hero for the winning Detroit Tigers was pitcher Mickey Lolich with three victories to McLain's one. The Series going seven games, it was actually a misjudged fly ball by the Cardinals' fine defensive outfielder, Curt Flood, that allowed two Detroit runs to score that made the difference. It would seem that 1968 was a pitcher's year, as only five National Leaguers and only one American Leaguer, Carl Yastrzemski, were able to top .300. Carl's .301 average was the lowest major league leading average of all time.

1968 was the last season under the original big league setups. With the National League moving into Montreal and San Diego for 1969, a divisional setup was approved for that season, with a best-of-five divisional playoff to determine the World Series participants. 1968 saw scoring drop to an all-time low. Runs and hits dropped to levels last seen in the dead-ball era. There were 330 shutouts, 82 of which were by the minimum 1 to 0 score. The overall major league batting average hit an all-time low of .237. Baseball Commissioner William Eckert resigned, and eventually Bowie Kuhn was selected as his successor. The move by Eckert was forced by the owners, especially the younger ones, who felt if baseball was to make progress against the growing rivalry with professional football it would need a strong and vigorous leader. Kuhn, at 42, a Wall Street lawyer, was a compromise candidate as the leagues could not decide among a number of other hopefuls.

Interestingly, not only were batting averages lower, but home run totals for 1968 were 300 less than 1967 and more than 1000 less than 1962. Baseball was losing its biggest offensive feature, something that has always been given credit for the resurgence of the game since the early 1920s when Babe Ruth began hitting home runs and turnstiles began humming at record rates. With ten major league clubs hitting less than 100 home runs, the majors began to look at the causes. We point this out so that when the reader begins to compare rookies strictly on figures in the record book, it is important to consider factors in the particular era the player is involved in. Just because a rookie in 1968 hit fewer home runs or appears to have pitched better, it does not necessarily follow that he was any better or worse than those who broke in during other years. I have long advocated that it is difficult and often unfair to attempt to compare players of different eras on the basis of statistics alone. Developments in equipment, care of playing fields, different rules, live vs. dead ball, types of pitches, and so many other reasons make it an impossible comparison. Today we emphasize the home run and offensive abilities over the defensive abilities, but that follows the overall trend of baseball and was not always the case. The baseball record books are full of players from the early years that are very deserving of recognition, and perhaps if they would have been born later would far have outshined some of the current players. These old-timers are probably lost forever in the pages of history as many of today's fans do not take the time to dig back into the past. Many of today's sportswriters fall into the same trap. How many old-timers are shut out of selection to baseball's Hall of Fame because of some of the current rules on selection or by the lack of interest in genuine research by the electors? A case could easily be made for the old third baseman Larry Gardner. Larry played from 1908 to 1924 and compiled a .289 batting average during an era when the standard average was not that high. In 17 years he hit only 27 home runs and therein may lie an answer. Ask anyone who played against or with Gardner and they will tell you of his value. The acknowledged third base leader in that era was Frank "Home Run" Baker, but several old-timers tell me they would never trade Gardner even-up for Baker or even trade ten Bakers for one Gardner. I point this out only so the reader will become appreciative of the changes in the relative short period we are covering in this book; to try to pick an all-time rookie or even to compare rookies may present an impossible task. As in everything else in this world, conditions are continually changing.

So why the drop in home runs in 1968? Various reasons have been put forth: pitchers were better trained, increased use of the slider, hitters were home run crazy and swinging wildly, the emergence of the relief specialist, larger fields, better gloves, dilution due to expansion, inconsistent calls by umpires, etc., etc. Whatever it was, baseball was concerned.

Detroit's champions actually won with a veteran ball club. They did have a rookie pitcher who contributed little to their cause in Jim Rooker. He was traded to K.C. where he starred for four seasons before he became one of the mainstays of the Pittsburgh Pirate staff. Pittsburgh did have some youngsters breaking in who would lead them and some other clubs into positions of contention in several years. Little 5'5", 140-pound Fred Patek, a shortstop (what else), played in his first of three seasons with the Bucs, then moved on to star on a couple of division-winning Kansas City Royal nines. A four-game appearance by outfielder Al Oliver signalled the start of a fine career for him in Pittsburgh. Right-handed pitcher Dock Ellis, a switch-hitting batter, also broke in with a 6-5 record and in 1970 pitched a no-hitter against San Diego. The highly touted third baseman, Richie Hebner, saw action in two games and returned in 1969 to become a Pirate fixture at third until his trade to the Phillies in 1977. They in turn sent him to the Mets, who peddled him to the Detroit Tigers in 1979. Journeyman catcher Carl Taylor caught the first of his six big-time seasons. The National League champion Cardinals introduced only a few new rookies but one, outfielder Joe Hague, had four hits in seventeen at bats, the first of the four was a home run off Los Angeles Dodger hurler Bill Singer. Another Cardinal rookie to see very limited action was catcher Ted Simmons, who was still two seasons away from becoming the Cardinal regular receiver, a position he has held on to for ten seasons, with some outfielding tossed in for good measure. A switch hitter, Simmons holds several National League records for home runs from each side of the plate. An excellent defensive catcher, he has consistently hit for a good average.

Other National League rookies included catcher Walt Hriniak and outfielder Dusty Baker with Atlanta. Walt had a short major league stay as a player, and Dusty, who has set several National League records, is still around. A good hitter, Ralph Garr also played his first game for the Braves and the lefty batter won the National League batting crown in 1974 with a .353 average. The Cincinnati Reds gave us Hal McRae, a good hitter and base stealer who was still playing with Kansas City (to whom they traded him in 1972) in the 1980 World Series. *The Sporting News* and the baseball writers chose Red catcher Johnny Bench as their rookie of the year for 1968. We met Bench briefly in 1967 when he appeared in 26 games for the Reds. In 1968 he took over as the first-string catcher and has been a fixture there ever since, except for games every now and then at first base, third base, and in the outfield. Bench has been one of the top defensive catchers in baseball history and one of the most durable, appearing in better than 114 games per season for 13 seasons. Holder of many club and league records, he was selected the league's MVP in 1970, and at 22 he became the youngest player to ever be so honored. He was a repeat MVP in 1972. Back problems have periodically bothered Bench during his career, and he has asked the Reds management to give him a few more days off in 1981. We will see!

Selected as the National League rookie pitcher of the year was the New York Mets' young left-hander Jerry Koosman with a brilliant 19-12 record for the ninth-place Mets. Jerry, like Bench, had a brief trial in 1967. Traded to the Minnesota Twins for the 1979 season, he turned in a 20-13 record, just one win short of his highest winning season for the twelve years he spent with the

Mets. His 1979 performance won him the Comeback Player of the Year Award. He had been 3-15 with the 1978 Mets. In winning twenty games he joined the Yankees' Tommy John as the 17th and 18th players to turn the trick in both major leagues. A strikeout artist, he also ranks high on that all-time list. In 1980 he was 16-13. The Philadelphia Phillies gave a trial to a husky outfielder named Larry Hisle. Larry hit for average and power and had fine speed on the base paths. A whiz in high school, Larry twice made the All-State basketball team and was named to scholastic All-American teams in both baseball and basketball. Another 21-year-old to appear in Philly was infielder Don Money who had gained All-Star honors in the PCL. He took over the regular shortstop job from Roberto Pena in 1969. Houston was giving the first of four brief trials to a big left-hand-hitting first baseman named John Mayberry, who they traded to Kansas City in late 1971. John developed into one of the majors' most feared hitters of the '70s when he was the Royals' regular first baseman. Another outstanding high school basket-ball player, John attended the same high school as Alex Johnson and Willie Horton. He is the Royals' leader in most offensive power-hitting categories, and is also a decent fielder. He was traded to Toronto in April of 1978 and has played well for them as a first baseman and a DH through 1980. Outfielder Danny Walton also got a trial with the Astros, and the journeyman has been popping up and down with clubs in both leagues ever since as a DH, catcher, first baseman, or a third baseman. First baseman Nate Colbert was back for a second try after a short stay in 1966, but the Astros let him go to San Diego where he starred for several seasons.

The Los Angeles Dodgers had two interesting rookie pitchers in 1968, both right-handers and better remembered today as American Leaguers than Dodgers. Mike Kekich did the bulk of his pitching with the Yankees, Indi-ans, Rangers, and Mariners rather than the Dodgers, and Vicente Romo was traded after one game in 1968 to the Indians and was better known in Cleveland, Boston (when they could find him), and Chicago in the AL before his trade to San Diego in 1973. The San Francisco Giants had a winner in rookie outfielder Bobby Bonds, up from Phoenix. This power-hitting out-fielder has spent most of his career with the Giants, but has also appeared with the Yankees, Angels, White Sox, Rangers, Indians, and in 1980 with St. Louis. He went on to join Willie Mays as the only player in history to hit 300 home runs and steal 300 bases, and he stands alone hitting 30 homers and stealing 30 bases five times. He was often a leadoff hitter and has hit more home runs from that spot than any other lead-off man. Until 1980 he had never played in fewer than 145 games per season. In his first major league game, third at bat, he hit a grand-slam home run (against the Dodgers) becoming the first 20th Century rookie to accomplish that feat. Many honors have fallen on the sometimes controversial Bonds. Hailing from an athletic family, his brother Robert was a 13th-round draft choice of the football Kansas City Chiefs in 1965 and his sister Rosie held the U.S. women's record in the hurdles and was a member of the 1964 U.S. Olympic team. The Chicago Cubs were giving a chance to catcher Bill Plummer, who went to Cincinnati in 1970 for eight seasons as Johnny Bench's backup and who wound up with Seattle in 1978.

The American League had a few decent rookies in 1968 also. The rookie of the year turned out to be the Yankees' pitching sensation, the 23-year-old right-hander Stan Bahnsen. Stan was 1-1 in 1966, but returned in 1968 to post a 17-12 record for the Yanks who climbed up to fifth place. His 2.06 ERA was the sixth best in the major leagues. Stan had pitched two minor league no-hitters, one a perfect game for Syracuse over Buffalo in 1967. He won All-American baseball honors at the University of Nebraska in 1965. In December 1971, the Yankees traded him to the White Sox who in mid-1975 sent him to Oakland. From the A's he was sent to Montreal in a May 1977 trade, and he was still pitching for the Expos in 1980. In 1972 at Chicago, Bahnsen was 21-16 and in a strange reversal was 18-21 for the same club in 1973. The Yankees had rookie Bobby Cox at third base replacing Charley Smith. After 85 games in 1969, Cox disappeared, replaced by Jerry Kenney (the Yankees were having as many problems at third base as the Mets). *The Sporting News* also selected Washington's Del Unser, an outfielder, as their rookie player of the year as Del hit .230. A graduate of Mississippi State with a degree in math, Unser could cover the ground that the Senators needed in a center fielder. He batted and threw from the left side, and his father was Al Unser, who was a scout for Atlanta and had caught with Detroit and Cincinnati during the war years. Enjoying a much longer career than his father, Del in 1972 played with Cleveland and in '73-'74 with the Phillies. In '75 he was with the New York Mets, in '76 with the Mets and Montreal where he remained through 1978, and then back to the Phillies again in 1979 where he set a major league record when he hit home runs in three consecutive pinch-hit appearances. In 1980 he helped the Phillies to the world championship by coming through with key hits on several occasions against the Kansas City Royals. Interestingly, when he was traded from the Phillies to the Mets in 1974, it was for Tug McGraw who also was a World Series hero for Philadelphia in 1980. Appearing in nine games for Washington was outfielder Gene Martin who was the first Vietnam War veteran to appear in a major league uniform. It was his only appearance in the big leagues.

Among the Oakland A's rookies was pitcher Rollie Fingers, who developed into one of the majors' best relief pitchers and who after nine seasons with the A's moved to San Diego. In 1980 Fingers was selected by *Baseball Magazine* as the "relief pitcher of the decade" for the '70s. Many times an All-Star pitcher, in 1975 he appeared in a unique four-pitcher no-hitter against California joining Vida Blue, Glenn Abbott, and Paul Lindblad in the 5-to-0 game. Also with the Athletics was infielder Tony LaRussa, recently the Chicago White Sox manager. The Boston Red Sox rookies of 1968 included shortstop Luis Alvarado, outfielder Joe Lahoud, and fireball pitcher Fred Wenz. The White Sox had the brother of Lee May, Carlos, who developed into a good-hitting outfielder. Right-handed pitcher Marty Pattin was 4-4 in his rookie year with California. He has been with four other American League teams, performing both as a starter and a reliever. From 1970 to 1973 Marty, an outstanding competitor, averaged fifteen wins per season, mostly in starting roles. An All-American baseball player at Eastern Illinois University, Marty is a member of the NAIA Hall of Fame. The Angels had another young right-hander in 1968 who while he was only 4-2 that season won 20 games for the Angels in 1971. Remember Andy Messersmith? Traded to the L.A. Dodgers after the 1972 season, he won 20 for L.A. in 1974 to become the National League's winningest hurler and to join that select circle of pitchers who have won 20 in both major leagues. One of the first free agents, he played out his option year in 1975 and signed with Atlanta for 1976. Atlanta sold him to the New York Yankees and when they released him in late 1978 he re-signed with the Dodgers. The Angels also recalled first baseman Jim Spencer from their El Paso farm club. Spencer's grandfather had been a professional baseball player for eighteen years, including a few games with the 1913 Washington Senators. The left-hand-hitting Spencer brought with him some very impressive minor league statistics. It would seem that this era was the one in which high school All-American basketball players would abound in the majors. Jim was another of that select group. Jim also was one of those rookies to get a hit in his first big league at bat. He also played with the Rangers and White Sox, but in 1978 was traded to the New York Yankees. Confessing to always have been a Yankee fan, Jim said his favorite player, however, was Ted Williams. In 1963 as a youngster, Jim played in a Hearst Sandlot game at Yankee Stadium and hit a home run. Still with the Yankees in 1980, he entered the season with a .996 lifetime fielding average which is the best in baseball history among first basemen who have played 1,000 or more games at that position. Outfielder Jarvis Tatum, the 1966 Rookie of the Year in the California League at San Jose was also up with the Angels for the first of three tries, none of which lasted very long. The Angels also had a good relief pitcher in left-hander

Tom Burgmeier. Burgy was originally signed by Houston in 1962, but they released him in 1964 and he signed on with the then Los Angeles Angels. In the 1968 expansion draft he was selected by the Kansas City Royals for whom he pitched until traded in 1973 to the Twins. He became a free agent in 1977 and was signed by the Boston Red Sox where, in his 11th major league season, he is still one of the majors' best relief pitchers. In 1967 he won the Rawlings Silver Glove as the minors' best fielding pitcher. A superb athlete, he is known as one who keeps himself in excellent physical shape. Outfielder Merv Rettenmund, who had been an outstanding football player at Ball State, chose 1968 to make his big time debut. He had been twice selected an All-Star center fielder in four minor league seasons. Joining Merv in Baltimore was a bright catching prospect named Elrod Hendricks who had spent three years south of the border playing in the Mexican League. The Orioles had drafted him from Seattle, a farm club in the Angels system. Ellie was the first-string Oriole catcher from 1969 to 1971.

1969 arrived and will forever be known as The Year of the Mets, the New York "Miracle" Mets. Before we get into that story, there were several other new developments on the major league scene for 1969. First and foremost, both leagues expanded from ten to twelve teams. The Montreal Expos and the San Diego Padres joined the National League and Seattle Pilots and the Kansas City Royals joined the American League. With this expansion, each league split into Eastern and Western Divisions. The divisional winners would meet in a best-three-out-of-five Championship Series, which has become known as the playoffs, the winners to meet in the World Series. This was baseball's answer to holding fan interest until mid-October, a spot traditionally held by football. The additional revenues were nothing to be overlooked either. Now since pitching had been dominating in recent years, the baseball world had to seek a method of juicing up the offense, another concern of those who had a more than passing interest in the gate receipts. After all, salaries were climbing, why not batting averages and home run output? To hopefully bring about a change, the pitching mounds were lowered five inches and the strike zone was shrunk from the top of the shoulder to the armpit and from the bottom to the top of the knee.

While all of these changes were important, it was nevertheless the year of the Mets, who not only won the National League East, but the playoffs, and then of all things the World Series to boot. In one of the more startling upsets in the history of the Series the Mets defeated the Baltimore Orioles four games to one. Never higher than ninth place since their birth in 1962, it was truly a miracle for the Mets to defeat Baltimore who had run over the American League with ease. The Mets had defeated the Atlanta Braves and the Orioles had beaten the Minnesota Twins to get into the Series. The Mets had finished 1968 in ninth place, 24 games behind the champion Cardinals, so as you can see, their rise was significant. Met manager Gil Hodges actually had been developing a number of young pitchers, most of whom we have spoken of. There were Tom Seaver, Nolan Ryan, Tug McGraw, Jerry Koosman, Gary Gentry, and Ron Taylor, with the catching being handled by Jerry Grote. They were backed up by infielders Ken Boswell and Bud Harrelson, Ed Kranepool and Wayne Garrett, and outfielders Cleon Jones, Ron Swoboda, and the former American League rookie of the year Tommy Agee. While the Mets' early years were marked by laughter, in 1969 things were turned around. The old veterans and the Marvelous Marv Throneberrys were gone, the youngsters had taken over.

Not to take credit away from this brilliant young Met club, the fan must remember that with the expansion drafts to stock the new teams, most clubs, except the Mets, were hurt; early in the season most developed some weakness. While the older pitching staffs in the league were tiring in the heat of July and August, the young Met hurlers kept up their pace, growing even stronger as they put more experience under their belts. Inspired by these events, Agee, who had been a disappointment since his rookie of the year season with the White Sox in 1966, came alive and helped put the Mets on top.

In the playoffs with Atlanta, a team which was not as great as it had been when based in Milwaukee, the Mets met a club with a great hitter in Hank Aaron and a couple of aging vets acquired by trade, Orlando Cepeda and Tony Gonzalez, who were the cream of the Atlanta nine. While these three ripped Met pitching, the Braves had too little pitching of their own to overcome the New Yorkers. The Baltimore batters could not solve the Met pitching and hit only a very poor .146 in the Series, while the Mets' .220 batting average wasn't much better. Except for a 5-to-0 third game all the contests were close. This was a tribute to a young Oriole pitching staff that was just coming into its own with such hurlers as Mike Cuellar, Dave McNally, and Jim Palmer. The Sixties were about to close on an exciting note, just as they had begun when the 1960 Pittsburgh-New York series started things off with such scores as 16-3, 10-0, 12-0 and 10-9. After all, it was the centennial year for baseball as it was exactly 100 years since the Cincinnati Red Stockings became the first professional team in 1869.

For a while it appeared that our rookies might be taking over on all the teams for the season as the veterans were threatening to boycott the season, especially spring training, to back up the demands of their Players' Association. Most of the rookies were not members of the association. The problem revolved around the players' pension fund and TV revenues. Rookie hopes began to sink when such veteran player leaders as Ron Santo of the Chicago Cubs and Carl Yastrzemski of the Boston Red Sox announced they would report to their respective training camps. Agreement was quickly reached on the issues and a new three-year contract signed between the owners and the players. So the fans became the winners, and many rookies who might have made debuts in 1969 returned to the minors to further their development.

There were many new faces introduced into the major leagues in 1969, the expansion, of course, having its effect. The San Diego Padres led the majors with 15 first-year players, while the American League champion Orioles listed only two first-timers. The world champion-to-be Mets with a young club only gave passing looks at pitchers Jack DiLauro and Bob Johnson, but gave the third base job to Wayne Garrett, a draftee from the Atlanta Braves organization, and took a good look at Rod Gaspar, a 23-year-old switch-hitting outfielder, who in 1968 while at Memphis had led the Texas League in hits, while batting .309 and stealing 25 bases. They also played rookie Bobby Pfeil at several infield spots after bringing him up in late June. The Mets' opponents in the playoffs, the Atlanta Braves, had little in the way of rookies. They did give a mid-September trial to first baseman Jim Breazeale who had been tabbed as the Western Carolina's circuit top prospect. He had been the Braves' number one draft choice in January 1968 out of high school in Houston. The Braves' catcher was rookie Bob "Hiya" Didier who had had only two seasons of limited minor league experience, but was rated as a solid catcher in the Western Carolina's League at Greenwood, although his hitting was suspect. His dad, Mel, was a former Atlanta scout and minor league pitcher and was, in 1969, the baseball coach at LSU. Bob was also the nephew of Gerald Didier, a former minor league infielder. Bob lost his regular catching job to the veteran Bob Tillman in 1970, but hung on with the Braves until 1972 and played a few games for Detroit in '73 and Boston in '74. Joining the Braves for an early look-see was third baseman Darrell Evans, player of the year in the Gulf Coast League in 1967 when he was an Oakland farmhand, later, drafted by the Braves. A lefty swinger, Evans was the heir apparent to Clete Boyer at third base for Atlanta. Traded to San Francisco in 1976, he has spent five seasons playing first and third bases and some outfield for the Giants. Evans has been a Candlestick Park favorite ever since he broke in there, and in 1973 endeared himself to Giant fans by joining Hank Aaron and Davey Johnson on the only teammate trio in baseball history with 40 or more home runs in a season. A selective hitter, he established a National League record in 1976 with walks in fifteen consecutive games. A better than average fielder, he also was part of a major league record 45 double plays at third base in 1974. Because of his resemblance to the television character

"Howdy Doody," his teammates nicknamed the former collegiate baseball and basketball all-star, "Doody." Ollie Brown's younger brother Oscar also played the first of his five seasons in 1969 with Atlanta as a reserve outfielder. Five other rookies made brief appearances for the Braves and were never heard from again.

The expansion San Diego Padres were grooming talent in a hurry and gave fifteen rookies a chance to get their names in big league box scores for the first time. Of this long parade of youngsters, only two really bear mentioning. Catcher Fred Kendall was the only original Padre still on their roster in 1980. After eight years on the roster, he moved on to Cleveland and Boston before returning in 1979. Fred was originally in the Cincinnati chain, but the Padres got him in the expansion draft. Once voted the Padre MVP, he has proven his worth by working with Padre youngsters, especially pitcher Randy Jones who credits Kendall for his success. Pitcher Clay Kirby was around long enough in 1969 to post a 7-20 record, but in fairness to Clay, it would have been difficult for anyone to turn in a winning record with that club. Kirby did have a couple of good years with the Padres and the Reds during his eight-year tour. Clay shouldn't feel bad though, as pitcher Steve Arlin, 0-1 in 1969, was 9-19 in 1971, and 10-21 in 1972. Arlin was one of the fifteen by the way.

Next to the Padres, the Philadelphia Phillies introduced eleven new players in 1969, none of whom would last long on the big team roster. One, however, looked and sounded like a winner, pitcher Billy Champion. He managed eight big league seasons with a not so champion 34-50 slate. The Phillie farm clubs did enjoy success in 1968 with only one finishing lower than second place, but the 1969 crop was not their best. They did have the prized rookies Don Money and Larry Hisle, whom we have already met. Those farm teams were, however, bursting with such future prizes as Larry Bowa, Denny Doyle, and Greg Luzinski, all of whom we encounter in the seasons ahead.

Among the hopefuls at Wrigley Field, Chicago, was pitcher Jim Colborn, who later became a 20-game winner for the Milwaukee Brewers and four years later, in 1977, won 18 for Kansas City. Joining Colborn was outfielder Oscar Gamble, who has been traded to many clubs since 1969 and was with the New York Yankees in 1980. Oscar has played for seven different clubs and has been with four clubs in the last four years. Among the feats this journeyman outfielder has enjoyed was the distinction of getting the last hit ever in old Connie Mack Stadium while a member of the Phillies in 1970. He had his best season in the majors in 1977, hitting .294 with 31 home runs and 83 RBIs while with Chicago, the White Sox that is. Bet the Cubs wished it was with them! His wife, Juanita, is a singer and once sang the National Anthem at Yankee Stadium prior to a 1976 Championship Series game.

One of Oscar's teammates on the 1980 Yankees was outfielder Lou Piniella, who was selected by the baseball writers as their American League rookie of the year for 1969. "Sweet Lou" was with the Kansas City Royals in 1969. Lou had originally been signed by Cleveland back in 1962, was drafted by Washington, who assigned him to Baltimore to complete a previous deal. He had a four-game try with the Orioles in 1964 and went back to the minors until 1968. From there he was traded to Cleveland, who gave him a six-game trial before Seattle drafted him and sent him to Kansas City where he gained rookie honors in '69. I wonder if Lou felt that no one wanted him, what with all that moving around? In December of 1973, the Royals traded him to the Yankees where he played in 1980. Not necessarily known for his speed or fielding prowess, he has become a Yankee favorite, whose fans greet him each time he bats with chants of "Lou, Lou." There were several other fairly decent rookies on the Yankees in '69, the highly regarded Ron Blomberg, who became the major league's first ever designated hitter and a couple of catchers named John Ellis and Thurman Munson. Ellis has been in the American League since, but with Cleveland and Texas. A fairly decent catcher, Ellis suffered a horrifying injury at Boston in 1976 when it was believed his career would be ended. Sliding into second base, John sustained a broken leg, a dislocated ankle, and torn ligaments. He was hitting .419 at the time. He recovered and is still around and contributing to the Ranger cause. Munson had a 26-game trial, and we will meet him in more detail when we discuss 1970.

While the baseball writers had selected Piniella as their American League rookie, a second baseman-shortstop with the Los Angeles Dodgers, Ted Sizemore, was their National League choice. Ted only remained in L.A. for two seasons, moving on to St. Louis where he was the Cardinal second baseman from 1971 to 1975. Then it was back to L.A. for 1976 before going to Philadelphia, the Cubs, and Boston. Ted, the opening day shortstop, was soon moved to second base. He started his pro career as a catcher having been all-Big Ten at the University of Michigan. At 5'9" and 160 pounds, perhaps the move from behind the plate was a wise one. Sizemore wasn't the only good young player to get a trial with L.A. in 1969, although he was the only regular among the group. You could build a pretty decent team around the likes of these rookies: A former Michigan State linebacker who had developed into a power hitting third baseman, Steve Garvey; or the top fielding, speedy outfielder, Bill Buckner; or a good-fielding base-stealing shortstop, Bill Grabarkewitz; or an outfielder who never played high school baseball and whose three-year career had been interrupted by college and military commitments, but who stole bases and whose bat showed a lot of power, Bill Russell; or a youthful outfielder with a sweetheart of a name who made the transition to shortstop and could also hit and steal bases, Bobby Valentine; or an excellent outfielder with only two abbreviated seasons of pro ball, Von Joshua. Here you have one of the best groups or rookies ever to arrive with one team in one year. Some expansion teams could have used this crew, proof that farm teams can pay handsome dividends.

San Francisco only broke in three rookies, and one is much better remembered as a Cincinnati Red than a Giant. Outfielder George Foster, who had had some incredible seasons on his way to becoming the top power hitter he is today, has been the backbone of the Reds for years. With the Reds in 1979, George had 19 game-winning hits which led him to say, "I wanted to be a 20-game winner, so I would have a chance at the Cy Young Award." I am sure the National League pitchers found nothing funny in his quip. One of the strongest men in the game today, George keeps himself in good shape all year round as a means of staving off injury. His 12-year career has netted him well over 1000 hits and 200 home runs. One day Philadelphia Phillie manager Danny Ozark, after seeing George hit a 475-foot home run, charged Foster with using a cork-filled bat. Answering the charge George replied, "It's not cork, but iron in here," pointing to his massive forearms. The next day George hit three homers in a twin bill against Ozark's Phillies.

Speaking of the Reds, they had decent newcomers in outfielder Bernie Carbo, shortstop Darrel Chaney, catcher Danny Breeden, and pitcher Jose Pena. Chaney was an impressive looking defensive performer; a switch-hitter. What he lacked in experience he overcame with aggressiveness. An All-American prep school football quarterback, he spurned 35 football scholarship offers, including Notre Dame, to concentrate on baseball. Carbo was the Red's first draft choice in 1965, ahead of Johnny Bench. Bernie, a left-han-hitting power hitter, had impressed the Reds' brass by hitting the longest home run in Asheville history, estimated at 500 feet, while he was playing for the farm club. Carbo starred all the way along the minor league trail. His major league career has found him moving to St. Louis, Boston twice, Milwaukee, and Cleveland, often leaving a trail of controversy behind him. Like a number of others, he too had been a three-sport star and a high school All-American.

The Sporting News selected their National League rookies as pitcher Tom Griffin of the Houston Astros and Coco Laboy of the Montreal Expos. Griffin was 11-10 with 200 strikeouts and, except for a 14-10 season in 1974, has never accomplished much in 12 major league seasons. He has been in both major leagues and was with the Giants in 1980. The Astros had several other rookies in 1969, one a pitcher with the unforgettable name of Scipio Spinks. Laboy, a third baseman, hit 18 homers and batted .258 and was a regular for two seasons with the Expos before weak hitting relegated him to three seasons in a utility role. Montreal also had outfielder Don Hahn, who is better remembered as a New York Met, and pitchers Carl Morton, Steve Renko, and Bob Reynolds. Renko has pitched some good ball for Montreal and in recent years has been with Boston. Reynolds was more effective in Baltimore than Montreal. The Pirates' only rookies of note were second baseman Dave Cash, who after five seasons with the Bucs became a regular with the Phillies, and outfielder Angel Mangual, who played more with the Oakland A's than at Pittsburgh.

The St. Louis Cardinals had among their pitching prospects two right-handers, Reggie Cleveland and Santiago Guzman, each of whom had a one-game appearance in 1969. Cleveland, a Canadian, was evaluated as needing one or two more minor league seasons plus an additional pitch to add to his repertoire, but definitely he had the tools to be a major leaguer. They said Guzman, who owned a major league fastball, needed a better curve and an improvement in his control. Both were back in 1970 and in the years that followed. After four tries, Guzman left with a 1-2 record, while Cleveland arrived to stay in 1971 and was in the Redbird uniform until traded to Boston in 1974. After four fairly successful years with the Red Sox, he was sold to Texas in early 1978. The Rangers sent him to Milwaukee for the 1979 season where he remained for 1980. We will meet Reggie again in 1971. Leron Lee, an outfielder, also broke in with the Cards for the first of eight major league seasons. Joining the St. Louis mound corps after an excellent year at Tulsa was a St. Louis native and a left-hander, Jerry Reuss. Jerry has been a consistent winner for twelve seasons in the National League with the Cardinals, Astros, Pirates, and for the past two seasons with Los Angeles. In 1980 he was the big winner on the Dodger staff at 18-6, his best season in the majors, and his 2.52 ERA was the lowest since his minor league days over ten seasons ago. He was chosen the starting pitcher for the National League in the 1975 All-Star Game and turned in a scoreless three innings of work.

In the American League there were also some pretty fine rookies. The Orioles had only one of note in first baseman Terry Crowley, who converted to an outfielder, but never as a regular. Washington had a budding star in shortstop Toby Harrah, who was drafted from the Phillies. Harrah's top thrill in baseball was a no-hitter he had pitched for his American Legion team at Marion, Ohio. Harrah, a good base stealer, has also established and tied a few fielding records. He was a regular at Texas from 1972 to 1978 and has put in some solid seasons with Cleveland. He has been an American League standout in recent years. Cleveland had little among seven rookies in 1969 as did Seattle among eight, although they had an outfielder with like first and last names in William Williams. Detroit, with a like number of rookies, couldn't find any with lasting quality. Joining the list of teams with eight newcomers, which seemed fashionable among American League teams, were the Minnesota Twins, who had a catcher named Rick Dempsey to whom they gave brief trials for four years before peddling him to New York as a backup catcher to Munson. The Yanks sent him to Baltimore where he developed into a pretty fair catcher. Shortly after joining the Birds, Dempsey tied a major league record by participating in three double plays in a single game. All were strikeouts with throws to Mark Belanger to retire would-be base stealers. Rick's parents were former vaudeville performers, and his father also played in the Broadway production of "Song of Norway" after World War II. Some of this show biz must have rubbed off on Rick, as he has put on some of the most memorable displays ever seen in the majors during rain-delay games. To the delight of the fans and indignation of the groundskeepers, he has mimicked at-bats, run around the bases on the tarps, sliding under imaginary tags, through puddles and into the mud.

The Chicago White Sox had the remarkable big right-handed pitcher Dennis O'Toole who gets the all-time rookie award for effort. Would you believe that after five seasons (1969-73) he still had not met the minimum requirements to qualify as a rookie? That's right, Denny had put in parts of five seasons with the Pale Hose, compiled a 4.94 ERA in 15 games with 31 innings pitched, giving up 45 hits, striking out 22, and walking 10. He never got a win, never took a loss, never started a game, and never had a save in his relief appearances—a truly remarkable record. The older brother of Washington's shortstop Ed Brinkman, one Chuck Brinkman, was a backup catcher for the Sox. His six years in the majors were about as distinguished as O'Toole's. Then there was Jose Ortiz, a highly rated speedster who had stolen 64 bases in the Midwest League in 1967. He was the fastest man in the Chisox camp. In three big league seasons, two with the Sox and one with the Cubs, he stole a total of three bases. It sure didn't seem like the White Sox year. But hold on, *The Sporting News* named a White Sox player their Rookie Player of the Year. Outfielder Carlos May, younger brother of the Reds' Lee May, won the honors. May had delightful offensive credentials and appeared to be the answer to the club's search for a power hitter. He had been in seventeen games with the 1968 White Sox and had hit a whopping .330 with Lynchburg of the Carolina League. Although he never delivered the power, he was good enough to patrol major league outfields for ten seasons.

The Sporting News American League Rookie Pitcher of the Year was a young Red Sox right-hander with a good curve ball, Mike Nagy. He had seen only limited action in the Sox system due to military service and arm trouble, but he turned out to be a pleasant surprise in Boston with a fine 12-2 record. He developed a good fastball to go along with his curve and made the jump from the Carolina League with only 39 games of professional experience. Of the 28 games he started, the Sox won 22. His freshman year remained his best as over five more seasons he was 8-11, never coming close to those rookie stats. He was joined by pitchers Mike Garman and Ray Jarvis, who did little to distinguish themselves. Jarvis was the early season surprise for the Sox with a very effective sinking fastball until arm trouble took its toll and he finished 5-6. Rushed up to the Sox in June from their Pittsfield farm club was pitcher Bill Lee. He made an immediate impression with his poise and effective screwball. There are some who will say that that pitch summed up Bill's Boston career, but while he had his moments off the field, he always gave his all between the foul lines. A standout at the University of Southern California, he led them to the 1968 NCAA championship by winning two big games on consecutive days. Bill won seventeen games three years in a row for Boston, 1973-75, and was a big factor in their 1975 pennant. A rather free spirit, he had his problems with management over the years and may best be remembered for his threat to quit when the Red Sox traded away his pal Bernie Carbo. He also had his fights on the field and under the stands; the best remembered would be his free-for-all with Yankees which netted him an injured arm. The Sox finally had enough and traded him to Montreal in 1978, where the lefty continued his winning ways, still the hero of the younger set. Known for his habit of jogging to the ball park, he has had his share of run-ins with Montreal taxis. Joining these pitchers was the younger brother of Tony Conigliaro, Billy. A most sought after high schooler, he turned down football scholarships to join the Red Sox system. 1970 and '71 found him appearing in over a hundred games for the Sox, but problems with management found him going to Milwaukee for 1972 and then to Oakland in '73. Highly rated left-handed first baseman Tony Muser and third baseman Syd O'Brien also joined the Sox. Another rookie in the Red Sox lineup for two games was a 21-year-old catcher from New Hampshire named Carlton Fisk. We will meet him again in 1973, but in '69 the Bosox brass was conceding, "He has a lot to learn, but has good power, a good arm, and does a good job of catching. We hope he'll advance well enough to qualify for the Eastern League." Fisk's older brother, Calvin, was a catcher in the Baltimore system. Out on the West Coast the Oakland A's were giving a trial to a pretty fair catcher of their own, Gene Tenace. Gene has appeared as a first baseman and third sacker in the majors and was also a pitcher while in the minors. Holder of a number of records, he played a major role in the A's World Series titles of 1972, '73, '74. He was the star of the 1972 World Series as he hit .348 against Cincinnati with four home runs and nine RBIs. Joining Tenace were four other rookies, the best of whom was a hard throwing 20-year-older, and a most valuable piece of Oakland property, Vida Blue. He had an impressive 231 strikeouts with Burlington of the Midwest League. Blue, the American League MVP and Cy Young Award winner in 1971, has been a top pitcher since winning 24 in '71, 20 in '73, 22 in '75, and 18 in '76 and '78. The A's traded him to San Francisco in March of 1978. He has appeared in numerous All-Star Game squads, and is the only hurler to start an All-Star Game for each league. He has been a hard-luck hurler in World Series play, losing a game in each of the three World Series he has appeared in. On September 21, 1975, he pitched a no-hitter against the Twins, and seven days later joined three teammates for a combined no-hitter against California. With a 14-10 record in 1980 and 46 total wins for the Giants, he has an outside chance to become the fourth pitcher in major league history to win 100 games in each league, a feat only Cy Young, Jim Bunning, and Gaylord Perry have accomplished. Once in high school Vida struck out 21 batters for all the outs in a seven-inning game. A left-handed quarterback in football, he set a record by throwing 35 touchdown passes for his Shreveport High School.

Among the rookies with the California Angels were two pitchers who developed into fairly decent big leaguers, Ken Tatum and Pedro Borbon. Borbon, of course, is better remembered as a member of the Cincinnati Reds, having pitched more games (531) than any pitcher in the Reds' 104-year history, most all of which were in relief roles. A native of the Dominican Republic and a veteran of that country's revolution, he plays baseball there each winter, but unlike his recent role with San Francisco, he appears as a starter there. He was originally signed by the Cardinals, was drafted by the Angels, traded to the Reds, and then to the Giants. Tatum won fourteen games in his first two years with the Angels, but in three seasons with the Red Sox and one with the White Sox picked up only two more wins. The Kansas City Royals had more rookies than any other American League club, which could be expected for an expansion club. Most of those rookies spent the season in Omaha. You may remember a 6'5", 210-pound catcher with a strong arm from New England who spent spring training in the service, but returned to hit .282 at Omaha, Fran Healy. He was drafted from the Cleveland system. Joining him were catchers Dennis Paepka and John Martinez. Pitchers with the Royals were rookies: Don O'Riley, a real competitor who was being molded into a relief pitcher; Jerry Cram, who had an outstanding curve and great control; Dick Drago, who is still pitching in the American League, but for the Red Sox; Al Fitzmorris, who enjoyed some successful years in the mid '70s; and Bill Butler, who put in seven American League seasons with a 23-35 record to show for it. The A's were trying outfielder Alfredo Rico, drafted from Baltimore, who showed promise in twelve games and retired to his offseason job as a barber. Another hopeful who managed only a 20-game look-see was Scott Northey, who could also play first base or shortstop and had been dazzling at Omaha on defense and in base running. He was the son of former major league outfielder Ron Northey. Utility infielder Juan Rios made an 87-game season his only one in the big time.

And so the decade of the sixties slipped into the baseball record books. It had been a good decade, lots of changes, lots of excitement, lots of new players, and lots of good rookies. It was on to the Seventies, a decade of continued changes in the old order of things in the world of baseball, as we shall see.

1970-73: A Time of Change and Turmoil

As the decade of the '60s slipped into history and the decade of the '70s arrived, baseball fans were about to witness a period of change and turmoil never before equaled in the history of the game. While many changes had taken place during the '60s, it would be nothing to the roller coaster ride baseball would start on in 1970. The 24 major league teams started the decade by attracting 28 million fans through their turnstiles, an all-time record. The Seattle Pilots moved into Milwaukee to take up where the Braves had left off when they moved to Atlanta in 1965. Actually, the move to Milwaukee was made only four days before the 1970 season began. The Pilots became the Brewers, and while it clearly was not a matter of love at first sight by the Milwaukee fans, they soon came to appreciate the efforts of the management to give them quality baseball. Before long the Brewers were the hit of the town. The Brewers were not all that was new in the baseball world. The National League presented two new ball parks, Three Rivers Stadium in Pittsburgh and Riverfront Stadium in Cincinnati. The tenants of those two stadiums responded by winning their divisional championships.

There were players in the news also, and the results of their actions were to be felt in baseball for many years to come. Detroit Tiger pitcher Denny McLain was setting records for suspensions. The two-time Cy Young Award winner was suspended three times during the 1970 season. Commissioner Bowie Kuhn sat him down after a national magazine, in a copyrighted story, revealed McLain had been involved in a bookmaking operation during the 1967 season and had become involved with mobsters. Kuhn originally suspended him indefinitely, but relented and restored McLain to duty as of July 1. Slightly more than a month later, McLain was back in the news when he doused a couple of Detroit sportswriters with water in the Detroit clubhouse. This led Tiger GM Jim Campbell to impose another suspension on his former ace hurler. Early September found a third suspension slapped on the pitcher, this time for flashing a gun in a Chicago restaurant. This time he was out for the season. The season had barely ended when the Tigers traded the controversial pitcher to the Washington Senators who were badly in need of a drawing card.

Another pitcher, Jim Bouton, formerly of the New York Yankees but more recently of Seattle and Houston, published a diary he had been keeping during the 1969 season. The work caused quite a stir for what it said about the private lives of some of his fellow players. While Bouton drew the censure of the commissioner's office for what he had written, all that was really accomplished was a stimulation of the sales of the books.

Detroit Tiger catcher Bill Freehan also wrote a book which was critical of some of his Tiger teammates. An embarrassed Freehan apologized to his fellow Tigers and refused to discuss his tome and the matter slipped from the news.

Veteran St. Louis Cardinal outfielder Curt Flood, however, presented a new and more far-reaching problem to the baseball world. The flyhawk's dispute with baseball was the result of his trade in late 1969 by the Cardinals to the Philadelphia Phillies. He refused to report and filed an antitrust suit against baseball's reserve clause, claiming he had the right to sign with any team he might choose. Flood eventually lost his case, but set the stage for similar future suits by other players like Andy Messersmith and Dave McNally. These suits finally resulted in players earning the legal right to play one season without a signed contract and then to enter the free-agent market to sell their services to a team of their choice, usually the highest bidder financially. This action, overthrowing the traditional reserve clause which bound a player to the team he had originally signed with or to a club he might be traded to, was the greatest change in baseball traditions to come along in many a year. As if Washington manager Ted Williams didn't already have enough problems, Flood signed a contract with the Senators, and Williams had the prospect of having both McLain and Flood for 1971.

The American League, after enduring the court battles related to the mess in Seattle and the transfer of that club to Milwaukee, won another significant battle when the National Labor Relations Board recommended dismissal of the complaints of former umpires Al Salerno and Bill Valentine. They had charged the league with firing them in 1968 for their activities in connection with helping American League umpires form a union.

The umpires assigned to work the playoffs at the end of the season staged a one-game strike, and the opening game of the Cincinnati-Pittsburgh series was worked by minor league umpires. There was also a threatened player strike over their dispute with the owners over the terms of their basic agreement which had expired on December 31, 1969. The dispute ended without the demonstration amounting to much.

The seeds for change were beginning to sprout, and before the decade would end there would be significant changes in player attitude. Up until this point, players followed the usual routes to the majors. Scouted and signed off college campuses and sandlots, the player found himself bound to the team he signed with unless traded elsewhere by that club. They would, in most cases, labor on the minor league level, polishing their skills for a number of years before reaching the major leagues. While most received little to sign, some were given good-sized bonuses in return for a signed contract. The decade of the Seventies would change all this with the instigation of a draft system, usually accompanied by some type of a bonus for signing There was a time when players were thankful enough just to get into professional baseball; more important than the money was the chance to play. While many players today will admit privately that this is still the case, it would appear that other things are sometimes more important. They want to make the majors in a much shorter time, and this has become a reality due mainly to expansion. They want more money and expect better treatment. While these may be good on one hand, you can't help but wonder what it has done to quality. The dissatisfied player chooses to go the free-agent route, no longer bound to one team. What this will eventually do to the balance of teams or the loyalty of fans remains an unanswered question.

There are other factors which effect our rookie of today, and perhaps they are a sign of the times in our fast-moving society. While it is not always the case, I have talked with many minor league rookies who, after playing three or four seasons, figure the parade has passed them by and they might as well hang up their spikes. I can think of several who are in the majors today that were on the verge of tossing in their glove, when to their surprise their break came along. Just last season I spoke with a young player who had been released from his triple A club and gone home discouraged. All he had left was a true love for the game. Many players would have wanted no part of baseball after that experience. It wasn't in this particular rookie's makeup, however. Shortly, it developed that the double A farm club in his team's system was hit with a number of injuries. Our rookie was called. Would he come back even if it meant a step down? Many would not have gone, but, sure, he would give it a try. He had the love for the game. I wish I could say this story had a happy ending, but I don't believe he will make it to the majors. However, as he has said, "What the hell, at least I am playing."

Then there was another rookie who was dissatisfied with his contract and decided to become a holdout. A call to his home revealed he was dying to go to spring training, but stubbornness was holding him back. Finally, after attending a local college game and receiving a few encouraging telephone calls from former teammates, he had rekindled his enthusiasm to an extent that he could resist no longer and sit home. He was off to spring training. Love of the game had won again. These are exceptions, but there are many others who go home disgusted, never to return.

There was another rookie who received a modest bonus to sign and was assigned directly to a high minor league club. This may have been a mistake. At any rate, by the Fourth of July he had packed up his belongings and headed home. Why? He didn't like the hand-me-down uniforms, the minor league living conditions, the bus rides, the poor lights and the bad infields. He didn't want it badly enough. I often wonder what will happen to him if he goes through life that way. On the other side of the coin, perhaps it was our society which made him that way. He was a product of over-zealous adults who from his Little League days had loaded him down with praise, fine new uniforms, good playing fields, trophies by the carload, award jackets, etc., etc. He found out he was no longer the hero. He had to struggle a little; he gave it up, whereas if he had stuck it out he might have gained greater satisfaction. Here we have an example of our rookie of today, not all of them, but more of this type are appearing on minor league rosters. Whose fault are the failures? Where once most of our athletes wanted nothing more than to play baseball (the minor league record books are filled with those who made a career on that level), the modern player has grown up with other interests and is not as willing to stay in organized baseball as his father or grandfather were.

While many players may have had their minds elsewhere in 1970, the Cincinnati Reds were having little difficulty with the Pirates. The Reds had a fine attack built around Pete Rose, Johnny Bench, and Tony Perez. While the Reds' lineup was basically a veteran one, there were several rookies of note on that 1970 club. In left field for the Reds was a young Bernardo "Bernie" Carbo who had been given a four-game trial in 1969. Bernie had been the American Association's batting champion in 1969, hitting .359 while with Indianapolis. He had also garnered that loop's MVP Award. His rookie year found him batting .310 while accounting for 21 homers and 19 doubles, and playing an important role in the Reds' pennant machine. Bernie's major league career has been a series of moves, as he has moved from the Reds to the Cardinals, to the Red Sox, to the Brewers, back to the Red Sox, to Cleveland, then back to the Cards. It was while at Boston in 1975 that Bernie supplied some dramatics in the World Series. Little remembered today is the fact that it was Bernie's clutch pinch-hit home run, with two out and two on in the eighth inning of game six, which tied the game and set the stage for Carlton Fisk's dramatic 12th-inning game-winning homer high into the nets at Fenway Park. Reds' manager Sparky Anderson had two minor league batting champions trying for his left field spot in 1970. The Reds had traded off their hard-hitting left fielder Alex Johnson and his left field spot was up for grabs between Carbo and Angel Bravo, who had been gleaned from the Chicago White Sox farm at Tucson where he had hit .342 to lead the Pacific Coast League.

Johnson, by the way, became the American League batting champion in 1970 with his new club, the California Angels, winning the crown by the razor thin edge of .0003 over Boston's Carl Yastrzemski, finishing at .3289 to .3286 for Yaz. It was a very controversial win, however, as Johnson left the final game early after pulling ahead of Yaz, whose team had completed the season a day earlier. Many felt Johnson should have finished the game in which he certainly would have made another plate appearance. Angel manager Lefty Phillips claimed that it was his decision to remove Johnson, however.

Back to Carbo, he won the left field spot and was named National League rookie player of the year by *The Sporting News*. The Reds were also trying to fill their shortstop position and were enjoying a four-way scramble between the tandem of Woody Woodward and Darrel Chaney, who had split the spot in '69, and rookies Frank Duffy and Dave Concepcion. Concepcion, the eventual winner, was only 21 and had batted .294 at Ashville before being advanced to Indianapolis where he hit .341 in 42 games for the Indians. Duffy, 23, an accomplished fielder, had hit .261 during a service-interrupted summer at Indianapolis. Concepcion was rated a surefire prospect, and the higher he moved in the Reds' system the better he hit, which was an indication of a future major leaguer. Duffy had been signed out of Stanford University as the Reds' number one draft pick in June 1967, and his minor league record established him as a solid shortstop. At Stanford he had played both baseball and football, and during his junior year he led Stanford to the Pacific Eight and NCAA district championships, and to a berth in the College World Series and in the process was named an All-American. A fine shortstop, Duffy played his best years in Cleveland, where he led American League shortstops in fielding during the 1973 and 1976 seasons.

The Venezuelan Concepcion had his best overall offensive year for the Reds in 1979 for whom he was still playing in 1980. He has maintained his status as baseball's best shortstop by continuing to win Gold Glove Awards for his fielding prowess. His spectacular play is so consistent that it is often taken for granted. When Dave reported to that first Reds' camp, he was a skinny all-arms-and-legs youngster, but over the years he has developed into a solid and strong adult. This fact was attested to in 1979 when he sent a Bill Lee pitch into the upper level red seats at Cincinnati's Riverfront Stadium, a feat that had been accomplished on only twelve previous occasions in that park's ten-year history. Dave's teammate, George Foster, who knows a thing or two about hitting home runs, was quoted as pointing out, "Dave doesn't have a home run swing, but he doesn't need one. He's got that good quick swing that will let him hit from fifteen to twenty home runs per year." A record holder, a good base stealer, and an All-Star selection, Dave remains one of the National League's premier players.

Joining in the Reds' 1970 rookie parade were several pretty decent pitchers, Wayne Simpson (14-3), Milt Wilcox (3-1), Mel Behney (0-2) and Don Gullett (5-2), all of whom except Behney put in more than one major league season. Gullett, at 19, struck out six consecutive Mets in a relief role to tie a National League record. He has had a successful, but injury plagued career, spending both 1979 and 1980 on the New York Yankees' disabled list. Described as the "all-American boy," he has a 109-50 lifetime record with a 2-3 Championship Series mark and a 2-2 World Series record.

Meanwhile the Reds' playoff opponents, the Pittsburgh Pirates, could find little among their crop of new rookies, except in a youngster being called "the new Johnny Bench." That would be 20-year-old catcher Milt May, the son of former major league infielder Merrill "Pinky" May. Milt became the most sought-after non-regular in the National League in 1973 when the Houston Astros offered any pitcher on their staff for him. The Pirates took Jerry Reuss, not a bad choice. Milt has enjoyed a successful career not only with both Pittsburgh and Houston, but with Detroit as well. The Bucs also had fair success with pitchers Ed Acosta, Fred Cambria, and Jim Nelson, along with outfielder Gene Clines, a good clutch-hitter.

The Reds' World Series opponents were the Baltimore Orioles, who had so unexpectedly dropped the 1969 Series to the Mets. 1970 was another story, however. Manager Earl Weaver had his Birds up for the season and they vented their frustrations of 1969 on the American League, winning the Eastern Division title by a wide margin and then trouncing the Minnesota Twins three straight in the playoff series. They continued their drive in the World Series, besting the Reds four games to one as their attack was led by the

Robinsons—Frank and Brooks—and big Boog Powell. The sensation of the
Series, offensively and defensively, had to be Brooks Robinson, something
Baltimore fans had known all along, but something a nation of TV viewers
were now well aware of.

The Orioles contributed little in the way of rookies for 1970, but in the
long run a couple proved to be excellent players. There was outfielder-first
baseman Roger Freed, who played with five clubs in seven years, catcher
Johnny Oates, four clubs in eight years, and then there was second baseman
Bobby Grich and outfielder Don Baylor, both of whom developed into solid
major leaguers. Baylor only received a look-see and spent most of the season
with Rochester where he won the Rookie of the Year title in the International
League, and Minor League Player of the Year by hitting .327 with 107 RBIs
and 26 stolen bases. Baylor was a regular with Baltimore for four years before
moving on to Oakland and California. With California, Baylor has perhaps
had his best years. In 1979 he was named MVP in the American League with
a .296 batting average, 120 runs scored, 33 doubles, and 36 home runs to go
along with a major league leading 139 RBIs. During one early-July stretch
he hit .423 with five homers and 13 RBIs, not bad for a week's work. A ballplayer's ballplayer, he once reflected, "I want to be out there every day. I
don't like to take a day off." During one period when the Angels were going
bad and the fans were taking out their frustration on Baylor, he refused to
fight back with any kind of a verbal barrage, which prompted his teammate
Bobby Grich to remark, "There isn't a finer gentleman around, and he
showed everyone what kind of a man he is." In his early career Baltimore
manager Earl Weaver once told Baylor, "You could be the most valuable
player in the league by 1978." Earl wasn't off-target by much. Perhaps Baylor
summed things up when he said, "Sure I've wanted the recognition. When
people sit down and talk about good ballplayers, I want my name to come
up. You spend money and it goes quickly. Respect as a player lasts a lot
longer."

Grich appeared in only thirty games for the Orioles in 1970 but was back
for good in 1972, and strangely, he also joined the Angels in 1977, the same
year Baylor did. They were both selected in the November 1976 re-entry draft
and signed by California. One of the league's leading second baseman since
1972, Bobby has put in considerable time at shortstop. In July 1977 he had to
undergo a back operation for the removal of a herniated disc, prompting him
to say, "It is never going to allow me to have the strength, endurance, or speed
I once had." This may be true; he is not the player he once was, he is better.
Countless hours spent at a rigorous reconditioning program have paid off
handsomely for this fine ballplayer. His manager with the Angels, Jim

Fregosi, summed it up well, "He makes the pivot, the double play, and the backhander going toward second as well as anybody." Grich proved that anything is within reach if you put your mind to it.

The Orioles' opponents in the playoffs were the Western Division champions, the Minnesota Twins, who had among eight newcomers, Graig Nettles' younger brother Jim and Steve Brye, both outfielders. Nettles was rated as having "an above average arm and good running speed," while Brye was not rated among the better Twins' rookies. It turned out to be the old story, as the less-acclaimed Brye turned out to be the better. Danny Thompson, a utility infielder, played the first of his seven big league seasons. There were several pitchers joining the Twins, one of whom had a name to confuse baseball researchers. His name was Steve Barber, and he was, of course, pitching at the same time as another Steve Barber. The one not with the Twins had been a hero for years in Baltimore, but in 1970 was with the Cubs and the Braves. The difference ended with their names, however. The Minnesota Barber pitched in two seasons with a 1-0 record, the better known Barber was 121-106 in 15 seasons. *The Sporting News* named Bert Blyleven of the Twins as their Rookie Pitcher of the Year in the American League for 1970, and what a good one he turned out to be. He was 10-9 in 1970 and has won in double figures every year since, until 1980 when he was 8-13. Bert spent six and-one-half seasons with the Twins before being traded to Texas. After a year and a half with the Rangers, he was traded to Pittsburgh for the 1978 season. In 1977, while with Texas, he pitched a no-hitter against California. Born in Holland, his real name is Rik Aalbert Blyleven. In 1980 there were only eight active pitchers who had tossed more career shutouts than Bert, and they averaged better than fourteen years of major league service to his ten. His thirteen games won by 1-0 scores is a feat bettered by only three pitchers in baseball history. A strikeout artist, he has struck out ten or more batters 37 times and twice has fanned 14 in a game. After he was traded to Texas, his initial two wins as a Ranger were both 1-0, 10-inning jobs, and the first of the two was a one-hitter over Oakland. Helping cement the rookie honors was the fact that he tied the American League record for the most consecutive strikeouts at the start of a game, as he fanned the first six batters in one game.

Three teams introduced only one rookie in 1970. The A's had infielder Jim Driscoll, the Padres, outfielder Dave Robinson, and the Braves, first baseman Earl Williams. Williams, who we will meet again, played for eight years; the others soon left the big league scene. The once proud Yankees had to settle for the likes of shortstop Frank Baker, outfielder Bobby Mitchell, and pitchers Loyd Colson, Gary Jones, and Steve Kline. The Chicago White Sox were similarly disappointed with such pitchers as Jerry Janeski, Don Eddy, Jim

Magnuson, Dick Maloney, and Virle Rounsaville, third baseman Charles McKinney, first baseman Carlos Blanco, catcher Art Kusyner, and first baseman-outfielder John Matias. Their National League counterparts, the Cubs fared a little better with three decent rookies among five. They included Larry Gura, another Arizona State product who had helped the Sun Devils win two NCAA titles and was the winningest pitcher in NCAA history. Their number one pick in the free-agent draft was shortstop Roger Metzger, and then there was utility man Terry Hughes. Houston also had five rookies appear in their lineups, only two of whom left any memorable impression, pitcher Ken Forsch, an Oregon State product, and outfielder Cesar Cedeno, who was the Astros' leading batter with a .309 average in 1980. Cedeno has appeared in numerous All-Star Games, won fielding honors, and is among the top three in every major offensive category in Astros' history. San Francisco had eight rookies, none of whom would be remembered today except by Giant die-hards, and Montreal had everyone's choice for Rookie Pitcher of the Year, Carl Morton. Morton originally had been signed by the Atlanta Braves as an outfielder and became Montreal's twenty-third selection in the 1968 expansion draft. He adapted to pitching so quickly that the Expos were willing to give him an eight-game trial in 1969, but the best he could do was an 0-3 record. Carl had begun his career in 1965, but never attracted serious attention until 1967 when he struck out 125 batters in 161 innings in the Carolina League. In 1970 he was 18-11, his best major league season. He stayed around for eight years, the last four of which were with his original club, Atlanta.

There was a toss-up for the American League Rookie of the Year. The baseball writers picked New York Yankee catcher Thurman Munson, who we have already met briefly, and *The Sporting News* chose Roy Foster, an outfielder with Cleveland. Foster showed signs of becoming a power hitter with 26 doubles and 23 home runs, while hitting .268. Two more seasons with dwindling power and average and he was gone. Munson turned out to be a far better choice for future honors. He was the captain and leader of the Yankees until early August of 1979 when he was tragically killed in an airplane crash. Munson had been appointed Yankee captain in 1976, the first to hold the title since Lou Gehrig during the '30s. He was a good clutch hitter, a fine catcher and handler of pitchers, and would occasionally make appearances in the Yankee outfield or infield. Named the American League's MVP in 1976, he became the first Yankee ever to win both rookie and MVP honors. Durable and rugged, he was a great all-around athlete and an ideal choice to lead the Yanks from the depths to which they had fallen. An All-American catcher at Kent State University, he had played only 99 games in the minors before reaching the Yankees to carry on their catching tradition of Dickey, Berra, and Howard. His sudden death shocked the baseball world and left a noticeable void on the Yankee club.

Teddy Martinez, a player who played many positions in eight seasons, Tim Foli, a fierce competitor and a perfectionist who believed he should make every play at shortstop and deliver a base hit every turn at bat, and outfielder Ken Singleton, a former basketball scholarship player at Hofstra University were the New York Mets' contribution to the 1970 rookie class. Foli, who had turned down scholarships to USC and Notre Dame has enjoyed a long major league career and was with the Pirates in 1980. Singleton has also had a long career and gained recognition as being one of the most valuable of the Baltimore Orioles. As fate would have it, the Mets traded Foli and Singleton along with Mike Jorgensen to Montreal for Rusty Staub in April of 1972.

The injury-plagued Philadelphia Phillies employed twelve new rookie players in 1970, the most of any major league club. Several of them turned out to be real finds. A 26-year-old left-hand-hitting second baseman, Denny Doyle, had been an all-star, MVP, and Rookie of the Year with the Eugene Emeralds of the Pacific Coast League. He was with the Phils for four seasons and wound up with the Boston Red Sox, via California, in 1975, helping the Bosox to a pennant that year. A burly first baseman who had been walloping tape-measure home runs at Reading and who appropriately hailed from Prospect Heights, Illinois, was Greg Luzinski. He was still with the 1980 edition from the City of Brotherly Love. Still a power hitter, Greg is known for his left field "Bull Ring" in Philly which provides $20,000 in tickets for underpriviledged children to see Phillie games. Nicknamed the "Bull," he has often represented the Phils in the All-Star Game. Joining these two was Doyle's keystone partner Larry Bowa, a small 5'10", 155 pounder. He had led the PCL with 48 stolen bases. A switch-hitter for the first time in his career, he hit a respectable .287 and was the league's All-Star shortstop. Larry stepped right into the shortstop job, moving sophomore Don Money over to third base. In 1980 he was still turning in fine seasons for the Phillies. An aspiring radio broadcaster, he hosts a weekly talk show on a Philadelphia station along with a twice-daily sports program. He also writes a weekly column for a Philadelphia newspaper. Like Luzinski, he is active in youth activities, raising funds for the Philadelphia Child Guidance Clinic. He owns the record for the highest lifetime fielding percentage among shortstops. An All-Star, a Gold Glove fielder and a brilliant all-around player, Bowa has remained a Philadelphia favorite for ten seasons. He also holds the National League record for the fewest errors by a shortstop in a season, nine, in 1972.

Close behind the Phillies with new players were the disappointing St. Louis Cardinals who had eleven newcomers, only two of whom showed any promise. Outfielder Jose Cruz, a lefty swinger, has played for eleven seasons, five with the Cards, and is still with the Astros to whom he was traded in 1975. He was the Astros' MVP in 1977. Like so many we have already met, he is the oldest of three ball playing brothers, Cirilio and Hector being the others. Joining Cruz was lefty relief pitcher Al Hrabosky, better known as "The Mad Hungarian." Al has been a good relief pitcher over the years and won the Fireman of the Year Award in 1975, when he registered 22 saves. He went to K.C. in 1978 and signed as a free agent with Atlanta in 1980. The colorful relief specialist is renowned for his flashy antics, as he goes behind the mound in tense moments for meditation to psyche himself up for the task at hand. In his first professional season, 1969 at Modesto, he had back-to-back 17 strikeout games.

The Los Angeles Dodgers'rookies of 1970 included pitchers Gene "Sandy" Vance, who was blessed with a major league curve and an excellent fastball, but was cursed with control problems, reliever Charlie Hough, a 23-year-old knuckleballer, and righty, Mike Strahler, who in 1973 was 4-5 with Detroit which was more of a record than he had in three trips with L.A. Joining them was a decent catcher who early on showed signs of brilliance, Joe Ferguson. Joe had started in the Dodger system as an outfielder. They traded him away in 1976, but he returned in 1978 by way of St. Louis and Houston. He has a couple of contrasting records to his credit. In 1973 he established a major league record for the fewest errors in a season, and in 1977 he led National League catchers in passed balls. Nationally he may be best remembered for his memorable throw in the 1974 World Series from right field to nail the As' Sal Bando at the plate in game number one. Nearing the end of his career, he has been fighting weight problems in recent years. Outfielder Tom Paciorek was another Dodger addition.

Joining an aforementioned Foster in Cleveland were a number of farm-hands. The best remembered would be pitcher Steve Dunning, who always seemed to be losing more than he won, and left-hand-hitting infielder John Lowenstein, who had been an outstanding hitter during his amateur days, but who never has done much of it in the majors. While he performed at all the infield spots, his major league career saw him play more in the outfield. In 1980 he hit .311 in 104 games for the Orioles. John was a second-team NCAA All-American at the University of California, Riverside.

The Boston Red Sox were seeking pitching help from rookies Norm Phillips, John Curtis, Dick Mills, and Roger Moret. Phillips and Mills contributed little. Curtis never really arrived until 1972 when he gave them eleven wins and followed it up with thirteen and was then traded to St. Louis, then to San Francisco. A free-agent route led him to San Diego and a 10-8 record in 1980. He was selected for the Pan American Games in 1967 and pitched the United States to a first-ever win over Cuba. He has worked as a columnist and staff writer for the *San Francisco Examiner* during the off seasons. Moret was a strange case, possessing a blazing fastball. He pitched very effectively at times for the Red Sox and at other times was quite ineffective. He was traded to Atlanta and then to Texas where mental problems got the better of him. His problems stunned the baseball world, as he was well-liked by all and it is hoped he will gain a complete recovery. Traded to Cleveland, he was unsuccessful in a 1980 trial. Arriving to catch these young hurlers was Bob Montgomery, a 26-year-old receiver who had spent a long nine years in the Red Sox minor league chain. Monty had been an International League all-star choice while at Louisville. The Red Sox had converted him to catching, although all his prior amateur experience had been as a pitcher, outfielder, and a first baseman. Montgomery retired after the 1979 season, having been a valuable backup catcher all those years. Also joining the Red Sox were outfielder-first baseman Mike Derrick and third baseman Carmen Fanzone. Fanzone had been involved in an unusual situation during the 1968 season as a rookie in the Red Sox farm system while playing for Pittsfield of the Eastern League. Fanzone had batted .270 in that tough pitcher's league, while his teammate and good friend Tony Torchia had hit higher. However, Tony did not have the required number of plate appearances to qualify for the batting crown, but when charged with 20 official at-bats to reach the requirement for qualification, Torchia's average was still higher, .294. Tony thus became the leader under the provisions of scoring rule 10:22. This situation brings to mind the similar dilemma surrounding Kansas City's George Brett's attempt to hit .400 and lead the American League in 1980. George, of course, did finally get enough at-bats to qualify. Fanzone moved on for three seasons with the Chicago Cubs, and Torchia remains until today as one of the highly regarded developers of the rookies in the Red Sox farm system.

The Milwaukee Brewers took a look at a couple of outfielders, Cal Smith and Pete Koegal, and a pair of pitchers, Ray Peters and Wayne Twitchell. Twitchell later gained some success with the Philadelphia Phillies. The Kansas City Royals were checking out shortstop Rich Severson and a trio of young pitchers, Ken Wright, Jim York and Paul Splittorff. Wright had four tries in K.C. and a brief appearance with the Yankees. Jim York was the most highly regarded of the trio. A right-hander, York had never started a game in organized ball, as he became a relief pitcher during his junior year at UCLA.

In seven major league seasons he started only four games, all in 1975 while with Houston to whom K.C. had traded him in 1972. York possessed a fine sinking fastball and a hard slider and appeared to be a sure bet to star in K.C. As so often happens, it was Splittorff, who had been rated "excellent," who became the best of the three. Paul was still with the Royals in 1980 and has enjoyed some fine seasons with them, winning 20 games in '73 and 19 in 1978. The big left-hander has become the winningest hurler in Royals' history. Having been a consistent mainstay in the Royals' starting rotation, he has relied on his baseball savvy, sharp control, and breaking ball to place his name at the top of most all of the club's all-time pitching charts. "Split" was an All-Star with each of his minor league clubs and had pitched for the United States team in the Pan American Games in 1967. His finest major league game may have come in 1975 against the Oakland A's. In that contest he allowed a one-out walk to Phil Garner and an infield hit to Claudell Washington and then retired 26 straight batters.

Among the rookies joining the Washington Senators was a decent outfielder who by 1980 was with the Chicago Cubs in his tenth big league season, Larry Biittner. The spelling of Larry's last name certainly must have caused him, various sportswriters, and typesetters their share of problems over the years. Larry was one of those Senators who moved with the club when they became the Texas Rangers in 1972. Larry was also a good basketball player and had enrolled at Drake University on a full basketball scholarship, but later decided to concentrate on baseball. A top clutch-hitter, he is known for his ability to come off the bench and fill, successfully, the pinch-hitter's role. Pitchers Bill Gogolewski, Dennis Riddleberger, Jackie Brown, and Dick Such all made appearances for the first time in the nation's capital. We met Such several chapters back when he had that embarrassing 0-16 record at York, but remember, he had a respectable 2.81 ERA. Senator pitching coach Sid Hudson was singing the praises of his tall right-hander who had put in several successful seasons since that 1967 year at York. Richard didn't live up to Hudson's hopes, as his only big league season showed a 1-5 record. Such is life I guess! The big man with the '70 Senators was Jeff Burroughs. Burroughs, who received a sizeable bonus to sign with the Senators, moved to Texas along with the franchise in 1972. The Rangers traded him to Atlanta in late 1976. Meanwhile Burroughs, a power hitter, had won the American League MVP Award in 1974 while batting .301 and knocking in 118 runs. Burroughs currently stands second on Atlanta's all-time home run list which may have fullfilled what his Washington manager Ted Williams had to say about him in 1970. Ted said, "He is one of the best natural young hitters I've ever seen." Don Zimmer, former Red Sox manager, at the time of Burroughs' trade to Atlanta said, "He can hit forty to fifty homers a year in Atlanta." Jeff hit three grand-slam homers in a ten-day span for the Rangers in 1973 and barely missed a record held by Babe Ruth and Mel Ott when he had RBIs in ten straight games in 1974. He also had eight straight hits in one streak during the 1978 season, two short of the National League record last accomplished by Kiki Cuyler many years earlier.

The Detroit Tigers had a pair of rookie catchers in 1970 in Gene Lamont and Tim Hosley and a shortstop with a long name in Ken Szotkiewicz. Lamont, the first free-agent draft choice in Tiger history, had worked his way up through the Tiger system and was well-rated. Perhaps the highlight of his five-year backup catcher role came in his first major league appearance, when he hit a homer against the Red Sox. The Tigers also had another player in what seems to be a never-ending line of good players from Arizona State in pitching ace Lerrin LaGrow. LaGrow had helped pitch the Tempe based Sun Devils to the 1969 NCAA World Series title. LaGrow has never enjoyed a really successful major league season, although he was the ace of the Chicago White Sox relief corps in 1977-78. He was still around in 1980 toiling for the world champion Phillies. Another pitcher with Detroit was Dennis Saunders. Moving up to Tiger Stadium after two seasons at Rocky Mount was Elliott Maddox, who appeared around the infield and in the outfield where he has performed for ten years with the Tigers, Washington, the Yankees, Orioles, and the Mets. A pre-law student at the University of Michigan, he had won the Big Ten batting title with a .467 average just prior to his being drafted by the Tigers. A series of injuries and time spent on the disabled lists have hampered his career over the years.

The California Angels had three pretty good newcomers among the seven that they introduced. Second baseman Doug Griffin was called up from Hawaii for 18 games and was traded to the Boston Red Sox at the conclusion of the season. His .326 average and league-leading 35 stolen bases at Hawaii prompted observers to hang a "can't miss" rating on him. An excellent fielder, he was rated as the best defensive second baseman in the league. After Doug was traded to Boston he did star for a number of years, although his career was plagued with injuries, including a Nolan Ryan fastball to the head. The second rookie of note with California was pitcher Dave LaRoche. LaRoche, a reliever, has played for the Twins, Cubs, White Sox, Indians, and has returned to the Angels. He had always turned in good seasons until 1979 when his record fell to 7-11 and his ERA ballooned to 5.57. Dave said "My pitching is just like the weather. It has to change." 1980 found him 3-5 and his ERA at 4.08. He did contribute four saves to place third on a disappointing Angels' club. At 30-years-old, LaRoche set an Angel record with 25 saves.

Primarily a fastball pitcher, Dave came up through the Angels' system and has been an American League All-Star Team member. The third Angel rookie of note was Mickey Rivers. Outfielder Rivers put in four partial and two full seasons with California before being traded to the New York Yankees for three years of glory before being sent to Texas. Mickey was regarded as the catalyst of the Yankee offense during his years in New York which brought three consecutive American League championships and two world championships to the New Yorkers. His 20-game hitting streak in 1976 was the longest by any Yankee batter since 1942, and his 43 stolen bases that season were the most any Yank could register since George Stirnweiss swiped 55 in 1944. Proving that speed pays dividends, Rivers led the league in triples in 1974 and 1975. Other Angel rookies were a tall Texan, Terry Lee Cox, fellow pitchers Greg Garrett and Harvey Shank, and outfielder Tom Silverio.

1971 was a season that saw major league attendance soar to better than 29 million, and it was the year that saw a World Series game played at night for the first time. It was the last season for a major league team in our nation's capital, as after the season the Washington Senators moved to Arlington, Texas, and were christened the Texas Rangers. Hank Aaron continued his assault on Babe Ruth's all-time home run record, as he hit his 600th round tripper. On September 1st, another major league milestone was reached when the Pittsburgh Pirates started a team of nine blacks. At the time, this fact went pretty much unnoticed, but it certainly marked the ultimate in baseball's integration. There were continuing rounds of legal battles for the major league clubs, involving players Alex Johnson, Tony Conigliaro, Clete Boyer, and Sam McDowell and his manager, Al Dark, but those are another story and do not involve our rookies. There was a somewhat smaller group of new players reaching the majors in 1971, although there were some of ability among the group.

The Sporting News selected the big Cleveland Indian first baseman Chris Chambliss as their American League rookie player of the year, while selecting Atlanta catcher Earl Williams as the National League rookie player of the year. We met Williams briefly earlier, as he had a ten-game trial for Atlanta in 1970 at the positions he had played the most in the minors, first and third bases. The Braves, however, converted Williams into a catcher for 1971. A power hitter, Earl hit 33 home runs and had 87 RBIs to go along with a .260 average, enough to win the rookie honors. He was traded to the Baltimore Orioles for the 1973 season, returned to Atlanta in 1975, and later was traded to Montreal and then to Oakland where he retired. Chambliss had been the American Association's rookie of the year in 1970 and, of course, carried on his honors after reaching the shores of Lake Erie. Actually, 1970 was his first year in organized ball, and the left-handed hitter was the first player in the history of the American Association to lead that league in batting in his first year as a professional. In 1971 he started the season with Wichita again, but after thirteen games was recalled by the Indians, where he showed some fine defensive play and batted .275. Chambliss remained with Cleveland until late April 1974 when he was traded to the New York Yankees. The Yanks sent him to Toronto in November of 1979, but before he could play a game there the Blue Jays traded him to Atlanta, where he hit a fine .282 with 18 home runs in 1980. A key player on the Yankees' 1976, '77, and '78 championship teams, many believe it was his determined play that carried them as far as they went. Few people will forget his homer which beat the Royals in the ninth inning of the final game of the 1976 American League playoffs. Before turning pro, Chris played at UCLA. setting school records for home runs (15) and RBIs (45). In 1978 he won a Gold Glove for his fielding, and his .997 fielding average tied him with Joe Pepitone for the all-time Yankee first baseman fielding mark. The son of a navy chaplain, Chris traveled much of his early life as he had during his major league career. In his first major league start, his two-run single defeated the Chicago White Sox. Williams and Chambliss were also the baseball writers' selections for rookie of the year.

The Sporting News, carrying on their tradition of naming rookie pitchers, selected Bill Parsons of Milwaukee in the American League and Reggie Cleveland of St. Louis in the National League. The 6'6" Parsons had been a high school All-American basketball player, but the right-hander chose a baseball career. and by his fine minor league ERAs it appeared he had made a good choice. The Riverside, California, native was 1.57 at Clinton, 2.57 at Billings, and 2.25 at Portland. Until Skip Lockwood came along, Parsons may have held the record for colleges attended, as he had gone to the University of Utah, Riverside City College, Cal Poly, and Arizona State. Lockwood, a right-handed pitcher who made a 27-game debut with Milwaukee in 1970, has attended eight colleges: Merrimack, Boston College, Bryant and Stratton, Marquette, Carroll, Emerson, Fairfield, and Columbia. Lockwood has also pitched for Milwaukee, California, the New York Mets, and the Boston Red Sox. Parsons put in two good years with Milwaukee, 13-17 in his rookie year and 13-13 in his second season. One more year with the Brewers and it was on to Oakland and retirement. Reggie Cleveland appeared in one game with the 1969 Cardinals, returned for sixteen games in 1970 and an 0-4 record, but his 12-12 record in 1971 earned him rookie honors. Reggie had two more good seasons before he was traded to the

Boston Red Sox for the 1974 season. After helping the Sox win the 1975 pennant, he put in two more decent seasons with them before they traded him to Texas in April of 1978. The Rangers traded him to Milwaukee in late 1978, and in 1979 he dropped to a 1-5 record, a low for him. In 1980 he reversed his form and registered an 11-9 season for the Brewers. He has been both a starter and reliever over the years. An outstanding track star in high school at Cold Lake in Alberta, Canada, he decided to follow a baseball career, thus making himself the second current Canadian to star in the major leagues, joining Ferguson Jenkins as hurlers from north of the border. In 1971, Reggie completed 10 of his 34 starts for the Cardinals and averaged six strikeouts per game. This all-around athlete, who starred at curling and set javelin records, also hurled a no-hitter for the Moose Jaw Phillies while in Babe Ruth League competition.

The San Francisco Giants introduced the most rookies in 1971 with nine. The Baltimore Orioles introduced the least, none. The Orioles also won the American League pennant, but lost the World Series four games to three to the Pittsburgh Pirates, who got some unexpected pitching from Steve Blass and some timely hitting from Roberto Clemente. The Buccos lost the first two games but came back to take four of the next five. San Francisco, the surprise winners in the National League West, lost to the Pirates in that league's playoffs. I am not sure what that might prove. All those Giant rookies didn't help, but again, Baltimore had none to help them.

Among those rookies who helped bring the National League West title to San Francisco was a most highly touted six-year vet of the Giant system, outfielder Jimmy Rosario. He was 26-years-old and rated a fine fielder with good speed and a reputation as a spray hitter. Chris Arnold was back from submarine duty to appear at second base, although most of his experience was at shortstop. There was Jim Howarth, an outfielder who had his first of four tries. Jim "J. B." Barr, a good right-hander, arrived and stayed until 1978 when he went the free-agent route and signed with the California Angels. His brother Mark was a pitcher in the Red Sox organization. If you think he wasn't a sought-after pitcher, consider this, he was drafted six times before inking a pact with the Giants. He had been drafted by the Angels in 1966, the Phillies in 1968, the Yankees in 1969, the Twins in 1970, and the Giants in the second draft of 1970. Jim established a major league record in August of 1972 when he retired 41 consecutive batters. The Angels signed him primarily as a short reliever, but as it turned out, he was not only used in short relief but long relief as well and as a starter. "It was a fun year," said Barr after posting a 10-12 record. In 1980 he dropped to 1-4 as the Angels wondered where the fun went. Statistics point out that he kept his club in the game with his fastball, slider, curve, and what he refers to as a sinker going off his slider. An aficionado of the current jogging craze, he and his wife run almost four miles daily.

Joining Barr were pitchers Jim Willoughby, a reliever who never gained a great deal of success with the Giants, Red Sox, or White Sox, and Steve Stone, a starting pitcher. Stone, a right-hander, bounced around to the White Sox, the Cubs, back to the White Sox, and to the Orioles where in 1979 he was 11-7. In 1980 he suddenly became the best pitcher in the American League, posting a great 25-7 record, and winning the Cy Young Award. Actually, in 1971 Steve joined the Giants in spring training as a non-roster player, but made the 25-man cut to stay with the club. In that first season he was 4-2 through May when control problems resulted in his being optioned to Phoenix. Before turning pro, he played for two years at Kent State University, where he was a battery-mate of the late Yankee catcher Thurman Munson. An all-around athlete, he was a standout tennis player, shot a hole in one in golf at age 11, and maintained a 180 bowling average while at Kent State. A well-rounded person, he has a teaching degree, writes poetry which has been published, and is part-owner in a group which owns and operates eight restaurants, the most famous of which is the "Pump Room" at the Ambassador Hotel in Chicago. Catcher Dave Rader was another rookie with the Giants in 1971, and we will meet him later on. Combination outfielder-first baseman and home run hitter deluxe, Dave Kingman made his bow also with the 1971 Giants. Dave had previously been drafted by the Angels and Orioles but chose not to sign with them. Up from Phoenix in 1971, he remained with the Giants through 1974. Since then he has been hitting home runs for the Mets, San Diego, California, the Yankees, and the Cubs. On four occasions Dave has hit three home runs in a game and along the way has tied several major league home run records. At USC he teamed up with Jim Barr to help the Trojans into the College World Series. In his first start with the Giants, he hit a Dave Giusti pitch for a grand-slam home run, and the next day he hit two more home runs off Dock Ellis and has been slamming home runs at record distances ever since. In 1979 he hit 48 for the Cubs, which topped Ernie Banks' 1958 total of 47 and put him second on the Cubs' all-time home run list next to Hack Wilson. Hack hit 56 in 1930 to establish the current National League high for home runs. The last rookie of '71 for the Giants was shortstop Chris Speier, who now plays for the Montreal Expos, having joined them after six seasons with the Giants. After only one season in the minors, he became a key factor in the Giants' 1971 pennant drive. On July 20, 1978, Chris hit for the cycle against the Braves. A standout athlete in high school, he also played baseball for the University of California at Santa

Barbara. Active in other affairs, Chris helped found the Athletes for Life movement.

The other West Coast National League entry, the Dodgers, had three rookies, two of whom were real winners. There were pitchers Doyle Alexander and Bob O'Brien and third baseman Ron Cey. O'Brien posted a 2-2 record in 1971 and passed from the scene. Alexander was traded to Baltimore in 1972. He pitched there for four-and-one-half seasons before being traded to the Yankees where he posted a 10-5 record in 1976 before being sold to Texas, where in 1977 he had a fine 17-11 record. In December 1979 he was sent back to the National League Atlanta Braves where he posted a 14-11 record in 1980. It would seem that like a good wine he improves with age. Ron Cey has remained with the Dodgers as a power-packed third baseman, continuing to produce 20 or more home runs and 20-plus RBIs per season. His 28 home runs in 1979 enabled him to become the all-time Los Angeles Dodger home run leader, and he has also tied the National League record for the fewest errors (nine) in a season by a third baseman. Cey's 30 home runs in 1977 made him part of a historic foursome (Baker, Garvey and Smith) the first quartet to hit 30 or more homers for a club in a single season in major league history. At one point in that year, he also had nine consecutive hits and holds the Dodger record for RBIs in a game, eight. He has played more games at third base than any other Dodger in history. The popular Cey has said, "I'm never satisfied. That's the way you should be. You should always try to better yourself, but team accomplishments are more important than anything I'll ever be able to do as an individual."

The Cardinals had pitcher Rudy Arroyo, who did little. The Phillies had similar success with outfielder Mike Anderson and pitcher Manny Muniz. The Braves had very little success with Leo Foster, a shortstop who later played with the Mets, and reliever Tom House who came highly rated. House is more remembered today as the bullpen crew member who caught Hank Aaron's historic home run number 715. The Reds had two pitchers, Steve Blateric, who accomplished little, and Ross Grimsley, who arrived with a "can't miss" tag. After three successful seasons with Cincinnati, Ross was traded to Baltimore where he continued to be successful. He became a free agent and signed with Montreal, where in 1978, he promptly became that team's first-ever 20-game winner. He slumped to ten wins in 1979 and to just two in 1980, yet in eight of his ten seasons he has won ten or more games. The Padres came up with little other than catcher Mike Ivie, who has tied several major league records, including the most grand-slam home runs in a season by a pinch hitter (two) and the most doubles in an inning (two). Although Ivie came up as a catcher, he has appeared in the outfield, all over the infield, but seems to be concentrating on first base lately. He was traded to the Giants in 1978 and has been brilliant while making significant contributions to the Giant cause. Mike made his debut less than a month after his nineteenth birthday.

The Montreal Expos were ballyhooing shortstop Rich Hacker, who they had acquired from the Mets, Terry Humphrey, a catcher who showed good progress along with a fine arm (he spent most of the season with the Winnipeg Whips), pitcher Ernie McAnally, a converted outfielder, who was 30-49 in four seasons at Montreal, and outfielder Stan Swanson who made 1971 his swan song. The Houston Astros were watching a parade of seven youngsters march through the Astrodome, most of whom kept right on going. Infielder Derrel Thomas was among them, but enjoyed more success in San Diego and San Francisco. There was, however, a strong young pitcher with what sounded like three first names, James Rodney Richard. Richard spent most of the 1971 season with Oklahoma City where he struck out 202 batters, an average of 10.53 per game. On the minus side, he led the league in walking batters with 105. Up and down until 1974, he became a 20-game winner in 1976 and posted 18 wins in each of the next three seasons until he was stricken with a stroke during pregame drills in early 1980. A successful operation for a blood clot has raised the hopes of the baseball world, and fans everywhere hope that J.R. will be able to return to the mound for the Astros in 1981. One of the best pitchers in baseball in recent years, the strikeout artist had a memorable year in 1969 while in high school. He had an unbelievable 0.00 ERA, and in one game he hit four consecutive home runs and drove in ten runs. Ten years later he established a modern National League record for right-handers by striking out 313 batters. By striking out 300-plus batters in both 1978 and 1979, he tied another modern National League record.

The New York Mets had people with famous baseball names like Dan Rose, a pitcher, Charlie Williams, a pitcher, and Fran Estrada, a catcher. Unfortunately for the Mets, they weren't the ones to make those names famous. There were three other Mets who have enjoyed some success: pitchers Buzz Capra (16-8 at Atlanta in 1974) and Jon Matlack who enjoyed some very good years at Shea Stadium. We will meet him again later. The third was decent outfielder, sometimes infielder, John Milner. Like the Mets, the Chicago Cubs had some who did and some who didn't make a contribution. Outfielder Gene Hiser filled utility roles for five seasons as did first basemen Pat Bourque and Hal Breeden. Of the rookie non-pitchers with the Cubs, Bill North has lasted the longest. After two partial seasons with the Cubs, he went to Oakland where he starred in the outfield before being traded to L.A. At L.A. he decided to try the free-agent route and moved to San

Francisco. North has been a steadying factor for young Giant outfielders since his arrival and has continued to utilize his abilities as a leadoff batter. The switch-hitter played with Oakland's World Series clubs of '73 and '74 and with the Dodgers' '78 championship team. North, a speedy runner, led the American League in stolen bases in 1974 and 1976 and missed by one in 1973. The '71 Cubs had several pitchers of note. Bill Bonham, who had doubled as a starter and reliever, put in seven successful seasons at Wrigley Field before going to Cincinnati where arm problems have cut down his efficiency. Joining him was Burt Hooton, who was fairly successful before he was traded to the Dodgers in May of 1975. Since then, he has done very well with the Dodgers. His gem of a game was a no-hitter against the Phillies in 1972 while a member of the Cubs. It came in only his fourth major league start. He was the Dodger ace in 1978 with 19 victories and at one point reached the ninth inning in 12 of 13 starts, while compiling a 10-1 record. His 12 straight wins for the Dodgers in 1975 broke the Dodger mark of 11 set by greats Sandy Koufax and Don Drysdale. Hooton made his first major league appearance nine days after signing with the Cubs and struck out the first hitter he faced, Lou Brock. Later that season he set a club record by striking out 15 Mets in one game. Farmed out only once in his career, he played for Tacoma of the Pacific Coast League and promptly set a league mark by striking out 19 batters in a game, matching a record that hadn't been approached since it was set in 1905. Dodger manager Tom Lasorda has nicknamed Hooton "Happy" because he seldom looks like he is. Still going strong in 1980, he turned in a 14-8 log. Also joining the Cub hill staff were Ray Newman and Chet Stephenson.

The Pirates, while only carrying five rookies in 1971, had good ones: Outfielder Richie Zisk, shortstop Frank Taveras, second baseman Rennie Stennett, outfielder Rimp Lanier, and pitcher Bruce Kison. All except Lanier have been major league stars ever since. Most of them had come from the Waterbury club of the Eastern League with high ratings. Kison was overcoming control problems. Stennett, a native of The Canal Zone, was very quick, and Zisk was rated a powerful thrower with potential to develop into a power hitter. All fulfilled their promise.

Over in the American League, the Boston Red Sox were introducing some very capable youngsters, and while they didn't develop until they had been traded to other clubs, all appeared first with the 1971 Bosox. There was Carlton Fisk's brother-in-law, outfielder Rick Miller, who the careful observer would have to rate as the tops among the defensive outfielders in the American League. Hitting was his weakness, nevertheless, he has starred for California. Ben Oglivie, an outfielder who has played first base in recent seasons, has been outstanding with Detroit and Milwaukee. He was joined by first baseman Cecil Cooper in Milwaukee, where Cooper has developed into one of the league's top first sackers. Cooper at .352 and Oglivie at .304 led the Brewers' batters in 1980. Then there was shortstop Juan Beniquez who starred in the outer garden and at first base for Texas, New York, and Seattle. Joining the group was second baseman Buddy Hunter, who is a manager in the Sox farm system now. I wonder if the Sox wish they had some of this talent back now? The New York Yankees had little in pitchers Roger Hambright and Terry Ley, but the big name in the Yankee camp was outfielder Rusty Torres, the International League's Rookie of the Year in 1971. A switch-hitter, he had a powerful, accurate arm and deceptive power for his size. He hit .385 with two homers in a nine-game September trial.

The West Coast entries had little, although Oakland's George Hendrick later had some success in Cleveland's outfield and California's pitcher Andy Hassler had fair success with a variety of clubs. K.C. pitcher Lance Clemons continued to get trials with other clubs for several years. People named Foor, Lane, Gilbreth, Young, Whillock, and Seelbach met little success with the Detroit Tigers. Joining Chambliss at Cleveland was infielder Kurt Bevacqua, who has been good enough to play backup roles with a number of clubs in both leagues. A very versatile player, Kurt has also played in the outfield. Another infielder, seasoned by eight years in the minors, was the popular switch-hitting Harold "Gomer" Hodge. Hodge joined Cleveland as a first baseman, but had been an All-Star with Waterbury in the Eastern League in 1968 at third base and in 1969 at second base. Other Cleveland hopefuls were outfielder Jim Clark, and pitchers Bob Kaiser, Mark Ballinger, Ed Farmer, and Charles Machemehl. The Milwaukee Brewers had, among other pitchers, Bill Parsons, who had two good and one poor year with the Brewers, Jerry Bell, four so-so years, and Jim Slaton who has been a valuable addition in Brewtown. Slaton never had an ERA above 2.92 in the minors. He was traded to Detroit in December 1977 where he had his best year in 1978, 17-11, but he played out his option and signed again with the Brewers. By 1980 he had slipped to 1-1. At times with Milwaukee in 1971 were Bob Ellis and Al Yates, outfielders, and Fred Auerbach and Ron Theobald, infielders. Arriving in Milwaukee from Danville was catcher Darrell Porter, more recently associated with the Kansas City Royals. Porter, who has been plagued by personal problems in recent seasons, is a solid, aggressive defensive receiver who owns a strong and accurate arm and has emerged as one of the game's best all-around catchers. His leadership and skills were important factors in leading the Royals to the 1980 American League pennant. Only 19 in 1971, he was only in his second professional season. As a prep school athlete, Darrell had received All-American honors as a football quarterback.

The Chicago White Sox had little to offer except pitcher Terry Forster, who today thrives in his role as a relief ace with the Dodgers. The Sox traded him to Pittsburgh in 1977, and then he signed as a free agent with the Dodgers for the '78 season. In 1974, while still with the White Sox, he was the American League fireman of the year. In 1972 he set the Chicago club record for saves with 29, breaking the great Hoyt Wilhelm's mark of 27 set in 1964. An interesting note to his record is that from 1971 until 1973 he hurled 138.1 innings in a row without permitting a home run and has, during his career, averaged only one homer for every 23 innings pitched. The first free agent ever signed by the Dodgers, he spent only one season in the minors. An all-around athlete, he played basketball in high school with NBA basketball star Bill Walton and football with NFL star Brian Sipe. Another reliever with Chicago was Rich Hinton. Five other rookies who had brief trials have not been heard from since.

Among those rookies with Washington were pitcher Pete Broberg, who hurled for three other clubs over an eight-year period but never had a winning season, and infielder Lenny Randle, who has also played with both New York teams, yet another product of Arizona State. The Minnesota Twins had as a rookie Eric Soderholm, an infielder who put in some good years with them and the Chicago White Sox before being traded to the Yankees for the 1980 season. In 1975 he set the all-time Twins record for fielding at third base, but an unexpected fall into a construction hole tore cartilage in his left knee and broke several of his ribs, causing him to miss the entire 1976 season. Refusing to believe that he would never play again, he underwent extensive rehabilitation and did make a comeback in 1978, receiving the American League's Comeback Player of the Year Award. His younger brother Dale is an infielder in the Twins' organization. Joining Soderholm was relief pitcher Ray Corbin and infielder Steve Braun. Braun has enjoyed moderate big league success.

1972 found the Oakland A's climb to the top of the American League and defeat the Cincinnati Reds in the World Series, 4 games to 3. It marked the first time such had happened to the A's since 1930 when they belonged to Connie Mack and were stationed in Philadelphia. The season started on a poor note, as the Major League Baseball Players' Association staged a 13-day strike, which delayed the season by 10 days and caused 86 regular season games to be cancelled. It was the first general strike of players in baseball history. As the strike ended, both players and owners were claiming victory. It should be noted that public opinion favored the owners. A ruling was made that if games affecting division races were among those lost, they would not be made up. The Detroit Tigers were thus able to win the American League East by half a game over the Boston Red Sox. It would appear that the Red Sox and their players were the losers in the strike. None of the other clubs were affected by the strike in their pennant races.

It was a year that saw Pittsburgh's Roberto Clemente get his 3000th hit and then meet his death in a plane crash. It saw Willie Mays head back to New York where he had begun his career, this time as a Met. The trade that brought Willie home was unusual in that Mays was allowed to sit in on the trade talks. The Senators bailed out of Washington for Texas, a move which did not get off to a good start as they failed to draw (what could you expect with a 54-100 record?). It left our nation's capital without a team for the first time in years. Player salaries continued to soar, as an estimated 24 hired hands reached the $100,000 bracket, led by Hank Aaron at $200,000 and Carl Yastrzemski at $167,000.

As for the top rookies of 1972, it was pretty much agreed that it was Boston Red Sox catcher Carlton Fisk in the American League and Jon Matlack, a pitcher for the New York Mets in the National League. *The Sporting News* added Cleveland pitcher Dick Tidrow and San Francisco catcher Dave Rader to their picks. We have met some of these players before in this work, but they still qualified as rookies in '72, their previous appearances being only brief.

Jon Matlack had pitched for five seasons in the minors before reaching the Mets, his final three at Tidewater in the International League. In 1971 he was 0-3 in seven games for the New Yorkers. In 1972 he posted a 15-10 record for the third-place Mets. He continued to pitch successfully for them for five more years before being traded to Texas. Primarily a fastball pitcher, Jon once threw about 80 percent fastballs, but recent years have seen him mix his pitches up a bit. Jon suffered a strange accident in 1979 which resulted in a 5-4 record. Just before the season began, he was warming up for his final spring outing before pitching the opener for Texas when he threw down the rosin bag and felt pain as he did; that was his last appearance until May. When he returned he was not the same Matlack, and it was little wonder as he had floating bone debris in his left elbow and suffered acute swelling after every outing. Surgery was performed, and he bounced back with a 10-10 record in 1980. San Francisco catcher Dave Rader had spent five seasons in the minors before he received a three-game look-see in late 1971 after having spent most of that season with Phoenix. Dave caught for the Giants until 1976, was with the Cardinals in '77, Cubs in '78, Phillies in '79, and the Red Sox in '80. Fielding-wise Rader wasn't rated as the best, but he was credited with a fine arm. Dave's final minor league season saw him win the Pacific Coast League batting crown with a .314 average and being named to that loop's All-Star team.

Carlton Fisk, known as "Pudge," was the first ever American League unanimous pick for rookie of the year. The Boston Red Sox catcher has proven to be one of the best and most durable catchers in baseball. A mastermind behind the plate, the Red Sox suffer when he is not playing. I once asked several Red Sox rookie pitchers what it was like to pitch to Fisk. "Like no other catcher, difference of night and day," was their reply. He has the reputation of keeping his pitcher alert and has developed his own style of setting up a batter, making the pitcher's job just that much easier. Fisk is one of five catchers in the history of baseball to score 100 runs and drive in 100 runs in the same year, joining such greats as Mickey Cochrane, Yogi Berra, Roy Campanella, and Johnny Bench in doing so. He will long be remembered for his dramatic twelfth-inning game-winning home run in game six of the 1975 World Series, a feat which has been voted as one of the all-time great moments of baseball. Fisk had received a two-game trial in 1969 and a 14-game look-see in 1971 before he arrived to stay in 1972. His .293 average, 9 triples, 28 doubles, and 22 home runs earned him the rookie honors. During his career, Pudge has been plagued by a number of serious injuries, including a mysterious elbow problem; but somehow he has always managed to bounce back. He has in the past been a Gold Glove winner, a tribute to his defensive skills. On opening day in April 1973 he hit two home runs to tie a major league opening day record. In 1980 he surpassed Sammy White as having played more games as catcher than any other Red Sox. A talented player, he takes an occasional whirl in the outfield or at first base. As we mentioned before, his brother-in-law is Angel outfielder Rick Miller, his brother Calvin caught in the Baltimore organization, and his cousin is the New York football Giants' punter, Dave Jennings.

Cleveland Indian pitcher Dick Tidrow was in his sixth professional season in 1972 when his 14-15 won-lost record and his 2.77 ERA won him rookie honors as the American League pitcher of the year. Tidrow had been selected in major league drafts by the Senators, Giants, and Reds prior to signing with Cleveland in 1967. In April of 1974 the Indians traded the right-hander to the New York Yankees where he first enjoyed success as a reliever and then as a starter. In May of 1979, the Yankees traded him to the Chicago Cubs. Before his trade to the Cubs he became the winning pitcher in the first game ever played in the "new" Yankee Stadium. With a reputation as always willing to take the ball and pitch whenever needed, he along with Bruce Sutter have given the Cubs two of the premier relievers in the National League.

While the 1972 rookie crop was up slightly in numbers over the previous several seasons, as it worked out there was not that lasting quality among the youngsters which occurs in some years. I suppose, except for the yearly few who make it big, things run in cycles. After all, there are only so many positions open on the major league rosters, and after several years of good newcomers it only stands to reason that there will be fewer spots available. Each year sees its share of openings occur due to illness, injury, and retirement, but every once in a while these reasons become minimal also. It should be noted that even the award winners, except for Tidrow, had had several previous trials without success, and Tidrow himself had been held in the minors for six seasons.

Let's take a look at the American League first. Joining Fisk in friendly Fenway were pitchers Lynn McGlothen and Don Newhauser, catcher Vic Correll, and outfielders Bob Gallagher and Dwight Evans. McGlothen, a big right-hander, started the season with the Red Sox farm club at Louisville and by late June had posted a fine 9-2 record with a neat 1.92 ERA. Those stats bore out the promise he had shown in four previous seasons in the Sox chain and earned him a promotion to the big club. He was not a disappointment, as he produced a good 8-7 record, including 112 strikeouts. An overpowering pitcher, he had logged 153, 202, and 151 strikeouts in three of his four minor league seasons. Lynn demonstrated versatility in all sports while in high school, earning 16 letters in baseball, football, basketball, and tennis. In 1970 he put together a super year as he was named the Carolina League Player of the Year by leading the league with 202 strikeouts, 16 complete games, and a 2.24 ERA to go along with a 15-7 record, while with Winston-Salem. This, of course, encouraged the Boston organization to move him up to Louisville. His first big league win was a 2-0 three-hitter over Minnesota on July 4, 1972. He started the 1973 season with Boston, but was soon sent down to Pawtucket for more seasoning. In December he was traded to St. Louis with whom he enjoyed his best success. He earned 44 victories in three years in St. Louis, including a career high of 16 in 1974. McGlothen, his former teammate Bob Gibson, and his 1980 teammate Bruce Sutter are the last three National League pitchers to strike out three consecutive batters in an inning on nine straight pitches. Traded to the Giants prior to the 1977 season, he spent most of that year on the disabled list. In mid-June of 1978 he was traded to the Chicago Cubs, where he has been a long relief pitcher. The last two seasons have found him with a combined 25-28 record for the Cubs. Newhauser did little except go off and on the disabled list and wear out the highway between Boston and Pawtucket, where the Red Sox' top farm club was located. Gallagher was dispatched to Houston and then to the New York Mets and did little for either club. Steady Vic Correll developed into a fine backup catcher for Houston and Cincinnati. Vic has accepted his role well, going to the ball park most days knowing that he is unlikely to get into the game. "I just want to be ready to plug the holes that need to be plugged," he said recently. The Sox had hopes that Dewey Evans might become the second rookie of the year in a row for them after his impressive 18-game late-season trial. He was the International League's MVP in 1972, and Bosox manager Eddie Kasko was already tabbing him as his right fielder for 1973, a big jump for the 21-year-old rookie. The handsome Evans has developed into one of baseball's best defensive outfielders and has shown an arm that many a runner has been leery of running on. A decent but sometimes streaky hitter, he will be in his tenth season with Boston in 1981.

The Chicago White Sox had eight rookies of whom only two developed into solid big leaguers. Their best prospect was an infielder who was a minor league standout in the field and at bat, Jorge Orta. The Mexican was an infield fixture with the Pale Hose until he was granted free agency in 1979 and signed up with Cleveland. Jorge's father, Pedro Orta, was an outstanding baseball player in Cuba. In 1974, his second full major league season, Jorge hit .316 and finished second to the league leader Rod Carew. He is also a member of the Mexican baseball Hall of Fame. The second standout for the White Sox was a 20-year-old right-hander, who had an outstanding record of 18-2 and a 1.83 ERA at Appleton of the Midwest League, named Richard Gossage (you know him as "Goose"). He was 7-1 at Chicago in 1972. The White Sox traded him after a 9-17 season in 1976 to Pittsburgh where in 1977 he had 26 saves matching his '75 high and league-leading total with Chicago. The New York Yankees made him their number one pick in the 1977 re-entry draft, giving the Goose a six-year contract. In three years with the Yankees, he has registered 27, 18, and 33 saves, much to the joy of the Yankee starters. In 1978 he was on the mound at the finish of the three most important Yankee wins, the playoff with Boston, the Championship Series clincher against K.C., and the World Series finale with the Dodgers. A little bit of trivia for you; while coming up in the White Sox organization his roommate and teammate was Bucky Dent. Was that just Mike Torrez who said, "So what?"

Speaking of the Yankees, they had a rookie pitcher named Larry Gowell, for whom things didn't, a third baseman named Celerino Sanchez, and outfielder, Charlie Spikes, who did better in Cleveland and was a top pinch hitter for Atlanta, and pitcher George "Doc" Medich, who in 1974 would win them 19 games. Medich played most of the season with the West Haven farm club, where he was 11-3. He was with the Yanks until 1975 when a December trade sent him to Pittsburgh. Since then he has been with Oakland, Seattle, the Mets, and Texas. Oakland presented pitcher Dave Hamilton, a fairly successful reliever in the mid '70s, and a first baseman, Gonzalo Marquez, who after several games with the A's and Cubs was gonzo. The

Brewers got little from their lone rookie, pitcher Gary Ryerson. Texas had little to brag about among Vic Harris, Steve Lawson, and Joe Lovitto, but pitcher Don Stanhouse has had some decent seasons since the Rangers traded him to Montreal, who in turn sent him to Baltimore. Could it be they didn't love Lovitto and couldn't stand Stanhouse? California had forgettables Chris Coletta, Dave Sells, Dick Lange, and Doug Howard. Joining Tidrow in the Cleveland teepee were Dave Bell, who didn't ring any, Larry Johnson, a catcher, and Jack Brohamer, an infielder who filled backup roles for the Chicago White Sox and Boston Red Sox after being a regular second base-man with the Indians. The Red Sox returned him to the Tribe in 1980. Of six rookies making their bows with the Minnesota Twins, only catcher Glenn Borgmann proved to be of value. The husky receiver, a former All-American at South Alabama under Eddie Stanky, was used mostly in backup roles with the Twins. A free-agency status allowed Glenn to sign with the White Sox for 1980, where he continued as a backup backstop.

The Detroit Tigers introduced the largest number of rookies of any Ameri-can League club in 1972. If anyone other than their mothers, loyal Detroit fans, or their teammates can remember any one of them, you qualify as a baseball expert. For the record and future baseball quizzes, here they are: pitchers Fred Holdsworth, Bob Strampe, Bill Slayback, Charles Meeler, and Don Leshnock; first basemen Joe Staton and Paul Jata; second baseman John Knox; shortstop John Gamble; and outfielder Isaiah Blessitt. Honest, that crew all gave it a try. Holdsworth, who Manager Billy Martin was high on, did have a 6-10 record after six years with three clubs. The Kansas City Royals had little success with pitcher Norm Angelini, but did get some value from Jim Wohlford once they got him off second base and into the outfield. He had been the American Association rookie of the year at second base while with Omaha. They had better results from pitcher Steve Busby, who had led the American Association with 211 strikeouts. He became the mainstay of the Royals' staff from 1973 to 1975 until shoulder problems limited his action. In 1977 he tried a comeback with Daytona Beach, and in 1978 with Omaha. 1979 found him back with the Royals and a 6-6 record. In 1976 he underwent surgery to repair a torn rotator cuff in his right shoulder and to correct a long-time knee problem. Steve is noted for his good command of all pitches and has developed a forkball to go with his fastball, slider, and curve. In 1974 he established an American League record by retiring 33 consecutive batters, but perhaps his most outstanding accomplishments are his two no-hitters. He is the first hurler to ever toss no-hitters in each of his first two full big league campaigns. His first no-hitter came in only his tenth major league start, in a game at Tiger Stadium in Detroit where there had not been a no-hitter in 21 years. A week later he came within eleven outs of back-to-back no-hitters. His second no-hitter took place at Milwaukee in 1974 and was close to a perfect game, as a walk to George Scott, who led off the second inning, represented the only runner to reach base. Busby was the selection of *The Sporting News* for rookie pitcher of 1973.

Baltimore had the most successful crop of rookies with outfielders Al Bumbry, who had led the International League in hitting at .345 while with Rochester, and Rich Coggins, a left-handed batter who hit .322 with the same club. We will meet Bumbry again. Another good arrival was first baseman Enos Cabell. Enos, who had played all the infield positions while a minor leaguer, was the rookie of the year in the Appalachian League in 1969, and was Texas League player of the year in 1971. Other Baby Birds were pitcher Ralph Scott and catcher Sergio Robles.

While the National League had more rookies in numbers, they were no more successful than their American League counterparts. Consider some of these: Cincinnati—Dave Tomlin, a pitcher; New York—pitchers Tom Moore, Bob Rauch, Brent Strom, and Henry Webb, catcher Joe Nolan, outfielder Dave Schneck and second baseman Luther Barnes; Atlanta—pitchers Ron Schueler and Jimmy Freeman, outfielder Rowland Office, infielders Larvell Blanks and Rod Gilbreath (Blanks and Office have had some moderate success and are still in the major leagues); Montreal—pitchers Joe Gilbert and Bob Walker, and outfielder Jose Mangual; San Diego—pitchers Steve Simpson, John Hilton, and Ralph Garcia, catcher Joe Goddard, outfielders Randy Elliott and John Grubb, and third baseman Dave Roberts. Grubb was successful for four-and-a-fraction seasons at San Diego before playing for Cleveland and Texas. Anyway, by now you get the picture.

The other National League clubs all had at least one rookie who met with success. The Pittsburgh Pirates had pitcher Jim McKee and infielders Chuck Goggin and Jose Gonzales. McKee was 1-1 in 17 games over two seasons, Goggin appeared in 72 games with three clubs in three years, but Gonzales, who is known by his middle name Fernando, has played with Pittsburgh on three occasions, sandwiched in between appearances with Kansas City, the New York Yankees, and San Diego. The Philadelphia Phillies gave a chance to catcher Bob Boone and third baseman Mike Schmidt among others. The Phils had found catching a tough spot to fill until they converted infielder Boone to that spot in the minor leagues. Bob's father, Ray Boone, had been a major league infielder who had converted from a catcher. Bob's manager at Eugene, Andy Seminick, a fine catcher himself, praised his young catcher saying, "Bob has advanced quicker than anyone I've ever had. He has a strong arm, stamina, is intelligent, and the big thing is, he hits the ball." A late-September trial found Boone throwing out the ace base stealer Lou Brock twice in one series. Often hampered by injuries, Bob has nevertheless been a real asset to the Phillies over the eight seasons he has been with them. Mike Schmidt, the hero of the Phillies' 1980 world champions, has been one of their most consistent players during the past eight campaigns. His 48 home runs in 1980 set a Phillies' one-season high. A consistent power hitter, he slammed 36 round trippers in 1973 and followed that up with 38 for three consecutive seasons in a row, dropped to 21 in '78, and rose to 45 in 1979. He has reaped a ton of individual honors, has set or tied many hitting and fielding records, and may be the National League's top player today. Consistency seems to be a Schmidt trait. He has walked more than 90 times and scored more than 90 runs seven straight seasons.

The San Francisco Giants had excellent rookies in two outfielders with the first name of Gary, Maddox and Matthews. We will meet Matthews later, but Maddox, after several good seasons with the Giants, was traded to the Phillies where he has continued to star as a Gold Glove fielder and a consistently good hitter. His fielding brilliance has been his trademark, and his mantle holds five of those golden gloves. A third outfielder up for a look-see was also named Gary, last name Thomasson. He has, like the other Garys, remained in the big leagues, alternating between first base and the outfield. The Giants traded him to Oakland in 1977, who sent him to the Yankees; but he is now back home in the National League with the Dodgers. Strange how the Giants could have presented an all-Gary outfield, and a talented one at that, had they not traded them all away. Thomasson has all the desire of an everyday player despite his platoon role. He can drive a ball as far as anyone on the Dodger club, and one of his home run balls now rests in the Baseball Hall of Fame. You see, his home run off Don Sutton's first pitch on opening day in 1977 sailed into the right field pavilion at Dodger Stadium, the first home run ever hit with the new Rawlings baseball that was introduced that season. The Giants also introduced pitchers Elias Sosa and Randy Moffitt (Billie Jean King's brother) and infielder Damaso Blanco.

Among seven Chicago Cub rookies were two who were ticketed for future stardom, outfielder-first baseman Pete LaCock and pitcher Rick Reuschel. LaCock, son of talk-show host Peter Marshall, put in four seasons for the Cubs before a trade sent him to Kansas City, where he has played four solid seasons. Pete, who never played organized baseball until he was fourteen, was a standout for several seasons in triple A ball, and in his first plate appearance for the Cubs he singled as a pinch hitter in a game at Pittsburgh. Reuschel, a big right-hander, has been one of the aces of the Cub staff every season since 1972, posting a 124-114 record, winning 20 games in 1977 and 18 in 1979. His minor league record was that of a winner. He made his first appearance a success, striking out the only batter he faced, Bobby Bonds. The very next day he recorded his first major league victory, a six-inning relief job. No slouch as a batter, he hit a double in his first major league at-bat, driving in his first RBI. A rare baseball phenomenon took place for Rick on August 21, 1975, against the Dodgers, when he and his older brother, Paul, combined to blank L.A. for nine innings, giving Rick the win and Paul the save.

Among three Houston rookies was a good catcher and sometimes first baseman, Cliff Johnson, who now owns part of several major league long-ball records. Joining the Cardinals, who had the most new faces in 1972, were second baseman Mike Tyson and pitcher Jim Bibby. The nine other rookies never panned out. Just to make things interesting, Ron Allen made a seven-game appearance to make yet another three-brother act to appear in the history of baseball. He was the brother of Richie and Hank. Tyson was named the Cardinal rookie of 1973 by the city's sportswriters. A steady fielder, he has always been among the infield leaders in picking up ground balls. In 1974 Mike teamed up with infield mates Joe Torre and Ted Sizemore to set a Cardinal record of 191 double plays. Bibby is just another in that long line of good pitchers who the New York Mets have traded away. While he never played with them, he was a product of the Met farm system. In two tries with the Cards, he had a poor 1-5 record and was traded to Texas where he had two full seasons, in one of which he was 19-19. Traded to Cleveland, he was a success, and then in 1978 he entered the free-agent draft and signed with the Pirates. After two winning seasons with the Bucs, he became their top hurler in 1980 with a fine 19-6 record. He can boast of a major league no-hitter, as he tossed one in 1973 against the world champion Oakland A's. Not a bad hitter for a pitcher, he is also proud of his two home runs in 1979. He is the brother of Henry Bibby, former UCLA basketball star, currently a strong performer in the NBA.

The Los Angeles Dodgers had several capable rookies in 1972 in infielders Lee Lacy and Davey Lopes and catcher Steve Yeager. Yeager had been named the outstanding rookie at Dodgertown in the spring and is still with the Dodgers. He has maintained his reputation as one of baseball's premier defensive catchers, as few opposing base runners attempt to steal on his arm and accuracy, which are among the most respected in baseball. He can hit the occasional long ball, but in recent years his batting average has tailed off. A competitive hitter, the bespectacled Yeager has said of his occasional slumps, "Sometimes a person has a tendency to try too hard, and I think that is my problem when I go into a slump at the plate. I have to learn to relax, do things naturally, and wait things out." On his success he says, "I can throw out anyone in the world if our pitchers give me half a chance." Good advice for youngsters to heed. No less than former St. Louis great Lou Brock agrees, "Yeager's the best throwing catcher in the league." Steve's aggressive plate play has resulted in many bone-jarring collisions, but one of the most unusual injuries in baseball history occurred to him at San Diego in 1976. He was wounded in the neck by a large part of Bill Russell's broken bat as he knelt in the on-deck circle. Nine splinters were removed from the wound, barely missing his windpipe, a major artery, and an area that controls nerve muscles in the arm. Infielder Davey Lopes has performed mostly at second base, but it has been his base stealing that has earned him honors. In 1975 he established a major league record by stealing 38 consecutive bases. A good power hitter, he hit 28 homers in 1979. Only two National League second basemen have hit more home runs in a season than Lopes, Hall of Famer Rogers Hornsby (42 in 1922) and Dave Johnson (43 in 1973). In 1978 and part of 1979 he served as the fifth-ever Dodger captain, but resigned the job in July 1979. Other Dodger captains? Reese, Snider, Wills, and Willie Davis. Dodger manager Tom Lasorda calls Lopes "One of the best clutch hitters in the game," and Wills, who should know, calls him "the greatest base stealer in the game today." In 1974 Lopes tied a 70-year-old National League record by stealing five bases in one game. Lacy has also proven to be a good utility infielder for the Dodgers. He was traded to Atlanta in November of 1975 and back to L.A. in June of 1976. A free agent after the 1978 season, he signed with Pittsburgh and hit a strong .335 for them in 1980. His debut was a good one as he hit in 12 of his first 13 games.

1973 continued to be a season of turmoil for baseball. Willie Mays called it a career, Richie Allen signed a record contract with the White Sox for $250,000 a year, two Yankee pitchers swapped wives, and the Yanks not only were sold to a Cleveland shipbuilder for a bargain price of $10 million, but at the season's end, the Yanks vacated Yankee Stadium and moved to Shea Stadium, home of the Mets, while "The House that Ruth Built" was being renovated. Slugger Hank Aaron came up one shy of Babe Ruth's 714 career home runs. Oakland topped the Mets 4 to 3 in the World Series, mainly on the batting of Reggie Jackson. A's owner Charlie Finley fired his substitute second baseman Mike Andrews after he made two costly errors in the second game, causing a player revolt which resulted in Andrews being reinstated. Three American League clubs, the Tigers, Yankees, and A's, fought over the services of managers Williams and Houk in an unprecedented tug-of-war.

Attendance climbed over the 30 million mark for the first time, and the American League adopted the designated hitter rule, which had little effect in the World Series as the A's hurlers, who were forced to bat, outhit the Met chuckers anyway. Angel pitcher Nolan Ryan topped Sandy Koufax's single-season strikeout record 383 to 382. The reserve rule was modified to give some veteran players the right to refuse a trade, a fact the Cubs' Ron Santo put to use by refusing a trade to California, but approving one to the White Sox. The American League had a record of twelve 20-game-winning pitchers. While the DH rule was being analyzed, there were two other strange statistics in 1973: Runners in the two leagues combined to steal over 2000 bases, the first time that had happened since the lively ball had arrived in 1920; and seven of the major leagues' 24 starting shortstops failed to hit a home run. Things were changing offensively. Perhaps there were signs of it back in 1972, when Rod Carew had won the AL batting crown without benefit of hitting a home run, the first such occurrence since 1918, when Brooklyn's Zack Wheat did it. Yogi Berra became only the second manager in history to win pennants in both leagues (Joe McCarthy was the first), as he led the most mediocre team in history to ever win a pennant, the Mets. Met 19-game winner Tom Seaver won the Cy Young Award over the Giants' 24-game winner Ron Bryant, which incensed fans everywhere but in New York. Detroit relief pitcher John Hiller recorded a record 38 saves (despite the DH rule which allowed starters to pitch longer), and just to show how zany the season was, consider that White Sox pitcher Wilbur Wood became the first 20-game winner and loser in the same season (24-20) in 57 years. What? Who was the Cleveland shipbuilder? That's right, George Steinbrenner.

There were more first-year players in 1973 than there had been for several seasons, and it was a quality group as we shall see. Unprecedented was the emergence of four amateurs as big league regulars. Three moved directly from the college campus to the big league dugout, pitcher Dick Ruthven (6-9) with the Phillies, pitcher Ed Bane (0-5) with the Twins, outfielder Dave Winfield with the Padres (.383), and pitcher David Clyde with the Rangers, who jumped from his high school mound to a starting job in Texas (4-8).

The rookies of the year were outfielders Al Bumbry of Baltimore and Gary Matthews of San Francisco, whom we have already met briefly. *The Sporting News* added pitchers Steve Busby of Kansas City, whom we have discussed, and Steve Rogers of Montreal. Matthews, of course, was the second San Francisco rookie in a row to take first year honors.

A word or two about the 1973 award winners. Al Bumbry, Baltimore's left-hand-hitting outfielder, was just another in what appeared to be a never-ending line of fine Bird rookies to arrive from Rochester. He led the

International League in hitting at .345 and in triples with 15. Though he didn't come up to Rochester until May, he stole 27 bases, and in 107 games he accepted 198 chances for a 1.000 fielding average. Rated as the fastest in the league, Bumbry appeared a sure-shot for the Bird outfield. He made it and has been in Baltimore since. He is one of the few players to go the free-agent route and re-sign with his original club. His outstanding catches have been one of the reasons the Baltimore outfield has been so fine in recent seasons. Al's .327 batting average carried him to rookie honors while his teammate Rich Coggins was runner-up for the award. Actually, it was Bumbry and Coggins in the outfield against right-handers and Don Baylor and Merv Rettenmund against lefties. Al didn't start playing baseball until his senior year at Virginia State College, where he had played four years of basketball. Joining Bumbry in Baltimore were three good pitchers, Wayne Garland, Jesse Jefferson, and Don Hood, outfielder Jim Fuller, and an all-star minor league third baseman, Doug DeCinces, the heir apparent to Brooks Robinson's job. Doug gained the job from the aging Robinson and by 1980 stood second to Brooks in games played for the Orioles at third base. There is a bit of irony between the two which many have forgotten. Doug hit a home run in his first at-bat in his first World Series (1979) just as his predecessor, Robinson, had done 13 years earlier. Ironically, Brooks had thrown out the first ball that night, and Doug was the one to whom he threw it.

In the National League, outfielder Gary Matthews of San Francisco, who had had a 20-game trial in 1972, took rookie honors. Gary has proven to be a good long-ball hitter and has been in double figures in round trippers in each of nine seasons. Like many others, he has improved with age. Now a member of the Atlanta Braves, in 1979 he enjoyed his best major league season with 1980 not far behind. His .300 average, 12 homers, and 58 RBIs won him the rookie award. Right-handed pitcher Steve Rogers of Montreal won the pitching honors for the National League rookies by posting a 10-5 record in 17 starts with a flashy 1.54 ERA. Steve has tossed four one-hitters in his career and holds all of the Expos' major pitching records, having appeared in more games on the mound than any other Montreal pitcher. In 1980, he was again the Expos' top pitcher with a 16-11 mark and a league-leading 14 complete games. Scott Sanderson also had a 16-11 record with seven complete games and a higher ERA than Rogers. Steve is the guy who surrendered Pete Rose's 3000th hit in 1978. Selected to the 1971 College World Series All-Star team, Steve had compiled a four-year 31-5 record at Tulsa University, from which he holds a degree in petroleum engineering. Perhaps that is why he never seems to run out of gas. Other rookies of note at San Francisco with Matthews were infielder Steve Ontiveros and pitcher John D'Acquisto. Montreal had the league's largest crop of rookies and among them were former minor league All-Star catcher Barry Foote, now with the Cubs, and good infielder Pepe Frias.

The Cincinnati Reds only had four rookies, but three have played important roles in recent Reds' history: Outfielder Ed Armbrister, who was at bat during the controversial play with catcher Carlton Fisk in the 1975 World Series; infielder Dan Driessen, who has taken over the first base chores and who hit .409 in 47 games at Indianapolis before being summoned to the Reds; fleet-footed outfielder Ken Griffey, whose .310 average tied him with Boston's Jim Rice and K.C.'s George Brett for fifth place among all major league hitters in the decade of the 70s; and outfielder Gene Locklear, who was traded to the Padres after 29 games. The New York Mets had among six rookies pitchers Bob Apodaca and Craig Swan. "Swannie" has been a productive hurler for the lads from Shea since his arrival, although he has been hindered at times by physical setbacks. He is known as a good control pitcher. Apodaca was 16-25 for five years. Joining them was catcher Ron Hodges, who did little in six seasons. The Dodgers also had six youngsters, two of whom contributed to the Dodger cause. Third baseman Jerry Royster, now with Atlanta, alternated between Albuquerque and L.A. for three seasons before his trade. He has been productive for the Braves and has tied Ralph Garr for the club record of 35 stolen bases. Pitcher Geoff Zahn enjoyed little success with L.A. and several other National League clubs, but has enjoyed some good seasons with the Minnesota Twins. An interesting career, he had been traded to the Cubs where a sore arm caused him to be released. Without a team, he asked for and received a trial with the Twins. Twins' manager Mauch liked what he saw, signed him, and he has been among the American League's top pitchers since.

The Chicago Cubs' Matt Alexander filled utility roles for several clubs, while showing a high total of stolen bases. Also joining the Cubs was a big first baseman with a seven-year minor league background, Andre Thornton. Traded to Montreal in 1976, he was then dispatched to Cleveland. Originally signed by the Phillies, he had also been a member of the Atlanta system. Today he is one of the top power threats in the American League. Recipient of many awards, he hit for the cycle against Boston in 1978, getting each hit off a different Bosox hurler. The San Diego Padres were talking about a first baseman named Randy Elliott, who played 14 games for them in '72, but it was another Randy, this one a pitcher named Jones who arrived to stay with a 7-6 rookie season. In '74 he dropped to 8-22, reversed his form in '75 and '76 when he was 20-12 and 22-14, capturing the Cy Young Award in '76 when he became the first man in his league since World War II to win 20 or more games without recording 100 strikeouts. He also tied Christy Mathewson's NL record of 68 consecutive innings without a walk. He seems to have recovered from arm problems which developed during the 1977 season. Joining Jones was outfielder Dave Winfield, who has been "Mr. Everything" with the Padres, except happy. As mentioned before, he moved directly to the Padres from the University of Minnesota with no minor league experience. Hitting with improved power and average since his start, he has also shown excellent defensive skills. He has set a goodly share of the Padres' team records. Noted for his contributions to underprivileged children, he established the Winfield Pavilion in right field at San Diego Stadium to provide tickets to selected games for them. Winfield is one of just two players (along with Nate Colbert) to rank in the current Padre top ten in every major career offensive category. Off to a good start, he hit safely in his first six games. At the University of Minnesota he was 13-1 as a pitcher while hitting over .400 in the outfield. He was named first-team All-American and MVP in the 1973 College World Series. He also starred in basketball for the Gophers and was drafted in three different sports—baseball (Padres), football (Minnesota Vikings), and basketball (Utah-ABA and Atlanta-NBA). Dave has just signed an extremely lucrative 10-year contract with the New York Yankees.

Among St. Louis Cardinal hopefuls were catcher Marc Hill, outfielders Hector and Cirilio Cruz, who were brothers and were joining yet another brother, Jose, who was already a regular outfielder with the Cardinals. Imagine all three playing in the outfield at one time (a headline writer's dream—"Cards Cruz to Victory"). Also up from Tulsa was Arnold "Bake" McBride, more recently a star and critic with the world champion Philadelphia Phillies. Bake, up for 40 games, went on to star in 1974 to become the baseball writers' pick for Rookie of the Year. He hit .309 and stole 30 bases, the second-highest stolen base total for a rookie award winner, five off the total of Sam Jethroe in 1950. He has been an important cog in the wheel at Philly. Heading the cast of rookies in St. Louis was outfielder Jim Dwyer, triple A ball's leading hitter with a .387 average at Tulsa, but only one HR. He was a baseball All-American at Southern Illinois, and he has shuffled around the big leagues with a number of clubs. The Pittsburgh Pirates presented as their rookie of '73 outfielder Dave Parker, and he has been one of their top players ever since. He has led his league in offensive departments many times, winning All-Star honors and the league's MVP Award in 1978 when he captured his second consecutive batting crown. Dave has hit several tape-measure home runs, including one in 1975 which traveled completely out of Chicago's Wrigley Field over the right-center field seats into an area few players have ever reached. The Houston Astros had little in their dugout in the way of rookies. Pitcher Jim Crawford put in two seasons in the Dome, went to Detroit for three more, and won more games for them than for the Astros. Outfielder Greg Gross was successful in Houston for four of six campaigns, then moved to the Cubs for two good years. In 1980, he was an important reserve for the world champion Phillies. He was *The Sporting News'* Rookie of the Year in 1974 with a .314 BA. Another outfield rookie was Mike Easler. He spent several seasons with the Astros, dividing his time between them and various farm clubs before they gave up on him and sent him to the St. Louis Cardinals, to whose farm system he had been on loan. After a season with Tulsa, the Cards traded him to the California Angels. After DHing with them for 21 games, he was traded to the Pirates. After ten games with them and a year with Columbus, he was mysteriously sent to the Boston Red Sox, where a poor spring training led to his being traded back to the Bucs. After a utility role in 1979, he emerged as their top batter with a .338 average in 1980. A very strange career to say the least. He also led the power-hitting club with 21 home runs and was second to Dave Parker with 74 runs batted in. Always a hitter for average in the minors, perhaps at 29 he has finally arrived. Over in Philadelphia, in addition to Dick Ruthven, the Phils came up with right-hander Larry Christenson, who in his first major league appearance, at age 19, defeated the Mets 7 to 1. Most of '73 and '74 were spent in triple A before coming to the majors to stay in 1975. Quite successful for the Phils, he won 19 games in 1975 and did well through 1979 when he entered a West Coast bike-a-thon and fell, breaking a collarbone. Catcher Larry Cox was never more than utility as was catcher Jim Essian until he went to the White Sox and Oakland. To confuse things, two Wallace boys were also given a trial by the Phillies, pitchers Dave and Mike, not brothers and not successful.

In the American League, the Red Sox were looking at Mario Guerrero, acquired from the Yankees, and people named Pole and Skok. The Yankees were looking at equally talented people named Buskey, Pagan, and Otto Velez, the latter being highly touted for his sizzling bat and outfielding. Both cooled off rapidly. The Oakland A's continued to produce good newcomers like triple A All-Star hurler Glenn Abbott, who earned a spot in the record books when on the final day of the 1975 season he combined with Vida Blue, Paul Lindblad, and Rollie Fingers to no-hit California. Taken by the Seattle Mariners in the 1976 expansion draft, he has been a winner with them and was their top chucker in 1980 with a 12-12 mark. Joining in was second baseman Manny Trillo, who was traded to the Cubs, where he won a spot before they traded him to the Phillies, where he won a Gold Glove. Actually, he was originally signed by the Phillies as a catcher and played at Huron of the Northern League for present Phils' skipper Dallas Green. He was a National League leading fielder for years until recent injuries have forced him into limited duty. Phil Garner was used mostly at second base by the A's, although advanced notices proclaimed him a third sacker. Believing the advance billing, Pittsburgh purchased him from the A's in 1977, hoping to use him in a void at third. It didn't work that way, and he wound up splitting his playing time between second and third. The former American League All-Star had a great postseason with the '79 Bucs, tying the record for the highest batting average in a seven-game series at .500. His twelve hits were one short of a series record. In 1978 he smacked two grand slams at Three Rivers Stadium on consecutive nights, making him the first National League player to accomplish the feat since Brooklyn's James Sheckard did it in 1901.

The Cleveland Indians came up with reserve catcher Alan Ashby, who has also been a reservist with the Blue Jays and Astros. Converted outfielder Craig Kusick was battling for the Minnesota Twins' first base job. He had been a Little All-American as a football tight end at Wisconsin's LaCrosse State College. Infielder Jerry Terrell was enjoying his best season in the major leagues as a Twin, and he was still around with the Royals in 1980. Never quite enjoying as good an offensive season as '73, he has turned in sparkling defensive work. Jerry has been considered a versatile defensive player, a scrappy hitter, and a good base runner. The outstanding American League relief pitcher of recent seasons, Bill "Soup" Campbell, made his debut with the Twins in 1973. Later a free agent, he signed on with the Boston Red Sox for 1977 when his 31 saves won him the Rolaids Relief Award for the second year running. In two seasons, '76 and '77, he had a combined 51 saves. With the Twins in 1976, he had a brilliant 17-5 record as a reliever. Soup was an All-Star at every minor league level he performed at.

Promising rookies abounded in the Kansas City Royal farm system. We have already met pitcher Steve Busby, and Royal brass was singing praises of: pitchers Gene Garber and reliever Dick Colpaert; American Association rookie of the year at second base, Jim Wohlford; hard-hitting first baseman Moose Ortenzio; outfielder Keith Marshall; lefty Mike Jackson, 21-year-old pitcher of the year in the American Association; relief specialist Mark Littell; and outfielder Tom Poquette. Less heralded was a young third baseman who had put in two decent seasons at Billings and San Jose. After posting a fairly good .284 average at Omaha, he was summoned to K.C. in early August to play in 13 games at third base. Back to Omaha he went to start the 1974 season, but he battled his way back to K.C. before long. His older brother Ken had already pitched in the majors for six seasons, and brother Bob had also done outfielding in the K.C. organization. George Brett has established himself today among the outstanding stars in baseball and turned out to be the best of all the '73 rookies, although little heard of back then. Defensively, he has good range, quick hands, and a strong arm, and his leadership abilities and offensive skills have been the foundation of recent Royal championship clubs. His consistency at the plate and aggressiveness on the base paths have made him one of the game's most exciting offensive performers. In the 25-year history of major league baseball in K.C., no one has exceeded the accomplishments of this multi-talented third baseman. His heroics in the 1979 and 1980 seasons have brought unprecedented awards and honors to him. He spent a good part of 1980 chasing the magic .400 batting mark, finally settling for a league-leading .390 average while clubbing 24 homers, 33 doubles, and driving in 118 runs. He was also the league's leading batter in 1976 with a .333 average. 1979 found him becoming the fifth player in major league history to join the exclusive 20-20-20 club for doubles (42), triples (20), and home runs (23). Others in that club are Jeff Heath (1941–Cleveland), Frank Schulte (1911–Cubs), Jim Bottomley (1928–Cardinals) and Willie Mays (1957–Giants). A tough clutch hitter, he seems to be at his best with men on base. In 1979 he also hit for the cycle against the tough pitching of the Baltimore Orioles. In winning two batting titles and league championships in hits (3 times), total bases (twice), doubles and triples (3 times), he matched feats only previously accomplished by Hall of Famers Ty Cobb and Lou Gehrig. He and Cobb are the only American League players to win three titles in both hits and triples. Consistently one of the toughest players to strike out, he has averaged only one strikeout in 23-plus at-bats. At 20-years-old in 1973, he was one of the youngest Royals ever to make a big league debut (Clint Hurdle in 1977 was younger). If George can continue the pace he has started out at, the least touted of K.C.'s 1973 rookies would appear headed for baseball's shrine at Cooperstown.

Because of injuries among the Chicago White Sox regulars, a number of rookies were promoted to that club in 1973. Among them was shortstop Bucky Dent, who is better remembered as a New York Yankee, although he was a White Sox for three-and-one-half seasons. Dent hit .248 and went 18 games and 101 chances without an error. There was Brian Downing, who played a number of spots, but was best behind the plate. He hit only .178 and had to overcome an injured leg, the result of a foul tip on his first big league play. Downing has perhaps the most unorthodox stance in baseball to go along with his great desire. He hits for average and his .326 average in 1979 was the third best in California Angel history, the team he now plays for (Rod Carew .331 in 1980 and Alex Johnson .329 in 1970 are better). While Downing credits his changed stance and a strength program ("I know I felt stronger far more into the season") for his high average, he has also improved defensively. He owns his own batting cage and pitching machine and has them set up in his backyard. About that right-handed batting stance he says, "Mine is really a radical stance. You'll see my left foot pointing toward the dugout. It's been the talk of the league. I'm practically facing the pitcher." Joining in at Chicago also was: first baseman Sam Ewing; switch-hitting Jerry Hairston, an outfielder-first baseman; Ohio State grad Bill Sharp, an outfielder who had only 139 games in pro ball; and catcher Pete Varney, a Harvard University product, who had hit 18 homers at the triple A level.

In the California Angel camp there had been more excitement about the addition of veterans to the roster than there was about some of the very promising youngsters. Some of the young Angels had appeared briefly in the California lineup but were nearing maturity down on the farms. Pitcher Andy Hassler, shortstop Rudy Meoli, catcher Charlie Sands, and outfielders Mickey Rivers and Bruce Bochte were all about ready to be hatched. Three highly regarded youngsters, however, did make their first big-time box score in 1973. Pitcher Frank Tanana arrived in early September after a 16-6 record at El Paso and a 1-0 slate at Salt Lake City. He was 2-2 for 26 innings pitched. We will meet him later. Well thought of was pitcher Terry Wilshusen, but he appeared in only one game and left the majors forever with an 81.00 ERA. Following along with Tanana, after playing in El Paso and Salt Lake City, was a very good shortstop, Dave Chalk. If numbers meant anything, then the Milwaukee Brewers should have had the junior circuit's best crop of rookies, as they introduced the largest group of new faces. It didn't work that way, however. Most soon passed from the majors. There were several who stayed around for a few years. Pitchers Kevin Kobel and relievers Edwardo Rodriguez and Carlos Velazquez, second baseman Pedro Garcia, catcher Charlie Moore, and outfielder Bob Coluccio were the better known among nine rookies. Kobel had little success and has alternated between majors and minors and the New York Mets. Rodriguez was the Brewers' most versatile and consistent pitcher for six years. He concluded his stay at Milwaukee among their career pitching leaders, including the all-time leader in appearances (235). After three seasons, his record stood at 23-11, but in many respects his initial season was his best, as he posted career highs in victories (9) and ERA (3.32), despite less than two previous seasons in the minors. He was sent to Kansas City in the spring of 1979. Velazquez was to get a good look after two successful seasons at Evansville. Garcia had led three minor leagues in an unusual category, repeatedly being the top man in being hit by the pitcher. Coluccio, highly rated, spent five big league seasons with a variety of clubs.

The Detroit Tigers were counting on a fine defensive center fielder, Dick Sharon, who they had picked up from the Pirates. They were hoping to cash in on Ron Cash, who could also play the outfield. Shortstop Tom Veryzer was also highly rated and has shown steadiness and durability with both Detroit and Cleveland. He had brief trials in '73 and '74, but became the regular shortstop in 1975 despite missing four weeks due to hand, eye, and foot injuries. His brother Jim also played in the Detroit system. The Tigers also had two rookie pitchers, Gary Ignasiak and Dave Lemanczyk. Gary never won a game, and Dave was sent to Toronto after the 1976 season. Down in Texas the Rangers had several good youngsters besides David Clyde who we met earlier. There was pitcher Rick Waits, who did nothing for Texas but went over to the Cleveland Indians in 1975 after only one game in '73 with the Rangers. He was twice a member of the Pacific Coast League All-Star Team before arriving in Cleveland where he has been a success. After nine excellent relief efforts, Rick was moved into the starting rotation. His '76 season got off to a bad start when his pitching arm (left) came up sore, but from then on he has been a top pitcher for the Tribe. Perhaps his biggest win came on the last day of the 1978 season, when he hurled a complete game in Yankee Stadium to beat New York 9 to 2 and force the historic playoff between the Yankees and the Red Sox for the American League East crown. Somewhat of a singer, Waits has sung the National Anthem and "O Canada" prior to Cleveland-Toronto contests on several occasions. The Rangers, who had the most successful farm system in baseball in 1973, also gave a look-see at some of the other fine products they were producing. First baseman Don Castle returned to the minors and became a fixture with the Eastern League West Haven Yankees. Pitcher Steve Foucault went on to a number of seasons of fine relief work. Castle's teammate at Spokane was pitcher Rick Henninger, and he was no more successful than Castle while down on the range. Pitcher Jim Kremmel did little either. Infielder Pete MacKanin did more for Montreal than Texas, but perhaps the best Texas rookie was infielder Bill "Mad Dog" Madlock. Texas kept him around for only 21 games, then sent him along with infielder-outfielder Vic Harris to the Chicago Cubs for pitcher Fergie Jenkins. Bill responded well to National League pitching, hitting at a .313 clip for '74 and then put together back-to-back batting championships, winning in '75 with a .354 average and at .339 in '76. He became the second-youngest player in National League history to win a batting title, as Tommy Davis won it at 23 in 1963. Madlock won his second title on the final day of the season, needing four hits in not more than five at-bats to edge the Reds' Ken Griffey. Bill went 4 for 4. The Cubs traded him to San Francisco after the '76 season, and he gave the Giants two .300-plus seasons before dropping to .261 and being traded to the Pirates where he took over the third base chores. Bill's single to center in the sixth inning of game five of the 1979 World Series drove in the winning run for an important win. The Pirates were down three games to one, and this single won their first of three straight victories needed to win the Series. Bill went 4 for 4 in that game to tie a Series record.

1974-76:
Records, Rookies,
and Rewards

It has been the premise in this book to jar the memory bank of those readers old enough to go back to the years covered and stir up some nostalgia about those players of the past, some well remembered and some long forgotten. By recalling some facts about their minor league careers and giving some insights into their big league stays, we arrived at a kind of "How did they do?" approach. As we arrive at what might be considered the current era, we find that many of our rookies are still in the majors or have had their first big trial but are back playing in the minors with a chance to return to the big time. There are others who may be just about ready to make it. The reader of the present will need no memory jogger, the reader of the future will. Since the returns are not in on all of the youngsters, we may treat some of them more briefly but with the realization that within a few seasons they may be the stars of the majors.

1974 found the Oakland A's winning their third consecutive World Series by upending the Los Angeles Dodgers, four games to one, behind the brilliant fielding of second baseman Dick Green. The A's were led by Al Dark, who had won a pennant with the 1962 Giants and thus followed Yogi Berra by a year in becoming the third manager to win pennants in both leagues. The pennant races were close in all divisions with the A's holding off the surprising Texas Rangers, the Orioles winning 28 of their last 34 games to overtake the Yankees, the Dodgers nosing out the Reds by four games, and Pirates edging the Cardinals by only a game and a half.

It was also a year that found the As' top pitcher, Catfish Hunter, win his free agency, and on New Year's Eve he signed a package in excess of $3 million with the New York Yankees for 1975. There was also a new procedure for salary arbitration, and 29 players took advantage of it with 13 winning salary increases. Another first found Frank Robinson being appointed the Cleveland Indians' manager for 1975, the majors' first black manager. Yankee owner George Steinbrenner was suspended for two years as a result of his conviction in a federal court for illegal corporate political contributions and attempting to persuade his ship building employees to give false explanations to the Feds. Detroit star Al Kaline got his 3000th hit and St. Louis' Lou Brock set a single-season stolen base record with 118 thefts. Slugger Hank Aaron surpassed Babe Ruth's 714 home runs. Rod Carew won his third consecutive AL batting crown, the first to accomplish that feat since Ty Cobb led the league in 1917-19.

The baseball writers selected Bake McBride of St. Louis as their National League rookie of 1974, and we met him in 1973. In the American League they selected first baseman Mike Hargrove of Texas. *The Sporting News'* picks were outfielder Gary Matthews of San Francisco, whom we have also met, Hargrove, and pitchers John D'Acquisto of San Francisco and Frank Tanana of California. D'Acquisto, a right-hander, gained a slot with the Giants in the final weeks of 1973 after posting a 16-12 season at Phoenix. His 12-14 record and 3.77 ERA in '74 won him the rookie honors. His record dropped to 2-4 in '75 as he had elbow surgery in June. The Giants traded him to St. Louis in October of 1976, and in May of 1977 he was traded to his hometown San Diego Padres, fulfilling a lifetime dream. Possessing an exceptional fastball, he has been both a reliever and a starter. John married a former Miss San Diego and has formed his own musical group called "Wild Pitch." Mike Hargrove has appeared at both first base and in the outfield. He never played baseball in high school and played in college only at the insistence of his father. There was an overwhelming surprise when Texas picked Mike in the 25th round, 572nd pick overall, in the June 1972 free-agent draft. In his first full year as a pro, he led Gastonia of the Western Carolina League with a .351 average, 60 points better than the runner-up. Invited to spring training with the Rangers in 1974, he hit .486 and made the jump from class A ball to the major leagues on that spring effort. He was named rookie of the year when he had what has been a career high average of .323. Texas traded him to San Diego in October '78, and by June 1979 he was back in the American League with Cleveland.

Frank Tanana, a fireballing left-hander, won 14 games as a 20-year-old rookie for California to take rookie honors. He started the 1973 season at El Paso where he was 16-6, moved to Salt Lake City where he picked up a win, before promotion to the Angels where he was 2-2. He has been a constant winner, and a much sought-after pitcher ever since his rookie season. In 1980 he was tied with Mark Clear for the most wins on the club at 11. It took him only a few seasons to establish himself as the top left-handed pitcher in the league, as he led the league with 269 strikeouts in 1975, had a career high 19 victories in '76, and a league-leading 2.54 ERA in 1977. During one stretch in 1977, he tossed 14 consecutive games, a marvelous achievement. This finally took its toll, and he developed what was described as a tired arm. 1978 found him no longer the strikeout artist, but a pitcher with great finesse who had matured in a hurry. Plagued with arm problems since, Tanana, a great competitor, has said, "I still have the confidence and ability to go out and win." He led the Angels to the 1979 Western Division title by winning the clinching game which he has said was his top thrill, especially coming before a home crowd. "After six years, after all the stuff I went through last year, winning the pennant is what you dream about," he said. "I was really happy to be able to come back and contribute."

Among the other rookies of 1974, the youngest was Milwaukee's 18-year-old shortstop Robin Yount and the oldest was a 29-year-old Cub hurler, Oscar Zamora. Yount had had only 64 games of previous experience at Newark of the New York-Penn League, and by 1976 he had a league-leading 104 double plays at shortstop. In seven seasons with the Brewers, Yount has averaged better than 140 games per season. In 1976 he played in 161 games with 638 at-bats becoming the youngest player in history to ever play that many games. Zamora pitched for four years, three with the Cubs and one with the Astros. 1974 found the largest group of first-year players since 1969, which was an expansion year.

It would appear that the two clubs with the most rookies of quality would be the Boston Red Sox and the Cincinnati Reds; perhaps this fact should be noted as it certainly paid dividends in 1975 as each club won their league's pennant. Newcomers to Boston included pitcher Steve Barr and catcher Tim Blackwell, neither of whom lasted too long, although Blackwell has proven to be a good backup catcher for several teams. Seldom does a club come up with three players in the same season who all go on to gain stardom and to rank among the best in the major leagues to boot. Consider then that Red Sox shortstop Rick Burleson and outfielders Fred Lynn and Jim Rice all arrived in 1974. Burleson took over the shortstop duties in May; Rice was summoned from Pawtucket in August and Lynn from the same club in September. Burleson battled for and won the shortstop post after Mario Guerrero had been given a trial. By far not the most polished shortstop in the beginning, Rick showed a steady improvement for several seasons and with a dramatic change became a complete shortstop by 1977 when he established himself as the league's best. He has won a Gold Glove and appeared on several All-Star squads and is tied with two others for the Red Sox high in fielding average for shortstops. Rick will never forget his first two major league games. He committed three errors in his first game, but came back the next day with a home run, single, and three RBIs. Jim Rice had a "can't miss" label on him. The 22-year-old was the Bosox top prospect and had been everyone's minor league Player of the Year and winner of the International League's triple crown (.337, 25 HR, 93 RBIs). Despite some fielding difficulties, the Bosox felt his superb hitting skills, which had also produced a batting title at Bristol in the Eastern League the year before, could overcome any shortcomings. Certainly Rice could stick as a right-handed designated hitter. Rice has developed into the most feared hitter in baseball, so strong that he once had the bat break off in his hand on a checked swing. His powerful line drives have been known to knock outfielders backwards and his towering home runs are legend. One such blast at Fenway Park caused the late Red Sox owner Tom Yawkey to remark that it was the longest home run he had ever seen at Fenway Park, and he had seen some real power hitters perform there. In 1979 Jim led the American League with 369 total bases for the third straight season to tie Ty Cobb and Ted Williams for the league mark. With his third consecutive 200-plus-hit season in 1979, he became the first American Leaguer to do so since John Pesky in 1947. He has led the majors in home runs, triples, slugging, and in 1978 was the first AL player since 1937 to have 400 total bases. In 1978 he became the first player to lead either league outright in home runs, triples, and RBIs. In 1978 he was the league's MVP. He has led his league in many areas and appears destined to become one of baseball's all-time great players. We will meet Fred Lynn, his Pawtucket teammate, a bit later on.

The Cincinnati Reds meanwhile had four pitchers arrive in 1974 that were to play important roles for them in 1975. Strangely, all came highly touted, played their parts in 1975, then faded away. There were three right-handers, Tom Carroll, Rawley Eastwick, and Pat Darcy, and lefty Will McEnaney. The Reds also had good glove men in third baseman Ray Knight and in shortstop Junior Kennedy, whose brother James Kennedy was a former minor league infielder.

Other National League hopefuls were at St. Louis, pitcher John Denny, shortstop Stan Papi, outfielders Jerry Mumphrey, Danny Godby, and Larry Herndon, and first baseman Keith Hernandez. Hernandez and Godby had been American Association All-Stars. Keith, of course, has starred for the Cards for years and was the National League's co-MVP in 1979, sharing the honor with Pittsburgh's Willie Stargell. His father, John, had been a former minor leaguer, and his brother Gary had also been in the Cardinal organization. In 1979 Hernandez became the first infielder in major league history to win both the batting championship (.344) and a Gold Glove for fielding in the same season. A lefty all the way, he made his first Cardinal appearance before the folks in his hometown of San Francisco. The Chicago Cubs had little to offer except pitcher Jim Todd (4-2), who went on to win more games in two seasons at Oakland then he did at Chicago, and a catcher with a great baseball name, Steve Swisher. Los Angeles had a fine prospect in shortstop Ivan DeJesus who at Albuquerque had hit .298, stolen 22 bases, cut down on his strikeouts, and was a defensive standout. DeJesus had signed a pro contract while still in high school. He never put in a full season in three tries with the Dodgers, who finally sent him to the Cubs where he had fans all over the league talking and marveling at his phenomenal catches and inspired hitting. Then in 1978 he seemed to improve even more, adding dazzling speed on the base paths. His 41 stolen bases were a high by a Cub since Kiki Cuyler's 43 in 1929 and Johnny Evers' 46 in 1907. Ivan holds a number of Cub team records. Joining him with the Dodgers was pitcher Rick Rhoden, who overcame osteomyelitis as a youngster and was one of the better Dodger pitchers during the mid-70s. Traded to Pittsburgh, he was 7-5 with them in 1980. At the age of 8, Rick was hurt in a freak accident where his right knee was cut by a rusty pair of scissors. Several months later he came down with osteomyelitis. For three years he had to wear a brace on his leg and later walk with a cane. He underwent surgery to remove part of his left knee so that his left leg would not outgrow his right. The rest is history, as he became a basketball and baseball star in high school and was drafted as a first pick by the Dodgers in June 1971. His battle against the odds can serve as an inspiration to all, young and old alike.

After just five years, the Montreal farm system began to pay dividends with the likes of: catcher Gary Carter, a converted infielder; Dale Murray, a fine relief pitcher; and Larry Parrish, a good glove at third base who made the jump from double A Quebec City. We will meet Carter again. The Mets came up with several rookies, the best of whom were a 21-year-old Dominican pitcher, Nino Espinosa, and an outfielder, Bruce Boisclair, who has also played some first base for the Mets. One of the Phillies' top prospects was a left-handed strikeout pitcher, Tom Underwood, whose brother Pat is a pitcher for Detroit, and whose father, John, was a minor leaguer in the Phillies' organization. Tom was a success with the Phils, Cards, and Toronto before a trade brought him to the Yankees in 1980, where he was 13-9. Originally a relief pitcher, he was converted to a starter and he once owned the Blue Jays' season strikeout record (140 in 1978) until Jim Clancy whiffed 152 in 1980. Joining Tom was yet another former Arizona State All-

American and baseball's number one selection in the January 1973 draft, outfielder-shortstop Alan Bannister. One of the most heralded college prospects ever, the two-time All-American holds a host of NCAA batting records. Arm and shoulder problems have plagued Alan's major league career. Traded to the Chicago White Sox, he has also played second base for them. Catcher John Stearns, who has gained more renown with the Mets, playing five different positions, and twice being selected for the All-Star Team, was a Phillie in 1974. A rarity among catchers, he can steal bases and ranks fifth on the all-time Met list. In 1978 he set the modern record for stolen bases by a catcher by stealing 25. The old record was set by the Cubs' Johnny Kling in 1902 and tied in 1903. Stearns was originally drafted by Oakland in 1969, but elected to accept a football scholarship to Colorado where he participated in four successive post-season bowl games as a defensive halfback. He also participated in baseball, and like his teammate Bannister, won All-American selection and was the NCAA home run champion in 1973. The Pittsburgh Pirates had an outfielder with speed to burn in Miguel Dilone. He had originally signed with the Bucs, but was later signed by the Cardinals who did not realize the Pirates held his contract, and back he went. In 1973 he set the Western Carolina's league stolen base record with 95. Before being called up by the Pirates, he had time to set the Carolina League record for stolen bases with 85. With the Pirates in 1977, he established a National League record for the most stolen bases without being caught stealing in one season at 12. He has also played with the Oakland A's and the Chicago Cubs. Joining Miguel were outfielder Ed Ott, pitcher Kent Tekulve, and shortstop Mario Mendoza. Ott was converted to a catcher during spring training in 1975 and has done a good job since. He turned down a football scholarship to Arizona State to play baseball. ASU sure seems to be tangled up in the baseball world one way or another. Ott will be remembered as riding a bicycle to spring training in 1979, from Philadelphia to Bradenton, Florida, in a charitable effort for Muscular Dystrophy sponsored by Phillie pitcher Tug McGraw. Tekulve, a sidearming submarine-ball-throwing relief pitcher did not pitch professionally until he was 22. He had been the mainstay of the Marietta College staff in Ohio. He holds the Pirate Club record for games pitched at 72, set in 1977 breaking the old record of 71 set by Pete Mikkelsen in 1966. San Diego had outfielder John Scott, their number two draft pick of 1970, but he didn't hit, and pitcher Dan Spillner who was 16-11 with Cleveland in 1980. Another strikeout artist, he had his career delayed in 1976 by back surgery, and was traded to the Indians in June of 1978. The San Francisco Giants not only had the rookie pitcher of the year, but they brought up four other pitchers who all turned out to be good finds;

one, John Montefusco, became the 1975 rookie hurler of the year. Joining him in 1974 were lefty reliever Gary Lavelle, righty Ed Halicki, and Butch Metzger. Lavelle has developed into one of the National League's top relievers, and when he joined the Giants, he had put behind him an eight-year minor league career. He has set club records for saves (20) and appearances (73), and as a member of the Fellowship of Christian Athletes is responsible for the club's Sunday chapel services both at home and on the road. Who can forget his two scoreless innings in the 1977 All-Star Game, which included strikeouts of Reggie Jackson and Carl Yastrzemski? Halicki, in only his 30th major league start, threw a no-hitter at the New York Mets on August 24, 1975, winning 6 to 0.

In the American League, righty reliever Dave Johnson, after splitting the season between the International League and Baltimore, was up to stay. At Minnesota, pitcher Jim Hughes was being looked at and responded nicely in 1975 with a 16-14 slate, but then it was all downhill. Cleveland had a top-rated prospect in 6'5" Jim Kern, who had been 17-7 (2.52 ERA) with Oklahoma City and had led his league with 220 strikeouts in 189 innings. Kern has not only developed into one of baseball's fine relief hurlers, but as befits a reliever, somewhat of a free spirit. Bearded, he is an awesome sight on and off the field. Frequently atop that big frame is a wide-brimmed black Amish hat. Now with the Texas Rangers, he is regarded as somewhat kooky, not a bad asset for a relief pitcher with a 100-mile-an-hour fastball. He can quote from Confucius, Castineda, and Aquinas, and while he may bay at the moon and live up to his nickname, "Emu" (the rare bird), when he runs in from the bullpen he's all business. Super hitter Al Oliver on Kern, "When he is right, the opposition can forget it." Joining Kern was second baseman Duane Kuiper who had hit .310 at Oklahoma City and led that league with 25 stolen bases. Duane had led his Southern Illinois University to the college NCAA finals in 1971, only to lose to USC in the final game. If you think he wasn't sought after, he had been drafted by the Yankees, Pilots, White Sox, Reds, and Red Sox before signing with Cleveland. In 1977 he had what has been considered the finest defensive season by any player in Cleveland history, as he was something to behold in the field. His first major league home run came in 1977 off Baltimore's Steve Stone at Cleveland Stadium and came after he had been to bat 1,382 times, the longest non-home run streak in baseball at that time.

The New York Yankees got little from hopeful pitchers Tippy Martinez and Dick Sawyer, or from outfielders Larry Murray and Terry Whitfield. The Milwaukee Brewers presented two pitchers who you might say "fit the bill" in Bill Castro and Bill Travers. Travers, hindered by an auto accident and arm problems in 1977, had a nerve transfer operation that December and returned in 1978 to post his first winning season as a professional (12-11), responded in '79 with a 14-8 mark, and was 12-6 in '80. Also joining the Brewers was fly-chaser Sixto Lezcano, who hit .325 with 34 HRs and 99 "ribbies" in the Pacific Coast League. In addition to Tanana, the Angels' formerly unproductive farm system produced pitchers Ed Figueroa and Don Kirkwood and outfielders John Balaz and a highly rated converted first baseman, Bruce Bochte, who had always hit .300 and was hitting .355 when called up from Salt Lake City. The Chicago White Sox were hoping to fill several reserve spots and find one starting pitcher among chuckers John Kucek, Joe Henderson, and Francisco Barrios and first baseman Lamar Johnson. The Kansas City Royals' top pitching prospect, Dennis Leonard, and a pitcher they had obtained from the Mexico City Reds, Aurelio Lopez, along with outfielder Al Cowens were all being made to feel welcome by that club. Leonard has emerged as one of the league's best hurlers, a consistent winner who mixes fastball, slider, and curve and has fine control for a power pitcher. Among the Royals' hardest throwers, he ranks among the league's top strikeout artists. Pitcher Mike Hooten, outfielder John "Champ" Summers, and the base stealing outfielder, Claudell Washington, were debuting in Oakland, while infielders Mike Cubbage and Roy Howell and catcher Jim Sundberg were pulling on Texas Ranger uniforms. Sunny has won a number of Gold Gloves and is considered by many the finest receiver in the majors.

What a grand year 1975 was for the baseball world. It was as if baseball had been reborn. There was the absence of a pennant race in three of the four divisions, and attendance, despite worsening economic conditions, held its own. It was, however, the World Series between the Cincinnati Reds and the Boston Red Sox that brought back the game as the number one sport in the country. A Series which must go down in memory as the most exciting of all time, it was almost a David vs. Goliath affair. The Reds, 108-game winners during the regular season and easy winners over Pittsburgh in the playoffs, were truly "The Big Red Machine." The Reds were loaded with future Hall of Fame candidates, Pete Rose, Johnny Bench, Joe Morgan, Tony Perez, Ken Griffey, and George Foster. If they had a weakness it may have been on the mound. The Red Sox, who handled the Athletics in three straight in the playoffs (the A's had won a 5th straight Western Division crown), were being led by two sensational rookies, Jim Rice and Fred Lynn, and two equally sensational veterans in Luis Tiant and Carl Yastrzemski. Backing up their quartet was catcher Carlton Fisk, an inspired Denny Doyle, and such steadies as Rick Burleson, Rico Petrocelli, Dewey Evans, Rick Wise, Bill Lee, and Reggie Cleveland. The two teams battled down to the sixth game, when it seemed that the Reds would wrap it up. Enter Bernie Carbo to hit a home run to tie things up and send the game into extra innings. Then in the twelfth inning came Carlton Fisk's dramatic home run off the foul pole and the Series was tied, forcing a seventh and final game. Pete Rose was quoted as saying, "Wow, I don't know who will win this, but isn't it great just being here." In the final game, the Sox held a three-run lead only to be tied and see the Reds win in the ninth inning on a Joe Morgan single. A year later that sixth game was voted to be the greatest game ever.

Recently arrived players would dominate the major league scene as such names as Bill Madlock, Greg Luzinski, Mike Schmidt, Dave Cash, Dave Parker, Jim Palmer, George Brett, Mickey Rivers, Jeff Buroughs, and Fred Lynn were among the season's leaders. A new crew was dominating the scene.

Another event which would have a lasting effect took place in 1975. Pitchers Andy Messersmith of L.A. and Dave McNally of Baltimore had played the season without signing contracts and declared themselves free agents. After a lengthy dispute, a ruling was handed down in their favor.

The American League Rookie of the Year Award was a toss-up between the two youngsters who had come up from Pawtucket to the Red Sox in late 1974. Jim Rice and his power hitting lost out to Fred Lynn's steady hitting and fantastic fielding. So good was Lynn that he was not only named rookie of the year, but also the league's MVP, something no other rookie had ever done. The only other rookie who came close was Pete Reiser of the 1941 Brooklyn Dodgers who was runner-up to teammate Dolph Camilli. Lynn took awards home by the carload and led the league in runs (103), doubles (47), and batted .331, second in the league to the Twins' Rod Carew (.359). In the MVP voting K.C.'s John Mayberry was second and Jim Rice third. Lynn won a Gold Glove for his fielding and was selected by Associated Press and United Press International as "Athlete of the Year." In a game in mid-June at Detroit, Lynn burst onto the national scene when he hit three home runs, a triple, and a single with ten RBIs and a record tying 16 total bases. Despite winning batting titles in youth leagues and high school, Fred entered USC on a football scholarship. Later he switched to baseball and was a three-year regular for Ron Dedeaux and made All-American in 1972 and 1973. He has continued his fine play over the years, and in 1979 he had a great year, leading the league with a .333 average and a .637 slugging average, becoming only the 16th player in American League history to accomplish that feat. Veteran Red Sox coach John Pesky was calling Lynn "The best young hitter since Williams." Reserved and confident, Lynn has gone about his job, often playing hurt, but giving it his all. He is one of baseball's premier players today.

Pitcher Dennis Eckersley of the Cleveland Indians was the choice for the American League rookie pitcher of the year. He had been an All-Star pitcher at San Antonio the year before with a league leading 14-3 record. The right-hander won rookie laurels off his 2.60 ERA, third best in the league behind Palmer and Hunter. The rookie right-hander ranked immediately as the ace of the staff, although he was only 21. His 13-7 record set him up as the spearhead of an Indian youth movement. Traded to the Boston Red Sox just prior to the 1978 season, he responded with a 20-8 record to lead that club into their now famous playoff with New York. "Eck" made his big league bow by shutting out Oakland 6 to 0 and did not allow an earned run in his first 28.2 innings, a major league rookie record. With his 200 strikeouts in 199 innings in 1976, he became only the eighth pitcher since 1900 to fan 200 in one season before the age of 22. In May of 1977, he tossed a no-hitter against California. He was also part of a 22.1 hitless string, the second longest in baseball history to Cy Young's 25.1 innings in 1904.

The National League rookie selections were John "The Count" Montefusco, a pitcher with San Francisco, and Gary Carter, a catcher with Montreal. John won 15 games and struck out 215 batters. He headed a well-stocked staff of Jim Barr, Ed Halicki, Mike Caldwell, and the '74 rookie John D'Acquisto. Actually, it was the fourth year in a row a San Francisco player had won a share of the rookie honors (Rader, Matthews, and D'Acquisto). When John graduated from high school nobody wanted him, but after his rookie season everyone desired him. As we said, as a rookie he was 15-9, setting San Francisco first-year records for wins and strikeouts. His 215 whiffs were the second best by a rookie in the National League. Only the great Grover Cleveland Alexander had had more back in 1911. Actually, Montefusco had appeared in seven games with a 3-2 record in 1974. He pitched a no-hitter against Atlanta in 1976 and had hit a home run in his first at bat in 1974. Gary Carter has been a workhorse among National League catchers since his rookie year. The Montreal Expo youngster set a club record with his 31 home runs, while leading the Expos in extra base hits (62) and game winning RBIs (13) in that rookie season. Coming to the Expos from Memphis, he was the International League's runner-up to Jim Rice in homers and RBIs. He has since become the first Expo to hit three home runs in a game, and he holds the single-season high in homers hit at Olympic Stadium. His rookie season also found him taking an occasional turn in the outfield.

It would seem that the San Francisco Giants had a corner on young players in 1975, some good, some not so good. There was the outfielder with the great name of Horace Speed, who maybe wasn't so fast after all, but he did pop up with Cleveland in 1978. Then there was the relief pitcher who perhaps should have played with Cleveland or Atlanta, Tommy Toms. Why didn't they call him Tom Toms? What a great public relations hit he would have made had he only been with the right team. There was the switch-hitting right-hander, Greg Minton, who had played American Legion ball with NFL kicker Tom Dempsey. Minton, a reliever, spent all of 1979 with the Giants, the first time in seven seasons he didn't change teams during the year. In 1980 only three Giant pitchers registered saves. Rookie Al Holland had 7, Gary Lavelle had 9, and Greg had 19. Shortstop Johnny Le Master, a fielding leader in the Pacific Coast League, arrived to become the 43rd player to hit a home run in his first at-bat, his coming on September 2, off L.A.'s Don Sutton. His cousin is Frank LeMaster, a linebacker with the Philadelphia Eagles. At age 19, Jack Clark made his debut, but it took him until 1978 to fulfill the predictions of stardom. He had an incredible year then, leading the Giants in all offensive categories and hitting in 26 consecutive games, breaking a Giant record set in 1930. His 46 doubles snapped a 47-year-old club mark set by Bill Terry in 1931 and tied by Willie Mays in 1959. Then there was the good hitting outfielder Glenn Adams, now a star at Minnesota. I guess the Giants couldn't keep all these good youngsters. Another who left was catcher Gary Alexander, who was the Texas League Player of the Year. After a few years with Cleveland, he was traded to the Pirates in late 1980. Two other joining the Giants were Pete Falcone and Dave Heaverlo. Falcone has been with St. Louis and is now with the Mets (7-10 in 1980). Heaverlo (who, if you like puns, has a great name for a pitcher, Heave-Her-Low, matching the old pitching axiom, "Keep it low") was on the Oakland roster where in 1979 he appeared in more games than any other A's pitcher (62).

The New York Mets had high hopes for outfielder Mike Vail, the International League Player of the Year, infielder Roy Staiger, Tidewater's fielding ace, and pitcher Randy Tate. Vail had a great bat in his first trial, and his arm was strong enough to cut down nine runners in 36 games. The Expos gave a try to a big outfielder who hit with authority, Ellis Valentine, and a pitcher, Dan Warthen, who was 8-6 in relief roles, but 2-10 as a starter in '76. The Phillies sent pitcher Randy Lerch to the mound directly from Reading in the Eastern League. The Reds, with little room for rookies, tried infielder Doug Flynn, who was not drafted but was later signed by the Reds. Now with the Mets, his defensive skills earned him a job. The Dodgers were watching Hank Cruz hit .266 in L.A. and .310 in the minors, and the Cubs had outfielder Joe Wallis, who had hit everywhere but Chicago. The Wrigley

Field crew also came up with pitcher Paul Reuschel who had spent eight years down on the farm. He joined his brother Rick with the Cubs, but was never as successful. He and his younger brother combined in a rare feat by beating the Dodgers, Paul getting a save and Rick a win. The Pirates had been looking at speedster Omar Moreno, who stole 230 bases in four years on the farm. Later, Moreno had six hits in the final two games of the 1979 World Series. It has been said that his speed and acceleration are so fast he can literally outrun baseballs. They also had an infielder named Willie Randolph, a prize who they traded off to the Yankees where he has battled injury problems until 1979, when he led the Yanks in many offensive categories. A claim to fame, he was the first rookie ever listed on an All-Star ballot. The Bucs were also testing pitcher John "Candy" Candelaria, a lefty. In 1977 John won 20 games for the Bucs, the first to do so since Vernon Law in 1960 and the first lefty since Wilbur Cooper in 1924. He also won pitching's triple crown (wins, ERA, and percentage) that season, the first pitcher to do so since Sandy Koufax in 1965. He also pitched a no-hitter against L.A. that season. His eleven wins in 1980 was second highest on the Pirates.

Over in the American League, the Oakland A's made room for Mike Norris and he became the 35th pitcher in major league history to pitch a shutout in a debut, his against Chicago. Bounced back to the minors until '78, he did little until 1980 and then came on like gangbusters, 22-9, with 24 complete games and a 2.54 ERA for Billy Martin's born-again A's. Mike lost the Cy Young Award to Baltimore's Steve Stone, 25-7, 3.23 ERA, and only nine complete games. There were many who felt Norris was the better pitcher. The Texas Rangers felt secure with catcher Ron Pruitt and shortstop Roy Smalley III, who is the son of Roy Smalley, Jr., a former major leaguer, and is the nephew of Gene Mauch, former big league player and manager. Smalley, drafted twice by Boston and once by Montreal, got $100,000 from Texas to sign. Traded to Minnesota in 1976, where Mauch was manager, he has been one of the league's best shortstops, setting several records and leading all shortstops in hitting home runs. Texas also looked at a decent pitcher in Jim Umbarger, another Arizona State product whom Texas traded to Oakland in March of 1977 and bought him back in August. The Boston Red Sox added third baseman Butch Hobson and second basemen Steve Dillard and Kim Andrew, a former Baltimore farm boy. Also in Boston were highly rated pitchers Rich Kreuger, who was better than his 6-15 record at Pawtucket, and Jim Burton, who was doomed to live forever as the pitcher who gave up Joe Morgan's game-winner in the World Series. In fairness, Jim was a fine pitcher and was 8-2 with a 1.54 ERA for a basement-bound Pawtucket team. The New York Yankees recalled a slender southpaw hurler from Syracuse who was strictly a reliever, his name Ron Guidry. His fastball, tabbed "Louisiana Lightning," helped him to a 16-7 record in starting roles in 1977. The following season, 1978, was one of the most remarkable years a pitcher in the history of baseball has ever had. He was 25-3, 16 complete games, 248 strikeouts and only 72 walks, with a major league leading 1.74 ERA. It had only been three seasons since he was 2-4 at West Haven in the double A Eastern League. He had come a long way. His 13 straight wins at the start of the season broke the previous Yankee high set by Atley Donald, the scout who had signed him. His nine shutouts also set a Yankee record and tied the AL record, and were the most by an American League lefty since 1916 when Babe Ruth also had nine. American League batters could only manage a .193 average against Guidry. His 18 strikeouts against the Angels in mid-June set a Yankee mark, breaking Bob Shawkey's record of 15 set in 1919, and set an American League mark for lefties. Those 248 Ks topped the Yankee record of Jack Chesbro (239) set way back in 1904, and his winning percentage of .893 was the best by a 20-game winner in baseball history. Needless to say, he was the 1978 Cy Young Award winner and was runner-up to Boston's Jim Rice for the MVP Award.

When Cleveland catcher Alan Ashby got hurt, they summoned a first-year professional up from Oklahoma City named Rick Cerone, a two-time NCAA All-American at Seton Hall University. Rick now catches for the Yankees. Joining Cerone was outfielder Rick Manning, who has emerged as a top defensive center fielder and base stealer. Detroit had a couple of rookies who have had very unusual careers, Ed Glynn and Fernando Arroyo. Every season since they made their first appearance had been split between Evansville and Detroit, although Glynn, who was traded to the Mets, spent part of '79 with Tidewater. The Brewers were counting on a Wisconsin native, southpaw Jerry Augustine, from a farm system that had little else ready. The Twins had two dandy outfielders in Lyman Bostock, who had been on an early season tear through the PCL (.391), and Dan Ford, who has done well for the Twins and Angels. He hit for the cycle against Seattle in 1979. Bostock was also traded to the Angels, and during his first season there was hitting only .147 in April with no homers when he decided to give his first month's pay to charities. Less than five months later, Bostock was dead, struck down by a gunman in Gary, Indiana. The intended victim was the gunman's estranged wife. Bostock had been visiting his uncle, who was riding in the car with him at the time of the fatal shot. Ford, recognized as a moody player while with the Twins, dispelled the image with the Angels. His manager, Jim Fregosi, says, "Ford gets everyone jumping. His enthusiasm rubs off." Ford can run, throw, and hit with power. Kansas City had a quarterback who turned down

30 football offers, including Notre Dame, to play baseball in Jamie Quirk. He spent two seasons in K.C., went to Milwaukee for a year, and returned to assume a pinch-hitting, late-inning defensive role. Lefty relief pitcher Bob McClure also joined K.C. in 1975.

The California Angels liked left-hand-hitting catcher Danny Goodwin, a former top draft choice. Lefty first baseman Dan Briggs, who hit .323 at Salt Lake but with only one homer, was also abroad. Pitcher Sid Monge had been 14-9 at Salt Lake City before taking the mound for the Angels, and backing him up was second baseman Jerry Remy. None of them stayed very long with the Angels. Briggs has been with the Indians and Padres, Goodwin with the Twins, Monge with the Indians, and Remy with the Red Sox. Monge holds the Cleveland record for single-season appearances by a pitcher at 76. Goodwin, the only player ever to be the nation's first pick in the free-agent draft on two different occasions, is now a first baseman. Remy, once the 453rd player picked in the draft (selected by the Washington Senators), and a member of the major league all-rookie team, has spent two seasons (79-80) with serious leg injuries. The Chicago White Sox were big on pitchers for 1975 with Bob Knapp, Tim Stoddard, Pete Vuckovich, and Ken Kravec. Kravec is the only one still with the Chisox, and his best game may have been his second big-time start, when he fanned ten Red Sox batters. Joining the pitchers was then third baseman, now outfielder, Chet Lemon, the White Sox top batter in 1980 with a .292 average, lower than his '79 team-leading .318. Chet has become one of the game's best defensive center fielders and has broken two 30-year-old records, which were held by former Red Sox centerfielder Dom DiMaggio—most chances by an outfielder (524) and most putouts (512).

The Orioles' farm system continued to develop talented players at the triple A level and in '75 were singing the praises of: Roy Stillman, a proven minor league outfielder; Bob Bailor, who was following in a long line of All-Star shortstops (Nordbrook, Grich, Belanger); outfielder Larry Harlow; pitchers Mike Flanagan, an All-Star lefty, and Dyar Miller, who was in his eighth minor league season when called up. Miller had gone to Utah State on a basketball scholarship and was originally a catcher; present K.C. manager Jim Frey converted him to pitching. Miller has been with California and Toronto as a reliever. His biggest thrill was his one major league start in May 1979 at Yankee Stadium. Stillman had a three-season 89-game career, two with Baltimore, one with Chicago. Harlow had some decent seasons as a backup outfielder and even tried his hand as a pitcher during one game in '78. Larry Harlow has had a strange career, an excellent hitter in April (.317) and in September-October (.318), the months in between have been his downfall (.202) and have prevented him from having an outstanding season (the figures are through the 1979 season). As Larry has said, "Defense is my strongpoint." He is now with the Angels (1980—.276 in 109 games). Bob Bailor has played infield and outfield for Toronto since they selected him in the expansion draft of '76. Still with the Blue Jays in 1980, his .310 average in 1977 was the best mark ever by a player on a first-year expansion team and the highest in either league for a rookie in 1977 (he still qualified). While Flanagan had several trials, it was not until '77 that he really arrived, posting a 15-10 record, which improved to 19-15 and then to a league-leading 23-9 in '79. He was 16-13 for 1980. The majors' winningest pitcher in '79, he brought the Cy Young Award to Baltimore for the fifth time in eleven seasons (Cuellar '69, Palmer '72, '75, '76). His success he credits to fellow Bird pitcher Scott McGregor, who in five minutes one day taught him how to throw a change-up. He was one of the famous three Mikes, all lefties, to defeat the Yankee pitcher Ron Guidry in his only losses of 1978. The other two were Mike Willis and Mike Caldwell. A native of New Hampshire, he played some basketball and was 12-1 in two years of baseball at the University of Massachusetts. Mike's father, Ed, was a pitcher (late '40s and early '50s) in the Red Sox system, and his grandfather had signed a pro contract in 1913.

We have talked about a good many rookies, and we have seen many of them set records; now, as this chapter suggests, what about the rewards? Some of our rookies got their reward by just being in the majors and leaving their name in the record book. There were, however, other rewards on the horizon as the 1976 season burst upon the baseball world. The exact date of the biggest change to ever take place in baseball was December 23, 1975. On that date, Peter Seitz, an arbitrator, handed baseball his ruling on the Messersmith-McNally case, to wit: a player who "plays out" his contract by not signing for a year has discharged his contractual obligations. Simple as that. Andy and Dave were free to sign with whomever they wished. Born were the free agents, and the baseball bidding wars for the services of the "free" ones was on. They were not free, however, as most cost the owners dearly. The players were the winners in this war. It is a whole other study to get into the effects of this decision, and we shall not attempt that here. Suffice it to say, a bitter collective bargaining struggle developed between the players and the owners, enough to cause a player lockout in spring training to kick things off for 1976. By mid-March, the camps opened and 1976 was underway. Thus began the era of baseball millionaires, the rewards. Those players who didn't become free agents often benefited by being offered inflated contracts. The farm system finally paid off for Kansas City, even though they lost the playoff to the Yankees, who finally made it back to the top with players developed by other clubs. The Yanks were no match for the homegrown Cincinnati Reds as the "Big Red Machine" swept them four straight in the Series. For the record, the first free-agent draft was held on November 4, 1976, and two days later Minnesota Twin relief ace Bill Campbell had the distinction of becoming the first free agent to sign with a new team. He became a Boston Red Sox, signing a four-year, one-million-dollar contract. Not bad considering his 1976 pay was $23,000.

1976 found the fewest number of rookies appearing in the majors for one season in the decade of the '70s. Some turned out to be of quality, despite the lack of quantity. Selected as tops in the American League were Detroit's irrepressible pitcher, Mark "The Bird" Fidrych, and Minnesota's tough catcher, Butch Wynegar. In the National League it was San Francisco outfielder Larry Herndon and a toss-up between pitchers Butch Metzger of San Diego and Pat Zachry of Cincinnati.

Without question the most refreshing rookie to arrive on the big league scene in many years was Detroit Tiger pitcher Mark Fidrych. With long curly blond hair, a toothy grin, and a 93-mile-per-hour fastball this youngster put "fun" back into the game. You couldn't help but like him no matter what team you rooted for. While many considered Mark somewhat flaky, there was nothing flaky about his 19-9 record. The 9-2 record and low earned run average he took into July earned him the starting role in the All-Star contest. This outing was no more successful than his first start; each was disastrous. The colorful youngster had an umimpressive start by permitting a game-winning hit to the only batter he faced in a game at Oakland. He was also hit hard in his two-inning All-Star stint. These games did nothing to dim the charisma that "The Bird" had over the baseball public. Tiger fans had taken to him with a passion, and on a day when he went to the mound, the turnstiles whirled at record paces. He was a virtual unknown until he appeared on a nationally televised game in late June, a game in which fans were tuning in to catch a glimpse of the "new look" Yankees. When they saw Fidrych, they stayed tuned to watch the kooky rituals he was going through. They saw his unorthodox delivery, no complete windup, just a short stuttering motion of clasping his hands up to his chest. He talked to his catcher, his fielders, repositioned them, talked to the ball, his glove, and himself. They saw him pat the dirt around the mound, doing his own groundskeeping. They saw him race full speed to and from the mound and dugout. They saw him act as a one-man cheerleading squad for his teammates, racing all over the field to congratulate or console them. At the ball park, fans refused to leave until he returned to the field for a bow. With anyone else these actions might have caused resentment among his teammates and opposing bench jockeys, but the players took to him just as much as the fans. It was apparent he was no hot dog, he was genuine. He showed remarkable control, kept the ball low, always around the plate, and was usually ahead of the batters. He pitched 24 complete games, beating every team in the league, and handled 78 fielding chances without an error. Injuries and arm problems have plagued him since that rookie season, but he keeps trying to come back. We can only hope for his sake and for the sake of baseball that he will make it one of these seasons, bringing with him those wonderful idiosyncracies. Joining him was his personal catcher Bruce Kimm, who has drifted off to the Cubs and White Sox in recent seasons, and two decent infielders, third baseman Phil Mankowski and a long-ball-hitting first baseman Jason Thompson. The Twins' contribution to rookie of the year was switch-hitting catcher Butch Wynegar, who made a big impression as he stepped right in behind the plate and into the clean-up spot in the batting order. His average dropped off a bit after being around .300 for half the season. "He's got power and handles himself and the pitchers very well," said Twins' manager Gene Mauch. He became, at 20, the youngest player ever selected for the All-Star Game and may well be the Twins' catcher for the next decade. A durable receiver, he has caught better than 130 games each season since his arrival. Second baseman Bob Randall and pitcher Pete Redfern were other top Twins' rookies.

In the National League, Larry Herndon, the San Francisco outfielder, made it five consecutive seasons for a Giant rookie to gain honors for his club. Not blessed with great power, he showed through most of the year that he could hit for average, being consistently around .300. Larry had a well-traveled minor league career, eight stops in five seasons, and had a brief trial with the Cardinals in 1974. A valued asset in the Giant organization, the speedy outfielder had continued to prove his worth. Larry hit safely in 24 of his first 26 games, including a 14-game streak, while his final average was .288. When it came to pitchers, it was hard to choose between Butch Metzger of San Diego, 11-4 and 2.93 ERA, and Pat Zachry of the Reds, 14-7, 2.74 ERA. Metzger had had brief trials with San Francisco in '74 and San Diego in '75. He established a major league record for the most games won at the start of a career for a relief pitcher at twelve and the most appearances by a pitcher in his rookie season at 77. Butch later pitched for the Cardinals and Mets. For Zachry, it was his first trial in the big time. Pat was traded to the New York Mets in mid-1977 in the deal for Met ace Tom Seaver. He has had his career curtailed by injuries with the Mets and has never repeated the heroics of his rookie season. After the '76 season, he had a hernia operation, which it is believed led to his falling into bad pitching habits in '77 and a 3-7 record when he was sent to the Mets. Winning seven of his next thirteen decisions, he became the only Met starter to wind up with a winning record. 1978 found him off to a good start until he fractured a foot by kicking a dugout step in disgust upon being removed from a game. He had just yielded a seventh-inning single to Pete Rose that tied the modern NL hit-streak mark at 37 games. The Reds also had rookie third baseman-outfielder Joel Youngblood, who has since joined Zachry with the Mets by way of the Cardinals. Joel started like a house afire with four hits in his first Red starting assignment. The Padres also had another good pitcher in Bob Owchinko, although he really didn't arrive until '77.

The St. Louis Cardinal shortstop Garry Templeton didn't come up until August 9, but from that point on he proved he had a future. He had led the American Association with 15 triples while hitting .321 before his recall. He showed tremendous speed, and batting second, between rookie Jerry Mumphrey and vet Lou Brock, he bolstered the Card offense. The Redbirds also had hope for pitcher Mike Proly, but the little right-hander has done better out of the Chicago White Sox bullpen. Speaking of the White Sox, they were hoping Kevin Bell would solve their third base problems (he didn't) or that the much-traveled Wayne Nordhagen might help out behind the plate or in the outfield. Originally Yankee property, Wayne has even appeared on the mound for the Pale Hose. Their crosstown rivals, the Cubs, were looking at two pitchers to go with catcher Ed Putman. They were Mike Krukow and Bruce Sutter. Krukow once pitched a no-hitter in amateur baseball while walking 17 batters. "The Polish Prince" has done a decent job for the Cubs and was 10-15 for them in 1980. Bruce Sutter has been the best relief pitcher in baseball in recent years. In five seasons he has registered 133 saves, and in 1979 his 37 saves tied the National League record of Clay Carroll and Rollie Fingers. That season he also tied a league mark by whiffing six consecutive batters, which included striking out the side in one inning on nine pitches. He was the Cy Young Award winner in 1979. In 1980 he dropped to 5-8 but still registered 28 saves, tops in the National League. Bruce has won two All-Star Games; only Lefty Gomez (Yankees) has won more (three).

The Cincinnati Reds got an 11-4 season from Santo Alcala, while Pittsburgh hoped for the same from Rick Langford, to no avail. He went to Oakland where he led the AL in wild pitches in 1979, although his ten straight complete games set an Oakland record. Pittsburgh's best defensive minor league outfielder was Tony Armas, a good hitter, but he like Langford was traded to the A's. Knee and shoulder injuries have slowed his progress. The Giants were hoping for brilliant things from lefty Bob Knepper, but didn't get them until 1978 when he was 17-11 with a league-leading six shutouts. The Mets said outfielder Lee Mazzilli could help them if he proves he can hit in the majors. He didn't, but returned in '77 to post .250, .273, .303, and .280 marks since then. Popular with the Met faithful, he broke in spectacularly by blasting a three-run homer in his second plate appearance. In addition to being a switch-hitter, he is also an ambidextrous thrower, although he has thrown only right-handed since turning pro. In 1975 in the minors, he once stole seven bases in a seven-inning game. Possibly an above-average player, he has yet to gain superstar status. the Yankees were looking to their super minor league shortstop, Mickey Klutts, but wound up right on looking. Los Angeles gave a look-see to pitcher Rick Sutcliffe (we will meet him later). The Phillies had hopes for outfielder Rick Bosetti and catcher Bill Nahorodny, but both have done better in the AL, the former with Toronto, the latter with Chicago. Bill was with Atlanta in 1980. The Expos had visions of Andre Dawson and Gary Roenicke in their outfield and Larry Landreth on their mound. Dawson made it as a power hitter, while Roenicke has done the bulk of his outfielding in Baltimore. Landreth was 1-4 in two seasons. Moving up to Atlanta was one of the minors' hottest prospects, catcher Dale Murphy. He has made good as a first baseman-catcher, although the highly touted youngster has had his share of injuries. Houston had excellent rookies in pitchers Joaquin Andujar, who has suffered reoccurring injuries, Mark Lemongello, known as a fierce competitor, and Joe Sambito, a fine relief pitcher.

In the American League, Texas was looking to first baseman Doug Ault and infielder Greg Pryor, who has played more with the White Sox as a utility man. His father played briefly with the NFL Baltimore Colts. Greg was a two-time All-American at Florida Southern. The Red Sox had a decent year from lefty pitcher Rick Jones, whose great potential quickly disappeared. Journeyman catcher Ernie Whitt also made a brief appearance at Fenway Park. Cleveland introduced highly rated shortstop Alfredo Griffin, who we will meet with the '79 Blue Jays. First baseman Wayne Gross and catcher Jeff Newman pulled on the green and gold of Oakland, while their West Coast neighbors, the Angels, tried out pitchers Paul Hartzell and Gary Wheelock and outfielder Carlos Lopez. Kansas City tested outfielder Ruppert Jones, who was selected by Seattle in the expansion draft. He tied a major league record for them with twelve putouts in an extra-inning game, while playing center field. He was traded to the Yankees for 1980, but was injured a good bit of the season. Catcher John Wathan has remained a key player on the strong K.C. bench. Outfielder Gary Woods has been a utility man with Toronto after his one season with K.C., but outfielder Willie Wilson has been a K.C. hero, batting .324 in '76, .315 in '79, and .326 in 1980, while displaying switch-hitting and base-stealing talents. He has an extremely high percentage of successful steals, setting records along the minor league trail and leading the American League in thefts. The Baltimore Orioles had a fine second baseman in Rich Dauer, who was the International League rookie of the year and MVP. In 1978 he set a record of 86 errorless games, while accepting 425 chances. Rich is another USC product nd holds a number of their records: homers (15), doubles (24), runs (70), RBIs (92), hits (108), and total bases (181), the last three also being NCAA one-season records. His teammates at USC included Roy Smalley, Steve Kemp, Pete Redfern, and Fred Lynn. The Birds also had fine pitchers in Scott McGregor and Dennis Martinez. Martinez, an excellent fielding pitcher, was the first Nicaraguan to play in the big leagues. In 1979 he led American League pitchers in starts (39), innings (292), and complete games (18). In McGregor, a former Yankee farmhand, the Orioles got an excellent pitcher. A 20-8 mark in 1980 only continued his winning ways; he was also tied for third place in shutouts (four). In late '78 and in '79 he had arm troubles, but his 1980 record would make it appear they are behind him. A control pitcher, he has averaged just slightly more than one walk per every nine innings. While pitching for West Haven in the Eastern League in 1973, Scott led that league in many pitching areas, including a 12-13 record and 14 complete games in a league-leading 27 starts. A gutsy pitcher, in 1979 he started a game against Boston and gave up a single, double, and home run to the first three batters, then retired 23 straight before giving up a hit with two down in the eighth. He won 5 to 3.

1977-79:
Baseball
Fever

1977 proved to be a year of some surprising record performances. The New York Yankees returned again to the World Series to capture a record 21st Series victory when they defeated their old rivals the Dodgers four games to two. The New Yorkers were led by Reggie Jackson, who hit three home runs in game six to insure a Yankee victory. All were hit on the first pitch. It was only the third time in Series' history a player had hit three homers; Babe Ruth had done it twice in 1926 and 1928. Two earlier homers gave Jackson five homers for the Series, a new record. Jackson had homered in his last at-bat in game five and walked in his first time up in game six, so that he actually had hit four home runs in four successive official times at bat.

Perhaps even more historic than Jackson's performance was that of the St. Louis Cardinals' Lou Brock when he stole his 893rd base, breaking a record which many baseball historians had considered untouchable—Ty Cobb's 892 lifetime stolen bases. When Brock was a rookie, he was considered, and rightly so, a long-ball hitter. Gradually his long-ball changed into singles and doubles, and his base-stealing prowess began to develop and grow. In 1974 Brock stole 118 bases, topping Maury Wills' Major League single-season record of 104.

Two new teams were added to the major leagues in 1977. The American League expanded from 12 to 14 teams, placing new franchises in Seattle and Toronto, a move that resulted in an imbalanced schedule. The result was that each American League club played each of the other clubs in its division 15 times, while meeting each team not in its division 10 times, except for two of these teams which they met 11 times. Previously, the schedule called for 18 games inside and 12 outside a team's division.

Major league attendance and salaries continued their upward climb in 1977, something many predicted couldn't happen the way the owners were tossing around their money after re-entry draft free agents. Atlanta Braves' owner Ted Turner turned self-appointed rookie manager for a day, one of the shortest reigns in managerial history. He was joined a little better than a month later in a similar one-day membership by Eddie Stanky at Texas.

The rookies of the year in 1977 were Montreal Expo outfielder Andre Dawson and San Diego Padres' pitcher Bob Owchinko in the National League and outfielder Mitchell Page of the Oakland A's, and first baseman Eddie Murray of the Baltimore Orioles along with pitcher Dave Rozema of the Detroit Tigers in the American League. They represented the cream of a banner year for newcomers. The primary reason for the large influx of rookies was, of course, the addition of Toronto and Seattle to the American League. A new world of opportunity opened up for the younger player. With 50 new jobs, a lot of youngsters who might have spent a year or two more in the minors were given a chance for early advancement. The expanded American League welcomed 96 first-time players, while the Nationals looked at 58.

In the American League in 1977, while there was no clear-cut sensation such as Mark Fidrych was in 1976, the Detroit Tigers came close again in bringing up a quality pitcher in Dave Rozema who was 15-7 for the season. The young right-hander was the most distinctive member of a Tiger team that went no place in 1977. There was no question, however, that he was the best of what would be a fine Tiger rookie crop, despite not receiving the raves from fans and press that Fidrych had basked in a year earlier. In 22 decisions, of which he won 15, Dave posted a 3.09 earned run average, striking out 92 batters in 218 innings. His most effective pitch was his baffling change-up, and he showed an adequate fastball to go along with a good breaking pitch while displaying exceptional poise and control for a rookie. Rozema had had a brilliant season in '76, leading the Montgomery Rebels to the Southern League pennant with a 12-4 record and a fine 1.57 ERA. Joining the Tigers in spring training as a non-roster player, he quickly gained a starting role and stepped right into the breach when Fidrych was sidelined with injuries. His first victory came when he shut out the Red Sox 8 to 0 on four hits. He followed that win up with two more before he lost his first game. After that loss, he reeled off seven straight wins. A postseason medical exam in 1976 disclosed that he had pitched much of that season with a broken elbow. Well-healed by 1977, his spring training record of 2-1 and 1.97 ERA earned him his stripes as a Tiger. His manager Ralph Houk remarked, "I don't know if his pitching has been a surprise, but you couldn't ask for more." In three seasons since his rookie year, he has never been able to turn in a better record.

Rozema was not alone as a rookie with Detroit in '77. Right-handed pitcher Bob Sykes got his chance and responded well. Another righty, Bruce Taylor, arrived in August to go unscored upon in his first six outings, as he posted a pair of saves and won his only decision. Also called up from Evansville was pitcher John Morris, who made his debut in an impressive four innings of relief work against Chicago. Promoted to a starting role, he soon came up with a sore arm. He could manage only a 3-5 mark in 1978, but after spending the first month of the season in the minors, he returned to become the ace of the Tiger staff with a fine 17-7 record. He remained the top winner in Detroit in 1980 with 16 victories; the replacement for injured Mark Fidrych had finally arrived. The Tigers were not done yet, as they called up the rapidly matured catcher Lance Parrish. Strong-armed with power, in his second major league game he walked, singled, doubled home three runs, and homered. After high school, Lance spurned a UCLA gridiron scholarship to sign a Tiger bonus contract. Lance had the interesting job during part of one offseason as a bodyguard for singer Tina Turner. A valuable catcher for Detroit, his 1980 batting average of .286 represented a career high. Then there was Bob Adams, another catcher who had converted from third base and the outfield. Like Parrish, he also had a football (fullback) scholarship to UCLA, which he accepted; but later he turned to baseball where he won many honors as a Bruin, including election to their Hall of Fame. Joining this long line of rookies was shortstop Alan Trammell and second baseman Lou Whitaker. They performed well together and gave the Tigers their best keystone combination in a decade. Trammell at 19, the Southern League's MVP and All-Star shortstop of '77, while setting a league record with 19 triples, made the jump to the majors successfully, although he was used primarily against right-handed pitching. Whitaker, who was the baseball writers' rookie of the year in 1978, also took a solid hold of his job in a September trial. In 1978 this combination combined on many of the Tigers' major league high of 177 double plays. Trammell was the leading Tiger batter in 1980 with a solid .300 batting average. Whitaker, a highly regarded infield prospect from the start, was moved from third base to second during spring training. With the best cast of rookies any club has ever had, the Tigers also were looking at an outfielder who in 1974 was an undrafted free-agent, Tim Corcoran. He was their hottest hitting prospect in spring train-ing (.378). A fine minor league batter, he was with Detroit for '78, part of '79, and returned to bat .288 for them in 1980. Joining Tim in the outfield was Detroit's hottest all-around prospect, Steve Kemp. With only one season of minor league ball, the left-handed batter had arrived to stay off a sensational year with Montgomery and Evansville. A collegiate All-American at University of Southern California, he dropped out of school after his junior year to become the number one draft pick in the nation. Manager Houk said Kemp reminded him of the Yankees' Mickey Mantle and Bobby Murcer, while his USC coach Rod Dedeaux called him "more of a pure hitter than Fred Lynn," another USC product. He hit .257 and drove in 88 runs in 1977. In 1979 he hit .318 with 26 homers and 105 RBIs; in 1980 he dropped to .293, 21 homers, and 101 RBIs. This superb gang of rookies has brought Detroit baseball back where it once was and they are, in large part, the reason for its recent successes. A fruitful year was 1977 for the Motor City nine.

The other American League rookies of the year were Mitchell Page at Oakland and Eddie Murray at Baltimore. Outfielder Page batted .307 with 154 hits, including 28 doubles, 8 triples and 21 home runs. In the process, the speedy Page set an American League record with 26 consecutive stolen bases. He finished the season with 42 steals. Oakland owner, Charlie Finley, was comparing Page favorably with his former stars Joe Rudi and Reggie Jackson, saying, "Here's a kid getting $18,000, who is producing as well as these millionaires. It goes to show you that it's not money that plays, but a ballplayer who has desire and eagerness to want to stand out." There was no doubt Mitch Page was an exceptional rookie. Mitch had been originally signed by the Pirates and played in their farm system. In recent seasons he has been slowed by injuries. Joining him in Oakland during 1977 were two good pitchers, including Matt Keough, a converted minor league All-Star infielder whose dad, Marty, was a former major leaguer and whose Uncle Joe had also been in the big time. Marty was 8-15 with 108 strikeouts for a poor 1978 Oakland Club. In 1979 he suffered through 14 straight losses and had the whole nation rooting for him to get a win at each start late in the string. Matt recovered in 1980, under American League manager of the year Billy Martin, to post a fine 16-13 record with a 2.92 ERA. Bob Lacey was 6-8 in relief roles, a position he has filled since joining the A's. He joined the A's after putting together 16 consecutive scoreless innings in 11 relief appearances at San Jose. Baltimore manager Earl Weaver was praising his power-hitting rookie first baseman Eddie Murray, who could also play in the outfield. "As far as I'm concerned, Eddie is a shoo-in for the rookie award," said Weaver. Murray did an outstanding job for the Orioles and showed promise of an outstanding future. His great knowledge of hitting was often demonstrated as he got hit after hit when needed. Appearing all over the field, he also served as a DH. Murray tied Lee May for the team leadership in home runs at 27, while setting a club rookie record for homers, surpassing the 22 of Ron Hansen

('60), Sam Bowens ('64), and Curt Blefary ('65). A natural right-handed hitter, Eddie made himself into a switch hitter in 1977, batting a neat .283. Since joining the Orioles and through the 1980 season, Eddie has missed only five Orioles games, proving his durability. Over the past several years he has been an Oriole leader in many fielding and batting areas. 1980 proved to be his best season, batting an even .300. He had 186 hits, scored 100 runs, drove in 116 with 36 doubles and 32 home runs. Eddie is one of five brothers, all of whom have played or are playing professional baseball. On his Locke High School team in Los Angeles, he was tri-captain of the baseball team. Oh yes, the other two captains? San Diego shortstop Osborn Smith and Minnesota pitcher Darrell Jackson, not bad for one high school.

Some of the other prospects of 1977 in the American League were pitchers Ken Clay and Larry McCall with the Yankees and hurlers Sam Hinds and Larry Sorenson at Milwaukee. Cleveland had 28-year-old outfielder Jim Norris off an outstanding triple A season. He had once starred at the University of Maryland and led the Tribe in stolen bases with 26. He had more injuries than most players would suffer in five lifetimes. It's a wonder he even survived to make the majors. He had spent 66 weeks in casts due to eight sports-related injuries. The Texas Rangers were giving a trial to Pat Putnam, a first baseman, who in 1976 was the minor league player of the year while at Asheville (.361, 24 HR, 142 RBIs), the first from a class A league to win such honors in 40 years. The Boston Red Sox were looking forward to big things from highly rated fastballer Don Aase, an aggressive right-hander Mike Paxton, and pitcher Bob Stanley. Stanley jumped up from double A Bristol, working in 41 games for the Sox, the most since Sparky Lyle appeared in 49 in 1968. The Bosox also introduced outfielders Sam Bowen and Dave Coleman to go along with rookie catcher Bo Diaz. One of the most memorable first-game performances belonged to Red Sox DH Ted Cox. His four consecutive hits (three singles and a double) on September 18 against Baltimore tied a major league mark for most hits and for most consecutive hits in a major league debut. Two hits in his first two at-bats the next day enabled Cox to set a major league record for the most consecutive hits at the start of a career, six. Kansas City had a productive hitter and hustler who was an outstanding fielder in Joe Zdeb. He could play all the outfield positions. Joining Zdeb, who hit .297, was U. L. Washington, a switch-hitting shortstop who had spent most of '77 with Omaha. The Minnesota Twins were looking to fill holes left by free agents who had moved elsewhere, with the likes of third baseman Larry Wolfe, second baseman Rob Wilfong, pitchers Jeff Holly, Gary Serum, and Paul Thormodsgard, and highly regarded outfielder Willie Norwood. Holly and Thormodsgard had been very impressive during spring training, with Paul jumping from A ball right into the starting rotation, but both had or would suffer arm problems. Wilfong was a line-drive hitter with speed, and Wolfe had a reputation as a good clutch hitter. In addition to Murray, Baltimore rated pitcher Randy Miller and catcher Dave Skaggs as future stars. Seattle looked to infielders Jose Baez and Julio Cruz, outfielder Luis Delgado, and a trio of pitchers, Greg Erardi, Rick Honeycutt, and Enrique Romo. The Toronto Blue Jays' left-hander Jerry Garvin got plenty of work and looked good, but was handicapped by pitching for a woefully weak team. Pitcher Jim Clancy also got plenty of work after a stint with double A Jersey City, and outfielder Alvis Woods made his debut. The California Angels boasted of a package of power named Willie Mays Aikens. A delivering physician had named him after Giants' outfielder Willie Mays when Aikens was born during the 1954 World Series. Outfielder Gil Flores emerged from anonymity in spring training to make a significant contribution to the Angel cause. Outfielder Ken Landreaux, Minor League Player of the Year at Salt Lake City and El Paso in 1977, carried a "can't miss" tag as he made a late-season arrival. He had been a super college star at, where else, Arizona State, hitting .413 to lead the Sun Devils into the 1976 College World Series.

In the National League, Montreal Expo outfielder Andre Dawson, a 22-year-old Florida A&M graduate won both *The Sporting News'* and baseball writers' acclaim with *TSN* also picking San Diego Padre pitcher Bob Owchinko for honors.

The overall farm system record of the Expos was the best ever enjoyed by the Canadians. The big reason was an American Association title won by their farm club at Denver. The driving force behind the Denver success was Dawson, who burned up the league with a .350 average and 22 home runs in 74 games after murdering double A pitching at Quebec City in the Eastern League, where in 40 games Dawson hit .357 with eight homers. He had begun his career by leading the Pioneer League, while with Lethbridge, in six offensive categories during the 1975 season. Andre was actually summoned to Montreal in late 1976 for 24 games. He possesses that rare combination of power and speed, a combo that paid immediate dividends for the Expos when he set a club mark for home runs with 19, tied the then Expos' record for triples at nine, and led the club in stolen bases, with 21. Dawson is now the all-time leader in stolen bases for the Expos, having passed the record formerly held by Larry Lintz. Atlanta Stadium, home of the Braves, has been a good luck charm for the friendly Expo, as it was there that he hit his first major league home run and where he tied a major league record by hitting two home runs in the same inning in 1978. Dawson captured the rookie honors with a .282 average to go along with his 19 home runs, nine triples, 26 doubles, and fine defensive skills. In 1979 he accomplished the rare baseball feat with at least 25 home runs and 25 stolen bases. His .308 average in 1980 led the Expos in hitting, and his 17 home runs were second to Gary Carter's team high of 29.

Bob Owchinko jumped right into double A ball at Amarillo of the Texas League from Eastern Michigan University and helped the Gold Sox win the 1976 Texas League title with a record of 6-2, 3.26 ERA. He had led Eastern Michigan to second place in the College World Series in 1976 and was named an All-American based on his 14-3, 1.95 ERA record. In his senior year, he was 4-0 in postseason competition; included among his wins were two shutouts over Big 10 champion Michigan and a 2-1 victory over top-ranked Arizona State. In 1977 he started the season at Hawaii and won a promotion to the Padres after posting a 5-1 won-lost record with a 1.43 ERA and four complete games in six appearances. Bob had a very brief trial in 1976, and he showed a good arm with an excellent curve and fine control. He ended up 1977 with a 9-12 slate and 101 strikeouts to cop the rookie honors. In mid-February of 1980, the Padres traded Owchinko to the Cleveland Indians where the left-hander's record fell to 2-9 with 66 strikeouts and a 5.29 ERA.

The Padres also had one of the most flexible pitchers in the National League make his start in 1977, Bob Shirley. Bob has been an equally fine starter and reliever. He had been with Owchinko at Amarillo and Hawaii before coming to San Diego, and his record with the Padres was 12-18. Bob's 11 wins tied him for the team high with Rollie Fingers. Texas seemed to be the state that had a hold on rookie shortstops during 1977. The American League Rangers had a fine one in Bump Wills, the son of the famous National Leaguer, Maury Wills, and the Houston Astros had Mike Fischlin, who was joined by the club's number one draft pick in 1976, pitcher Floyd Bannister. Floyd proved that his selection off the campus of Arizona State was well worth the hefty chunk of dough he received. Also joining Houston was outfielder Terry Puhl, a good all-around player who could run well, and Craig Cacek, a first baseman who had enjoyed three excellent minor league seasons in a row.

Elsewhere in the National League, outfielder Warren Cromartie, after two previous short trials, made it in Montreal, and the same held true for outfielder Jack Clark at San Francisco. With Cromartie joining Dawson and Ellis Valentine in the outfield, Montreal was presenting one of the fine young outfields. Cromartie and Dawson hit for the identical averages of .282 while Valantine came up 11 points higher. Clark was one of the more pleasant developments in an otherwise so-so Giant season, as he hit .252 and demonstrated some power with 13 round trippers. More than that, he proved himself one of the better right fielders in the league, with an excellent and accurate arm. Clark has improved his home run totals over the past three campaigns, and while he dropped off a few in 1980 his 22 were still good enough to lead the club.

The New York Mets had an early season sensation in outfielder Steve Henderson, who had been acquired in the Seaver deal with the Reds. Along with Steve came the previously mentioned Pat Zachry, infield vet Doug Flynn, and outfield hopeful, Dan Norman, who summered at the Met farm at Tidewater. Henderson took over the regular left field duties in early July and led the club in RBIs (65) and tied John Stearns and John Milner for the club lead in homers at 12. He was runner-up to Dawson for National League rookie honors. The Mets were also impressed by righty Jackson Todd, who had already overcome a bout with cancer and was 13-9 at Tidewater. The Pirates presented third baseman Dale Berra, Yogi's son, and pitchers Al Holland and Ed Whitson. San Diego, in addition to Owchinko, had a decent keystone combination in shortstop Bill Almon and second baseman Bill Champion. The Phillies came up with pitcher Warren Brusstar, a reliever who gave them a 7-2 season, and first baseman Dane Iorg, who they traded off to the Cardinals. St. Louis had hopes for third baseman Taylor Duncan, and Chicago for pitcher Willie Hernandez, who was 8-7 in relief roles and was impressive. He was a former Phillie farmhand. In Los Angeles, they were singing praises for infielder Rafael Silvialdo Camilo Landestoy and pitcher Jeff Leonard, both of whom they raised in their farm system, but were sent to the Houston Astros for 1978. The Reds were hoping to bolster their pitching corps with Tom Hume, Mario Soto, and Paul Moskau. Atlanta had out-fielder Barry Bonnell, who later was switched to third base and back to the outfield, third baseman Alvin Moore, who also played some second base, and pitchers Joey McLaughlin, Larry Bradford, and Mickey Mahler. Of the trio, only Mahler could win or lose a game, and was 1-2.

In 1978 baseball adapted the theme "Baseball Fever-Catch It," and my how the baseball public caught it! Attendance records were broken in all areas, as baseball was enjoyed by more people than had ever come out to the ball yards before. The National League champion Los Angeles Dodgers became the first club to top the three million home gate barrier, while major league attendance topped by almost two million, its previous high. Actually it was the third record-breaking season in a row, with both leagues setting new marks for attendance. Attendance wasn't the only thing climbing, as player salaries also pushed on to new heights, led by Pete Rose's $800,000-plus per year with the Phillies. A fearful Commissioner Bowie Kuhn reported that the average player salary was in excess of $95,000 when all bonuses and deferred compensation were considered, a fact, he said, which could well threaten the financial structure of the game. Marvin Miller, executive director of the Players' Association took an opposite view, stating that revenue had increased at a higher rate than the leap in player salaries.

There was basically peace among owners and players, but the umpires took a turn at labor problems and staged a one-day strike in August. There was continual turmoil in New York, as the Yankee manager Billy Martin resigned after criticizing his boss George Steinbrenner and his right fielder Reggie Jackson. Five days later, prior to the annual Old Timer's Day at Yankee Stadium, it was announced that he would be back at the helm in 1979. The Yankees, the eventual American League champions, had to do it the hard way. After the Boston Red Sox got off to a fast start, looking unbeatable, they saw their craft begin to flounder, and when the season ended the Bosox and Yankees were in a dead heat, each having won 99 games while losing 63. For the second time in American League history and only the sixth time in major league history, a playoff was necessary. The Sox had lost the first American League playoff to Cleveland in 1948, and holding true to form, dropped this game to the New Yorkers and the most unlikely hero, the weak-hitting former White Sox shortstop, Bucky Dent. It was Dent who belted a drive off Mike Torrez, which managed to just make the net above Boston's famed left field wall to erase a 2-to-0 Boston lead. As two teammates scored ahead of him, Dent became an instant hero. In the last half of the final inning, the Red Sox, now trailing 5 to 4, had the tying run at third and the winning run aboard; a whole season was down to one final inning and one batter. It ended for Boston right there. The Yankees went on to defeat the Dodgers four games to two in the Series.

When you stop and think a minute, 1978 becomes a year of contrasts, the old way against the new. The winning pitcher in that playoff game was Ron Guidry, a product of the old way; scouted, signed, and developed by one club, in this case the Yankees. The loser was Mike Torrez, a much-traveled product, with his fifth club in as many seasons, a free agent, a representative of the new era in baseball. The era of inter-league trading, free agents, designated hitters, franchise shifts, and expansions. What will the rookies of the future face?

The rookies who walked off with top honors in 1978 were third baseman Bob Horner of the Atlanta Braves, second baseman Paul Molitor of the Milwaukee Brewers, second baseman Lou Whitaker of the Detroit Tigers, and pitchers Don Robinson of the Pittsburgh Pirates and Rich Gale of the Kansas City Royals.

We have already met Whitaker and learned how he teamed up with Alan Trammell to form one of baseball's newest and most exciting keystone combinations. Lou arrived late in 1977 after a fine season on the Tiger farm at Montgomery. "Sweet Lou" capped his first full season by gaining the baseball writers' nod for rookie of the year along with many other rookie honors. Flashy at the plate and in the field, Lou hit .285 and committed just 17 errors in 139 games, while leading his Tigers in triples and sacrifice bunts. The nickname "Sweet Lou" was hung on him by his Tigertown teammates. While Lou was winning honors, the Tigers were bringing up pitchers Kip Young and Sheldon Burnside. Burnside learned his baseball on the sandlots of Toronto, and he brought with him a hard slider, which was very effective against lefties, and a record of steady improvement through the Tiger system. He did little for the Bengals. Righty Kip Young posted a 6-7 slate and was the surprise rookie for the Tigers. His first appearance was in a relief role; then he reeled off 13 consecutive starts, winning the first four, all complete games. Composure on the mound and pinpoint control were his trademarks. Outfielder Dave Stegman joined them and hit fairly well in a late-season trial. A former Arizona all-American, he doubled in his first big league at-bat. A fine defensive outfielder with speed, he may be a future fixture at Tiger Stadium.

Bob Horner arrived in Atlanta directly off the Arizona State University campus with no minor league experience, and in his first game he homered and singled. Rookie of the year honors went to him off his 23 homers, 17 doubles, and .266 average. He homered once in every 14 at-bats, a better average than any previous rookie of the year winner. He impressed all observers and had Montreal manager Dick Williams exclaiming that he appeared to be another Harmon Killebrew. The Braves had originally planned to start him at Savannah, but Horner talked them into letting him stay in Atlanta. This may be a dominant trait, as in 1980 when he got off to a slow start, the Braves wanted to farm him out, but he refused to report to the minors. After considerable hassle they let him stay, and he proceeded to hit .268 with 35 homers, second in the league to Mike Schmidt's 48. Horner had also hit an NCAA record 25 homers at ASU. Impressive defensively at third base, he lived up to his advanced billing. As a rookie, he set an Atlanta team record with nine sacrifice flies. His manager, Bobby Cox, said, "This kid is going to make it and make it big. He has ability, the confidence, and the poise." Joining Horner in Atlanta late in the season was his Arizona State teammate Jerry Maddox, a fast-improving glove man in the infield. At ASU Jerry had broken all of Reggie Jackson's single-season home run records, and they stood until Horner broke them. An outstanding second baseman, Glenn Hubbard was recalled by the Braves in mid-July. Hubbard is comparatively small by today's standards at 5'9", 160 pounds. When Hubbard became injured, the Braves reached down to Richmond and came up with Chico Ruiz, who had been a minor leaguer since 1970. An excellent utility infielder, he responded by hitting .333 over a ten-game span when he played regularly and wound up hitting .283.

The big right-hander Don Robinson pitched his way onto the Pirates during spring training and then into the starting rotation, finishing up 14-6 and tied for club high in wins with a 3.47 ERA, while whiffing 135 batters. His .700 winning percentage was third among the National League leaders and tops for the Bucs. Spending most of the '77 season with the Pirate farm at Shreveport, he was a non-roster invitee to spring training in '78 and was rated as inexperienced but with a good arm. The Pirates had hoped Steve Nicosia, a squatty catcher who had also played some outfield at Columbus, might arrive to catch Robinson; he didn't. Dorian "Doe" Boyland, a former basketball player (6'4", 204 lbs.) at the University of Wisconsin, where he was primarily a pitcher in baseball, switched to the outfield and first base, but had no chance to move veteran Willie Stargell in his trial at Pittsburgh.

Second baseman Paul Molitor moved up to the Milwaukee Brewers after just one season in the minors at Burlington of the Midwest League, where he was MVP, league-leading batter, and gained a "can't miss" tag. He was a major factor in the Brewers' midseason title push when he teamed up with young shortstop Robin Yount to form a strong double-play combination. A fine fielder, Molitor demonstrated enough speed to lead the Brewers in stolen bases with 30, the highest by any Brewer since Tommy Harper stole a club record of 38 in 1970. Fielding, speed, and hitting (.273) won him rookie honors. Joining Molitor were rookie pitchers Mark Bomback, a six-year veteran of the Red Sox farm system, and Andy Replogle, a former St. Louis farmhand who the Brewers had obtained from Baltimore. Andy was the best of the two hurlers, posting a 9-5 record. Also up for a brief try with the Brewers was outfielder Jeff Yurak who had had two fine seasons at Holyoke, where he had led the Millers in many offensive areas and had been the Eastern League's MVP. The Western Division champion Kansas City Royals added their fine right-handed pitcher Rich Gale to the rookie award winners. Gale would have been called up in 1977, except for a fracture of his right wrist, but that seemed to do little to hold back the potential he possessed. Rich stands 6'7" and weighs 227 pounds, which accounts for his nickname of "Big Red." A University of New Hampshire product, he gained honorable mention All-American from that New England school, not necssarily noted for its baseball programs. A hard thrower, he complements a good fastball with a curve and a slider. One of the top pitching prospects in the country in

1978, he has not disappointed the Royals. He won 11 of his first 14 decisions and pitched sensationally. On two occasions he held the Rangers hitless until late in the game; he tossed a two-hit win at the hard-hitting Red Sox; and on another occasion he struck out ten Angels. His 14-8 record earned him rookie honors. K.C. manager Whitey Herzog said, "I am not sure where we would have ended up without him. We think he has a great future," and teammate Dennis Leonard echoed Whitey, "Thank God for Rich Gale. I'd hate to think where we would be without him."

The 1978 rookie standouts, while overall not as sturdy a group as some years, were worthy enough. The Chicago Cubs were pitching right-hander Dennis Lamp, who had a brief try in 1977. Dennis really hasn't been too bad with a mediocre Cub nine, 7-15 in '78, 11-10 in '79, and 10-13 in '80. Actually, if his teammates had gotten him some runs he might have been 15-7 and with a little luck 19-3. He was beaten 1 to 0 three times, 2 to 1 twice, and 3 to 1 and 4 to 1. Joining him late in the season was outfielder Carl Pagel, up from Wichita. The Dodgers had a possibility behind the plate in Brad Gulden, who possessed a fine arm and had been showing steady improvement in the minors. Classified as a pure hitter was infielder Pedro Guerrero, obtained in 1974 from the Cleveland organization. Pedro had batted better than .300 five straight years. Outfielder Rudy Law made his L.A. debut in '78. A speedster, he had set a modern Pacific Coast League record while with Albuquerque when he stole 79 bases, the most that league had seen since 1923, while hitting a fine .319. Joining these Dodgers was a fine right-handed pitcher Bob Welch who gained the esteem of the nation for his fine work in post-season play as a reliever in three games of the World Series. "I see a lot of Don Drysdale in Bob," said Dodger skipper Tom Lasorda. There was, of course, the difference that Welch came in over the top, while Drysdale was a sidearmer. His first World Series relief job was the classic dual between the rookie and the veteran, in this case the Yankees' Reggie Jackson. The rookie prevailed, striking out Jackson to save the game. Welch was signed out of the same school, Eastern Michigan, as our rookie pitcher of '77, Bob Owchinko. Yes, they were close friends. The New York Mets had little to offer, except catcher turned part-time infielder Alex Trevino, who had a late-season trial. Alex was rated the most improved player in the Met system. He started his career in the Mexican League and really doesn't appear to be the answer to the Mets' catching situation. The Mets also looked at catcher Butch Benton and pitchers Juan Berenguer, "Mr. Fastball" in the International League Dwight Bernard, and Neives Cornejo.

The Montreal Expos were looking at pitcher Scott Sanderson, whose trial marked the end of a rapid and dramatic rise from double A Memphis, to triple A Denver, to the Expos. In 1980, Scott won 16 games to tie for tops on the team with Steve Rogers. To catch, the Expos brought along Bob Reece and Jerry Fry. Reece was strictly a catcher, but Fry had been signed as a shortstop and played third and the outfield. The Padres were hopeful that Tony Castillo, who had a fine record in the Texas League, might do their catching. San Diego did come up with their regular shortstop, a rookie with only 68 games of pro experience, in Ozzie Smith, who had only played at Walla Walla of the rookie Northwest League. Next to Horner, Smith was probably the top National League rookie of 1978. Not on the 40-man roster when spring training started, Manager Al Dark gave Smith the job and his successor as manager, Roger Craig, reaped the benefits. Smith stole 31 bases in his first 38 attempts 40 overall, and helped the Padres turn in one of the league's best double-play records. Smith led the League with 28 sacrifice hits. Manager Craig said, "Ozzie is the best young infielder I've ever seen." The Houston Astros had lefty swinging Jim Obradovich, a first baseman who was an impressive hitter in the International League where he did more DHing than playing first. Jim had a long minor league career starting in 1967 with two years out for military service. He was originally signed by the Twins. Catcher Bruce Bochy, who was born in France, opened the season as a backup catcher at Columbus, but became number one when Reggie Baldwin moved up to the Astros, and later his good hitting earned Bruce a July call-up to Houston.

The St. Louis Cardinals gave trials to catcher Terry Kennedy, who was working at becoming a switch-hitter and had ten homers and a .330 average in triple A ball. In 1977, he had been selected the College Player of the Year while at Florida State. The Cards also checked in pitchers George Frazier and Silvio Martinez, both right-handers. Martinez had been obtained from the White Sox with whom he put in 10 games and 21 innings in 1977. He did some excellent hurling for the Cards, tossing two one-hitters and two two-hitters, all complete games. In his first National League start he one-hit the Mets. His season record was 9-8, and it seems he was either very good or very bad. The Giants had a good rookie catcher in Dennis Littlejohn who was a noted defensive specialist. In only his second season as a pro, pitcher Phil Nastu showed signs of a promising major league future. The young lefty had been a walk-on at the '77 Giant minor league camp, not having been drafted after a fine career as a basketball and baseball player at the University of Bridgeport in Connecticut. The Cincinnati Reds were high on: First baseman Arturo DeFreites, a hitter with good power; shortstop Ron Oester, one of the finest infield prospects in baseball; pitcher Mike LaCoss, who had moved up quickly through the Reds' system; and Harry Spilman, who had played first and third bases in the minors, where he was an excellent hitter posting a .373 average with Three Rivers in the Eastern League. The Phillies were high on an excellent shortstop named Todd Cruz, young outfielder Lonnie Smith, who we will meet later, relief pitcher Kevin Saucier, a lefty who helped them to the 1980 world championship with a 7-3 record, and catcher Keith Moreland, noted as a good contact power hitter and a former All-American third baseman with the University of Texas, the 1975 national champions.

Of all the National League rookies, Pittsburgh's Doe Boyland made the most unusual debut. He was sitting on the bench when he struck out in his first at-bat. A lefty batter, he had been sent to the plate to hit against the Mets' Skip Lockwood. However, Lockwood left the game with an arm injury after the count had reached one ball and two strikes. Lockwood was replaced by lefty Kevin Kobel. Boyland was called back in favor of right-hand-hitting Rennie Stennett, who struck out on Kobel's first pitch. Under the scoring rules, Boyland was debited with the strikeout.

While the American League didn't have such a bizarre incident among their rookies, California's shortstop Dave Machemer did become the 46th player to homer in his first major league at-bat. Joining Machemer was Carney Lansford, one of the best infielders to come up in the Angel organization in years. Carney, a good hitter, batted second most of the season, but moved down a notch to third upon the untimely death of Lyman Bostock. The Boston Red Sox were looking for pitching in their quest to stay on top of the league and gave trials to Jim Wright, who pitched several nice games for them, and Al Ripley, whose father once pitched for the Red Sox. Al did little. Then there was Bobby Sprowl, a left-hander. Sprowl made the jump from A ball at Winter Haven to Boston in less than two seasons. At Boston, he was put to the test by being sent against Baltimore and New York, and while he looked good, he was not the answer. Plagued with an unexplainable case of wildness in the '79 spring training camp, he was traded to Houston. Bobby may be heard from yet. The Sox also gave a gander at outfielder Garry Hancock. Baltimore, with a set lineup, also had only pitchers on their mind and they were right-handers Dan Ford and Sammy Stewart. With pitchers always in demand, the White Sox were hopeful but southpaw moundsman Ross Baumgarten would help them. Ross had played at every level, from A to majors, in one season with an 18-8 record for the year. Winning a game at every level of baseball in the same season is a unique feat. Joining Baumgarten on the mound were a big lefty, Britt Burns, signed on newspaperman's tip to owner Bill Veeck, Steve Trout, another impressive left-handed youngster whose dad, Dizzy, had once been a good pitcher in the majors, and yet a third lefty in Dick Wortham, a hard thrower. The White Sox also called up from Appleton the diminutive Harry Chappas, who made an impressive showing with his fielding wizardry and hitting ability. The switch hitter is one of the smallest players ever to appear in the majors at 5'3", 150 pounds. Another infielder was the Southern League batting champion at .333, Joe Gates. With all those pitchers, it was only natural that catchers would be needed so the White Sox gave two a chance, Mike Colbern a right-hand hitter, who was an all-star outfielder at Arizona State and now one of the most promising newcomers, and the left-hand-hitting Marvis Foley, who was impressive at Chicago.

Up from San Jose with the Seattle Mariners was first baseman-outfielder Charlie Beamon, who had been drafted from the Kansas City Royals (his father was Charlie Beamon, Sr., who had pitched for the Orioles, 1956-58), and short-reliever Shane Rawley, who came from the Cincinnati farm at Indianapolis, but had originally signed with Montreal. He appeared in 52 games, all but two in relief. The Toronto Blue Jays' hopefules were pitcher Vic Cruz and catcher Brian Milner, who was placed on the major league roster directly from high school and was the youngest player in the majors at the time of his signing. He spent very little time with the Jays, but had four hits in nine at-bats. Not bad at all considering his age. Speedster Willie Upshaw, out of the Yankee organization, appeared in the outfield, and he was joined by another former Yankee farmhand, second baseman Garth Iorg, Dane's brother. The New York Yankees finally came up with some good rookies, running them back and forth to the minors at a great rate. They were catcher Mike Heath, second basemen Brian Doyle and Damaso Garcia, third basemen Domingo Ramos and Dennis Sherrill, and pitchers Jim Beattie, Ron Davis, Bob Kammeyer, and Dave Rajsich. Most of these rookies have been on the merry-go-round for the past several seasons, although some are now with other clubs. In 1978 Beattie probably contributed the most, while 6-9 during the regular season, he started and won a game in the Championship Series and the World Series. Doyle proved to be one of the Yankee World Series heroes with a .436 average. He was the replacement for the injured second sacker Willie Randolph. He is the younger brother of former major leaguer Denny Doyle.

Rookies cracking the Minnesota Twins' lineup included a fine right-handed pitcher who, right from spring training, would obviously make it. Roger "Pudge" Erickson didn't miss a start all season, wound up tied with K.C.'s Gale for the most wins by a rookie (14-13), and led the Twins' staff with 37 starts, 14 complete games, and 121 strikeouts. He unveiled a remarkably good pickoff move for a right-hander, nabbing ten men off base for a

Twins' record. He was joined by lefty Darrell Jackson who had started the season with Class A Orlando. What a start it was, his first in pro ball; he pitched nine innings of no-hit ball in an opening night extra-inning game! His impressive work continued leading him to the Twins' mound. It may seem redundant, but he too pitched for and was drafted from Arizona State. Pitcher Greg Thayer also made an appearance. While outfielder Dave Edwards was getting a September trial after a fine season at Toledo, his twin brother, Marshall, was doing well for Milwaukee's farm club at Holyoke in the Eastern League. Their other brother was Mike, who did so well at second base for the Oakland A's. Looks like another three-brother act on its way to the major leagues. If they get Marshall into the Twins' system puns will fly all over—"Twins play for the Twins." David did an unusual thing against Pittsburgh farmhand pitcher Fred Breining of Columbus; he faced Breining only three times, hitting a home run each time. The Oakland A's had one of those quantity if not quality years, although some of these youngsters may still make a mark, pitchers Tim Conroy, Alan Wirth, and John Henry Johnson, catchers Scott Meyer and Bruce Robinson, first baseman Dave Revering (.290 with fifteen home runs in 1980), infielder Darrell Woodward, and outfielder Dwayne Murphy. The Texas Rangers promoted pitchers Danny Darwin, who responded by striking out the first four batters he faced in his first start (he was their leading pitcher in 1980 at 13-4, 2.62 ERA), and Steve Comer, who had been ignored in the draft and was a long-shot to even stick in baseball, but his Cinderella story turned out okay, as he was still with the Rangers in 1980. Pitcher Paul Mirabella was a Ranger in 1978 and now is doing a good job with Toronto. Other Ranger rookies in 1978 were infielders Nelson Norman, Bill Sample, and LaRue Washington, who was a speedster having stolen 93 bases in two years at Tucson. Sample was rated the best young hitter in the Texas farm system and hit .467 in his eight-game appearance with the Rangers.

1979 found the Pittsburgh Pirates capture the National League flag and gain World Series honors by becoming only the fourth team to win a seven-game World Series after trailing three games to one, as they bested the American League winners, the Baltimore Orioles. In other events, the leagues got started without their regular umpires. They were out on strike, and substitutes were brought in. After 45 days, the regulars returned when an agreement was worked out regarding their demands. It seemed it was the New York Yankees who were continually making the baseball news in 1979, and most of it was not of the happy variety. First there was the illness of the popular coach Elston Howard, which laid him up for the year. That was followed by the Cliff Johnson-Goose Gossage clubhouse scuffle which put

Gossage out of commission and may have led to the Yankees' not gaining a third successive pennant. It also led to the trade of Johnson. The saga continued when manager Bob Lemon was kicked upstairs and controversial Billy Martin returned to the helm. This led to the rekindling of the Martin-Jackson feud. Next, president Al Rosen had his problems with owner Steinbrenner and resigned. Then Yankee catcher Thurman Munson met his death in a plane crash. Martin was back in the news when it was charged that he ordered rookie hurler Bob Kammeyer to hit Cleveland Indian batter Cliff Johnson and that a cash reward was given for doing it, a charge denied by Martin. Next it was Martin fighting a marshmallow salesman and being fired. A trouble-filled year for the Yanks who tumbled to fourth place.

For the fourth consecutive year attendance reached new highs, and it appeared the owners and players might have some problem reaching contract agreement before the 1980 season would arrive. Veterans Lou Brock and Carl Yastrzemski each collected their 3000th hit. The 40-year-old Brock also stole 21 bases for a career total of 939, an all-time record. With 400 homers to his credit Yaz became the first American Leaguer to have 3000 hits and 400 homers. Pete Rose with 200 or more hits for the tenth time broke Ty Cobb's record of nine. Manny Mota at 41 got his 147th pinch hit and 40-year-old Phil Niekro won 21 games for Atlanta while brother Joe of Houston also won 21, thus becoming the first two brothers to win 20 in the same league during the same season.

There was one other case which may well affect our future rookies. When Atlanta signed Bob Horner, they gave him a standard contract, plus bonuses. He claimed they did not live up to their contract when they offered him a new pact at what amounted to less when the bonuses were considered. It was his contention that the combination made up his first year contract. The Braves claimed the bonuses were over-and-above his contract. The ruling finally handed down was in Horner's favor. This could affect bonus arrangements with rookies of the future.

The rookies of the year for 1979 selected by *The Sporting News* were first baseman Pat Putnam of the Texas Rangers and pitcher Mark Clear of California in the American League and outfielder Jeff Leonard of Houston and pitcher Rick Sutcliffe of Los Angeles in the National League. The baseball writers agreed on Sutcliffe, but chose co-winners in the American League in third baseman John Castino of the Twins and shortstop Alfredo Griffin of the Blue Jays.

We spoke of Pat Putnam earlier as the Minor League Player of the Year in 1976, when he was the first such recipient in an A league. A good-sized first baseman, Pat was playing his first full year in the major leagues in 1979 after two previous trials with the Texas Rangers. The 25-year-old made little impression in those two previous brief shots, but in '79 took over the first base job after the trade of Mike Hargrove. "He's given us some power and does a good job in the field," said Ranger manager Pat Corrales. Putnam was among the top Texas hitters most of the season and finished with 18 home runs and a .277 average. His hitting was really no surprise, as he proved to be a slugger at every minor league level, but his improvement at first base made him an excellent candidate for the rookie award. His eighteen homers allowed him to share the team's home run leadership with Buddy Bell, and he was the club's most proficient pinch hitter, batting .381 in that role. Two of the team's five pinch-hit homers were off Pat's bat.

Gene Autry, owner of the California Angels, finally saw some return on the millions he had been doling out of his saddlebags when his young right-handed relief specialist Mark Clear picked up some rookie gold. Better than half of the 1979 major league rookies were pitchers, and Clear was the standout among them. Originally signed by the Phillies, but dumped after one year in the minors, he played a key role in the Angels' Western Division championship. His bullpen work helped tide the Angels over, when ace starters Frank Tanana and Nolan Ryan were hurt. Without him, the Angels might never have made their successful bid for the title. He posted 14 saves, an 11-5 record, and a 3.63 ERA, as well as a fine strikeout record of 98 in 109 innings. Not bad for a youngster who didn't have his picture on a bubble-gum card the year before. Mark's uncle is Bob Clear, the Angels' bullpen coach, who continually works with him on his mechanics. While he relies on his fastball like most relievers, he also has a slider and a curve which some people call a "slop drop." A hard thrower who moves the ball around well and is not afraid to pitch the best hitters inside, he was the Angels' top hurler in 1980 with an 11-11 record and a 3.31 earned run average.

You might think that baseball's worst team, the Toronto Blue Jays, wouldn't have much in the way of prospects, but shortstop Alfredo Griffin destroyed that myth. Acquired by the Jays from Cleveland in December of 1978, Griffin was a standout among rookie infielders. Despite three short trials with the Indians, Alfredo still enjoyed rookie status and was a standout with his glove. One of the better Toronto hitters, he combined his speed with other skills to pull down a share of rookie honors. He combined beautifully with rookie second baseman Danny Ainge to give Toronto a very promising double-play combination. Undoubtedly Toronto's most pleasant surprise, Griffin wound up hitting .287 and setting club seasonal records for hits (179), runs (81), triples(10), and stolen bases (21) while helping the Blue Jays set a team record for double plays. A switch-hitter, Griffin hits equally well from both sides of the plate. Dan Ainge (rhymes with range), the second baseman of the combo, was in his second season of pro ball, having started his career with Syracuse at the triple A level. He demonstrated good range in the field for a man big enough to play on Brigham Young's varsity basketball team in the offseason. Prior to the 1978-79 basketball season, *Sports Illustrated* named him as one of their ten "super sophs."

John Castino took over the regular third base job on the Minnesota Twins, particularly impressing manager Gene Mauch with his deftness in the field. He also proved no slouch at the plate hitting .285. John tied in the baseball writers' voting and was awarded Co-Rookie of the Year with Griffin. Right from spring training, John showed that his defensive play was going to be something to behold. He started the season splitting the third base post with Mike Cubbage, but when Mike became injured, John stepped right in and took over the spot on a regular basis. Although John was guilty of a throwing error from time to time, it was his range, both left and right, that had them talking around the league. Interestingly, both Castino's and Griffin's first major league home runs were of inside-the-park variety.

The Houston Astros' divisional-title push would have been impossible without Jeff Leonard, particularly after Cesar Cedeno became hampered with illness and Jeff replaced him. Not a power hitter, he can hit for average as his .290 mark showed. He has speed, a fine arm, and can cover the outfield exceptionally well. Bob Watson, before his trade to Boston, said he felt Leonard had a chance to become one of baseball's superstars. Jeff was originally the property of the Dodgers and had a look-see with them in 1977, but in September 1978 was traded to the Astros. His first three at-bats in the brief Dodger trial resulted in three hits. Toronto wanted him, but the Dodgers wouldn't let him go until they got the catcher they needed to back up Steve Yeager, the Astros' Joe Ferguson.

The Dodgers had a tall (6'7") hard-thrower in Rick Sutcliffe, who manager Tom Lasorda was touting for pitching rookie honors. "He's come in and done the job when our pitching staff needed help. He's pitched like a veteran, giving us consistency in his starts," said Lasorda. In the spring the rookie right-hander was considered a long shot for a Dodger job, but they kept him on as a long man out of the bullpen and he worked his way from there into a starting role. He accomplished a lot on his way to rookie honors, leading the staff in wins with 17, innings pitched at 242, and tied for the club lead in shutouts with 11. Only four rookies in Dodger history had more victories: Henry Schmidt, 21 in 1903; Oscar Jones, 20 in 1903; Jeff Pfeffer, 23 in 1914; and Dazzy Vance, 18 in 1922. Rick had had trials in 1976 and 1978 with L.A.

Other National League rookies of note in 1979 included John Fulgham of the Cardinals, who went from a June 19th complete-game debut victory against the Padres to a 10-6 record and a .253 ERA. Frank Pastore jumped from double A to the Reds in a relief role, returned to the minors, and came back in a starting role, finishing with a 6-7 record. Right-hander Dickie Noles had a similar experience with the Phillies. Although he was strictly a starter, he showed he could also relieve as he did with Oklahoma City. He was 3-4 in Philadelphia. The Astros were pinning their future hopes on reliever Pete Ladd, a former Red Sox farmhand, catcher Al Knicely, outfielder Tom Wiedenbauer, who hit .667 in a brief trial, and pitchers Randy Nieman (3-2), Gordon Pladson, Gary Wilson, and Bert Roberge. Despite a 6-10 record, the New York Mets found a fourth starter in Neil Allen, a right-hander with exceptional athletic talents. Switched to a reliever, he gave them a team-leading 22 saves in 1980. The Mets opened the season with Kelvin Chapman at second base, but a weak stick sent him back to Tidewater. Following the same route was Jesse Orosco, a non-roster player in spring training who earned a berth, then faltered. Elevated to the Mets after an impressive stay with the Tides was righty Jeff Reardon (1-2, 1.71 ERA). His 8-7 record was good for second high in Met wins in 1980, and his 2.62 ERA was tops among Met regulars.

The Dodgers switched righty starter Joe Beckwith to a reliever in 1979, and he responded with a 3-3, 1.95 ERA in 1980. They were also high on third baseman Mickey Hatcher and rated him their most promising prospect for the future. He was an All-American high school football and baseball player at his Mesa, Arizona, high school. The Montreal Expos couldn't help but be joyous over the work of Bill Gullickson (we will meet him later on). Tony Brizzolara won six and lost nine for Atlanta, but his ERA was on the high side. Rick Matula was 8-10 for the same Braves, another non-roster player in spring training to make good. Rick was 11-13 in 1980, as he remained in the big time as a control pitcher. One of the hardest throwing pitchers in baseball, a former Cardinal and Red farm boy, Bill Caudill pitched well for the Cubs, although his 1-7 record didn't reflect it; he is a strikeout pitcher with a future. The Cubs also looked quickly at Texas League all-star infielder Steve Macko. Twenty-five-year-old Joe Strain was promoted from Phoenix in June to take over the second base chores for San Francisco. Joe had a good base-stealing record in the minors, where he had won a number of awards. Another Giant speedster with future potential was outfielder Max Venable, a former Dodger minor leaguer who was making remarkable strides toward the majors.

In the American League, the Boston Red Sox were featuring "The Boys from Pawtucket," catchers Gary Allenson and Mike O'Berry, pitchers John

Tudor, Joel Finch, Chuck Rainey, and Win Remmerswaal. O'Beery and Allenson were alternating until the injured Carlton Fisk could return to action. O'Berry was good defensively but not offensively, and was sent to the Cubs for 1980. The pitchers all had potential; the lefty Tudor turned in some good efforts and was 8-5 in '80. Rainey looked great and was the ace of the 1980 staff at 8-3 until arm problems knocked him out at midseason. Finch gave the Sox some good efforts in tough situations against K.C. and New York. He started the 1980 season at Pawtucket where he was hampered by a bad back and then a broken finger, losing a whole season. A couple of excellent showings at the season's end could signal his recall to Boston for 1981. Remmerswaal, a Dutchman born and raised in Holland, is the first player on a major league roster who was raised and learned his baseball in Europe, and he has been effective at times in relief roles. The death of Yankee catcher Thurman Munson thrust Jerry Narron into a regular job, although Munson's injuries had given Jerry a fair amount of previous work. The Bronx Bombers were also continuing their merry-go-round of '78 and had catcher Dennie Werth, outfielder Darryl Jones, and pitchers Rick Anderson, Mike Griffin, Dave Righetti, and Roger Slagle on it. Kansas City pitcher Craig Chamberlain jumped from double A level into the K.C. rotation. With his fastball and control he reeled off three straight complete-game wins, but finished 4-4. Other K.C. hopefuls were pitchers Gary Christenson, Renie Martin, and Craig Eaton, along with relief specialist Dan Quisenberry. Quisenberry helped put the Royals into the 1980 World Series with his sidearm motion, from which comes a good sinkerball and slider that worked effectively against left or right-handed batters. Pitcher Eric Wilson started 14 games for Cleveland, completed none, and was 2-4. The Indians also introduced Sandy Wihtol, another pitcher.

The Texas Rangers tried pitcher Brian Allard in various roles, learning that he was an intelligent hurler with good command of all the basic pitches. Pitchers Bob Babcock and Jerry Gleaton had brief appearances with Texas also. The Seattle Mariners had little luck with pitchers Rafael Vasquez, Jim Lewis, or Roy Branch, but outfielder Rod Craig, the first player signed and developed in the Mariner organization to play in the major leagues, caught everyone's eye as he hit safely in his first seven games and 14 of the 16 he played, while batting .385.

The Minnesota Twins had little luck with a host of rookies, except Castino and outfielders Gary Ward and Rick Sofield. Ward hit .286 in 10 games and Sofield .301 in 35 games. Baltimore's league champions had little room for rookies on their veteran club, but were interested to see if highly regarded second baseman Wayne Krenchicki had recovered from injuries suffered at

Rochester, or if outfielder Mark Corey's bad knee would allow him to become an everyday player. The Birds also looked at first baseman Tom Chism and pitcher Jeff Rineer. The Chicago White Sox had seven rookie pitchers in and out of their 1979 lineup, none of whom could boast of a winning record. Randy Scarbery may have been the best, despite a 2-8 record, as he led the Sox staff in appearances, making forty in relief and five as a starter. Most of the seven bounced between Iowa or Knoxville and Chicago. Dick Dotson was 2-0, hurling a shutout in his second start. Reliever Guy Hoffman (0-5) was effective in spots, as was Fred Howard (1-5), but Mark Esser, Dewey Hoyt, and Dewey Robinson did little. Robinson, after an early season try, was returned to Iowa where he won the American Association's outstanding pitcher's award. The lone non-pitcher among the Chisox was outfielder Russ Kuntz, whose five-game trial proved little. The Oakland A's recalled a very talented and speedy youngster from their Ogden farm club in Rickey Henderson. Henderson stole 79 bases and hit .310 with Jersey City of the Eastern League in 1978. In 1977 he stole 95 bases for Modesto. His combined Ogden-Oakland total showed 77 thefts. He moved immediately into one of the starting outfield spots, and while not a power hitter, showed up well at the plate hitting .274. Certainly one of the stars of the American League in 1980, he stole an even 100 bases, far outdistancing any other player, and while doing it, he broke Ty Cobb's record, 96 stolen bases in 1915, to set a new American League record. The A's used Derek Bryant as a defensive outfield replacement and got a nice 8-7 record from fireballing right-hander Brian Kingman. In 1980 Kingman had the misfortune of losing 20 games while matching his eight wins of 1979.

The Toronto Blue Jays, in addition to Ainge and Griffin, were impressed with Phil Huffman, another non-roster pitcher who showed up well in spring training and earned a try. He gained the opening day win for the Jays and spoiled Yankee manager Billy Martin's return by turning back the Yankees. He finished with a deceptive 6-18 record. Outfielder Bobby Brown got into four games before his trade to the Yankees along with outfielder Ted Wilborn, who appeared in 22 Blue Jays' games. Pitchers Butch Edge and Dave Stieb were impressive, and Stieb, an excellent fielder, was also used as a pinch runner on several occasions. The Detroit Tigers were again making themselves felt in the American League and had some capable material looking to crack their lineup. Perhaps the most unusual rookie debut occurred to their 22-year-old left-handed pitcher Pat Underwood, as his mound opponent was his brother Tommy, a pitcher for Toronto. It was the first time two left-handed brothers had opposed each other, and the first time that anyone had pitched his first game with his brother hurling for the opposing team. Detroit and Pat won the game 1 to 0. Underwood's 6-4 record was typical of the success of other rookie pitchers in Detroit; Mike Chris and Bruce Robbins were 3-3, and Dan Petry was 6-5. All showed very rapid development and much-hoped-for future successes. Tom Brookens played a steady third and second base after his recall from Evansville, as did the versatile infielder-outfielder Rick Peters. The balance of the Tiger youngsters were outfielders, including the much sought after and highly regarded Kirk Gibson. Also appearing were Altar Greene, Lynn Jones, and Dan Gonzales. The AL West champions, the California Angels, in addition to Mark Clear, brought up catchers Tom Donohue, who had spent eight years on the farm, and Brian Harper, and pitchers Ralph Botting, Steve Eddy, Bob Ferris, and Dave Schuler. Outfielder Bob Clark appeared in a few games, filling in for injured Joe Rudi. First baseman John Harris made it into one game, and infielder Dick Thon appeared to need more time to sharpen his defensive skills.

Let's go back a minute and think about that Texas right-hander Bob Babcock. He could serve as an inspiration to those rookies laboring in the minors. When he made his first appearance, he was one month shy of 30-years-old, not the oldest rookie ever, but one who proves that it is never too late. So ended the decade of the '70s.

1980:
The Ninth
Inning

The 1980 major league season was marred by a threatened player strike, a threat so real it appeared that rosters would have to be filled entirely by youngsters. Suffice it to say, the action was averted and 1980 settled down to be, for the most part, a normal season. With the luster beginning to wear off the free agents and their big money contracts, more and more teams were starting to realize the wisdom of growing their own players, and it would appear the farm clubs will again become the main supply system of talent during the '80s. As we can see from the decade of the '70s, the successful teams were the ones who continued to depend upon their own farm team players. Consider the successes of the Dodgers, Reds, Red Sox, Orioles, and Pirates. The Orioles, who especially have lost players to the re-entry draft, always seem to have a new face waiting in the wings to take their place. Of course, if there is a drawback it is that the rookies of the early '80s may well become the free agents of the late '80s; but for a while they are on their way and will benefit the clubs to which they are called.

The top rookies of 1980 appear to be Cleveland Indian outfielder Joe Charboneau, who won all of the American League rookie honors, Philadelphia Phillies' outfielder Lonnie Smith, and pitchers Britt Burns of the Chicago White Sox and Bill Gullickson of the Montreal Expos. It was, from all appearances, a vintage year. We will take a look at these four and speculate on the rest, as from among them will come the stars of the new decade, or will they? It's certain some of the heroes of the '80s are not yet even in professional baseball, and some will be those we met in the late '70s.

Joe Charboneau stirred more fan excitement in Cleveland than any recent ballplayer to appear on the shores of Lake Erie. You might be safe in saying he put life back into the Indian teepee, which seemed to be folding up in recent years. The 25-year-old rookie made the team after an impressive spring training and only three-and-one-half seasons of minor league experience. Originally signed by the Phillies, Joe was traded to Cleveland in December 1978. His progress through the minors had been steady and rapid, and he clearly has proven his ability to hit at all levels. He paced double A Chattanooga with a .352 average in '79, the second straight year that he had hit for high average, batting .350 at Visalia in '78. He broke in with a bang for Cleveland by hitting a home run in his second at-bat and again in his first game at Cleveland while going 3 for 3. Known as "Super Joe" to the Cleveland faithful, he hit 23 homers, drove in 87 runs, and batted .289, appearing in 131 games. He suffered a groin pull, forcing him out of left field and into the designated-hitter role. The injury worsened in the latter stages of the season, forcing Joe into a pinch-hitting role. Cleveland manager Dave Garcia has had nothing but praise for his popular rookie, stating, "No matter how we have used him, he has come through." It has also been Joe's off-the-field antics which have gained him a share of greatness. Among his more famous feats have been bench pressing 401 pounds, fighting bare-knuckle matches for a few bucks, opening beer bottles with his arm muscles and off his eye socket bones, removing his own tattoos, straightening his own nose, pulling one of his teeth, drinking beer through his nose, stitching up his own wounds, being stabbed by an anti-American with a ball pen while in Mexico, eating lighted cigarettes, swallowing uncracked eggs (shell and all), appearing on a poster in a superman outfit, and having a record, "Go Joe Charboneau," make the disco charts in Cleveland. Certainly he qualifies as the most colorful of players to come along in a long while, one who also has on-the-field abilities as well, a rare combination. The 6'2", 200 pounder bats right-handed.

Britt Burns, a 21-year-old left-hander, was a pleasant surprise for the Chicago White Sox in 1980 after a brief six-game, five-inning trial in 1979. The 6'5", 215 pounder never had an impressive minor league record, but possesses a lot of raw talent and displayed good control. A strikeout record of 92 in 110 innings with only 37 walks while at Knoxville went a long way in calling the attention of White Sox officials. The number three draft choice of the Sox in 1978, he came to them with a very impressive high school record in his hometown of Birmingham, Alabama. Britt, whose first name is Robert but he prefers his middle name, credits his father's coaching during Britt's early youth for his success. His father saw him strike out 292 batters in 139 innings, walking only 30 and allowing only 30 hits with a 0.12 ERA and an 18-game winning streak in high school. In his first full year in the majors, he worked 238 innings, allowing 213 hits, striking out 133, while walking only 63 and posting a 15-13 record for a club that won only 70 games. His 2.84 ERA was third best in the league. Britt's star Burns brightly over Comiskey Park.

Outfielder Lonnie Smith of the world champion Philadelphia Phillies, like Charboneau, literally forced his way into the lineup by his heavy hitting and consistent play. With six good minor league seasons behind him (.308 average and 239 stolen bases), he hit a fine .330 at Oklahoma City in 1979 after an early-season 17-game tryout with the Phils. Believe it or not, it was his fourth season with Oklahoma City, and he had had impressive stats each year. It seemed no one in Philly had faith in him. How wrong they were. Rated an excellent speedster, his minor league manager Lee Elia said, "He can carry a ball club and make things happen when he gets on base." The 24-year-old right-handed batter was sent down in 1979 after several fly balls got the best of him, but when Dallas Green took over the Phils he gave Smith a chance and the rookie didn't let him down. In 100 games he hit .339 to lead the Phillie regulars in batting while stealing 33 bases, which broke Richie Ashburn's Philadelphia rookie record of 32 set in 1948. Lonnie appeared in all three outfield positions, while moving his average above the .300 mark in April and never letting it dip below that mark the rest of the way. There was talk just prior to spring training of 1980 of trading Smith to the Orioles, but Green luckily put his foot down against such a move. His faith paid off. Smith batted .600 against Houston in the playoffs and .263 against K.C. in the World Series. As Green has said, "Lonnie puts pizzazz into your offense."

The National League rookie pitcher for 1980 as selected by *The Sporting News* was a 21-year-old right-hander from the Montreal Expos, Bill Gullickson. Bill was 10-5 with a 3.00 ERA in 141 innings. He joined the Expos in late May after winning six consecutive games at Denver, but it took him seven weeks before he got his first win and to the end of July before he cracked the rotation. The modern record for strikeouts in a nine-inning game is 19, held by such notable pitchers as Nolan Ryan, Tom Seaver, and Steve Carlton. Gullickson almost joined that select group, as on September 11, he struck out 18 Chicago Cubs, including whiffing the side in three of the first four innings, to set a rookie record for strikeouts in a nine-inning game. Overall, he struck out 120 batters while walking only 50 for the season. Bill uses a lively fastball, a fine curve, and what his catcher Gary Carter calls "an awesome slider." Bill first drew national attention when he pitched six no-hitters for his Joliet, Illinois, high school. Never one to be discouraged, he learned in the spring of 1980 that he was a diabetic, a fact which would have been a terrible blow to many a player, but not Bill. His attitude might be reflected by the following: When he was told he would have to watch what he ate, he replied that was okay, he would probably stay in better shape.

There were many other fine rookies in the 1980 crop, and if we can draw a comparison with the past, it may be one or two of these non-award winning youngsters who will emerge as the top prize of the bunch. Let's take a brief look at what may well be the stars of the '80s.

The Boston Red Sox came up with several fine newcomers, although a couple found their way into the lineup due to injuries to regulars. It could be, however, that they will become the regulars off their fine play. When third baseman Butch Hobson's ailing arm failed to respond to treatments, Glenn Hoffman was installed at his position and gave a fine account of himself in the field and at bat with a .285 average. When second baseman Jerry Remy became injured, the Sox put Dave Stapleton in his slot. Dave had an excellent spring training, finished the season hitting .321, and was perhaps the major league's most underrated rookie of 1980. He seems certain to be the leading candidate for a long and successful future, and was runner-up to Joe Charboneau in the balloting. Waiting in the wings for the Bosox were such hopefuls as pitchers Bruce Hurst, Steve Crawford, Joel Finch, Bobby Ojeda, Keith MacWhorter, Danny Parks, and relievers Luis Aponte and Mike Smithson. The Sox also appeared to have an outfielder with a future in Reid Nichols and gave a late-season trial to the keystone combination of Julio Valdez and Chico Walker. Pawtucket third baseman Wade Boggs was a batting leader a good part of the season in the International League and may be heard from. Should Carlton Fisk falter, young catchers Rich Gedman or John Lickert might step in.

Speaking of catchers, the Baltimore Orioles came up with Dan Graham, who proved to be a valuable backup to regular Rick Dempsey. He proved to be a surprise at the plate with a .278 average after hitting only .213 at Toledo in 1979. Matching Graham's batting average was outfielder Mark Corey. Joining him on the Oriole list of hopefuls were outfielder Drungo Hazewood, catcher Floyd Rayford, infielder Chick Krenchicki, and reliever Dave Ford, who combined the hard-to-throw knuckle curve with a fine fastball, slider, and change-up. The New York Yankees, despite a pitching staff loaded with fine lefties, came up with Tim Lollar, yet another portsider, and righty Mike Griffin, while waiting for a try on the Stadium mound are Tim Lewis, Dave Righetti, Bob Kammeyer, Andy McGaffigan, and Chris Welch. It would seem the Yanks are deep in young arms. Outfielder Joe Lefebvre appeared ready to join the Yankee outfield, as he filled in capably whenever regulars became injured. Marshall Brant, a first baseman and former Met, catcher Dennis Werth, and infielders Roger Holt and Dennis Sherrill may not be far behind.

It is an old baseball axiom that you can never have enough pitching, and while the majors came up with a good crop of young arms in 1980, it was the Chicago White Sox with an already young staff that added three more very capable arms. We have already met Britt Burns, but they also added Richard Dotson (12-10) and Lamarr Hoyt (9-3) who both had brief trials in 1979. Dotson pitched a shutout in his second big league start, and in 1980 his 109 whiffs were second to Burns' 133. Hoyt, former Yankee property, joined the White Sox organization in the Bucky Dent deal. Reliever Robby Robinson and Guy Hoffman or Arnaldo Contreras may be ready to add their arms to the Sox' fine young staff. Outfielder Harold Baines, with three good minor league seasons behind him, won the regular right field spot and hit .255, not quite up to what had been expected of him, but he showed enough raw talent at bat and in the field that experienced baseball men were predicting future stardom for him. Baines was first noticed by Chisox owner Bill Veeck when Harold was just 12-years-old and playing in a Maryland Little League not far from Bill's home. Baines, who Sox farm director Paul Richards called a kid with the potential to be a great hitter, maybe one of the best ever in baseball, became the tenth player in the 72-year history of the American Association to hit two home runs in the same inning during 1979. The White Sox were also looking at Fran Mullins, a fine infield prospect, Leo Sutherland, a good hitting and speedy outfielder, catcher Ricky Seilheimer, a former first-round draft choice, and Randy Johnson, an outfielder of some talent. Meanwhile the California Angels, who were a disappointment after their 1979 American League West first place finish, had really only one rookie shine for them in 1980, pitcher Fred Martinez, who had been selected from Mets' organization in the minor league draft and who appeared to be a definite prospect to follow in the footsteps of Mark Clear. Freddie was 7-9, not bad considering how the Angels fell. Joining him but with little success were lefty Dave Schuler and right-handers Bob Ferris and Jim Dorsey, all with future promise. Outfielders Gil Kubski and Bob Clark, infielder John Harris, and catcher Stan Cliburn also were given a look-see. Harris is a power-hitting first baseman. Cliburn has had his problems at the plate. Clark, also a power hitter, popped five homers in 78 games. Kubski is a line drive hitter who hit .254 and showed good speed and a fine arm (his father is K.C. scout Al Kubski).

The Detroit Tigers had one of the most highly touted rookies in years in Kirk Gibson, a former football All-American flanker from Michigan State who appeared to win the center field post at Tiger Stadium. Gibson, a natural all-around athlete, had displayed power and speed until injuries and light hitting put him out of the line-up, and in his place emerged Ricky Peters who had hit .320 at Evansville in 1979. The versatile Peters, not a power hitter, hit a fine .291 and convinced manager Sparky Anderson that he was up to stay. A good fielder, Anderson is convinced that Peters may some day become an outstanding player. The Bengals also look for future heroics from former Arizona All-American outfielder Dave Stegman and fly chasers Dan Gonzalez and Jim Lentine. On the mound, the Tigers will be looking for more help from Roger Weaver and Bruce Robbins in 1981. Weaver, who has a good slider, fits in well as a reliever, and Robbins, who started eight games for the Tigers in 1979, has made a rapid rise to the majors. The Toronto Blue Jays picked up the slick-fielding Damaso Garcia, who was a .265 hitter in four seasons in the Yankee farm system, and put him at second base. Teamed up with Alfredo Griffin, the Jays' 1979 great rookie, they blended into one of the American League's fine double play combinations, leading the majors in that category. Toronto coach Bobby Doerr, once a great second baseman himself, was praising Garcia for his great hands and fielding ability before the season ever got underway. Garcia's .278 batting average was second only to Al Woods' .300 for the Jays, which seems to show that that quick stroke of his is going to hit major league pitching. The arm, range, and speed along with the hitting makes Garcia appear to have a good future. The Blue Jays also look to catcher Pat Kelly, outfielders Paul Hodgson (a native Canadian), and Lloyd Moseby (.322 at Syracuse) and infielder Garth Iorg to help their cause. Pitching is thin, but perhaps Luis Leal or Ken Schrom will help.

In Cleveland, Charboneau was the whole rookie show as the Tribe came up with little else in newcomers, but then how many Joe Charboneaus can you expect in one season, or a dozen for that matter. The closest the Indians could come was Jerry Dybzinski, who hit .230 in 114 games with little power. A native Clevelander, he has always been a good glove man. "Dybber" was the MVP in the Dominican Republic League in the 1979-80 season as a shortstop. Reliever Sandy Wihtol, hurlers Mike Stanton or Tom Brennan, along with first baseman Gary Gray or catcher Chris Bando may be the ones to team up with "Super Joe" to lead the Indians to the promised land. Bando, brother of long-time major leaguer Sal, led the Southern Association in hitting with a .349 average and hit 12 home runs. He is yet another Arizona State NCAA All-American. With a relatively young club, the Milwaukee Brewers produced little to go with their already strong lineup, but how do you break into a lineup that already contained Lezcano, Oglivie, Cooper, Molitor, Yount, and "Stormin'" Gorman Thomas? Infielder Ed Romero, catcher Ed Yost, and outfielder Mark Brouchard all tried to find the answer, while pitchers Dan Boitano, Dave LaPoint, and Ricky Keeton met with little success on the mound.

The Texas Ranger pitchers Don Kainer, Jerry Gleaton, Bob Babcock, Brian Allard, and John Butcher couldn't average one win among them. Butcher at 3-3 was the best, and he wasn't on the roster in the spring. Still there are some good arms among the group with, hopefully, some future Ranger victories in them. Infielders Odie Davis and Mike Richardt struggled at the bat. The year before, Richardt looked like a comer hitting .412 in spring training, .311 for Ashville, and .327 at Tulsa. Mike did hit .279 while playing third base at Charleston, W.V., and Davis .243 at shortstop for the same club. The Seattle Mariners, who won only 59 games while dropping 103 for baseball's worst record, had outfielder Reggie Walton, who for a while looked like he might be an answer for the problems in the Kingdome. Although he trailed off, his .277 average was second to Bruce Bochte's .300. Walton had once been recruited by Arizona State as a football player. Drafted by the Giants, he was signed by the Mariners after a year in the Mexican League. He came to them with a fine string of minor league batting averages. Outfielder Rod Craig, who we met earlier, still had rookie status and hit .238. Up for a look-see was Jim Allen, who had hit .294 with Spokane but only .165 at Bellingham in 1979. The youngster managed .235 in 23 games for Seattle. He plays second base and the outfield. Dave Edler, another non-roster hopeful, was recalled for 28 games after hitting .288 as Spokane's third baseman. The only rookie pitcher to appear for the Mariners was Rick Anderson, a former Yankee farmhand, and he had no record in five games, but was 6-0 at Spokane. Among the fine crop of second basemen to appear in 1980 was Oakland's Jeff Cox, a speedster who in 1979 stole 45 bases at Ogden, and in 1977 had set the Southern League mark at 68 while with Chattanooga. Despite that fine start, he managed only eight for the A's in 59 games. Cox, a five-year minor leaguer, may be ready. Also ready might be outfielder Mike Davis, who turned down a full scholarship to Arizona State to sign with the A's, and long-time minor leaguer Ray Cosey, another outfielder. The A's introduced a host of young pitchers, none who did much except Jeff Jones whose five saves were second high on Billy Martin's staff. Other hopefuls among the group were Dave Beard, Ernie Camacho, Dick Lysander, and youngsters Souza and Bordi.

The American League champions, the Kansas City Royals, came up with a fine pitcher in Renie Martin, who could only manage an 0-3 record in a late '79 trial. He was 10-10 for them in 1980, helping them to the pennant. The big right-hander struggled somewhat in his relief role but helped. Then, after 120 consecutive professional ball relief appearances, manager Jim Frey tried him in a starting role, and off his fine curve ball Renie came through to help the Royals run away with the flag. Joining him were fine prospects Gary Christenson (3-0), Mike Jones (0-1), and Jeff Twitty (2-1). With a set lineup, the Royals had little in the way of openings for other rookies, but were high on infielders German Barranca, a product of the Mexican League, Ken Phelps, who has demonstrated solid offensive ability in five minor league seasons, Onix Concepcion, a fine defensive infielder, and Manny Castillo, a switch-hitting utility infielder picked up from the Cardinal farm system. The Minnesota Twins had two very fine rookies in the running for rookie honors in pitcher Doug Corbitt and outfielder Rick Sofield. Sofield got to play regularly in left field and displayed fair power while hitting .247 and fielding adequately. In 1979 he had made a brief appearance with the Twins as a fill-in for Hosken Powell, who had broken a wrist. A fine minor league season in 1979 earned him his shot in 1980, and he was one of seven first-round draft picks on the Twins' roster. That first-round draft pick caused Rick to pass up a football scholarship to Michigan, where he would have competed with Rick Leach for the starting quarterback role. Corbitt was a standout reliever with an 8-6 record and a 1.99 ERA to go along with 23 saves. A right-hander, Corbitt was a real find for the Twins, who had drafted him during the winter from the Reds' organization. Doug had been a standout in relief for two seasons at Indianapolis and had originally been signed by the Royals. How did he ever slip through the Reds' and Royals' organizations? At his best when worked often, he should prove a plus for years to come out of the Twin bullpen.

Joining the Twins pitching staff also was former first-round draft pick Bob Veselic, a hard-luck pitcher whose career was seriously jeopardized in a California auto accident after the 1979 season. It was his second brush with death, as he was hit in the jaw by a line drive while pitching in the Midwest League in May 1977. Bob has an impressive string of strikeouts. Joining in were Terry Felton, Mike Kinnunen, and Al Williams, all pitchers. Williams, recalled from Toledo in late July, finished up at 6-2 with 3.51 ERA in relief and may have a fine future. A Nicaraguan, Williams fought for the Sandista guerrillas against Somoza in that Latin American country. Outfielder Gary Ward spent most of the summer at Toledo and hit .282, but in 13 games and 41 at-bats for the Twins banged the ball at a .463 rate. The Twins have a good backup catcher for regular Butch Wynegar in Sal Butera, an eight-year minor league vet, and are hoping outfielder Jesus Vega can improve his stick work and shortstop Len Faedo can show enough to stay around.

Meanwhile, in the National League, the defending champion Pittsburgh Pirates brought up few of the talented rookies they have in their farm system, and what they did bring along paid very slim dividends. Catcher Tony Pena hit .429 for eight games and 21 at-bats, and non-roster shortstop Vance Law contributed. The fine-fielding pitcher Rod Scurry proved his seven-year minor league record meant little, although his fastball struck out 28 in 38 innings. Pascual Perez, perhaps the only major leaguer from Haina, accomplished nothing in his trial. Haina is in the Dominican Republic. Don't be fooled by this crew, as the Bucs have a host of top minor leaguers soon to burst on the scene at Three Rivers Stadium. Names like Nicely, Garnett, Law, Gilbreath, Skinner, Anderson, Britt, Long, Ortiz, Boyland, and Vargas may soon be known in Pittsburgh. Imagine another Law and Skinner there!

Over in the eastern end of Pennsylvania, the Philadelphia Phillies were capturing the National League flag and eventually the 1980 World Series. In contrast to the former champs, they used a number of rookies on their way to the championship. The best of the bunch turned out, at least in 1980, to be Lonnie Smith, who we met at the beginning of this chapter. Joining Lonnie was right-hander Bob Walk, who won seven of his first eight games, finishing with an 11-7 slate, but with a relatively high 4.56 ERA. Manager Dallas Green was not all that convinced at first that Walk could make the jump from the pitching leader in the Eastern League at Reading to the Phillies. Walk had only three years of pro experience, but in '78 at Peninsula he had struck out 150 and in '79 at Reading had set down 135. When the Phils were hurting for starters, Green went with the youngster and was rewarded by Bob coming through for him. Bob's 94 strikeouts were second high among Phillie chuckers, but miles behind the old ace Steve Carlton's 286. However, Steve hurled 304 innings to Bob's 152. There were other young arms to appear for Philadelphia, some who may bear watching. Marty Bystrom was 5-0, 1.50 ERA, 21 strikeouts, and one shutout in six games. Two other rookies appeared briefly, Scott Munninghoff and Mark Davis. To catch this group the Phillies brought along catcher Keith Moreland, a good hitter at Oklahoma City in 1979 with a .302 average, 20 homers, and 109 RBIs. Backup for first-string catcher Bob Boone, Moreland continued his fine hitting by batting .314. Keith had been summoned in late 1979 to take over the regular catching duties when Boone suffered a knee injury. A good clutch hitter, Keith had been an All-American third baseman at the University of Texas in 1975 and has certainly come a long way since the Phillies switched him to catching. Brief "hellos" were also said to catchers Don McCormack and Ozzie Virgil, infielders Jay Lovigilo and Luis Aguayo, and outfielders Orlando Isales, Bob Dernier, and George Vukovich.

In the National League West, the Houston Astros with a strong and relatively young club were taking the honors, and like the Pirates, they did not rely on rookies to any extent, except for pitcher Dave Smith. Outfielder Danny Heep got into 33 games and hit .276, and Scott Loucks and Al Knicely made brief appearances. On the pitching side, Bobby Sprowl was back for a brief trial, but it was Dave Smith who turned in a fine performance with seven wins against five losses and a neat 1.92 ERA. He also had 85 strikeouts and registered 10 saves. Dave had been used almost exclusively as a starting pitcher in the Astros farm system until 1979 when the right-hander got in some relief work. His minor league record was good but not exceptional. Seems he arrived suddenly in 1980. Seven-year veteran of the minors, right-hander Gordy Pladson was not as successful (0-4) in 12 games. In 1979 at Charleston, Gordy had the rare experience of earning a decision in every game in which he appeared for the Charlies, 13-14 in 27 games, all but one as a starter.

The Cincinnati Reds were searching for youngsters to bolster their club and came up with a couple of good ones, pitcher Charlie Leibrandt and second baseman Ron Oester. Leibrandt, a lefty, was an important factor in keeping the Reds in contention for the National League West title with his 10-9 record. His future appears to be bright for the Rhinelanders. Charlie moved up very rapidly through the Reds' system after his signing in 1978 by stopping briefly at Eugene, Tampa, and Indianapolis. He was so advanced the Reds gave him a brief try in 1979 and used him in the Championship Series against Pittsburgh as a replacement for injured Bill Bonham. A polished pitcher, he fit in well in the Reds' rotation. A good fielder, he gained valuable experience at Miami University in Ohio. With second baseman Joe Morgan gone to the Astros, Oester, 23, who is a native of Cincinnati, moved into that slot. A .281 average at Indianapolis earned him a late-season trial in 1979. Ron had been a shortstop during his minor league career, but made the change easily to second. A switch hitter, he hit a fine .277. He first caught the eye of baseball scouts with his excellent range and powerful and accurate arm. The Reds also gave a look-see to outfielders Paul Householder and Eddie Milner. Joining Leibrandt on the mound was Bruce Berenyi, a righty with a fine minor league record and nephew of former American League pitcher Ned Garver, and Geoff Combe another righty and former Southern League pitcher of the year at Nashville where he had 27 saves in 1979. Rookie pitchers Sheldon Burnside and Jay Howell also made brief appearances.

The National League's West Coast teams were not to be left out of the rookie sweepstakes, as each one came up with at least one good newcomer. The San Francisco Giants acquired a hard-throwing southpaw from Pittsburgh in 1979 in Al Holland, and he responded by coming out of the Giant bullpen to save seven games while compiling a 5-3 record and an excellent team-leading 1.76 ERA. Holland should improve and remain the key reliever for the Giants. Mike Rowland, a right-hander, responded well as did righties Fred Breining and Jeff Stember and lefty Bill Bordley. Al Hargesheimer, with only two years of minor league experience, won four and lost six while showing future potential. Rich Murray, younger brother of the Baltimore Orioles' Eddie Murray got a chance at first base when Willie McCovey decided to retire and Mike Ivie quit for a brief period. Highly rated, Murray lived up to his advanced billing as a fielder, but slipped to a career low .216 batting average. Joe Pettini played mostly at shortstop, but appeared to be on his way to becoming a valuable utility infielder. Catcher Dennis Littlejohn, a noted defensive specialist, could be ready to stay, and his minor league teammate Chris Bourjos may join him. Bourjos, overlooked in the 1976 draft, was signed after an impressive showing at a Giant tryout camp. Infielder Guy Sularz was recalled from Phoenix for a brief trial and did well. The Los Angeles Dodgers continued their seemingly never-ending string of good rookies. Third baseman Mickey Hatcher was highly touted, but he had the impossible task of moving vet Ron Cey off third, which meant he spent more time in the dugout than he might have with a few other teams. Hatcher may prove to be good trade bait for the Dodgers. Mickey had hit .371 for Alburquerque to lead the Pacific Coast League in batting in 1979, the third straight year he was over the .300 mark. The Dodgers also looked at rookies Pedro Guerrero, Gary Weiss, Jack Perconte, Bob Mitchell, Mike Scioscia, and Rudy Law. Guerrero, an outfielder by trade, also filled in at second base and hit .322. Pedro, a six-year veteran of the Dodger farm system, spent his first minor league season in the Cleveland organization. Rudy Law, a highly rated outfielder, appeared to be the regular Dodger center fielder, and while he hit well (.260), he showed little power and his weak throwing arm eventually cost him his first-string job. Nevertheless, his speed still makes him a strong possibility for future trades or stardom in L.A. In fairness, injuries have hampered his advancement. Pitching, always a strong point with the Dodgers, was bolstered by young Steve Howe, a bullpen operative who posted a 7-9 record with a team-leading 17 saves. It was Howe who stepped in to keep the Dodgers in the pennant race when the aces of their pen, Terry Forster and Don Stanhouse, suffered injuries. The left-handed Howe may well become the ace reliever of the '80s, and was named National League Rookie of the Year by the baseball writers. Two other rookie pitchers showed promise. Fernando Valenzuela was in ten games, saved one, won two, and had an ERA of 0.00, while Joe Beckwith switched from starting to relieving and was 3-3 with a 1.95 ERA. The San Diego Padres' top rookie was second baseman Tim Flannery, who hit .240 but with little power. With only two minor league seasons, Tim was summoned by the Padres in September 1979 after he hit .345 at Amarillo following a .350 year at Reno. An avid guitar player and singer, Tim performed to packed audiences at a local nightclub near the Padres' spring training base at Yuma, Arizona. A close friend of Atlanta's Bob Horner, he played at Bob's wedding also. Joining the Padres was catcher Craig Stimac, who had seen three seasons of duty with Hawaii. Relief pitcher Tom Tellman appeared in six games, winning three and losing none, and posted a good 1.23 ERA. He was joined by sinkerball pitcher Gary Lucas, who seemed to have recovered from a 1979 broken wrist and was 5-8 with three saves. Juan Eichelberger, a former collegiate standout at the University of California, was 4-2 and was highly thought of by Padre brass.

Up in Canada, the Montreal Expos were boasting of second baseman-shortstop Tony Bernazard, who hit a weak .224 but did have five homers in 82 games. Tony will be remembered for his 1978 performance at Denver of going six for six, a performance that included three doubles, two home runs, and six RBIs, the 24th player in American Association history to turn that trick. Catcher Roberto Ramos, infielder Tim Raines, and outfielder Bob Pate are a few other Expo rookies to watch. In the pitching department, we have met the Expos' top rookie of 1980, Bill Gullickson, but Steve Ratzer and Charlie Lea may replace him as the rookie pitcher of 1981. The St. Louis Cardinals gave long looks at infielders Tom Herr and Mike Ramsey, outfielder Terry Landrum, and short looks at catcher Joe DeSa, infielder Ty Waller, and outfielders Jim Lentine and Keith Smith. But perhaps the best non-pitching newcomer was first baseman Leon Durham. Leon, who batted .310 with 23 home runs at Springfield in the American Association in 1979, had to face the problem of moving the 1979 National League batting champion Keith Hernandez, a fixture at first base in St. Looie. Durham couldn't do it, but managed to play some at first and some in the outfield for 96 games and batted a good .271, with eight homers and 42 RBIs while stealing eight bases. He will bear watching as a National League star of the future with the Chicago Cubs, to whom he was sent as part of the Bruce Sutter trade. On the mound, the Cardinals had Andy Rincon in four games, and he responded with a 3-1 record, striking out 22 along the way. Perhaps the best young pitcher for St. Louis was John Littlefield, who had put together five seasons as a reliever at both double and triple A levels. John posted a 5-5 record, but led the Redbirds in saves with nine. Right on John's heels was Kim Seaman with a 3-2, four-save record. Kim, originally a Met, began his pro career as a starter, but the Cardinals switched him into relief roles and in 1978, his third minor league season, saw him come into his own. Other rookie hurlers for the Cards were Olmsted, Little, and Martin.

Atlanta had little in the way of rookies in 1980, and that may explain in some part why owner Ted Turner would appear to be turning to the free-agent market, although his team is relatively young. A couple of those young players we have already met turned into a very powerful home run duo in 1980. Bob Horner hit 35 homers while Dale Murphy banged out 33, and they may become the best one-two home run punch in the majors. They were topped only by Milwaukee's Gorman Thomas and Ben Oglivie, who hit 79 round trippers between them during the 1980 season. The rookie who was used the most by the Braves was Rafael Ramirez, a shortstop who converted from the outfield while at Bradenton in 1977. Spending a good part of the season at Richmond where he hit .281, he managed a .267 mark with the Braves in 50 games and at times can show surprising power for a player of his size. Joining him, but having spent most of the summer in the minors, were outfielders Gary Cooper and Terry Harper and infielder Manuel Ruiz. The Braves used only one rookie pitcher, Mickey Mahler, a switch-hitting left-hander, who was Richmond's top hurler at 12-6 before moving to Atlanta where he had no record. The Chicago Cubs were also shuffling players between Wichita and Wrigley Field. Catcher Mike O'Berry, a former Red Sox, just qualified for rookie status, but after the season they traded him away. The top rookie in the Cub fold was Jesus Figueroa, who had been drafted from the Yankee West Haven club in 1977. The Dominican Republic native had an excellent season at Wichita in 1979 hitting .291, while showing a fine arm and excellent running speed, stealing 28 bases. Coming close to playing every day in either center field or as a pinch hitter, Figueroa appeared in 115 games, posting a .253 average. Carlos Lezcano, cousin of Brewer outfielder Sixto and a former Florida State All-Star, also saw some action in the outfield. After spending the entire 1978 season on the disabled list, he returned to Midland in 1979 to hit .326. First baseman Jim Tracy appeared in 42 games, the same number as Lezcano, but outhit Carlos .254 to .205. Infielder Steve Macko and catcher Bill Hayes also made token appearances. Pitcher Lee Smith was 2-0 in 18 games, but fellow hurlers Randy Martz and George Riley contributed little, although both have good backgrounds. Riley, while a high schooler in Philadelphia, once pitched four no-hitters in a row, and Martz, who went to the University of South Carolina on a football scholarship, helped pitch the Gamecocks into second place in the 1977 College World Series, earning a place on seven different All-Star teams.

The New York Mets, who spent the 1980 season fighting it out with the

Cubs for last place in the East, did, however, come up with some fine rookies who in the '80s may well play a part in moving them up in the standings. The three with the most promise spent most of the season at Tidewater where they were among the International League's top batters. Shortstop Wally Backman, a switch hitter and a number-one prospect for future major league stardom, hit .293 for the Tides and .323 for the Mets. Not a power hitter, he has always hit for average and is a fine base stealer. Infielder Hubie Brooks, another Arizona State All-American and like Backman a Mets' first-round draft choice, gave the Tides a .297 season and hit .309 for the Mets. Joining them was the popular outfielder William Hayward Wilson better known to all as "Mookie." Drafted behind Backman in June of 1977, "Mookie" is also one of the prime candidates to become a full-fledged major leaguer in the '80s. Completing his second season with the Tides (Wilson led them in most every offensive category in 1979), he led the League with 152 hits, while compiling an average of .295. Once drafted by the Dodgers, but not signing with them, the speedster may become a Shea Stadium fixture. Other rookies making brief Shea Stadium appearances were infielders Mario Ramirez and Jose Moreno. Moreno, a utility infielder and part-time outfielder, hit .280 at Tidewater and has speed. Ramirez, a good glove man, led International League shortstops in fielding in 1979, and has also played second base. Luis "Papo" Rosado, a catcher with a long minor league record and a previous trial with the Mets, was up again for appearances in two games, as was catcher Butch Benton. Benton hit .263 for the Tides, but could do little with National League pitching in 21 at-bats. He has a history of shoulder prob- lems. Two of the Mets' fine rookie pitchers gave good accounts of themselves. Jeff Reardon, a right-hander who came to the Mets in late 1979, won eight while losing seven, and struck out 101, eight off the 1980 high for Met pitchers. He also had six saves to go along with his 2.62 ERA. Then there was Mark Bomback, another righty, who was 10-8 to become the winningest Met hurler for 1980. Mark was originally signed by the Boston Red Sox back in 1971 and pitched for their farm system until 1976 when he decided to retire. Basically a breaking ball pitcher now, he was talked out of retirement by the Milwaukee Brewers in 1977 and appeared briefly with them in 1978. Sent to Vancouver for 1979, he posted a fine 22-7 record and was acquired by the Mets for 1980, a move which kept the Mets from becoming cellar dwellers. The New Yorkers also looked over Scott Holman, John Pacella, and Ed Lynch, all right-handers.

Now, no book on rookies would be complete without mentioning one minor leaguer, who believe it or not, has pitched in professional baseball in six different decades. When Hub Kittle took the mound for Springfield against Iowa in an American Association game on August 27, 1980, the 63-year-old accomplished this feat. A minor league pitching coach for the St. Louis Cardinals, he needed only ten pitches to get through the first inning, showing a fastball, slow curve, forkball, and a change-up. He threw one pitch in the second inning and was replaced on the mound after conceding that the ball felt like a ton of lead. Originally signed by the Chicago Cubs in 1936, he won fifteen and lost three in his first season for a Catalina Island semi-pro club sponsored by the Cubs. He has pitched for Los Angeles, San Francisco, and Oakland of the old Pacific Coast League, and in 1939 won 20 games for Yakima of the Western International League. Active through the '40s and '50s, he pitched one game for Austin of the Texas League in 1966 and one for Savannah of the Southern League in 1969. In 1973, while a pitching coach for the Houston Astros, he was called upon to protect a lead in the ninth inning in an exhibition game against the Detroit Tigers. A truly amazing record and person.

The Kittle story is perhaps a fitting end to our story of the rookies. Of course, at one time every major leaguer was a rookie, and while I couldn't mention each one, I hope your favorite has been among them. For the older reader, I hope some memories of seasons past have been revived. For the younger reader, there are lessons to be learned from the trials of our rookies; the ups and downs, the determination, the seeking of a goal and going after it. Truly in the story of the rookies are the keys to "how to make it in the major leagues." The skills these ballplayers used and the obstacles they overcame will serve as examples to any youth who would like "to make the big time." Here in the grass roots of baseball are the examples followed by all who have made the major league rosters.

When we started our journey, there were only 16 big league teams, free agents were unheard of, the reserve clause hadn't been challenged in fifty-some years, and our rookies of the '80s hadn't been born. The star of today will, like those who went before them, become more legendary as time passes and sooner than we would like become yesterday's memories. Some will make baseball's Hall of Fame, most will not, but there won't be one among them who will not be able to say he played in the majors, no matter how briefly. Our rookies of the 1980 season will be able to tell the story of the major leagues in the '80s and so hopefully will you, and what a story it promises to be!

APPENDIX

Rookie
Records

The following are the rookie records in various categories based on the players first season in the major leagues.

Batting-Rookie Season

High Average
.373   George Watkins—St. Louis Cardinals 1930 (NL), 119 games
.343   Dale Alexander—Detroit Tigers 1929 (AL), 155 games
.408   Joe Jackson—Cleveland Indians 1911 (AL), 147 games

Most At-Bats
679   Harvey Kuenn—Detroit Tigers 1953 (AL), 155 games
661   Ken Hubbs—Chicago Cubs 1962 (NL), 160 games

Most Runs
133   Lloyd Waner—Pittsburgh Pirates 1927 (NL), 150 games
132   Joe DiMaggio—New York Yankees 1936 (AL), 138 games

Most Hits
223   Lloyd Waner—Pittsburgh Pirates 1927 (NL), 150 games
217   Tony Oliva—Minnesota Twins 1964 (AL), 161 games

Most RBIs
145   Ted Williams—Boston Red Sox 1939 (AL), 149 games
119   Wally Berger—Boston Braves 1930 (NL), 151 games

Most Singles
198   Lloyd Waner—Pittsburgh Pirates 1927 (NL), 150 games
167   Harvey Kuenn—Detroit Tigers 1953 (AL), 155 games

Most Doubles
52   John Frederick—Brooklyn Dodgers 1929 (NL), 148 games
47   Fred Lynn—Boston Red Sox 1975 (AL), 145 games

Most Triples
22   Paul Waner—Pittsburgh Pirates 1926 (NL), 144 games
15   Dale Alexander—Detroit Tigers 1929 (AL), 155 games
15   Joe DiMaggio—New York Yankees 1936 (AL), 138 games

Most Home Runs
38   Wally Berger—Boston Braves 1930 (NL), 151 games
38   Frank Robinson—Cincinnati Reds 1956 (NL), 152 games
37   Al Rosen—Cleveland Indians 1950 (AL), 155 games

Most Total Bases
374   Hal Trosky—Cleveland Indians 1934 (AL), 154 games
374   Tony Oliva—Minnesota Twins 1964 (AL), 161 games
352   Richie Allen—Philadelphia Phillies 1964 (NL), 162 games

Most Games
162   Jake Wood—Detroit Tigers 1961 (AL)
162   Bobby Knoop—Los Angeles Angels 1964 (AL)
162   George Scott—Boston Red Sox 1966 (AL)
162   Richie Allen—Philadelphia Phillies 1964 (NL)

Most Walks
107   Ted Williams—Boston Red Sox 1939 (AL), 149 games
100   Junior Gilliam—Brooklyn Dodgers 1953 (NL), 151 games

Most Intentional Walks
14   Willie Montanez—Philadelphia Phillies 1971 (NL), 158 games
13   George Scott—Boston Red Sox 1966 (AL), 162 games

Most Strikeouts
152   George Scott—Boston Red Sox 1966 (AL), 162 games
152   Larry Hisle—Philadelphia Phillies 1969 (NL), 145 games

Fewest Strikeouts
17   Buddy Hassett—Brooklyn Dodgers 1936 (NL), 156 games
25   Tom Oliver—Boston Red Sox 1930 (AL), 154 games

Most Stolen Bases
56   Gene Richards—San Diego Padres 1977 (NL), 146 games
49   Rollie Zeider—Chicago White Sox 1910 (AL), 136 games

Most Caught Stealing
21   Mike Edwards—Oakland A's 1978 (AL), 142 games
20   Greg Gross—Houston Astros 1974 (NL), 156 games

Highest Slugging Average
.621   George Watkins—St. Louis Cardinals 1930 (NL), 119 games
.609   Ted Williams—Boston Red Sox 1939 (AL), 149 games

Consecutive Games Batting Safely
26   Guy Curtright—Chicago White Sox 1943 (AL), 6/6 to 7/1
23   Joe Rapp—Philadelphia Phillies 1921 (NL), 7/7 to 7/30
23   Richie Ashburn—Philadelphia Phillies 1948 (NL), 5/9 to 6/5
23   Al Dark—Boston Braves 1948 (NL), 6/20 to 7/11
23   Mike Vail—New York Mets 1975 (NL), 8/22 to 9/15

Most Long Hits
89   Hal Trosky—Cleveland Indians 1934 (AL), 154 games: 45 doubles, 9 triples, 35 homers
82   John Frederick—Brooklyn Dodgers 1929 (AL), 148 games: 52 doubles, 6 triples, 24 homers

Most Hit by a Pitch
20   Frank Robinson—Cincinnati Reds 1956 (NL), 152 games
17   Henry Manush—Detroit Tigers 1923 (AL), 109 games

Pitching-Rookie Season

Most Games
77   Clarence Metzger—San Diego Padres 1976, (NL)
69   Bill Kelso—California Angels 1967, (AL)

Most Complete Games
41   Irv Young—Boston Braves 1905 (NL)
36   Roscoe Miller—Detroit Tigers 1901 (AL)

Most Shutouts
8   Ewell Russell—Chicago White Sox 1913 (AL)
7   Irv Young—Boston Braves 1905 (NL)
7   Grover Alexander—Philadelphia Phillies 1911 (NL)
7   Jerry Koosman—New York Mets 1968 (NL)

Most Strikeouts
245   Herb Score—Cleveland Indians 1955 (AL)
227   Grover Alexander—Philadelphia Phillies 1911 (NL)

Most Strikeouts in First Game
15   Karl Spooner—Brooklyn Dodgers 9/22/54 (NL)
15   J. R. Richard—Houston Astros 9/5/71 (NL)
12   Elmer Myers—Philadelphia Athletics 10/6/15 (AL)

Most Walks
149 Bobo Newsom—St. Louis Browns 1934 (AL)

Most Innings Pitched
378 Irv Young—Boston Braves 1905 (NL)
316 Ewell Russell—Chicago White Sox 1913 (AL)

Consecutive Scoreless Innings—Start of Career
25 George McQuillan—Philadelphia Phillies 1907 (NL)
22 Dave Ferriss—Boston Red Sox 1945 (AL)

Most Games Lost
26 Bob Groom—Washington Senators 1909 (AL)
25 John McIntire—Brooklyn Dodgers 1905 (NL)

Most Consecutive Games Lost
13 Guy Morton—Cleveland Indians 1914 (AL)
12 Henry Thielman—Cincinnati Reds 1902 (NL)
12 Pete Schneider—Cincinnati Reds 1914 (NL)

Most Games Won
28 Grover Alexander—Philadelphia Phillies 1911 (NL)
24 Ed Summers—Detroit Tigers 1908 (AL)

Most Consecutive Games Won
12 Atley Donald—New York Yankees 1939 (AL)
12 George Wiltse—New York Giants 1904 (NL)

The Baseball Writers' Association Rookie Awards

The Baseball Writers' Association began naming their selection of the top
rookies in 1947, and for the 1947 and 1948 seasons named a combined
American-National League selection as the rookie of the year. The recipients
were both from the National League in those two seasons. In 1949 they began
naming the top rookie in each league, whether a pitcher or a fielder: It is a
distinction that made no difference; simply name the top player. The writers
conduct a voting poll to determine the winner, a system which resulted in a
tie in the National League in 1976 and the American League in 1979.

The following are their selections:

Both Leagues

1947 Jackie Robinson—Brooklyn, 1B   1948 Al Dark—Boston (NL), SS

American League

	American League	National League
1949	Roy Sievers—St. Louis, OF	Don Newcombe—Brooklyn, P
1950	Walt Dropo—Boston, 1B	Sam Jethroe—Boston, OF
1951	Gil McDougald—N.Y., 3B	Willie Mays—N.Y., OF
1952	Harry Byrd—Phila., P	Joe Black—Brooklyn, P
1953	Harvey Kuenn—Detroit, SS	Junior Gilliam—Brooklyn, 2B
1954	Bob Grim—N.Y., P	Wally Moon—St. Louis, OF
1955	Herb Score—Cleveland, P	Bill Virdon—St. Louis, OF
1956	Luis Aparicio—Chicago, SS	Frank Robinson—Cinn., OF*
1957	Tony Kubek—N.Y., INF-OF	Jack Sanford—Phila., P
1958	Albie Pearson—Wash., OF	Orlando Cepeda—San Fran., 1B*
1959	Bob Allison—Wash., OF	Willie McCovey—San. Fran., 1B*
1960	Ron Hansen—Baltimore, SS	Frank Howard—L.A., OF
1961	Don Schwall—Boston, P	Billy Williams—Chicago, OF
1962	Tom Tresh—N.Y., OF-SS	Ken Hubbs—Chicago, 2B
1963	Gary Peters—Chicago, P	Pete Rose—Cincinnati, 2B
1964	Tony Oliva—Minn., OF	Richie Allen—Phila., 3B
1965	Curt Blefary—Balt., OF	Jim Lefebvre—L.A., 2B
1966	Tommie Agee—Chicago, OF	Tommy Helms—Cincinnati, 3B
1967	Rod Carew—Minn., 2B	Tom Seaver—N.Y., P
1968	Stan Bahnsen—N.Y., P	Johnny Bench—Cincinnati, C
1969	Lou Piniella—K.C., OF	Ted Sizemore—L.A., 2B
1970	Thurman Munson—N.Y., C	Carl Morton—Montreal, P
1971	Chris Chambliss—Cleveland, 1B	Earl Williams—Atlanta, C
1972	Carlton Fisk—Boston, C*	John Matlack—N.Y., P
1973	Al Bumbry—Baltimore, OF	Gary Mathews—San Fran., OF
1974	Mike Hargrove—Texas, 1B	Bake McBride—St. Louis, OF
1975	Fred Lynn—Boston, OF	John Montefusco—San Fran., P
1976	Mark Fidrych—Detroit, P	Butch Metzger—San Diego, P
		Pat Zachry—Cincinnati, P
1977	Eddie Murray—Balt., DH-1B	Andre Dawson—Montreal, OF
1978	Lou Whitaker—Detroit, 2B	Bob Horner—Atlanta, 3B
1979	John Castino—Minn., 3B	Rick Sutcliffe—L.A., P
	Alfredo Griffin—Toronto, SS	
1980	Joe Charboneau—Cleveland, OF-DH	Steve Howe—L.A., P

The Sporting News Rookie Awards

In 1946 the sports publication *The Sporting News* began recognizing the rookie of the year with their "rookie award." For the first three years that they gave this award they selected the one outstanding rookie from both major

---

*Unanimous selection.

leagues. As it turned out, a National League rookie captured the honors for each of the years. In 1949 *The Sporting News* decided on the selection of the top rookie in each major league, but in 1950 returned to the combined selection again. The year 1951 saw them revert to naming the top prospect in each league. In 1957 they adapted a system of naming the top rookie pitcher and top rookie player in each league, although they named no pitcher in the American League for that season. For the 1959 and 1960 seasons they returned to the single-selection system; but in 1961 returned to the dual-award system for a year. Finally, 1963 saw another return to the dual system, which has been in effect since.

Both Leagues

1946 Del Ennis—Phila. (NL), OF
1947 Jackie Robinson—Bklyn., 1B

1948 Richie Ashburn—Phila., OF

American League
1949 Roy Sievers—St. Louis, OF
1950 Whitey Ford—N.Y. (AL), P
1951 Minnie Minoso—Chicago, OF
1952 Clint Courtney—St. Louis, L
1953 Harvey Kuenn—Detroit, SS
1954 Bob Grim—N.Y., P
1955 Herb Score—Cleveland, P
1956 Luis Aparicio—Chicago, SS
1957 Tony Kubek—N.Y., INF-OF
      No Pitcher named
1958 Albie Pearson—Wash., OF
      Ryne Duren—N.Y., P
1959 Bob Allison—Wash., OF
1960 Ron Hansen—Balt., SS
1961 Dick Howser—K.C., SS
      Don Schwall—Boston, P
1962 Tom Tresh—N.Y., OF-SS
1963 Pete Ward—Chicago, 3B
      Gary Peters—Chicago, P
1964 Tony Oliva—Minn., OF
      Wally Bunker—Balt., P
1965 Curt Blefary—Balt., OF
      Marcelino Lopez—Calif., P
1966 Tommie Agee—Chicago, OF
      Jim Nash—K.C., P
1967 Rod Carew—Minn., 2B
      Tom Phoebus—Balt., P

National League
Don Newcombe—Brooklyn, P

Willie Mays—N.Y., OF
Joe Black—Brooklyn, P
Junior Gilliam—Brooklyn, 2B
Wally Moon—St. Louis, OF
Bill Virdon—St. Louis, OF
Frank Robinson—Cinn., OF
Ed Bouchee—Phila., 1B
Jack Sanford—Phila., P
Orlando Cepeda—San Fran., 1B
Carlton Willey—Milwaukee, P
Willie McCovey—San Fran., OF
Frank Howard—L.A., OF
Billy Williams—Chicago, OF
Ken Hunt—Cinn., P
Ken Hubbs—Chicago, 2B
Pete Rose—Cinn., 2B
Ray Culp—Phila., P
Richie Allen—Phila., 3B
Bill McCool—Cinn., P
Joe Morgan—Houston, 2B
Frank Linzy—San Fran., P
Tommy Helms—Cinn., 3B
Don Sutton—L.A., P
Lee May—Cinn., 1B
Dick Hughes—St. Louis, P

1968 Del Unser—Wash., OF
Stan Bahnsen—N.Y., P

1969 Carlos May—Chicago, OF
Mike Nagy—Boston, P

1970 Roy Foster—Cleveland, OF
Bert Blyleven—Minn., P

1971 Chris Chambliss—Cleve., 1B
Bill Parsons—Milwaukee, P

1972 Carlton Fisk—Boston, C
Dick Tidrow—Cleve., P

1973 Al Bumbry—Baltimore, OF
Steve Busby—K.C., P

1974 Mike Hargrove—Texas, 1B
Frank Tanana—Calif., P

1975 Fred Lynn—Boston, OF
Dennis Eckersley—Cleve., P

1976 Butch Wynegar—Minn., C
Mark Fidrych—Detroit, P

1977 Mitchell Page—Oak., OF
Dave Rozema—Det., P

1978 Paul Molitor—Milwaukee, 2B
Rich Gale—Kansas City, P

1979 Pat Putnam—Texas, 1B
Mark Clear—Calif., P

1980 Joe Charboneau—Cleve., OF-DH
Britt Burns—Chicago, P

Johnny Bench—Cinn., C
Jerry Koosman—N.Y., P
Coco Laboy—Montreal, 3B
Tom Griffin—Houston, P
Bernie Carbo—Cinn., OF
Carl Morton—Montreal, P
Earl Williams—Atlanta, C
Reggie Cleveland—St. Louis, P
Dave Rader—San Fran., C
Jon Matlack—N.Y., P
Gary Matthews—San Fran., OF
Steve Rogers—Montreal, P
Greg Gross—Houston, OF
John D'Acquisto—San Fran., P
Gary Carter—Montreal, OF-C
John Montefusco—San Fran., P
Larry Herndon—San Fran., OF
Butch Metzger—San Diego, P
Andre Dawson—Montreal, OF
Bob Owchinko—San Diego, P
Bob Horner—Atlanta, 3B
Don Robinson—Pitts., P
Jeff Leonard—Houston, OF
Rick Sutcliffe—L.A., P
Lonnie Smith—Philadelphia, OF
Bill Gullickson—Montreal, P

Most Hits in Rookie Season

American League

1954	Tony Oliva—Minnesota	217
1929	Dale Alexander—Detroit	215
1953	Harvey Kuenn—Detroit	209
1936	Joe DiMaggio—New York	206
1934	Hal Trosky—Cleveland	206
1942	John Pesky—Boston	205
1929	Roy Johnson—Detroit	201
1943	Dick Wakefield—Detroit	200

National League

1927	Lloyd Waner—Pittsburgh	223
1899	Jim Williams—Pittsburgh	219
1929	John Frederick—Brooklyn	206
1964	Richie Allen—Philadelphia	201

The First Black Player with Each Original Major League Club

1.	Brooklyn Dodgers—Jackie Robinson	4/15/47
2.	Cleveland Indians—Larry Doby	7/5/47
3.	St. Louis Browns—Hank Thompson	7/17/47
4.	New York Giants—Hank Thompson	7/8/49
5.	Boston Braves—Sam Jethroe	4/18/50
6.	Chicago White Sox—Sam Hairston	7/21/51
7.	Philadelphia A's—Bob Trice	9/13/53
8.	Chicago Cubs—Ernie Banks	9/17/53
9.	Pittsburgh Pirates—Curt Roberts	4/13/54
10.	St. Louis Cardinals—Tom Alston	4/13/54
11.	Cincinnati Reds—Saturnino Escalera	4/17/54
12.	Washington Senators—Carlos Paula	9/6/54
13.	New York Yankees—Elston Howard	4/14/55
14.	Philadelphia Phillies—John Kennedy	4/22/57
15.	Detroit Tigers—Ossie Virgil	6/6/58
16.	Boston Red Sox—Pumpsie Green	7/21/59

Rookie-Year Home Run Leaders by Team

American League		*National League*	
Baltimore—Eddie Murray, 1977	27	Atlanta—Earl Williams, 1971	33
Boston—Walt Dropo, 1950	34	Boston—Wally Berger, 1930	38
California—Kent Hunt, 1961	25	Brooklyn—Del Bissonett, 1928	25
Chicago—Zeke Bonura, 1934	27	Chicago—Billy Williams, 1961	25
Cleveland—Al Rosen, 1950	37	Cincinnati—Frank Robinson,	
Detroit—Rudy York, 1937	35	1956	38
*Kansas City—Woody Held, 1957	20	Houston—Joe Morgan, 1965	14
Kansas City—Bob Oliver, 1969	13	Los Angeles—Frank Howard,	
Milwaukee—Darrell Porter, 1973	16	1960	23
Minnesota—Jimmie Hall, 1963	33	Montreal—Andre Dawson,	
New York—Joe DiMaggio, 1936	29	1977	19
Oakland—Wayne Gross, 1977	22	New York (Giants)—Bobby	
Philadelphia—Bob Johnson,		Thompson, 1947	29
1933	21	New York (Mets)—Ron	
*Seattle—Steve Hovley,		Swoboda, 1965	19
Dan Walton	3	Philadelphia—Willie Montanez,	
Seattle—Rupport Jones, 1977	24	1971	30
Texas—Pat Putnam, 1979	18	Pittsburgh—John Rizzo, 1938,	
Toronto—Doug Ault, 1977	11	Ralph Kiner, 1946	23
*Washington—Bob Allison, 1959	30	St. Louis—Ray Jablonski,	
Washington—Don Lock, 1962	12	1953	21
		San Diego—John Grubb, 1973,	
		Mike Ivie, 1975	8
*Original team.		San Francisco—Jim Ray Hart,	
		1964	31

Players Hitting a Home Run in First At-Bat in the Major Leagues

American League

Baltimore	Buster Narum	May 3, 1963
Boston	Bill Lefebvre	June 10, 1938
	Ed Pellagrini	April 22, 1946
California	Don Rose	May 24, 1972
	Dave Machemer	June 21, 1978
Cleveland	Earl Averill	April 16, 1929
Detroit	Hack Miller	April 23, 1944
	George Vico	April 20, 1948
	Gates Brown	June 19, 1963
	Bill Roman	September 30, 1964
	Gene Lamont	September 2, 1970
	Reggie Sanders	September 1, 1974
Kansas City	Bert Campaneris	July 23, 1964
Minnesota	Rick Renick	July 11, 1968
	Dave McKay	August 22, 1975
New York	John Miller	September 11, 1966
Oakland	Joe Keough	August 7, 1968
Philadelphia	Ace Parker	April 30, 1937
St. Louis	Bob Nieman	September 14, 1951
Toronto	Al Woods	April 7, 1977
Washington	John Kennedy	September 5, 1962
	Brant Alyea	September 12, 1965

Note: Alyea, Campaneris, Rose, and Vico all accomplished it on the first pitch.

National League

Boston	John Bates	April 12, 1906
Brooklyn	Clise Dudley	April 27, 1929
	Gordon Slade	May 24, 1930
	Ernie Koy	April 19, 1938
	Dan Bankhead	August 26, 1947
Chicago	Frank Ernaga	May 24, 1957
	Cuno Barragan	September 1, 1961

Cincinnati	Clyde Vollmer	May 31, 1942
	Ted Tappe	September 14, 1950
Houston	Jose Sosa	July 30, 1975
Milwaukee	Chuck Tanner	April 12, 1955
New York (Giants)	Buddy Kerr	September 8, 1943
	Whitey Lockman	July 5, 1945
	Les Layton	May 21, 1948
	Hoyt Wilhelm	April 23, 1952
	Bill White	May 7, 1956
New York (Mets)	Ben Ayala	August 27, 1974
Philadelphia	Bill Duggleby	April 21, 1898
	Emmett Mueller	April 19, 1938
	Ed Sanicki	September 14, 1949
Pittsburgh	Don Leppert	June 18, 1961
St. Louis	Ed Morgan	April 14, 1936
	Wally Moon	April 13, 1954
San Francisco	Johnnie LeMaster	September 2, 1975

Note: Dudley, Morgan, Tanner, and Vollmer all accomplished it on the first pitch.

Players Making Their Major League Debuts Since 1969

Year	American League	National League	Total
1979	78	45	123
1978	80	68	148
1977	97	58	155
1976	48	58	106
1975	77	53	130
1974	67	77	144
1973	62	69	131
1972	57	65	122
1971	60	53	113
1970	71	69	140
1969	85	98	183